The ILLUMINATI

THE SECRET SOCIETY THAT HIJACKED THE WORLD

ABOUT THE AUTHOR

 **Jim Marrs** is an award-winning journalist and author. After graduating from the University of North Texas with a degree in journalism, he worked for and owned several Texas newspapers before becoming an independent journalist/author. He is the author of the *New York Times* bestsellers *Crossfire: The Plot That Killed Kennedy*, which was a basis for the Oliver Stone film *JFK*, and *Rule by Secrecy*. His in-depth overview of the UFO phenomenon, *Alien Agenda*, is the top-selling non-fiction book on UFOs in the world, and it is available in several foreign languages. He is a frequent guest on national radio and television talk-show programs. Marrs lives in Wise County, Texas.

The ILLUMINATI

THE SECRET SOCIETY THAT HIJACKED THE WORLD

JIM MARRS

Bestselling author of *Rule by Secrecy*

VISIBLE
INK
PRESS

Detroit

ALSO FROM VISIBLE INK PRESS

"REAL NIGHTMARES" E-BOOKS BY BRAD STEIGER

PLEASE VISIT US AT VISIBLEINKPRESS.COM

THE SECRET SOCIETY THAT HIJACKED THE WORLD

Visible Ink Press®
43311 Joy Rd., #414
Canton, MI 48187-2075

Visible Ink Press is a registered trademark of Visible Ink Press LLC.

Most Visible Ink Press books are available at special quantity discounts when purchased in bulk by corporations, organizations, or groups. Customized printings, special imprints, messages, and excerpts can be produced to meet your needs. For more information, contact Special Markets Director, Visible Ink Press, www.visibleink.com, or 734-667-3211.

Managing Editor: Kevin S. Hile
Art Director: Mary Claire Krzewinski
Typesetting: Marco DiVita
Proofreaders: Larry Baker and Aarti Stephens
Indexer: Shoshana Hurwitz

Cover images: Albert Pike photo courtesy Brady-Handy Collection, Library of Congress; Levite priests illustration courtesy Jim Marrs; Aachen Cathedral photo by Trexer (Wikicommons).

Library of Congress Cataloging-in-Publication Data

Names: Marrs, Jim, author.
Title: The Illuminati : the secret society that hijacked the world / Jim Marrs.
Description: Detroit, MI : Visible Ink Press, 2017.
Identifiers: LCCN 2017008995 (print) | LCCN 2017011102 (ebook) | ISBN
    9781578596195 (paperback) | ISBN 9781578596508 (kindle) | ISBN
    9781578596492 (epub) | ISBN 9781578596485 (PDF) | ISBN 9781578596485
    (pdf)
Subjects: LCSH: Illuminati—History. | Freemasonry—History. | Secret societies—
    History. | BISAC: SOCIAL SCIENCE / Freemasonry. | BODY, MIND & SPIRIT / Mythical Civilizations.
Classification: LCC HS142 .M37 2017 (print) | LCC HS142 (ebook) | DDC 366--dc23
LC record available at https://lccn.loc.gov/2017008995

Printed in the United States of America.

10 9 8 7 6 5 4 3

TABLE OF CONTENTS

Photo Sources ... [ix]
Introduction ... [xi]

PHOTO SOURCES

Osama Shukir Muhammed Amin FRCP(Glasg): p. 28.

Johann Valentin Andreae: p. 74.

Art Institute of Chicago: p. 193.

Biblioteque Nationale de France: p. 58.

Brady-Handy collection, Library of Congress: p. 159.

Brooklyn Museum: p. 23.

Das Bundesarchiv: pp. 135, 280, 284.

Mathieu Chaine: pp. 115, 315.

Chatham House: p. 138.

The Conmunity—Pop Culture Geek: p. 333.

Crates (Wikicommons): p. 4.

Cyan22 (Wikicommons): p. 196.

Sophie Delar: p. 343.

Evert A. Duyckinick Portrait Gallery of Eminent Men and Women in Europe and
    America: p. 96.

A. Elfwine: p. 36.

T. K. Ellappa: p. 25.

Federal Reserve Board: p. 85 (right).

FEMA: p. 297.

Michael Foran: p. 293.

George Grantham Bain collection, Library of Congress: p. 132.

Google Maps: p. 177.

Heritage Auctions: p. 269.

Kevin Hile: p. 174.

Historijski Arhiv Sarajevo: p. 319.

Jastrow (Wikicommons): p. 9.

Jewish Historical Institute: p. 189.

Jjbowks (Wikicommons): p. 6.
Jrtayloriv (Wikicommons): p. 81.
Kunsthistorisches Museum: p. 299.
Library of Congress: pp. 78, 257.
Carrie Lorraine: p. 2.
The Louvre: p. 128.
Michal Manas: p. 13.
Jim Marrs: pp. 165, 175, 178, 181, 200, 243, 288, 335, 337.
Marsyas (Wikicommons): p. 50.
Metropolitan Museum of Art: p. 232.
Montclair Film Festival: p. 338.
NASA: p. 306.
National Archives and Records Administration: p. 316.
National Gallery of Ireland: p. 208.
Nflravens (Wikicommons): p. 309.
NsMn (Wikicommons): p. 77.
Pamukcho (Wikicommons): p. 12.
Reiss-Engelhorn-Museen: p. 119.
Rockefeller Archive Center: p. 116.
Royal Collection, Windsor Castle: p. 235.
Wolfgang Sauber: p. 160.
Philip Scalia: p. 332.
Dominique Signoret: p. 330.
David Stanley: p. 29.
Sustructu (Wikicommons): p. 150.
Trexer (Wikicommons): p. 176.
United Kingdom Government: p. 221.
U.S. Air Force: p. 41.
U.S. Department of Defense: p. 186.
U.S. Government: pp. 38, 240.
U.S. Navy: p. 313.
Daniel Villafruela: p. 66.
White House Historical Association: p. 182.
Wikileaks: p. 44.
Messer Woland: p. 88.
Yale University Art Gallery: p. 238.
Yale University Manuscripts & Archives Digital Images Database: p. 311.
Kenneth C. Zirkel: p. 85 (left).
Public domain: pp. 18, 20, 31, 34, 47, 51, 55, 61, 63, 69, 72, 91, 107, 109, 111, 112, 124, 126, 130, 146, 148, 167, 172, 185, 210, 213, 215, 218, 228, 230, 246, 248, 251, 253, 259, 261, 264, 267, 274, 275, 277, 291, 302, 304.

Introduction

Hesitantly, the candidate crept down the long, dark passageway. It was the day of his initiation and sweat beaded on his forehead from both fear and expectation. His anxiety had continued to rise as he moved through the massive medieval château with its four distinctive turrets and surrounding moat.

Entering an immense hall draped in black cloth, he found the ornate candelabras were dark. In the faint light of lamps along the walls, he was just able to discern what appeared to be corpses draped in shrouds. But they moved. Silently. Leaving a foul odor in the air.

In the center of the dark hall squatted an eerie altar built of human skeletons. He cringed as two of the shrouded figures approached him and tied a pink ribbon smeared with blood on his forehead. A crucifix and an amulet were hung around his neck. His clothes were removed and crosses painted on his naked body in blood. He winced, not daring to move, as his genitals were bound with string.

Five other shrouded figures approached, bloodstained and mumbling incoherently. They threw themselves down in supplication, as if in prayer. There was sudden light as a funeral pyre was lit. He watched wide-eyed as his clothing was tossed into its fire. As the pyre blazed higher, a large form seemed to rise from the flames. The booming voice of a priestly initiator spoke out. Low, but distinctly. With great authority. The initiate could not determine its source but found himself repeating the words of the oath:

> In the name of the crucified one, I swear to sever all bonds which unite me with mother, brothers, sisters, wife, relatives, friends, mistress, kings, superiors, benefactors or any other man to whom I have promised faith, service, or obedience;

I name the place in which I was born. Henceforth I live in another dimension, which I will not reach until I have renounced the evil globe which has been cursed by Heaven;

From now onwards I shall reveal to my new chief all that I have heard or found out; and I shall also seek out and observe things which might otherwise have escaped me;

I honor the *aqua tofana* [a poison developed by Giulia Tofana, executed in Rome in 1659 for killing the husbands of abused women]; it is a quick and essential medium of removing from the earth, through death or robbing them of their wits, of those who oppose truth, and those who try to take it from our hands;

I shall avoid Spain, Naples, and all other accursed lands, and I shall avoid the temptation to betray what I have now heard;

Lightning will not strike as rapidly as the dagger, which will reach me, wherever I may be, should I betray my initiation.

Next, a seven-branched candelabrum, bearing seven black candles, was set before the candidate, along with a bowl containing human blood. The candidate washed himself in the blood, and even drank a quantity of it. The string around his genitals was removed and he was placed in a bath to undergo complete ablution, after which he was served a meal of root vegetables.

So was described an Illuminati initiation at Le Château d'Ermenonville near Paris in a 1789 book entitled *Essai sur la Secte des Illuminés* ("Essay on the Cult of the Illuminati") by Jean-Pierre-Louis de Luchet.

For a visual approximation of such rites with a more modern and erotic viewpoint, see director Stanley Kubrick's controversial film *Eyes Wide Shut*. Of particular interest is that this was Kubrick's last picture (he died in 1999 before its release), and it was filmed in Mentmore Towers, which was built outside London between 1852 and 1854 as a summer home for English businessman Baron Mayer de Rothschild. Many believe that the portrayals of the sensual rituals are reflections of actual events within the Illuminati of today. If the chilling initiation described above seems odd and antiquated, consider what few details have been made public about the Chapter 322 Order of the secret society Skull and Bones on the campus of Yale University, which has inducted members from a core group of about twenty-five families of what has been called the "liberal Eastern Establishment." These include such familiar names as Harriman, Rockefeller, Payne, Davison, Whitney, Lord, Phelps, Wadsworth, Allen, Bundy, Adams, and Bush. It is said that initiates lie naked in a coffin masturbating as they reveal to the members the most intimate details of their sexual exploits. More on this order later.

The Illuminati: The Secret Society that Hijacked the World

The Order was brought from Germany to Yale in 1832. Could it be that Skull and Bones is a modern incarnation of the infamous Bavarian Illuminati, which has cast such a lasting influence right up until today?

"Type 'Illuminati' into an Internet search engine and you will wind up with an impossible aggregation too numerous and contradictory to be useful," noted author William H. McIlhany, who, after research at the British Museum and in Ingolstadt, Germany, wrote a primer on the Illuminati for *The New American* magazine. "A search on Ask.com yields 1.4 million entries, while the same at Google produces 12 million entries, and Yahoo! gives 33 million entries! A small percentage of these deal with genuine historical documents and reliable research by reputable scholars, but the vast majority, unfortunately, deal in fanciful fiction (of the sci-fi or mystery-action-adventure variety) or misinformation and deliberate disinformation posing as fact and serious scholarship."

So what exactly is the Illuminati?

Many researchers and Internet pundits continue to view the fabled Illuminati in much the same way as American businessman, financial adviser, and *Rich Dad, Poor Dad* author Robert Kiyosaki does. He described the Illuminati this way:

The Illuminati began as a secret society under the direction of Jesuit priests. Later, a council of five men, one for each of the points on the pentagram, formed what was called The Ancient and Illuminated Seers of Bavaria. They were high order Luciferian Freemasons, thoroughly immersed in mysticism and eastern mental disciplines, seeking to develop the super powers of the mind. Their alleged plan and purpose is world domination for their lord—which is the fallen Lucifer. The Illuminati are alleged to be the primary motivational forces forcing the global governance, a one-world religion, and centralized control of the world's economic systems. Organizations such as the United Nations, the International Monetary Fund, the World Bank, and the International Criminal Court are seen as tentacles of the Illuminati. The Illuminati are the driving force behind the brainwashing of the mindless masses, blatant mind control, manipulation of beliefs, scientific dumbing-down of society, chemical poisoning of food, water and air (globally known cancers like aluminum salts [chemtrails], aspartame, sodium fluoride, melamime, etc.); also, the Illuminati are revealed to have total and complete control over all the mainstream media of the modern world, all the information, all the food, all the money, most of the world's military forces. The Illuminati's power vehicles are the big banks, and the manipulation of all the money and wealth of the planet. The Illuminati have a private board of elite, interlocking delegates who control the world's major banks. They create inflations, recessions, depressions, and manipulate the world markets, supporting certain leaders and coups and undermining others to achieve their overall goals. The goal behind the Illuminati conspiracy is to create and then manage crises that will eventually convince the masses that globalism, with its centralized economic control and one-world religious ethic, are the necessary solution to the world's woes. This structure, usually known as The New World Order, will of course be ruled by the Illuminati. There are many end times prophecies in the Bible that are interpreted by most to point to an end times one-world government, one-world monetary system, and one-world religion. Many Bible prophecy interpreters see this "New World Order" as being controlled by the antichrist, the end-times false messiah. However all believers in Christ should remember this: God has sovereignly allowed all these developments, and they are not outside of His overall plan. God is in control, not the Illuminati.

But is it really all that?

Many disbelieve that the Illuminati were anything more than some eighteenth-century intellectuals having fun with their own secret society. Skeptics, such as British journalist David Aaronovitch, author of *Voodoo Histories: The Role of the Conspiracy Theory in Shaping Modern History*, has written that such beliefs in an overreaching world plot are "formulated by the politically defeated and taken up by the socially defeated." In other words, losers.

"The Illuminati have become a touchstone for every pseudohistorical, delusional, right-wing, fundamentalist, militia nutjob, and the term is used today as shorthand for a variety of anti-Semite, racist, homophobic, and otherwise distasteful bigotry, but this simply reveals the intellectual poverty of the paranoid conspiracy movement," proclaimed author Joel Levy in his small 2012 tome, *The Little Book of Secret Societies: 50 of the World's Most Notorious Organizations and How to Join Them*. Levy, however, may have approached the truth when he added, "In reality, the Bavarian Illuminati were a short-lived group of little consequence in practical terms, although their ideas and aims … may well have exerted important influence on subsequent intellectual and social developments."

The New England Skeptical Society (NESS) also sees the Illuminati as mere fever dreams of conspiracy-minded reactionaries. It states: "In the paranoid mind, the Illuminati succeeded in their goals, and have now infiltrated every government and every aspect of society. They are responsible for every evil and every unjust act that ever occurs anywhere; the fact that absolutely no evidence of their existence can be found only serves to make them stronger and more frightening. They are the demon in the closet, and will probably never disappear from the paranoid fantasy world of right-wing conspiracy theorists."

Dr. Steven Novella, in an article for the NESS, explained that conspiracy theories exist because "humans have a well-documented propensity for pattern recognition. We seek out patterns as a way of making sense of the complex world around us. Sometimes we see patterns that are not there. Humans also have a natural, and evolutionarily adaptive, paranoia."

He tips his hand as a dedicated debunker of conspiracy by admitting that "a 1992 *New York Times* survey [showed that] 77 percent of Americans hold the demonstrably wrong belief that the JFK assassination was the work of a conspiracy." Novella explained, "The assassination of JFK had enormous consequences; therefore it could not have been the insane act of a lone nut. It must have had an equally enormous cause—a conspiracy. The more elegant view is that we simply live in a wacky world and sometimes stuff happens."

Novella failed to point out that a Gallup Poll in 2003 showed 75 percent of those responding still believe Kennedy's death involved more than a lone individual. Today, most people acknowledge a conspiracy in that tragedy. Most members of current American society have never even heard of the Illuminati, except through the entertainment media, and most could not care less. Those literate enough to have read about the Illuminati generally fall into two distinct categories: the first are those who, like Dr. Novella, cling to a coincidence theory of history. They argue that nothing much is planned, bad stuff just happens, and it is usually merely the result of poor planning, greed, or malfeasance.

One who believes in coincidences is historian Mitch Horowitz, a self-described long-time student of esoteric spirituality and the occult, who wrote in early 2016 about conspiracy theorists. He said, "Rather than looking to grossly flawed policies, negligent and repressive governance, futile and horrific warfare, and administrative incompetence, they looked toward an easier answer in the existence of a 'hidden hand'—anti-church, anti-monarchial and transnational in reach. Conspiracists had little trouble marrying this view to long-standing attitudes of anti-Semitism and xenophobia.

"… [L]et me be clear: The concentration of wealth and power in today's world stems from corrupted policies and a lack of accountability and transparency—not bloodlines of wealth, underground cabals, or secret clubs, talk of which necessarily leads to very dark places and zero political progress."

He concluded, "No, Virginia, secret societies do not run the world. Jury-rigged politics and citizen apathy are the cause of our current dilemmas. We do not need to unmask cloak-and-dagger elites; we need a public that demands accountability, and understands where the real problems lie."

Horowitz's argument is all well and good, but a close examination of the second category of those knowledgeable about the Illuminati—those who hold the idea that the world is being tightly controlled by a handful of powerful personages—cannot be brushed off so lightly when one considers a 2011 study in Switzerland that confirmed the worst fears of conspiracy theorists.

The idea that a small group of international yet interconnected individuals can control the worlds of finance and commerce was confirmed by scientists at the Swiss Federal Institute of Technology in Zurich. Combining mathematics used to model natural systems with comprehensive corporate data, they traced the ownership of forty-three thousand transnational corporations. From a database of thirty-seven million companies and investors, the Swiss team constructed a model of which companies controlled others through shareholding networks, coupled with each company's operating revenues, to map the structure of economic power.

In their analysis of the relationships between these transnational corporations, they identified a relatively small group of companies—primarily banks—with unprecedented centralized control over the global economy.

The Swiss study, published in the October 19, 2011, edition of *New Scientist,* revealed "a core of 1,318 companies with interlocking ownerships. Each of these firms had ties to two or more other companies, and on average they were connected to 20. What's more, although they represented 20 per cent of global operating revenues, the 1,318 appeared to collectively own through their shares the majority of the world's large blue chip and manufacturing firms—the 'real' economy—representing a further 60 per cent of global revenues."

One of the authors of the study, Dr. James B. Glattfelder, stated, "When the team further untangled the web of ownership, it found much of it tracked back to a "super-entity" of 147 even more tightly knit companies—all of their ownership was held by other members of the super-entity—that controlled 40 per cent of the total wealth in the network. In effect, less than one per cent of the companies were able to control 40 per cent of the entire network." The Swiss researchers only limited their study to corporations and never sought to determine the family, social, business, and secret society relationships between owners and stockholders.

Glattfelder added, "Reality is so complex, we must move away from dogma, whether it's conspiracy theories or free-market. Our analysis is reality-based."

History tends to support the conspiratorial view. One need only look at world and national events and place them into an historical context to see the tell-tale signs of conspiracy. A growing number now view human history as one long series of conspiracies. Accidents occur all the time. Planes and cars crash, ships sink, and victims fall off ladders. But if an action cannot be ascribed to an accident or an act of God, then someone planned it. It's a conspiracy. President Franklin D. Roosevelt once remarked, "In politics, nothing happens by accident. If it happens, you can bet it was planned that way."

Other world figures have spoken out regarding conspiracies. In 1856 British prime minister Benjamin Disraeli told the House of Commons, "It is useless to deny, because it is impossible to conceal, that a great part of Europe—the whole of Italy and France and a great portion of [then-fragmented] Germany, to say nothing of other countries—is covered with a network of these secret societies.... And what are their objects? They do not attempt to conceal them. They do not want constitutional government ... they want to change the tenure of land, to drive out the present owners of the soil and to put an end to ecclesiastical establishments [churches]."

World events do not occur by accident. They are made to happen, whether it is to do with national issues or commerce; and most of them are staged and managed by those who hold the purse strings," explained Denis Healey, the British Labour Party minister who once served as the UK's secretary of state for defense.

As far back as 1922, the late New York City mayor John F. Hylan stated, "The real menace of our Republic is the invisible government which like a giant octopus sprawls its slimy length over our city, state and nation.... At the head of this octopus are the Rockefeller-Standard Oil interests and a small group of powerful banking houses generally referred to as the international bankers [who] virtually run the U.S. government for their own selfish purposes."

President John F. Kennedy addressed the ticklish issue of secret society control in a speech before the American Newspaper Publishers Association on April 27, 1961, when he stated, "The very word 'secrecy' is repugnant in a free and open society; and we are as a people inherently and historically opposed to secret societies, to secret oaths and to secret proceedings. We decided long ago that the dangers of excessive and unwarranted concealment of pertinent facts far outweighed the dangers which are cited to justify it."

Kennedy went on to say, "For we are opposed around the world by a monolithic and ruthless conspiracy that relies primarily on covert means for expanding its sphere of influence—on infiltration instead of invasion, on subversion instead of elections, on intimidation instead of free choice, on guerrillas by night instead of armies by day. It is a system which has conscripted vast human and material resources into the building of a tightly knit, highly efficient machine that combines military, diplomatic, intelligence, economic, scientific and political operations. Its preparations are concealed, not published. Its mistakes are buried, not headlined. Its dissenters are silenced, not praised. No expenditure is questioned, no rumor is printed, no secret is revealed."

Many at the time thought Kennedy was talking only about the spread of communism, but considering the connections between communism and Illuminism, coupled with his mention of secret societies, it would appear that Kennedy may have known more about control within the U.S. government than most people could have guessed.

After all, his father, Joseph P. Kennedy, was quoted in the July 26, 1936, edition of the *New York Times* as saying, "Fifty men have run America, and that's a high figure. Fifty men … have within their power, by reason of the wealth which they control…[the ability to] paralyze the whole country, for they control the circulation of currency and can create a panic whenever they will." Apparently, the Kennedy family understood better than most the secret societies and brotherhoods beneath the surface of American life.

Another government insider who confirmed that a plot was afoot was America's first secretary of defense, James Forrestal, who may have paid with his life for his forthrightness. Beginning in 1947, Forrestal voiced his concern that government leaders were consistently making decisions that were not in the best interests of the nation. "These men are not incompetent or stupid. They are crafty and brilliant. Consistency has never been a mark of stupidity. If they were merely stupid, they would occasionally make a mistake in our favor," he noted. In 1949, Forrestal, reportedly in a strange daze, was ordered to Bethesda Naval Hospital by President Harry S. Truman. There, he either fell, jumped, or was thrown from a sixteenth-floor window to his death.

More recently, in 1973 Colonel L. Fletcher Prouty, who served as a Focal Point liaison officer between the Pentagon and the CIA from 1955 to 1963, was able to witness the control mechanisms over both intelligence and the military and wrote about a "Secret Team" that controlled the United States as an "inner sanctum of a new religious order" answerable only to themselves. "The power of the Team derives from its vast intra-governmental undercover infrastructure and its direct relationship with great private industries, mutual funds and investment houses, universities, and the news media, including foreign and domestic publishing houses," explained Prouty, adding, "All true members of the Team remain in the power center whether in office with the incumbent administration or out of office with the hardcore set. They simply rotate to and from official jobs and the business world or the pleasant haven of academe."

And we must not forget Dr. Carroll Quigley, a prominent historian, professor of history at the Foreign Service School of Georgetown University and President Bill Clinton's academic mentor, who wrote in his book *Tragedy and Hope*: "There does exist, and has existed for a generation, an international Anglophile network which operates, to some extent, in the way the radical Right believes the Communists act. I know of the operations of this network because I have studied it for 20 years and was permitted for two years, in the early 1960s, to examine its papers and secret records. I have no aversion to it or to most of its aims and have, for much of my life, been close to it and to many of its instruments.... [I]n general my chief difference of opinion is that it wishes to remain unknown, and I believe its role in history is significant enough to be known."

James Paul Warburg, the son of Paul Moritz Warburg, the German-born first chairman of the Federal Reserve System, gave the game away in 1950 when he told a Senate committee, "We shall have World Government, whether or not we like it. The only question is whether World Government will be achieved by conquest or consent."

The above speakers are credible men and were in positions to know about the subject on which they spoke. Lesser-known contemporary researchers also see a conspiracy afoot to control the world.

Ken Adachi, editor of the *Educate Yourself* website, after viewing the progression of recent history, saw the term "New World Order" as signifying "a worldwide conspiracy being orchestrated by an extremely powerful and influential group of *genetically-related individuals* (at least at the highest echelons) [emphasis in the original] which include many of the world's wealthiest people, top political leaders, and corporate elite, as well as members of the so-called Black Nobility of Europe (dominated by the British Crown) whose goal is to create a One World (fascist) Government, stripped of nationalistic and regional boundaries, that is obedient to their agenda. Their intention is to effect complete and total control over every human being on the planet and to dramatically reduce the world's population by 6.5 Billion people to 500 million. " It might be noted that the term "New World Order" has been used by both President George H. W. Bush and Adolf Hitler.

Johnny Cirucci, a career U.S. Marine, published a book in 2015 titled *Illuminati Unmasked: Everything You Need to Know about the "New World Order" and How We Will Beat It*. Cirucci traced the lineage of the Illuminati from ancient Babylon to the present. He also outlined some of the more notorious claims against the modern Illuminati.

Cirucci described "how the Illuminati have co-opted the United States at every level of government; Barack Obama's shocking ties to this Mystery Religion—and it's not Islam; How American politics have been rigged and who has the power to control every level of your government; All of America's external threats—illegal immigration, pandemics, terrorism—orchestrated by the same people; Who was really behind 9/11 and how they have far worse planned; America's top leaders from both Parties bow to this secret power; The worst days in America can all be traced back to them. American Patriots have been framed and murdered by them and assassination is their specialty."

It is easy to dismiss as conspiracy theory any subject that grates against an individual's core beliefs. However, as has been pointed out, belief is not a valid argument. While everyone is entitled to their beliefs, this does not constitute knowledge. For example, despite evidence of fabrication, Adolf Hitler believed the much-maligned *Protocols of the Learned Elders of Zion* were a genuine document. In *Mein Kampf* he wrote, "They are supposed to be a 'forgery'; the *Frankfurter Zeitung* moans and cries out to the world once a week; the best proof that they are genuine after all … the best criticism applied to them is reality. He who examines the historical development of the past hundred years, from the points of view of [the *Protocols*], will also immediately understand the clamor of the Jewish press. For once this book has become the common property of a people, the Jewish danger is bound to be considered as broken."

Hitler sensed a real conspiracy but in his belief system this conspiracy stemmed from Jews. Some researchers believe there is evidence indicating that the *Protocols* may have originally been an Illuminati document only later fabricated as anti-Jewish propaganda. There will be more to be said about this later.

To add to all this confusion, certain individuals on the Internet seem to be there only to deny, denigrate, and generally distract legitimate conversation concerning secret societies, but especially the Illuminati. Known as "trolls," some are actually paid by government agencies or private organizations—both foundations and corporate entities—while many others are simply naysayers and narrow-minded, argumentative types. Let's begin by taking a look at the word "conspiracy."

The word comes from the Latin *conspirare*, which literally means "to breathe together." In a 1940 edition of *The Modern Webster Dictionary*, the word "conspiracy" is defined simply as "a plot." The terms "plan" or "plot" are essentially neutral words. A surprise birthday party is a plan kept secret from the honoree. But it is not sinister or evil.

Following the assassination of President John F. Kennedy in 1963, many people believed his death was the result of a conspiracy, not a lone-nut assassin as proclaimed by the federal government's Warren Commission. Responding to this growing belief, in April 1967, a CIA official named Clayton P. Nurnad wrote a dispatch to the agency's "Chiefs, Certain Stations and Bases." The dispatch was marked "psych" and "CS"—the former shorthand for "psychological operations" or "psychological disinformation," and the latter referring to the agency's "Clandestine Services" unit (CIA Document No. 1035-960). This memo revealed the CIA's intention to brand any view of the assassination dissenting from the official version as unreasonable conspiracy theory. Nurnad argued, "Just because of the standing of the [Warren] Commissioners, efforts to impugn their rectitude and wisdom tend to cast doubt on the whole leadership of American society. Moreover, there seems to be an increasing tendency to hint that President [Lyndon] Johnson himself, as the one person who might be said to have benefited, was in some way responsible for the assassination. Innuendo of such seriousness affects not only the individual concerned, but also the whole reputation of the American government. Our organization

[CIA] itself is directly involved: among other facts, we contributed information to the investigation. Conspiracy theories have frequently thrown suspicion on our organization, for example by falsely alleging that Lee Harvey Oswald worked for us."

"The aim of this dispatch is to provide material countering and discrediting the claims of the conspiracy theorists, so as to inhibit the circulation of such claims in other countries," Nurnad concluded.

An indication of the effectiveness of this CIA effort is the 1986 *Webster's Third New International Dictionary*'s first definition of conspiracy as "an illegal, treasonable, or treacherous plan to harm or destroy another person, group or entity." A search for the definition today on Google yields the first response as "a secret plan by a group to do something unlawful or harmful."

So a relatively neutral word like "conspiracy"—after all, a proprietary business strategy is a conspiracy—has become a pejorative term used against anyone who would dare question the government's pronouncements on the JFK assassination or any other problematic issue. Until the attacks of 9/11, which obviously involved a conspiracy, the term "conspiracy theory" was connected by the corporate mass media to any statements or claims they considered anti-government, perhaps even unpatriotic.

It has been said that "conspiracy theorist" is a term used today as a derogatory slur to dismiss any person who is a critical thinker.

One such critical thinker is Carl Oglesby, political activist and author of the influential 1976 book *The Yankee and Cowboy War: Conspiracies from Dallas to Watergate*. He wrote, "Conspiracy is the normal continuation of normal politics by normal means."

Many conspiracy theories, such as claims of a Nazi base on the moon or that all TVs are being used to spy on us, fall short of solid evidence. Others, such as questions surrounding the Apollo 11 moon landing or Adolf Hitler surviving World War II, while given no serious consideration by the public at large, nevertheless contain persuasive and puzzling aspects to the official story. Critics of the official account of the 9/11 attacks are decried as conspiracy theorists, yet the official 9/11 Commission narrative fails to even mention, much less explain, how two aircraft can bring down three separate buildings—World Trade Centers one, two, and seven (seven being also known as the Salomon Brothers Building), which collapsed at 5:25 P.M. on the afternoon of September 11, 2001.

In fact, in his 2009 book, *The Ground Truth: The Untold Story of America under Attack on 9/11*, John Farmer, senior counsel to the National Commission on Terrorist Attacks upon the United States (better known as the official 9/11 Commission), wrote, "In the course of our investigation into the national response to the attacks, the 9/11 Commission staff discovered that the official version of what had occurred that morning [September 11, 2001]—that is, what government and military officials had told Congress, the Commission, the media, and the public about who knew what when—was *almost entirely, and inexplicably, untrue* [emphasis added]."

To make certain there was no misunderstanding his message, Farmer later stated, "At some level of the government, at some point in time, this book concludes, there was a decision not to tell the truth about what happened."

Such skepticism, as expressed by Farmer, is healthy and should be encouraged. However, simply pleading skepticism cannot always shield dedicated conspiracy deniers. As Jonathan Elinoff, writing for *Infowars.com*, noted, "Skeptics are important in achieving an objective view of reality. However, skepticism is not the same as reinforcing the official storyline. In fact, a conspiracy theory can be argued as an alternative to the official or 'mainstream' story of events. Therefore, when skeptics attempt to ridicule a conspiracy theory by using the official story as a means of proving the conspiracy wrong, in effect, they are just reinforcing the original 'mainstream' view of history, and actually not being skeptical."

Elinoff said it is common for "hit pieces" or "debunking articles" to address the most fringe conspiracy theories. "This in turn makes all conspiracies on a subject matter look crazy," he wrote. "*Skeptic* magazine and *Popular Mechanics*, among many others, did this with 9/11. They referred to less than 10 percent of the many different conspiracy theories about 9/11 and picked the less popular ones—in fact, they picked the fringe, highly improbable points that only a few people make. This was used as the 'final investigation' for looking into the conspiracy theories. Convenient, huh?"

Elinoff joined many others in pointing to events once thought to be just conspiracy theory that later investigation proved to be true. Just a few examples include:

- French artillery officer Alfred Dreyfus was convicted of selling military information to the Germans in 1894 and sent to Devil's Island in French Guiana. Dreyfus protested his innocence and claimed he was being used as a scapegoat because he was a Jew. Many people began to support him but were accused of being conspiracy theorists. The argument over his role grew over the years and divided France. A second trial again brought in a guilty verdict but by 1906 enough evidence had been gathered to prove his innocence and show that ranking military officers had lied and fabricated evidence against him. Dreyfus was exonerated and reinstated as a major in the army. However, the French Army did not officially admit his innocence until 1995.

- Following the August 1964 Gulf of Tonkin incident, which prompted President Lyndon Johnson to push through Congress a resolution allowing him to continue the Vietnam War without a formal declaration of war, conspiracy theorists claimed there was no attack on U.S. warships (the official excuse for war). They were belittled and called unpatriotic. However, in 2005, the National Security Agency (NSA) finally released an internal study showing that of two reported attacks on American ships, one was instigated by the United States and the other was only false images caught on radar. In 1984, *U.S. News & World Report* described the event as "the phantom battle that led to war."

- By the late 1960s, conspiracy researchers were whispering that the CIA was assassinating its enemies around the world. Irate citizens claimed that the United States would never engage in such activities, only seen in places like Nazi Germany and Soviet Russia. However, in 1975, during hearings by the U.S. Senate Select Committee to Study Governmental Operations with Respect to Intelligence Activities, headed by Senator Frank Church, it was learned the CIA had violated its charter to perform only intelligence gathering outside the United States. The committee learned of the controversial "suicide" of Salvador Allende in Chile in 1973 and the CIA-supported overthrow of Mohammad Mossadegh in Iran in 1967, as well as other Central and South American leaders and revolutionaries. The committee discovered that CIA agents used a variety of largely undetectable killing methods such as the injection of cancer and staging suicides, along with car, skiing, and boat accidents, and even the use of a "Heart Attack Gun."

- For years, researchers claimed that major U.S. media were being infiltrated with CIA assets who managed, even distorted, the news. Just such activity, Operation Mockingbird, was documented by the Church committee, and in 1977 famed Watergate reporter Carl Bernstein revealed this conspiracy with a well-documented, 25,000-word exposé in *Rolling Stone* magazine entitled "The CIA and the Media."

- Similar claims of government misconduct came during the anti-Vietnam War demonstrations of the 1960s and 1970s. Peace activists claimed government provocateurs were infiltrating the peace movement causing disruption and violence. They were dismissed as hippie conspiracy theorists. A program just as described was successfully kept secret until 1971, when a group called the Citizens' Commission to Investigate the FBI burgled an FBI field office in Media, Pennsylvania, and took files exposing the FBI's Counterintelligence Program (COINTELPRO), a secret project aimed at surveilling, infiltrating, discrediting, and disrupting domestic political groups. Even with this evidence available, some major media refused to print the story.

- Since the attacks of 9/11, a growing number of people have claimed the events of that day were false-flag actions (actions designed to shift blame from the true perpetrators), instigated by individuals within the U.S. government to provide a pretext for war in the Middle East and to erode civil liberties at home. Dismissed as wild conspiracy theory, many argued that government leaders would never support an attack on their own citizens. However, Operation Northwoods documents discovered and released by Congress's Assassination Records Review Board (ARRB) revealed that in 1962 the Northwoods plan was secretly approved by the Joint Chiefs of Staff. This plan called for sinking ships in the Caribbean, firing on boats of Cuban refugees, hijacking airliners, setting off bombs in American cities, and even assassinating citizens in such a manner as to place the blame on Fidel Castro and incite renewed public support for another invasion of Cuba. Apparently, Northwoods was stopped only by orders of President John F. Kennedy.

- Speaking of Kennedy, despite years of pounding the lone-assassin theory onto the American public by the corporate mass media, which also lambasts those who see a plot behind JFK's death as witless conspiracy theorists, national polls beginning in 1964 and into the twenty-first century show a majority of citizens disbelieve the idea of a lone assassin. A Gallup poll in 1963 showed 52 percent thought more than one person was involved in the assassination. By 2001, this number had reached a high of 81 percent.

As far back as 1928, famed author H. G. Wells joined the ranks of conspiracy theorists by proclaiming plots behind world events. Writing in his book *The Open Conspiracy*, Wells stated:

Not only are the present governments of the world a fragmentary competitive confusion, but none of them is as simple as it appears. They seem to be simple because they have formal heads and definite forms, councils, voting assemblies, and so forth, for arriving at decisions. But the formal heads, the kings, presidents, and so forth, are really not the directive heads. They are merely the figure heads. They do not decide. They merely make gestures of potent and dignified acquiescence when decisions are put to them. They are complicating shams. Nor do the councils and assemblies really decide. They record, often very imperfectly and exasperatingly, the accumulating purpose of outer forces. These outer really directive forces are no doubt very intricate in their operation; they depend finally on religious and educational forms and upon waves of gregarious feeling, but it does not in the least simplify the process of collective human activity to pretend that it is simple and to set up symbols and dummies in the guise of rulers and dictators to embody that pretense.

Once a Fabian Socialist in England, Wells outlined a plan for a New World Order that intimated Illuminati influence:

> We have now sketched out in these blue prints the methods by which the confused radicalism and constructive forces of the present time may, can, and probably will be drawn together about a core of modernized religious feeling into one great and multifarious creative effort…. Whenever possible, the Open Conspiracy will advance by illumination and persuasion. But it has to advance, and even from the outset, where it is not allowed to illuminate and persuade, it must fight. Its first fights will probably be for the right to spread its system of ideas plainly and clearly throughout the world.

Wells concluded, "A time will come when men will sit with history before them or with some old newspaper before them and ask incredulously, 'Was there ever such a world?'"

We see in Wells's words his solid conviction of ongoing conspiracy and they echo the Illuminati doctrine for changing the world, a doctrine that first coalesced with the creation of the Bavarian Illuminati in 1776 Germany.

Yet, while much has been written and electronically produced regarding the Illuminati, very little of documented substance has reached the public.

The curtains of Illuminati secrecy parted somewhat in 2009, when TrineDay published a book of more than 500 pages by Canadian author Terry Melanson, who studied old works in French, German, and Italian and presented what well may be the most thorough and authoritative overview of the Order yet produced.

TrineDay publisher Kris Millegan explained the results of the lack of documented information on the Illuminati thusly:

> The dearth of validated material about this secretive group has helped to create a ferociously adaptive "conspiracy-theory-of-the-day" phenomenon, with many employing the Illuminati as their prime covert antagonist, muddying the waters of history and creating wakes of disinformation, misinformation, and just plain wrong information. This state of affairs has generally hidden the true nature of the Illuminati, and their place in history.

One irreverent author, the late Robert Anton Wilson, elaborated in his 1977 book, *Cosmic Trigger: Final Secret of the Illuminati,* upon many of the myths concerning that Bavarian Order. He wrote a succinct overview of the Order. After presenting a brief synopsis of the creation of the Illuminati by Adam Weishaupt in 1776 and its suppression by the Bavarian government less than ten years later, Wilson wrote:

It has been claimed that Dr. Weishaupt was an atheist, a Cabalistic magician, a rationalist, a mystic; a democrat, a socialist, an anarchist, a fascist; a Machiavellian amoralist, an alchemist, a totalitarian and an "enthusiastic philanthropist." (The last was the verdict of Thomas Jefferson, by the way.) The Illuminati have also been credited with managing the French and American revolutions behind the scenes, taking over the world, being the brains behind Communism, continuing underground up to the 1970s, secretly worshipping the Devil, and mopery with intent to gawk. Some claim that Weishaupt didn't even invent the Illuminati, but only revived it. The Order of Illuminati has been traced back to the Knights Templar, to the Greek and Gnostic initiatory cults, to Egypt, even to Atlantis. The one safe generalization one can make is that Weishaupt's intent to maintain secrecy has worked; no two students of Illuminology have ever agreed totally about what the "inner secret" or purpose of the Order actually was (or is …). There is endless room for spooky speculation, and for pedantic paranoia, once one really gets into the literature of the subject; and there has been a wave of sensational "ex-poses" of the Illuminati every generation since 1776. If you were to believe all this sensational literature, the damned Bavarian conspirators were responsible for everything wrong with the world, including the energy crises and the fact that you can't even get a plumber on weekends.

The name of the Illuminati has apparently meant many things to many different people. But regardless of their position, most agree that Illuminati—and those who follow Illuminati doctrine—have attempted to gain some measure control over their fellow humans as well as the religious and political institutions of their time. This compulsion to control others is not limited to the Bavarian Illuminati. Many persons down through history, from dictators like Hitler and Stalin down to political and corporate leaders of today, have followed the tenets of Illuminism—the founding Illuminati doctrine that they alone had developed a personal enlightenment not accessible to the rest of humankind. This theology included the desire to control others, to operate in secrecy, and adhere to the idea that the end justifies the means. Thus, the shadow of the Illuminati has been cast right up to the events of today. So, we find that any reference to the Illuminati must distinguish between the old Bavarian organization, which is now defunct, and the theology of Illuminism, which is very much alive. But to fully comprehend Illuminism, one must trace the antecedents of this philosophy back through history to its origins.

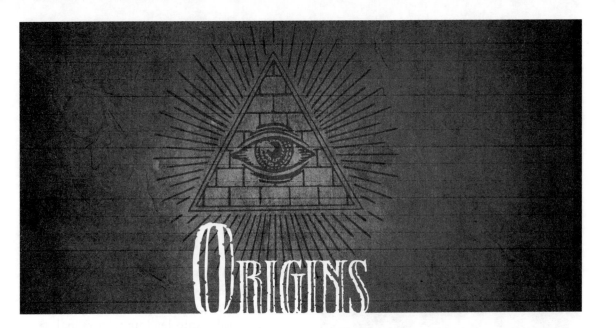

Origins

Conspiracies and secret societies have been with us since the dawn of humankind. After all, humans are social animals. They prefer, even need, companionship with another person. From the beginning, humans have banded together, first as families, then as tribes, communities, and nations.

Even in education systems it is important to belong to some group. This might be a popular organization such as the school ball team, pep squad, science club, or band. Or it may be in a less reputable group such as hipsters, Goths, and stoners. Even loners band together.

Following school life, there is still the need for companionship, to belong. It is this drive that fills churches, Lions and Rotary Clubs, honky-tonks, and sports bars.

In some individuals, the desire to lead is more powerful than the desire to simply belong. In the distant past, the mightiest warriors became chiefs while the more intellectual tribe members became soothsayers and shamans. Both the hunters and the shamans would form cliques, bound together by shared experiences and comradery.

Secrecy has always played a role in any collection of humans, from prehistoric hunters, who felt themselves above other tribe members, to chamber of commerce members, who keep their business strategy hidden from competitors. In almost all areas of life there is the suspicion that only well-connected persons get the choice jobs. Everyone occasionally has the feeling of being left out, be it from some social group or the plans of others.

"Whether it's a child in his own special club of two or three members, or whether it's a businessman in the Freemasons, there's nothing unusual about wanting to belong to a secret society," writes David V. Barrett, a British sociolo-

Publisher Adam Parfrey of Feral House has said there are over 600 secret societies operating today.

gist who has worked with the U.S. National Security Agency (NSA), in *A Brief History of Secret Societies*. "It can be fun; there is the delight in knowing secrets that few others know; the satisfaction of being included in the in-group; a feeling of importance, and sometimes of power; and sometimes there is genuine power through being one of the decision-makers, one of the elite."

Barrett defines a secret society as having the following characteristics: carefully graded and progressive teachings, training available only to select members, teaching that leads to some hidden truths, the practice of rituals not open to nonmembers, and membership leading to personal benefits beyond the reach and even the understanding of the uninitiated.

Adam Parfrey, the founder of Feral House, a publisher of books on subjects generally ignored by the mainstream, defines a "secret society" as a social group that demands an oath of allegiance to join. "That's our perspective; we know that others may feel differently," said Parfrey, the author of *Apocalypse Culture*. "Some service-oriented organizations, like Lions or Elks, have a great deal of secret ritual within its structure. Rotary and Kiwanis, less so, but these organizations, like the Masons, require oaths of allegiance. No oath, no membership."

Parfrey said he has identified more than 600 secret societies existing today and that the number just in the United States provides a "snapshot of America" as they address many and disparate concerns. These include labor unions, business groups, rural/agrarian organizations, religious and occult organizations, sobriety groups, drinking groups, and both immigrant and anti-immigrant organizations. As we all know, at the beginning of history, humans were primitive and only modern man is civilized. At least that's what the vast majority of people believe. "It is, however, one of the most egregious fallacies conceivable," wrote Brian Heatley, an Irish-born New Age writer who uses the pen name Michael Tsarion. He explained:

> A second cataclysmic wave, so to speak, has likewise swept from existence august Druidic colleges that once operated throughout the world. These colleges had been restoring, for the good of all, elements of technology from a devastated bygone age of the

gods. These colleges and their creators are equally lost, buried and forgotten. In the place of primordial sanctums of knowledge and culture there arose institutions and teachings that seek not to improve and enlighten, but confuse and mislead.... It might be said that history is the story of the conflict between the Servants of Truth and the virtue-less ones; between magicians and sorcerers. The obliteration of the gnosis of the primordial caste of Elders was a man-made holocaust largely unknown today. It is this calamity that has damaged and oppressed the peoples of the world more than any series of natural disasters, terrible as they might have been. To the Elders of old, a twisted darkened mind was a horror worse to behold than a broken lightless world.

But remnants of this lost knowledge were passed down within the secret societies found in ancient clans and communities, which continued to grow as nomadic tribes evolved into cities and states, then into nations and empires. At one time or another, even major religions like Christianity and Islam were considered secret societies, operating clandestinely and banned by the regime then in power.

The deepest secrets of secret societies all seem to trace back to ancient Sumer in Mesopotamia. This was the first known great civilization and was located between the Tigris and Euphrates rivers at the headwaters of the Persian Gulf. In biblical times, it was called Chaldea or Shinar. Today, it is known as Iraq, which derived its name from the ancient Sumerian city of Uruk. The Sumerian culture seemed to appear from nowhere more than 6,000 years ago and before it ended, it had greatly influenced life as far east as the Indus River, which flows from the Himalayas through Pakistan to the Arabian Sea, and the Nile of the later Egyptian kingdoms. Sumer was an amazing and fully evolved civilization that handed down the basics for all ensuing western cultures— from language and law to mathematics, agriculture, and astronomy.

Virtually nothing was known about the Sumerians until about 150 years ago when archeologists, spurred on by the writings of Italian traveler Pietro della Valle in the early 1600s, began to dig into the strange mounds that dotted the countryside in southern Iraq. Beginning with the discovery of Sargon II's palace near modern-day Khorsabad by Frenchman Paul-Émile Botta in 1843, archeologists found buried cities, broken palaces, artifacts, and thousands of clay tablets detailing every facet of Sumerian life. By the late 1800s, Sumerian had been recognized as an original language and was being translated. Despite today's knowledge, the general public still has been taught little about this first great human civilization, which suddenly materialized between the Tigris and Euphrates rivers.

It is fascinating to realize that it may be possible to know more about this 6,000-year-old civilization than we may ever know about the more recent Egyptians, Greeks, and Romans. The explanation lies in the Sumerian cuneiform writing. Whereas the papyrus of other elder empires disintegrated over time or was destroyed by the fires of war, cuneiform was etched onto wet clay tablets with a stylus to create a wedge-shaped script. These tablets were then dried, baked, and kept in large libraries. About 500,000 of these clay tablets have now been found and have provided modern researchers with invaluable knowledge of the Sumerians, although only about 20 percent have been translated. These tablets are stashed within various museums around the world and are largely unseen by the public.

Conventional history tells us Sumer grew out of a collection of hunter-gatherer clans who banded together to form the first human civilization within the Tigris-Euphrates Valley about 4000 B.C.E. Archeological studies have shown that by 3300 B.C.E., the Sumerians had developed an amazing and advanced society that included drained marshes, lengthy canals, and dams and dikes, and they had built a large-scale irrigation system next to gleaming cities containing huge pyramidal structures called ziggurats.

Sumer was invaded from the west and north by Semitic tribes about 2400 B.C.E., and by 2350 B.C.E. it was captive to the warrior king Sargon the Great, who founded the Semite Akkadian dynasty, which stretched from the Persian Gulf to the Mediterranean. After years of warfare and population displacement, the lands of Sumer were united under Hammurabi of Babylon, whose famous "Code" of laws may have been instituted to discipline the mass migrations of people taking place at that time due to wars and geophysical catastrophes. It is now clear that the Code of Hammurabi was drawn from laws set down by the Sumerians centuries earlier, particularly the earliest law code yet discovered, issued by the Sumerian king Ur-Nammu.

In addition to a legal system, the Sumerians also gave us mathematics based on a sexagesimal system (a numeral system with a base of 60), which permitted a precise method of measuring large quantities by area and volume. This system was passed down to the Babylonians and is still in use today, with some modifications, to measure time, angles, and geographic coordinates. The Sumerians also were able to determine the relationship of the hypotenuse to the lengths of the other two sides of a right triangle, a theorem only much later rediscovered by Pythagoras.

Alan Alford, author of *Gods of the New Millennium: Scientific Proof of Flesh &*

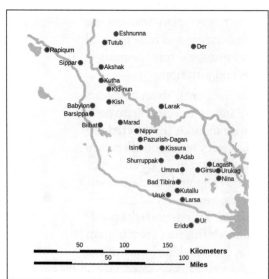

The Sumer civilization extended across the Tigris-Euphrates Valley about 6,000 years ago.

Blood Gods, regarded the Sumerian knowledge of astronomy as both amazing and puzzling. "(T)he whole concept of spherical astronomy, including the 360-degree circle, the zenith, the horizon, the celestial axis, the poles, the ecliptic, the equinoxes, etc., all arose suddenly in Sumer," he noted. Sumerian knowledge of the movements of the sun and moon resulted in the world's first calendar, used for centuries afterward by the Semites, Egyptians, Greeks, and the Illuminati.

Alford wrote that few people realize that we owe not only our geometry but also our modern timekeeping systems to the Sumerian base 60 mathematical system. "The origin of 60 minutes in an hour and 60 seconds in a minute is not arbitrary, but designed around a sexagesimal (based on the number 60) system," Alford reported, adding that the modern zodiac was a Sumerian creation based on their twelve "gods." They used it to chart a great precessional cycle—the division of the 360-degree view from the Earth's North Pole during its twelve-month orbit around the sun into twelve equal parts—or houses—of 30 degrees each. Taking into account the slight wobble in Earth's orbit, movement through this complete cycle takes 25,920 years, an event known as the Platonian Year, named for the Greek scholar Plato, who inspired future secret societies such as the Knights Templars, the Illuminati, and Cecil Rhodes's Round Tables. Alford posited, "The uncomfortable question which the scientists have avoided is this: how could the Sumerians, whose civilization only lasted 2,000 years, possibly have observed and recorded a celestial cycle that took 25,920 years to complete? And why did their civilization begin in the middle of a zodiac period? Is this a clue that their astronomy was a legacy from the gods?" Before it strangely vanished, the Sumerian culture had greatly influenced life from the Indus River to the peoples of Palestine and the later Egyptian kingdoms. The biblical patriarch Abraham brought the knowledge of Sumer to Egypt by means of cleverly coded information found within the Torah and other old Hebraic texts such as the *Sefer Yezirah* (Book of Creation) and the *Sefer HaZohar* (Book of Light).

> Before it strangely vanished, the Sumerian culture had greatly influenced life from the Indus River to the peoples of Palestine and the later Egyptian kingdoms.

These books predate the Talmud, a compilation of older Jewish laws and traditions first written down in the fifth century C.E. but produced centuries before the time of Jesus. According to the Book of Light, God gave Adam the "mysteries of wisdom" while Adam was still in the fabled Garden of Eden. These elder secrets were then passed on through Adam's sons to Noah and on to Abraham long before the Hebrews existed as a distinct people. According to the Bible, Abraham was a Sumerian nobleman from Ur of Chaldea, the ancient term for Iraq. Other Sumerians traveled frequently and widely and are thought to have brought their advanced technology of ship building and mapping to the early Phoenicians, who settled along the eastern

Mediterranean coast in what is now Lebanon. Historians have been left with the question of how the early primitive humans of almost 6,000 years ago suddenly transformed from small packs of hunter-gatherers into a full-blown civilization—advanced even by today's standards. Even the writers of *The New Encyclopedia Britannica* acknowledged that serious questions remain concerning the Sumerian histories and cautiously explained that such queries "are posed from the standpoint of 20th century civilization and are in part colored by ethical overtones, so that answers can only be relative."

Since we now have thousands of translated Sumerian tablets along with their inscribed cylinder seals, perhaps we should allow the Sumerians themselves to explain. The answer is that they claimed everything they achieved came from beings who came from the skies. "All the ancient peoples believed in gods who had descended to Earth from the heavens and who could at will soar heavenwards," explained Middle Eastern scholar Zecharia Sitchin in the prologue to the first book of a series detailing his translations and interpretations of Sumerian accounts of their origin and history. "But these tales were never given credibility, having been branded by scholars from the very beginning as myths."

Russian-American author Zecharia Sitchin believes that the technology of ancient Sumer was brought there by the extraterrestrial Annunaki.

Recognizing that even the most learned researcher before the turn of the twentieth century could not possibly have begun to think in terms of concepts we accept as commonplace today, Sitchin reasoned, "Now that astronauts have landed on the Moon, and unmanned spacecraft explore other planets, it is no longer impossible to believe that a civilization on another planet more advanced than ours was capable of landing its astronauts on the planet Earth sometime in the past."

It is most significant that the Sumerians never referred to the beings who brought them knowledge as "gods." This was a later interpretation by the Romans and Greeks, who fashioned their own "gods" after the earlier oral traditions.

Most people think of the ancient empires of the Sumerians, Babylonians, Akkadians, Phoenicians, and Assyrians as separate civilizations. However, a close inspection of history will show that each was a degraded version of its predecessor.

First came Sumer with its amazing ziggurats, agriculture (they had four types of beer!), and written language. The Sumerian cuneiform tablets, more than half a million still cached away in museums across the world, state that civilization was brought to them by beings who could fly through the air. These god-like beings were called the Anunnaki, translated as "those who came from the heavens to the Earth." Many who follow the writings of Sitchin are convinced the Anunnaki were extraterrestrial visitors.

"An astonishing array of scientific and technological feats are described in the Sumerian tablets, such as genetic engineering and cloning, interplanetary travels around their nomad planet, instantaneous distant communication, and the ubiquitous use of techno-magical chips called ME's—erroneously translated as 'formulas' before the Sumerian and biblical expert Zecharia Sitchin brought in a revolutionary perspective on this high-tech civilization of our ancestors," wrote Chris H. Hardy, author of *Wars of the Anunnaki: Nuclear Self-Destruction in Ancient Sumer.* In her book, she presents very human-like descriptions of the sky gods as well as the evidence of nuclear attacks in our distant past—from radioactive corpses to vitrified stones in diverse places, indicating the possibility that they were fused by great and sudden heat, most probably from atomic blasts.

Others, such as authors Philip Gardiner and Gary Osborn in their well-researched book *The Shining Ones: The World's Most Powerful Secret Society Revealed,* state that these enlightened beings might have alternatively come from inner Earth or from some earlier destroyed civilization akin to fabled Atlantis. The tradition of gods who acted in very human ways—they envied and hated each other, schemed against their relatives, even fought wars among themselves using humans as pawns—has been carried down through the religions of the Egyptians, Greeks, and Romans. Gardiner and Osborn attempted to determine if secret societies, such as the Illuminati, Freemasons, Rosicrucians, Knights Templar, Knights of Malta, Opus Dei, and others revolved around the same center. They concluded they do.

According to Gardiner and Osborn, "We had discovered that down the ages many organizations, however seemingly diverse and contradictory, had all been various fronts or derivatives of the Shining Ones. It was as if they were all part of a wheel. The outer rim is the face of the group or society. One side of the rim cannot see what the other side is doing, or even that it exists. The center can see what is happening in all directions but is distanced from it, while still holding all the spokes in its grasp.

"The same is true in the world of secret or exclusive societies. The world sees the groups from the rim, but that is all. But we are just like those on the rim—we cannot see the center of the wheel from our prospective."

Gardiner and Osborn concluded: "They [secret societies] have all essentially arisen from the same hub or stem: The Catholic Church, which in turn, in our view, can be traced back to ancient Sumer and the Shining Ones....

The secret doctrines of the Shining Ones have steered the development of humankind for possibly 50,000 years, and continue to do so today."

A close examination of the astounding similarities in character between the gods of ancient times appears to go beyond mere coincidence. While the names change with the different languages, the descriptions remain remarkably similar.

The god who ruled from the heavens was Anu to the Sumerians, Amen-Ra to the Egyptians, Cronos to the Greeks, and Saturn to the Romans. The wife of the Heavenly Father for the Sumerians was Antu, for the Egyptians was Mut, for the Greeks was Hera, and for the Romans was Juno. The ruler over the Earth was the Sumerian god Enlil, the Egyptian Set, the Greek Zeus, and the Roman Jupiter. This deity's wife was the Sumerian Ninhursag, the Egyptian goddess Isis, and the Greek and Roman goddesses Athena and Minerva. A brother and builder of monuments on Earth was the Sumerian Enki, the Egyptian Osiris, the Greek Apollo, and the Roman Vulcan while a rival warrior god was the Sumerian Marduk, the Egyptian Horus, the Greek Ares, and the Roman Mars. The goddess of love and nurturing was Asherah, Hathor, Aphrodite, and Venus. Could these various "gods" be describing the same living beings, individuals who once communed with men and lived beyond human years? The racial memory of interacting with actual beings might explain the fervor and durability of some religions. Authors Gardiner and Osborn pointed out that regardless of these beings' origin, "... whatever scientific knowledge was passed on was originally based on fundamental spiritual principles, and more importantly, *one's attainment of the higher states of consciousness* [emphasis in the original]—the spiritual awakening the ancient Hindus named *kundalini*."

> A close examination of the astounding similarities in character between the gods of ancient times appears to go beyond mere coincidence.

"Of course not everyone who lived during this now forgotten epoch [the time of the Anunnaki] understood this knowledge," they added, "only those who had earned the position of 'adept' or 'master' understood it and utilized it ... a shamanic priesthood of some kind which we have now identified and who were known as the Shining Ones."

Gardiner and Osborn said their in-depth research into world civilizations and cultures led them to believe that knowledge, however imperfect, of these ancient Shining Ones constitutes a global phenomenon in which dissimilar names but similar descriptions have been applied to "certain intelligent beings" that have existed around the world emerging at different periods of history. In the Middle East, remnants of Anunnaki/Shining Ones' knowledge and some bits of their technology were passed down to the Akkadians, a Semitic race that assimilated with the Sumerians, yet kept the Sumerian language because it was thought to be from the gods. The Akkadian state broke into the empires of the Hittites, the Assyrians, and the Babylonians. The knowledge and beliefs of what had been the Sumerian Empire made their way to Egypt, largely though the travels of the biblical patriarch Abraham, who was from Chaldea, a previous name for the residents of southeastern Mesopotamia known for their interest and study of astronomy and astrology. By 3100 B.C.E., the technology of the ancient gods brought the fledgling Egyptian Empire into a prominence that lasted for more than thirty centuries. The greatness of Egypt was to be followed by the renown civilizations of Greece and later Rome.

Dr. Arthur David Horn, who resigned as a professor of biological anthropology at Colorado State University after he concluded that the con-

The Akkadian king Narâm-Sîn is shown on a victore stele celebrating a victory against the Lullubi. The king wears a helmet with horns, which represented divinity because kings ruled by divine right.

ventional explanations for man's origins he taught were "nonsense," wrote in his book *Humanity's Extraterrestrial Origins*, "Let us make clear, once again, that we do not believe the ancient Sumerian and other Mesopotamian stories are 'absolutely true' history. These stories that have come to us through thousands of years of oral tradition and writing are bound to be somewhat distorted—probably in some cases deliberately distorted by the Anunnaki. But, I feel these ancient stories are probably as close as we'll come to the truth today...."

One should consider what current events will sound like 2,000 years from now—the greatest nation on Earth bombing some of the smallest and weakest for no clear reasons, people starving in parts of the world while farmers are paid not to plant crops in others, technophiles sitting at home playing electronic golf rather than the real thing, and police forces ordered to arrest people who simply desire to ingest a psychoactive weed. People of that future era will likely laugh it all off as fantastic myths just as many of us do concerning ancient aliens.

> These ancient wars became the metaphorical basis for the struggle between the new monotheistic God and his evil counterpart, Satan.

Yet searchers for truth cannot afford to laugh off the accounts of the Sumerian reporters who have been proven accurate in so many of their records. Just as the overwhelming evidence of conspiratorial control exists in government, business and the media cannot be ignored. Already breakthroughs in astronomy, anthropology, archeology, and Egyptology have only tended to support the thesis of ancient nonhuman intervention.

Researchers have found that the Anunnaki firmly established the dominance of the priesthoods and the divine right of kings in the earliest civilizations. By the time of the ancient Egyptians, religions were well established and had merged with the prevailing political structure. Anointed priests who worshiped one god exhorted their followers to demonize the worshipers of the others. Anyone who failed to offer allegiance to his or her one true god was castigated as a blasphemer, heathen, devil worshiper, or worse.

The Earth, or at least the Near East, was devastated at some point, either through natural cataclysms or some prehistoric war. The Anunnaki gods withdrew from overt human contact. As these gods dropped from sight, the religions they created became metaphysical. The concept of God evolved from a physical being to an omnipresent yet anthropomorphic supernatural entity. The conflicts between the ancient astronauts, who commanded armies of human subjects, were faithfully recorded in the Old Testament. These ancient wars became the metaphorical basis for the struggle between the new monotheistic God and his evil counterpart, Satan.

Baptist minister and author Paul Von Ward noted, "Here [in Mesopotamia] religions that grew out of absentee-[Advanced Being or Anunnaki]-cults that described their gods as immortal, magical beings took the next step toward supernaturalism."

Let us consider historically how human populations have been controlled. Throughout the ages, there have been two predominant methods for controlling humankind—religion and finance. These well-honed control mechanisms may well be of extraterrestrial origin, according to a growing number of researchers. Early humans instinctively sensed some unseen guiding force behind the order of life and developed spirituality. But with the advances of scientific knowledge over the centuries, such blind faith should have fallen away. But it hasn't. Today, most of the world's population continues to follow one religion or another, often leading to conflict, wars, and genocides. What is it that has made religion so important in the minds of so many?

Some believe that most religions, certainly the Judeo-Christian beliefs found in western nations today, can be traced back to Sumer, the world's earliest recorded civilization, and, interestingly enough, one of the few places on Earth to which Americans cannot easily travel.

According to ancient Sumerian tablets, the Old Testament, Egyptian papyrus, and the accounts of the Greek and later Romans, there was a time when humans experienced face-to-face encounters with their gods. Virtually every ancient culture in this world contains legends of gods who came from the sky and taught them fundamentals of civilization—language, mathematics, astronomy, chemistry, law, and architecture. These include Native American tribes; the Mayans, Aztecs, and Incas of Central and South America; the ancient Chinese, Egyptians, and Greeks; the aborigines of Australia; and certain African tribes such as the Dogons. The Masonic historian Walter Leslie Wilmshurst gave clues to the hidden history of Freemasonry when he wrote of a "Golden Age" when "men were once in conscious conversation with the unseen world and were shepherded, taught and guided by the 'gods'...." He noted that humankind lost its way after a "fall" due to its attempt to gain the same knowledge as its creators, a concept comparable with the biblical "fall from grace."

This "fall" of mankind, according to Wilmshurst, was not due to any individual transgression but to "some weakness or defect in the collective or group-soul of the Adamic race," so that "within the Divine counsels" it was decided that "humanity should be redeemed and restored to its pristine state," a process that required "vast time-cycles for its achievement." He added that this restoration also required "skilled scientific assistance" from "those gods and angelic guardians of the erring race of whom all the ancient traditions and sacred writings tell."

The earliest accounts in religious writings have become garbled over the centuries. For example, it should be noted that in the original texts, there was nothing spiritual about angels. In the Greek translations of original documents,

A painting of the angel Gabriel by Leonardo Da Vinci is typical of how many people thing of such beings. The word "angel" comes from a Greek word simply meaning "messenger."

the word *angelos* (*angelus* in the Latin) simply meant "messenger." So an angel of the Lord becomes a messenger of the Lord.

Many in the past have seen a more down-to-earth aspect to the ancient accounts. The thirty-third-degree Scottish Rite Mason Manly Palmer Hall, in his seminal book *The Secret Teachings of All Ages*, acknowledged early contact between humans and others by writing, "In the remote past the gods walked with men and they chose from among the sons of men the wisest and the truest. With these specially ordained and illumined sons they left the keys of their great wisdom, which was the knowledge of good and evil … these illuminated ones founded what we know as the Ancient Mysteries."

So one inner secret of the Freemasons is awareness of prehistoric "gods" who bestowed their knowledge on certain humans, thus illuminazing them. This knowledge was passed down through ancient Mystery Schools to the founders of both the Jewish and Christian religions, whose traditions were learned by the Knights Templar and brought to the inner core of modern Freemasonry and on into the Illuminati.

In both early Eastern and Western cultures, rulers gained power and wealth from religion. However, with the advent of the printing press, more people could read the Bible for themselves and a more sophisticated understanding grew in the public while religious control waned, especially in highly developed nations.

Today, the favored control mechanism is through the lending of money. By joining the lending of money with religion, as if money itself were God-ordained, an international class of bullion brokers was created. It remains a powerful control mechanism over humanity today.

The power that comes with exchanging money can be traced back to the Near East where people called money changers were prevalent, exchanging the currencies of the various cities and nations into money acceptable to the temple priests. Money therefore became closely connected to the temples of religion, which also doubled as centers for the study of astronomy and astrology. Recall that it was only in the temple at Jerusalem that Jesus, the "Prince of Peace," turned violent—and this was against the money changers. The conflict between the money changers and the human population has continued down through the ages.

A growing number of people today are quite seriously considering the idea of ancient astronauts—nonhumans who visited the Earth millennia ago. This is a concept that gained popularity in the 1970s with the publication of Swiss author Erich von Daniken's best seller *Chariots of the Gods*. Further details on this theme, gleaned from Sumerian literature, were offered by the scholar and author Zecharia Sitchin in his multivolume series on the twelfth planet and ancient astronauts called the Anunnaki, or "Those Who from Heaven to Earth Came."

Any in-depth study of this issue shows the evidence for such alien visitation—found in sacred sites, ancient art, and anomalous artifacts—is quite compelling, almost overwhelming. Indeed, some of the earliest religions may have been based on a reality that has since been long forgotten.

While this concept may sound preposterous to many, even scientific minds have offered similar suggestions. The British molecular biologist Francis Crick, a Nobel Prize winner for his codiscovery of the structure of DNA in the 1950s, speculated in his book *Life Itself* that space-faring beings from another solar system brought the seeds necessary for life to Earth in the distant past. Our primitive ancestors most likely felt awe and reverence toward technologically advanced visitors who came from the heavens. These visitors could fly through the air and perform feats that must have seemed like magic. These visitors were originally considered merely watchers or messengers from the heavens. Such accounts are found in the ancient cuneiform tablets of Sumer that predate the Bible by more than 2,000 years. They recount how the Anunnaki initiated the concept of organized religion and appointed rulers over humanity.

Rather than deal directly with the burgeoning human population, the ancient gods ordained an administrative body or priesthood to pass along edicts and instruction as well as interpret policy. Once such clerics got a taste of wealth and power, they were loath to relinquish it. Religion soon evolved into a rigid structure of dogmas, catechisms, tithing, and obedience. "Apparently, these extraterrestrials performed 'great feats' in order to be worshipped as 'gods.' The reported next step was to pro-

Author Erich von Daniken penned *Chariots of the Gods*, which popularized the idea that aliens visited Earth and passed knowledge on to ancient peoples.

vide technology to these Earth humans so that these humans could create impressive looking 'rich' structures of religious worship, laid with gold and other mined mineral resources, of religious worship to these extraterrestrial 'gods,'" wrote researchers Peter Jiang and Jenny Li in *The Canadian*.

Many esoteric and occult traditions—including those within the Freemasons and Rosicrucians—are thought to have originated with the Mystery Schools of the ancient Greeks and Egyptians. Many researchers believe the Mystery Schools carried within them secrets handed down from the Anunnaki of Sumer. Conspiracy writer Dr. Henry Makow reported that a woman who claimed to have been a former prominent member of the Illuminati said she was told the Order dates back to ancient Babylon and the Tower of Babel. "When the Cabalists' plans for a tower reaching to heaven were foiled by God, they instigated their centuries-long vendetta against Him and vowed to hijack His Creation," Makow wrote.

Perhaps one of the most prized technologies of the Anunnaki sky gods was the creation and use of monatomic gold.

Ancient Technology

The accidental discovery of single atom elements by a Phoenix-area cotton farmer in the 1970s may have actually been a rediscovery of technology in use by the ancient astronauts. This involves the manipulation of energy at the atomic level and may have opened the door to limitless free energy, cures for AIDS and cancer, longevity, faster-than-light speeds, anti-gravity, and much more, perhaps even interdimensional and time travel. This discovery may have precipitated new governmental policies and even war in the struggle to gain control over this new technology. And, while this discovery has been startling to modern science, it appears to be nothing new.

As stated in Ecclesiastes 1:9, "What has been will be again, what has been done will be done again; there is nothing new under the sun."

Today, several scholars have linked this amazing discovery to the mythology and legends of the far distant past, especially the Anunnaki in ancient Mesopotamia. Interest in this new technology grew rapidly and by 2003, some researchers were even claiming that the U.S. invasion of Iraq may have had more to do with this new discovery than with oil, weapons of mass destruction, or regime change. This discovery of monatomic matter and its connection with narratives from the ancient past with its possible role in current world events have garnered increased interest from researchers. It appears as though these elemental secrets were lost centuries ago, though vestiges of this knowledge may have been passed down through the years by a series of secret societies culminating in the Illuminati.

This story began with David Hudson, a self-styled conservative Republican and cotton farmer from Phoenix, Arizona. By the mid-1970s, Hudson had found farming in the parched baked soil in that area a hardscrabble. He began to look for other means of making a living even as he began injecting sulphuric acid into the soil in an effort to break up the dry crust. He found that by spraying his soil samples with a cyanide solution, he could obtain traces of metals from the ore, including gold. "[W]e had been doing soils analysis [when we thought of] this concept of literally piling ore up on a piece of plastic and spraying it with a cyanide solution, which dissolves selectively the gold out of the ore," Hudson told a Dallas audience in 1995. "It trickles down through the ore until it hits the plastic and then runs out of the plastic into the settling pond. It's pumped up through activated charcoal where the gold adheres to the charcoal and then the solution is returned to the stack.... The concept seemed pretty simple. I decided, you know a lot of farmers have airplanes, a lot of farmers have race horses, a lot of farmers have race cars.... I decided I was going to have a gold mine."

After checking out several locations, including abandoned gold mines, Hudson found the site near Phoenix he was seeking. "I had a lot of earth movers and water trucks and road graders and backhoes and caterpillars and these kinds of things on the farm and I had equipment operators, so I decided I was going to set up one of these heap leach cyanide systems."

Hudson got much more than he had bargained for.

"[W]e began recovering the gold and silver and we would take the charcoal down to our farm. We'd strip it with hot cyanide and sodium hydroxide. We'd run it through an 'electro-winning cell' to get the gold out. And then we would do what's called a 'fire assay,' where you run it through a crucible reduction to get this gold and silver bead.... This is the time honored procedure for recovering gold and silver and, basically, it's been performed for 250–300 years. It's the accepted standard in the industry," he explained.

But, along with small amounts of gold and silver, Hudson also recovered small beads of a material that complicated their attempts at analysis. "Something was recovering with the gold and silver [that] we couldn't explain," he said.

This "something" turned out to be elements heretofore unknown to modern science, elements composed of a single atom. This monatomic matter is found in virtually everything around us, including the food we eat and the water we drink.

Hudson found such elements could be retrieved from noble metals such as gold, silver, copper, cobalt, and nickel, along with platinum, palladium, rhodium, iridium, ruthenium, and osmium.

He also found that the nuclei of such monatomic matter acted in an unusual manner. Under certain circumstances, they began spinning and creating oddly deformed shapes. As these nuclei spun, they began to come apart on their own.

It was found, for example, that in the element Rhodium 103, the nucleus became deformed in a ratio of two to one, twice as long as it is wide—like a Coke bottle—and entered a high spin state. "It's inherent in the stuff," noted Hudson. "It isn't anything you do from the outside."

After a two-year study of this material, an Arizona analytical chemist informed Hudson that what he had found was not any of the normal elements on the periodic table. Referring to one sample, the chemist said, "What we have here is something that I know is pure rhodium and yet none of these spectroscopic analyses are saying it's rhodium." Hudson explained that iron could be a reddish-brown chloride, but silica, aluminum, and calcium do not form colored salts at all. "And yet if you take the material that they claim is silica and calcium and re-dissolve it through a fusion and hydrochloric acid, and you got the red brown chloride again. Now where did it come from?" asked Hudson.

> He ... found that the nuclei of such monatomic matter acted in an unusual manner. Under certain circumstances, they began spinning and creating oddly deformed shapes.

The chemist told Hudson, "Dave, this makes absolutely no sense at all. This is defying everything I have been taught in college, everything I have been taught in graduate school. I'm going to send this back to my graduate professors at Iowa State." He sent the red-brown chloride salts to Iowa State University where he asked chemists, "What is the metal that's present in this salt?" The Iowa State experts reported that chlorine was present in the samples. "Chlorine's a gas," noted Hudson. "Well, fine, there's chlorine, but what is the chlorine reacting with that makes it a crystalline material? And they said, 'There's chlorine present." And we said, "Yes, but what's the metal that's holding the chlorine?" They couldn't tell us.

"So we decided that we were really going to get sophisticated.... When we did the spectroscopy, I told you at 70 seconds these elements begin to burn, well at 68 seconds we stopped the burn. Okay? Now there shouldn't be anything there other than these elements and carbon and the electrode. We dug the metal bead out with a little knife and we sent it off to Harwell Laboratories over in London, which is the government, you know, the government labs over in London, and they did neutron activation. "Now neutron activation does not care what state the electron orbitals are in, it actually analyzes the nucleus itself, of the element. The results come back, 'No precious elements detected.' They did see some carbon, but no precious elements detected. You know, this is really getting serious here. I probably got the best credentials money can buy. I got a man that worked, now, a total of 9 1/2 years, he's a Ph.D. analytical chemist, he physically can separate and quantify everything known to man. And he says, 'Dave I can't explain this. This is not explainable.' So we finally order from Johnson Matthey, pure standard materials of rhodium and iridium, platinum, palladium, ruthenium and osmium and we learn how to make them disappear. We could take pure rhodium chloride and analyze it to be pure rhodium, and through a process of repeated evaporation with salt, we could make the rhodium disappear from the instrumental analyses. It still is a blood red chloride, you still can perform all the chemistry, it still was in solution but it didn't analyze to contain any rhodium. And this was pure rhodium standard. The way it disappeared was a process of disaggregation."

So the learned men at Iowa State could not identify the material within the sample, and the neutron activation analysis in England also failed to identify the elements.

Hudson finally located a source of information in the Soviet Academy of Sciences in Russia. Through specialized equipment, scientists there determined that his mysterious white substance was composed entirely of platinum group metals in a single atom form previously unknown to modern science.

Something quite new and unusual was revealing itself.

Working with United Technologies, Hudson's new material was placed in fuel cells being developed there. Although analysis showed the material contained no rhodium, when mounted on carbon and placed in a fuel cell, it performed as only rhodium could.

Hudson was told that if he could explain how to obtain his strange white powder from commercially available material, he could patent the process. In 1988, he did just that, filing both U.S. and worldwide patents on eleven monatomic elements.

He coined the term "Orbitally Rearranged Monatomic Elements" (ORMEs) to describe this newfound matter. Such material in a pure monatomic state forms a snow-white powdery substance, in appearance not unlike ordinary cooking flour.

Then the study of this odd material took an even stranger turn.

"The amazing thing about it," explained Hudson, "is the weight of the material. It was very difficult to weigh.... They want things very precise at the patent office [but] we couldn't get consistent results with the material. It kept gaining weight and gaining weight."

Using thermo-gravimetric analysis, it was found that when samples of the material were reduced to the white powder state, it lost 44 percent of its original weight. By either heating or cooling the material, it would gain weight or lose weight. "By repeated annealing we could make the material weigh less than the pan weighed it was sitting in," said Hudson. "… Or we could make it weigh 300–400 times what its beginning weight was depending on whether we were heating or cooling it.… If you take this white powder and put it on a quartz boat and heat it up to the point where it fuses with the quartz, it becomes black and it regains all its weight again. This makes no sense, it's impossible, it can't happen. But there it is."

By the early 1990s, the Niels Bohr Institute and Argonne National and Oak Ridge National Laboratories published scientific papers substantiating the existence of these high-spin, monatomic elements and their power as superconductors.

Hudson also met with Dr. Hal Puthoff, director of the Institute for Advanced Studies in Austin, Texas. Puthoff performs cutting-edge research into zero-point energy and gravity as a zero-point fluctuation force. He and other scientists have theorized that enough energy exists in the space found in the atoms inside an empty coffee cup to boil all the oceans of the Earth if fully utilized. Puthoff had also theorized that matter reacting in two dimensions should lose about 44 percent of its gravitational weight, exactly the weight loss found by Hudson.

The Niels Bohr Institute at the University of Copenhagen in Denmark is one prestigious research facility that has substantiated that Hudson's high-spin, monatomic elements exist.

When it was found that Hudson's elements, when heated, could achieve a gravitational attraction of less than zero, Puthoff concluded the powder was "exotic matter" capable of bending time and space. The material's anti-gravitational properties were confirmed when it was shown that a weighing pan weighed less when the power was placed in it than it did empty. The matter had passed its anti-gravitational properties to the pan.

Puthoff has published papers developing Andrei Sakharov's theory concerning gravity, namely that gravity is not a gravitational field. There may be no real gravitational field but instead what we experience as gravity may be the inter-reaction of matter, protons, neutrons, and electrons with the zero point, or vacuum, energy. In Puthoff's calculations and in his mathematics, when matter is resonance connected in two dimensions, it no longer interacts in three dimensions but rather two dimensions. Puthoff calls this the "jitterbug motion," and it loses 44 percent of its gravitational weight, exactly as found in Hudson's work. This means the material is a resonance-connected, quantum oscillator, resonating in two dimensions, which just happens to be the definition of a superconductor. Hudson related that when he met Puthoff, he was told, "Dave, you know what this means. It means when you can control space-time, if you control gravity, and if you control gravity, you are controlling space-time. And so literally what these atoms are doing is they are bending space-time...." Puthoff added, "There are theories in the published journals, credible journals, about moving faster than the speed of light, from one place to another. But to do it you must have what's called exotic matter, matter that has no gravitational attraction at all."Iridium at 70 degrees Fahrenheit has no gravitational attraction at all; 70 degrees Fahrenheit and above is the temperature of your body. So it is suspected that at or above body temperature, the human body becomes filled with the light. Commenting on the white power of gold, Hudson said, "We can literally eat this until our light body exceeds our physical body, then we supposedly become light beings."

Adding to their amazement, it was found that when the white powder was heated to a certain degree, not only did its weight disappear but the powder itself vanished from sight. When a spatula was used to stir around in the pan, there apparently was nothing there. Yet, as the material cooled, it reappeared in the same configuration as when originally placed in the pan. This amazing matter, which could be changed from solid gold to the white powder, had not simply disappeared, it apparently had moved into another dimensional plane.

As if all this were not amazing enough, a relative directed Hudson to a book on alchemy. Being a practical man, a farmer, and a metallurgist, Hudson disdained any reference to the occult. But he quickly became intrigued by the similarities between his newly discovered monatomic elements and accounts from the past.

"The Alchemist in Search of the Philosophers Stone," an eighteenth-century painting by Joseph Wright of Derby, depicts the quest for a substance that would turn base metals to gold.

Alchemy is the centuries-old attempt to discover the relationship between a human and the universe and to benefit from an understanding of the basics of life. Alchemical theory determined that some substance must exist that could bring about the transmutation of certain metals. Foremost among these metals was gold. This mysterious catalyst was sometimes referred to as "the tincture," but more often as "the powder." This term, as it passed from the Arabic language into Latin, became known as the "elixir of life" and more commonly as the "Philosopher's Stone."

According to the *Encyclopedia Britannica*, this stone, "which is not a stone," was sometimes called "a medicine for the rectification of 'base' or 'sick' metals, and from this it was a short step to view it as a drug for the rectification of human maladies."

Such rectification may have been confirmed. Monatomic researchers theorized that carefully administered amounts of the white powder can actually provide benefits to human health. "I'm not a doctor so I can't practice medicine," Hudson told a Dallas audience. "Anything that is administered to someone for the purpose of curing a disease is medicine. So therefore I can't tell you on tape what's been done with it, what the doctors who have given it have done with it, but I can tell you that at 2 mg [milligrams or one thousandth of a gram] it totally has gotten rid of Karposi Sarcomas [KS] on AIDS patients, at 2 mg per day. Two mg per day! There's 32,000 milligrams in an ounce, 2 mg is nothing. And it gets rid of KS. I can tell you that people who have taken it, at 2 mg injections, within two hours their white blood cell count goes from 2,500 to 6,500 white blood cells. I can tell you that stage four cancer patients have taken it orally, and after 45 days have no cancer anyplace in the body. We're not gonna go into any more specifics than that. I will talk to you about it later when the cameras aren't running."

The idea that the famed "Philosopher's Stone" is actually monatomic gold was attested to by seventeenth-century alchemist Thomas Vaughn, who took the name Eirenaeus Philalethes. Vaughn wrote, "Our Stone is nothing but gold digested to the highest degree of purity and subtle fixation...." He said this was called a stone because of its fixed nature and resistance to fire, but that its appearance was that of a very fine powder.

Everyone knows of the alchemists' search for the formula of changing base metals into gold, but few have wondered why exactly they wanted gold. It has been assumed that the alchemists wanted riches. But a close study of alchemy and occultism reveals that these men and women of the past were attempting to recover the ancient knowledge of the sky gods, long since lost in the mists of time.

Had David Hudson found the fabled Philosopher's Stone?

The Phoenix farmer was further astonished when he asked a local rabbi, "Have you ever heard of the white powder of gold?"

"Oh, yes," came the unexpected reply, "but to our knowledge no one has known how to make it since the destruction of the first temple [Solomon's Temple]. The white powder is the magic, which can be used for white magic or black magic."

In one of his last public appearances, Hudson remarked, "Now if that isn't heavy enough for you, ... I found out that the name for the golden tree of life was the ORME, ormus, or ormes. And the name of my patent is Orbitally Rearranged Monatomic Elements [ORME]. In the Book of Isaiah, it says a latter-day David, a descendant of the Davidic bloodline, will be the one who's to plant the Golden Tree of Life. My cousin, bless her soul, joined the Mormon Church, and they had her do her genealogy, and my great-great-great grandmother was Hanna de Guise, daughter of Christopher de Guise, brother of Charles or Claude de Guise, who if you got a copy of *Holy Blood Holy Grail* you will find Charles or Claude de Guise is in the book. Nostradamus worked for the de Guise family and Nostradamus prophesied by 1999 the occult gold will be known to science. Very specific prophecy, very exact dates, very precise. "And I didn't know any of this when I filed my patent. And so when you realize what this is, and you realize what it does, and you realize why it's here, then you realize why my job is not to make money with it. I can't make money with it. My job is to tell those people who are ready for it what the state of things are and when it's going to be available. I can't sell it. I will solicit donations to cover our costs in producing it. But it has to be made available for those people who are ready for it."

By 2004, David Hudson had dropped from sight after promising audiences that he intended to manufacture his monatomic white powder for the benefit of all humanity. His disappearance from the public scene engendered much speculation. Had he just been a hoaxer who slinked back into the shadows before he was exposed? Or had the people who so profited from medical treatments and pharmaceuticals and who had so much to lose due to his discov-

By 2004, David Hudson had dropped from sight after promising audiences that he intended to manufacture his monatomic white powder for the benefit of all humanity.

ery found a way to neutralize him? Or had he taken some of the amazing gold powder himself and shifted to another dimension?

Meanwhile, the connection between his gold powder and ancient legends caught the attention of a growing number of scholars and researchers. Today, monatomic gold is being offered on many websites but the buyer should be cautioned that there is yet no conclusive way to ensure the purity or effectiveness of such offers. Buyer beware. Some have even warned that monatomic gold is an Illuminati plot to damage the human DNA chain.

British author Laurence Gardner, in his book entitled *Lost Secrets of the Sacred Ark*, noted that the oldest complete book in the world—the Egyptian *Book of the Dead*—tells of the pharaohs ingesting "the bread of presence," also called "schefa food," while making the ritualistic journey to the afterlife. At each stage, the pharaoh would ask, "What is it?"

This has been compared to the biblical account of Moses and the Israelites in the desert following the exodus from Egypt. Egyptian history matches the story of Moses in the Bible but with some significant differences. Some researchers contend that Moses (Mosis) is not a name but a title that means "the rightful heir of Tuthmosis," the third pharaoh of Egypt's eighteenth dynasty. In true royal Egyptian tradition, Tuthmosis's son married his sister Sitamun to inherit the throne as Amenhotep III. He later wed Tiye, daughter of the chief minister. It was decreed that no son of Tiye could inherit the throne and when Tiye became pregnant, it was ordered that if the child was a son, he should be killed. Tiye indeed bore a son and she and the royal midwives conspired to spirit the child away by bundling him in a basket of bulrushes and floating him down the Nile to the Jewish relatives of her half-brother Levi. The boy was educated by this Jewish family and given the royal education befitting his position as a potential pharaoh. As he grew, Aminadab or Amenhotep ("Amun is pleased" in Hebrew) changed his name to Akhenaten (servant of Aten, the one true god).

Meanwhile, as Amenhotep III sickened, Akhenaten married Sitamun's daughter Nefertiti in order to become eligible for the role of pharaoh. With the old king's death, Akhenaten became Amenhotep IV. With his belief in one god, thanks to his Hebrew upbringing, Akhenaten angered the priesthood by closing the temples of the other Egyptian gods and replacing them with temples dedicated to Aten. After some conflict, Akhenaten was forced to abdicate the throne to his cousin Semenkhkare, who later was succeeded by Akhenaten's young son Tutankhaten. As he was considered a god himself, Akhenaten could not be killed, but he could be exiled.

In leaving Egypt, Akhenaten, now Moses (rightful heir to the throne), took not his birth parents but the Hebrew servants who had raised him. Either because of second thoughts about leaving Moses alive to challenge his right to the throne or angered by the fact that the children of Israel took with them anything not nailed down, the reigning pharaoh chased after Moses with his army but became mired or destroyed in the Sinai Desert near Lake Timsah. This pharaoh is actually unknown but is believed to be Ramesses II, primarily because the Bible mentions the building of the city of Ramesses, which occurred during his reign.

Interestingly, both Akhenaten and Nefertiti are said to have suffered from a genetic abnormality, namely elongated skulls just like those being found today in Peru. Often in history such elongated skulls were covered by large conical hats or helmets. This is thought by some to be a sign of a lineage from ancient astronauts—the Anunnaki, also known as the biblical Nephilim.

To sustain themselves during their long sojourn in the wilderness, Moses and his people ate a white, powdery substance they called manna. This manna was ground by hand into small cakes then baked or boiled. In Hebrew, "manna" literally means "What is it?," the same term used by the pharaohs.

Gardner noted that it is of particular significance that, irrespective of today's costly and extensive research in the area of these monatomic elements, the secrets of this mysterious powder were known many thousands of years

Brooklyn Museum's Wilbour Plaque depicting Akhenaten and Nefertiti.

ago. "They knew there were superconductors inherent in the human body," Gardner wrote. "They knew that both the physical body and the light body [the spirit or soul] had to be fed to increase hormonal production and the ultimate food for the latter was called *shem-an-na* by the Babylonians, *mfkzt* by the Egyptians and *manna* by the Israelites. This was manufactured by the priestly Master Craftsmen of the temples (the guardians of the House of Gold) for the express purpose of deifying the kings."

It has been reported that Moses/Ankhenaten constructed a temple on Mount Sinai, also known as Mount Horeb or the Mount of Moses. This mountain sits in the southern part of the Sinai Peninsula and houses the Egyptian temple of Serabit el Khadim, established as the royal House of Gold for the Egyptian dynasties, although no metallic gold has ever been found there, only enigmatic white powder.

According to the *Holman Bible Dictionary*, "The entire peninsula takes the shape of an inverted triangle whose base is 150 miles long and is bounded on the east by the north end of the Red Sea and on the west by the Gulf of Aqaba. The Gaza strip lies directly north. This peninsula contains 23,442 square miles and has a population of approximately 140,000 at time of publication [1991]. The central and southern parts are extremely mountainous, ranging from 5000 to about 9000 feet, and the land today is valued for its oil fields and manganese deposits."

Researchers of the ancient astronauts theory claim the Anunnaki maintained their spacefaring facilities in the Sinai but it was destroyed in an atomic fire about the same time as the destruction of Sodom and Gomorrah.

An immense cavity is found in the center of the Sinai Peninsula along with fracture lines. The surrounding area is covered with blackened stones, indicating vitrification, the changing of rocks into a glass-like state usually only found at atomic bomb test sites. Furthermore, higher-than-normal radiation has been found at the south end of the Dead Sea, thought by many to be the location of the destroyed cities of Sodom and Gomorrah.

In his 1975 book *Footprints on the Sands of Time: The Truth about the Super Race from the Stars*, author L. M. Lewis argued that hardened salt around the Dead Sea is evidence of a nuclear explosion. "When Hiroshima was being rebuilt, stretches of sandy soil were found to have been atomically changed into a substance resembling a glazed silicon permeated by a saline crystalloid," reported Lewis, who added that if the salt pillars around the Dead Sea were ordinary salt, they would have been washed away by rain. Instead, they are a "special, hardened salt, only created with a nuclear reaction such as an atomic explosion."

The late Philip Coppens, author of *The Ancient Alien Question: A New Inquiry into the Existence, Evidence, and Influence of Ancient Visitors*, noted, "Another candidate for a nuclear explosion, so far left untouched by most of the 'ancient astronaut proponents,'" is the Indus River Valley, where towns such as Harappa and Mohenjo Daro flourished in 3000 B.C.E., but were then quickly abandoned. One answer that has been put forward is that the ancient cities might have been irradiated by an atomic blast. If true, it would be impossible to ignore the conclusion that ancient civilization possessed high technology.

Passages from the Hindu *Mahabharata,* one of two major Sanskrit tales of ancient India, in addition to descriptions of flying machines termed *vimanas,* suggest the use of nuclear weapons in the distant past. These controversial excerpts include: "— (the weapon was) a single projectile charged with all the power of the Universe. An incandescent column of smoke and flame as bright as the thousand suns rose in all its splendor.... An iron thunderbolt, a gigantic messenger of death, which reduced to ashes the entire race of the Vrishnis and the Andhakas ... the corpses were so burned as to be unrecognizable. The hair and nails fell out; pottery broke without apparent cause, and the birds turned white ... after a few hours all foodstuffs were infected ... to escape from this fire, the soldiers threw themselves in streams to wash themselves and their equipment...."

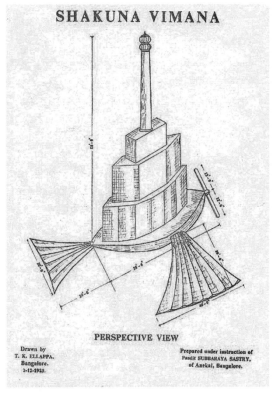

SHAKUNA VIMANA

PERSPECTIVE VIEW

Drawn by
T. K. ELLAPPA,
Bangalore.
3-12-1923.

Prepared under instruction of
Pandit SUBBARAYA SASTRY,
of Anekal, Bangalore.

A 1923 illustration of a vimana drawn by an artist in Bangalore, based on Indian mythology. This one sports moving wings and tail.

And it is true that excavations of Harappa and Mohenjo Daro (Mound of the Dead) revealed human skeletons scattered about the cities, unburied with many holding hands and sprawling in the streets as if a horrible, sudden death had overtaken them. There was no apparent cause of death for these people, nor had they decayed or been consumed by animals. Most telling was the fact that these skeletons are among the most radioactive ever found, matching those at Hiroshima and Nagasaki.

A news item in the New York *Herald Tribune* of February 16, 1947, noted that archaeologists digging in the Euphrates Valley uncovered evidence of an agrarian society dating back more than 8,000 years. Under this was a layer of a herding culture and under that evidence of cavemen. Under all this was a layer of sand fused into green glass. This was evidence of nuclear fire as such fusion was also found at the New Mexico Trinity site used for the testing of the first atom bomb.

But prehistoric nuclear warfare aside, there is further evidence of esoteric technology being used in our distant past. The biblical story in Exodus tells how Moses became angered upon his return from the mountain where he was given tablets by his God. It seems in his absence the Israelites had taken most of the gold in their possession and had melted it down to make a calf, which they then worshipped. They knew there was a magical aspect to gold but, like the alchemists who came after them, they did not know the means of reducing it to powder.

Exodus 32:20 [*New International*] states, "And he [Moses] took the calf they had made and burned it in the fire; then he ground it to powder, scattered it on the water and made the Israelites drink it." Since swallowing molten metal would be lethal, Moses, who had been well educated in Egyptian esoteric knowledge, knew the secret of making the high-spin monatomic gold powder.

Confirmation that such was the case came in 1904 when British archeologist Sir William Flinders Petrie discovered a large smelting facility in the temple on Mount Horeb, which some scholars believe is the actual location of the Mount of Moses mentioned in the Bible.

Mount Horeb, or Mount Sinai, interestingly enough has been interpreted to mean "shining"—as in the "Shining Ones." The name is thought to have been derived from the word "sin," the Babylonian moon god who equates to Nannar, the first Anunnaki leader born on Earth to the Anunnaki commander Enlil and his wife, Ninlil.

It was on Horeb that Petrie discovered an enclosed temple composed of adjoining halls, shrines, and chambers, all filled with carvings, pillars, and stelae depicting Egyptian nobility and mentioning the mysterious *mfkzt*. Most surprisingly was the discovery of a metallurgist's crucible along with a considerable amount of pure white powder cleverly concealed under some flagstone. Unconcerned with the baffling powder, Petrie allowed it to blow away in the Sinai winds.

David Hudson noted that in the Bible he found the Hebrew people reporting fire and smoke on Mount Sinai. "It was if a forge was going up on Mt. Sinai. But when you recall that Moses had been there previously and in the area of Sinai is where copper was being mined and smelted. And in fact, I believe there was a forge going on Mount Sinai, because at 1,160 degrees the white powder of gold can be melted to a transparent glass of gold. It literally becomes a glass as clear as window glass, and yet it is pure gold, it's not a gold compound, its pure gold. You can take it in a mortar and pestle and grind it right back to the white powder … it looks absolutely like glass," he said.

Several engravings in this ancient temple depict various Egyptian rulers, among these Tuthmosis IV and Amenhotep III, along with the god Hathor. In these carvings various persons are offering the king a conical loaf. Was this the legendary white powder known as *mfkzt*?

The answer appears to be yes, as the figure offering the powder can be identified as an Egyptian treasurer named Sobekhotep, elsewhere described as the man who "brought the noble Precious Stone to his majesty."

This leads to the connection with Iraq. It is clear to many researchers and scholars today that the Egyptian civilization, far from being the world's first great culture as once popularly believed, was in fact a mere remnant of the much older and fascinating culture—that of Sumer. The Sumerians wrote about the Anunnaki, who presented the early humans with the knowledge of writing, farming, astrology, and even politics. They too were also most probably the source of knowledge concerning the miraculous white powdered gold.

Since some authorities believe that white powdered gold can regenerate the human DNA, it is theorized that it might also provide a cure for diseases and even old age itself. If this is true, the biblical stories of Methuselah living nearly 1,000 years may not be as farfetched as some believe. Anti-gravity, longevity, cures for AIDS and cancer, limitless free energy, faster-than-light space travel—no wonder certain persons would go to any lengths to obtain, or conceal, such knowledge. As detailed in this author's "underground bestseller" *Rule by Secrecy*, the United States has long been governed by men connected to secret societies such as the Council on Foreign Relations, the Trilateral Commission, the Bilderbergers, the Illuminati, and the Freemasons. All of these groups can be traced back to even earlier societies, all with a particular interest in alchemy and the occult. It may well have been this interest and knowledge that prompted certain U.S. leaders with secret society connections to desire sending troops into Iraq in 2003.

In these carvings various persons are offering the king a conical loaf. Was this the legendary white powder known as *mfkzt*?

This interest may have been intensified after ABC News reported that nearly 400 ancient Sumerian artifacts were discovered in 1999 in the southern Iraqi town of Basmyiah, about 100 miles (160 kilometers) south of Baghdad. The Iraqi News Agency said the objects ranged from animal and human-shaped "toys" to cuneiform tablets and even "ancient weapons." At least one cylinder seal depicted a tall person thought to represent the ancient King Gilgamesh. The antiquities were dated to about 2500 B.C.E., said excavation team leader Riyadh al-Douri. Further discoveries in Iraq were made in 2002 and early 2003 by archeologists from the Bavarian Department of Historical Monuments in Munich, Germany, using digital mapping technology. According to spokesman Jorg Fassbinder, a magnetometer was utilized to locate buried walls, gardens, palaces and a surprising network of canals that would have made Uruk a "Venice in the desert." This equipment also located a structure in the middle of the Euphrates River, which Fassbinder's team believed to be the tomb of Gilgamesh, the ancient Sumerian king who claimed to be two-thirds god and only one-third human. An

One of the tablets containing the epic of Gilgamesh, a tale about a demigod that historians believe originates from a real king who lived thousands of years ago.

epic poem describing Gilgamesh's search for the secret of immortality was inscribed on clay tablets more than 2,000 years before the birth of Christ and is thought to be one of the oldest books in history.

Reportedly, other astonishing finds were being made during this time by both German and French archaeological teams given permission to excavate by Saddam Hussein. It may be worth noting that Germany and France were the two nations most opposed to the U.S. invasion in 2003. The new discoveries were added to those stored in the Iraqi National Museum in Baghdad, which had been closed to the public since the first Gulf War in 1991. Scholars around the world lamented the loss of priceless antiquities in that nation because of the 1991 Gulf War and subsequent embargo of Iraq.

McGuire Gibson, with the Oriental Institute of the University of Chicago, bemoaned, "The aftermath of the war witnessed the looting and sometimes the burning of nine regional museums and the loss of more than 3,000 artifacts, only a few of which have been recovered. "The loss of the objects, although grave, was not as destructive as the change that the attacks on the museums will have on the future relationship of museums to the people of Iraq. It is unlikely that there will ever again be an effort at public education about archeology on the scale that was represented by those regional museums." Gibson added that almost all archeological research in Iraq came to a halt because of subsequent wars and embargos.

In addition to the American bombing of historical artifacts, such as the the giant ziggurat at Ur, and the losses due to construction by U.S. troops at Tell al-Lahm, economic conditions caused by the American embargos have caused an increase in the illegal trading of Iraqi artifacts.

It is most intriguing to some researchers to realize that travel to Iraq, most probably the cradle of human civilization if not the starting point for all humanity, is today prohibited unless the travelers are part of the U.S. military.

By mid-2002, President George W. Bush was clearly intent on invading Iraq despite assurances from United Nations chief weapons inspector Hans Blix, the International Atomic Energy Agency, and even Scott Ritter, who had resigned as the U.S. weapons inspector, that Iraq had no weapons of mass destruction.

Protest marches were reported in almost every major American city and a poll conducted for the *New York Times* and CNN in early 2003 showed half of those queried were uneasy at the prospect of war with Iraq.

None of this seemed to sway President Bush, who pronounced, "There's no negotiations, by the way, for Mr. Saddam Hussein. There's nothing to discuss. He either gets rid of his weapons and the United Nations gets rid of his weapons—he can either get rid of his weapons and the United States can act, or the United States will lead a coalition to disarm this man."

On March 20, 2003, Bush made good on these words by launching U.S. forces across Iraq's borders. Unlike previous military campaigns where armies captured key cities and objectives, then consolidated their forces before moving on to the next objective, U.S. forces made a beeline for Baghdad, bypassing most of the country. They left the Iraqi military forces in place with their weapons;

The Iraq National Museum was attacked when American protection was withdrawn and looting began. Many precious artifacts were lost. It has since reopened.

later, many of these soldiers became insurgents. Once the capital was in American hands by late April 2003, looters took at least 50,000 priceless artifacts and tablets from the Iraqi National Museum in Baghdad. Evidence indicated that some of these looters were highly organized with an agenda of their own.

Despite prior attempts to alert American military officers of the danger of losing artifacts dating back 7,000 years, American authorities failed to prevent the wholesale looting of humankind's most ancient treasures. "It was my impression that the Department of Defense had made provisions for the safeguarding of monuments and museums," lamented Maxwell Anderson, president of the Association of Art Museum Directors. Anderson was among a group that in January 2003 alerted Pentagon and State Department officials to the importance of these antiquities.

Furthermore, according to an *Associated Press* report, the thieves had keys to the museum and its vaults. McGuire Gibson said what appeared to be random looting actually was a carefully planned theft. "It looks as if part of the theft was a very, very deliberate, planned action," he said. "They were able to obtain keys from somewhere for the vaults and were able to take out the very important, the very best material. I have a suspicion it was organized outside the country. In fact, I'm pretty sure it was."

"I believe they were people who knew what they wanted," agreed Dr. Donny George, head of the Baghdad National Museum. "They had passed by the gypsum copy of the Black Obelisk. This means that they must have been specialists. They did not touch the copies."

"Glass cutters not available in Iraq were found in the museum and a huge bronze bust weighing hundreds of pounds … [that] would have required a fork lift to remove it indicate that well organized professional cultural thieves were mixed in with the mob," noted Christopher Bollyn in the *American Free Press*.

The fact that some display cases were empty without being broken indicated that some of the precious materials may have been taken out prior to the arrival of the looters. "It was almost as if the perpetrators were waiting for Baghdad to fall to make their move," commented a writer for *BusinessWeek*. All this was confirmed by Colonel Matthew Bogdanos in early 2004. Colonel Bogdanos headed an investigation of the looting as deputy director for the Joint Interagency Coordination Group originally assigned to seek out weapons of mass destruction in Iraq. After gaining permission from General Tommy Franks, the group probed the museum looting. In an interview published in the January/February issue of *Archeology*, Colonel Bogdanos was asked what is still missing from the Iraqi National Museum. He replied, "You have the public gallery from which originally 40 exhibits were taken. We've recovered 11. Turning to the storage rooms, there were about 3,150 pieces taken from those, and that's almost certainly by random and indiscriminant looters. Of those, we've recovered 2,700. So there's about 400 of these pieces, excavated pieces, missing.

"The final group is from the basement. The basement is what we've been calling the inside job. And I will say it forever like a mantra: it is inconceivable to me that the basement was breached and the items stolen without an intimate insider's knowledge of the museum. From there about 10,000 pieces were taken. We've only recovered 650, approximately."

When the looting began on April 17, 2003, one Iraqi archaeologist summoned U.S. troops to protect the national museum. Five Marines accompanied the man to the museum and chased out some looters by firing shots over their heads. However, after about 30 minutes, the soldiers were ordered to withdraw and the looters soon returned. Apparently the only building in Baghdad to receive full American protection was the Ministry of Oil.

"Not since the Taliban embarked on their orgy of destruction against the Buddhas of Bamiyan and the statutes in the museum of Kabul—perhaps not since World War II—have so many archaeological treasures been wantonly and systematically smashed to pieces," reported British newsman Robert Fisk, who toured the museum shortly after the incident.

The preventable looting prompted three members of the White House Cultural Property Advisory Committee to resign, disgusted that the alerted American military had failed to protect the Mesopotamian treasures. "This tragedy was not prevented, due to our nation's inaction," wrote committee chairman Martin E. Sullivan in his resignation letter.

Prior to the American invasion of Iraq, it was widely reported that Saddam Hussein believed himself to be the reincarnation of King Nebuchadnezzar, the ruler who performed wondrous achievements in construction such as the Hanging Gardens of Babylon, in an attempt to communicate with ancient Mesopotamian gods from the heavens. To further this attempt, the Book of Daniel states that Nebuchadnezzar II built a tall narrow structure of gold 27 meters high and 2.7 meters wide near Babylon, mistranslated as a "fiery furnace." It would seem Nebuchadnezzar had produced some sort of energy field based on sky god technology. Whatever he created was dangerous. He threatened to destroy anyone who would not worship his golden calf by throwing them into the structure. When three Hebrew scholars/priests who had been

The late Iraqi president Saddam Hussein was said to have believed himself to be the reincarnation of King Nebuchadnezzar II, the Babylonian ruler who destroyed the Temple in Jerusalem.

appointed by the prophet Daniel to administrate over Babylon, Shadrach, Meshach, and Abednego, refused to serve his gods, they were thrown into the nearby crucible. But after clothing themselves in hats, coats, and "other garments," the trio survived the fire.

Oddly enough, when Nebuchanezzar checked to see if the three were dead, he said, "Lo, I see four men loose, walking in the midst of the fire, and they have no hurt; and the form of the fourth is like the Son of God [*King James Bible*]." Although no further mention is made of this fourth god-like person, the three Israelites survived and were honored by the king. They prospered under his kingship and were promoted to positions of power in Babylon. Obviously, there is something much more to this golden structure than ornamental jewelry and wealth. Had Nebuchanezzar somehow created a dimensional doorway, a space/time portal or black hole?

Could the rush to war with Iraq, the hurried rush to Baghdad, and the "inside job" at the Baghdad museum have something to do with gaining control over recently discovered ancient knowledge, and perhaps even technology, which might undo modern monopolies in science and even disrupt cherished beliefs in religion?

Could the millennia-long veneration of gold have more to do with ancient knowledge of its intrinsic power than with its monetary worth? Could Saddam Hussein have been working on unlocking the secrets of the white powdered gold? Could the possibility that he might succeed have contributed to the rush to war with Iraq? Dr. Michael E. Salla, who has taught at American University and George Washington University in Washington, D.C., and the Australian National University in Canberra, believes this is indeed the case. "This study provides an exopolitical analysis of the policy dimensions of an historic extraterrestrial presence that is pertinent to Iraq and a U.S. -led preemptive attack. It will be argued that competing clandestine government organizations are struggling through proxy means to take control of ancient extraterrestrial (ET) technology that exists in Iraq, in order to prepare for an impending series of events corresponding to the 'prophesied return' of an advanced race of ETs. The *Columbia* space shuttle may well have been a high-profile victim of such a proxy war intended to send a message to U.S.-based clandestine organizations over the preemptive war against Iraq," he wrote in a 2002 research paper. "Rather than being an unsubstantiated 'conspiracy theory' with little relevance to contemporary policy issues such as a preemptive US war against Iraq, it will be argued that an exopolitical analysis can provide a more comprehensive understanding of what motivates the Bush administration in launching a preemptive attack against Iraq." Arguing that the strongest evidence for an historical ET presence in Iraq are the numerous cuneiform tablets directly recording the beliefs and activities of the ancient Sumerians, Salla wrote, "Most of these cuneiform tablets relate stories of the Sumerians interacting with their 'gods.'

Most archeologists initially accepted that these were merely myths and attached little importance to them other than giving insight into the mytho-religious beliefs of the ancient Sumerians."

The recent discovery of exotic monatomic elements, the ages-long quest for both gold and its alchemical secrets, ancient texts that speak of life-giving powder, and the proximity of Iraq to the source of knowledge concerning this certainly provides one possible motive for the invasion and looting of Iraq.

The intense search for exotic, or even extraterrestrial, knowledge to include anti-gravity may also play a part in the covert search for ancient technology, which may have begun in earnest beginning before World War II.

> The intense search for exotic, or even extraterrestrial, knowledge to include anti-gravity may also play a part in the covert search for ancient technology....

Prior to the war, Nazi Germany mounted expeditions to points around the world—Tibet, Antarctica, Egypt, etc. They were searching for ancient relics and knowledge as depicted in the first Indiana Jones film, *Raiders of the Lost Ark*. And there is no question that Germany produced a number of scientific breakthroughs in their quest for war technology. The V-1 Buzz bombs (an ancestor of today's cruise missiles), the V-2 rockets that terrorized London, and the Messerschmitt 262 (the world's first operational jet fighter), three of the most famous examples.

Later, influence of the Illuminati on the rise of the Nazis will be presented. While a number of books and documentaries have suggested that the Nazi hierarchy dabbled in occult practices, there is no question that the Germans were experimenting with a variety of innovative aircraft and propulsion systems toward the end of the war and that they at least contemplated building a flying saucer. There are tantalizing bits of evidence that Nazi Germany indeed added a flying disc to its inventory of secret super weapons. But there is no indication of what became of it.

The solution to this puzzle may be found by studying the man in charge of Germany's high-tech weapons programs—SS *Obergruppenfuehrer* Dr. Hans Kammler.

General Dr. Hans Friedrich Karl Franz Kammler was born in Stettin, Germany, on August 26, 1901. He studied civil engineering at the Technische Hochschule in Danzig from 1919 to 1923 and was awarded his engineering doctorate in November 1932. Kammler joined the Nazi Party that same year and was given a variety of administrative positions, particularly in the Aviation Ministry. In 1940, he joined the Nazi SS (the *Schutzstaffel* or Defense Squadron) where from 1942 he worked at designing facilities for the extermination camps, including gas chambers and crematoria. He soon became administrator for *Amtsgruppe D*, which directed the concentration camp system. In the aftermath of the 1943 revolt in the Warsaw Ghetto, Kammler was put in charge of the ghetto's demolition in retaliation. It is claimed Kammler designed and constructed cremation facilities at the Auschwitz-Birkenau Concentration Camp, as part of the camp's conversion to an extermination camp, although no such facilities were found at the war's close and nor were any mentioned by the thousands of Auschwitz survivors.

In mid-1943, SS chief Heinrich Himmler sent a letter to Albert Speer, Germany's minister for armaments and munitions. "With this letter, I inform you that I, as SS *Reichsfuehrer* … do hereby take charge of the manufacture of the A-4 instrument," it read. The A-4 rocket was later designated by Hitler as the V-2—V for Vengeance—weapon, the V-1 Buzz bomb being the first. The V-2 was Germany's most secret high-tech weapons system. Himmler then placed Kammler in overall command of the rocket program.

According to Speer, Kammler insinuated his way into all phases of the V-2 program until Hitler finally put him in charge of all air armaments to include any possible secret saucer or anti-gravity project. "Thus—just a few weeks before the end of the war—he had become commissioner general for all important weapons," wrote Speer, who bemoaned the fact that as the war drew to a close, Himmler's SS gradually assumed total control over Germany's weaponry, production, and research.

SS officer Hans Kammler, who would oversee the V-2 missile program.

Working closely with Kammler on the V-2 project were Wernher von Braun, who was director of America's National Aeronautics and Space Administration (NASA) from 1960 to 1970, and his superior, *Luftwaffe* Major General Walter Dornberger, who later was vice president of Bell Aircraft Company and Bell Aerosystems Company in the United States.

Alarmed by progress on the V-2 rockets, Britain's Bomber Command sent 597 bombers beginning the night of August 16, 1943, to raid Peenemünde—Germany's top secret rocket facility built on an island at the mouth of the Oder River near the border of Germany and Poland. Because so much of Peenemünde was underground or well-camouflaged, much was left undamaged. Author Brian Ford described the results: "Even so, over 800 of the people on the island were killed…. After this, it was realized that some of the facility had better be dispersed throughout Germany; thus the theoretical development facility was moved to Garmisch-Partenkirchen, development went to Nordhausen and Bleicherode, and the main wind-tunnel and ancillary equipment went down to Kochel, some 24 miles (38 kilometers) south of Munich. This was christened *Wasserbau Versuchsanstalt Kochelsee*—experimental waterworks project—and gave rise to the most thorough research center for long-range rocket development that, at the time, could have been envisioned." It has been noted that a certain portion of top-secret Nazi weaponry development was moved to an area near Blizna, Poland—the same area where Allied aircrews first encountered the "Foo-Fighters," flying balls of light thought by Allied airmen to be Nazi secret weapons.

Their purpose was to continue Nazi goals long after the military defeat of Germany.

As Kammler, von Braun, Dornberger, and others worked feverishly to perfect the V-2s and other secret weapons, Himmler was taking steps to separate his SS from normal party and state control. "In the spring of 1944 Hitler approved Himmler's proposal to build an SS-owned industrial concern in order to make the SS permanently independent of the state budget," wrote Albert Speer.

In moves that were to be copied in later years by America's Central Intelligence Agency, SS leaders created a number of business fronts and other organizations—many using concentration camp labor—with an eye toward producing revenue to support SS activities. These highly compartmentalized groups headed by young, ambitious SS officers neither required nor desired any connection with Germany's high-profile leaders. Their purpose was to continue Nazi goals long after the military defeat of Germany.

Speer mentioned one SS scheme in 1944 for a secret weapon plant requiring 3,500 concentration camp workers. "The Fuehrer protocols make no mention whatsoever of this new weapon," Speer wrote. "(But) It was certainly not the 'flying saucers,' which extreme right-wing circles now claim were secretly produced by the SS toward the end of the war and concealed from me." However, he conceded that there were weapons development programs he knew nothing about.

Toward the end of the war, Kammler was put in charge of the Nazi Reich's most advanced and secret projects, including both the V-2 and A-10 rocket program and *die Glocke* (the Bell) experiments. These experiments involved a bell-shaped object that was housed in a concrete chamber hundreds of feet underground. Made from very hard metal, the cylindrical-shaped bell held a semicircular cap and hook or clamping device on top. Huge quantities of electricity were fed into it through thick cables dropping into the housing chamber from the outside. Inside the Bell was a thermos-like tube encased in lead and filled with a metallic liquid. During operation the Bell was covered by a ceramic material, apparently to act as insulation. Inside, two contra-rotating cylinders filled with a mercury-like and violet-colored substance spun a vortex of energy that emitted a strange phosphorescent blue light and made such a buzzing sound that operators nicknamed it the *Bienenstock* or Beehive. Due to the phosphorescent light and reports that operators suffered from nervous system disruption, headaches, and a metallic taste, it was speculated that the Bell's operation involved iodizing radiation as well as very strong magnetic fields of energy. The scientists experimenting with the Bell would place various plants, animals, and animal tissue within its energy field from November to December 1944. Almost all the samples were destroyed by the experiment. Kammler and his top-secret Nazi energy Bell device have been tracked to the Wenzeslaus Mine, located about 215 miles (346 kilometers) west of Warsaw in Lower Silesia near the border with Czechoslovakia. The mine is in Ludwikowice Klodzkie, formerly Ludwigsdorf, a perfect location for security purposes as it was outside Germany yet within the Greater Third Reich. Additionally, Kammler spoke fluent Czech. With the occupation of Poland, the mine was reconditioned by the Nazis as a gigantic science center. The area sits in a deep valley, accessible only through two mountain passes. Remnants of watch-towers can be seen and the valley, about 300 yards (274 meters) across, is bisected by rail lines. Also still visible are the ruins of a variety of structures, including concrete bunkers and guard stations, many covered with dirt and trees as camouflage. Today the entire site is overgrown with trees and vegetation.

A V-2 rocket on display at the Historical Technical Museum in Peenemünde, Germany. The V-2 was considered one of the Nazi's *Wunderwaffen* ("Wonder Weapons").

Formerly classified Soviet documents detailed the interrogation at the end of the war of Rudolf Schuster, who had been a member of the *Reichssicherheitshauptamt* or Reich Central Security Office, Nazi Germany's version of the Homeland Security Department. Schuster revealed that in June of 1944, he was transferred to a special evacuation *Kommando* called "General Plan 1945," formed by Hitler's private secretary, Martin Bormann, to evacuate valuable science and technology from the *Reich*. Schuster, who was not privy to the plan's overall agenda, nevertheless located many of these evacuation activities in the area of the Wenzeslaus Mine. Here were found remnants of what once had been the secret SS testing and production facility, to include what may have been a giant early superconductor. Almost everything known about the

Wenzeslaus Mine and the Bell came from SS General Jakob Sporrenberg, the officer commanding the "northern route" of General Plan 1945. Sporrenberg's testimony and affidavits, the only known description of the strange experiments at the mine, were given during a postwar trial in Poland. He was found guilty of war crimes and executed. Very little is known for certain about the Bell except it was given the highest—and perhaps most unique—classification possible in the Third Reich. In a few captured documents, experimenters with the Bell were said to be working on something *Kriegsentscheidend,* or Decisive for the War. Most top-secret German weapons, including the V rockets, were merely classified *Kriegswichtig,* or Important to the War. One major reason that so little is known about the Bell was the loss of the scientists involved in the project. Polish investigator Igor Witkowski explained, "They were taken out and shot by the SS between the 28th of April and the 4th of May, 1945. Records show that there were 62 of them, many of them Germans. There were no survivors, but then that's hardly surprising.... It's quite clear that someone had gone to great lengths to clean up."

Considering the new knowledge of monatomic elements, vortex energy fields, and the possibility of nonhuman technology in the distant past, it is reasonable to theorize that the Nazis may have been experimenting with new forms of energy, the control of matter at the atomic level, and even interdimensional or time travel. What a concept—Nazis tinkering with the building blocks of the universe.

There is also much evidence indicating that, contrary to conventional belief, in the closing days of the war Nazi scientists may have developed a working atomic bomb. In early 1945, the American effort to produce enriched uranium by centrifuge was proving slow and inefficient. The scientists working on the top-secret Manhattan Project had only produced enough enriched uranium for one bomb and it needed testing. The scientist also had a problem in that American proximity fuses were too slow to ignite an atomic explosion.

Then on May 14, 1945, just six days after the German military surrendered (no member of the Nazi Party was present at this event), the Nazi submarine U-234 was taken into captivity by the *USS Sutton* off the east coast of the United States having passed unhindered through war zones. On board were two Japanese officers who committed suicide, two dismantled ME-262 jet fighter planes, gold-lined cylinders containing 560 kilograms of uranium, and, perhaps most importantly, Dr. Heinz Schlicke, the inventor of fast fuses capable of setting off an atomic bomb.

On July 16, 1945, just two months after the seizure of the U-234, America set off the first atomic bomb at Alamagordo, New Mexico, to prove it could do it and later that same day the *USS Indianapolis* set sail from San Francisco for the Pacific island of Tinian bearing atomic bomb parts. It arrived on July 25 and twelve days later the B-29 *Enola Gay* left Tinian to drop the bomb on Hiroshima. By this timeline it would seem that "Little Boy," the first atomic bomb dropped on Japan, was not tested by the Americans because there was no need—it had already been tested by the Germans. This idea is supported by the statement of German authors Edgar Mayer and Thomas Mehner, who reported that J. Robert Oppenheimer, the "father of the atomic bomb," maintained that the bomb dropped on Japan was of "German provenance."

It should also be noted that Nazi Germany had the means, though they lacked the accuracy to deliver an atomic weapon. The Luftwaffe (the Nazi Air Force) had a feasibility study of an atomic bomb blast on Manhattan Island available in mid-1943. On August 27, 1943, a giant six-engined Junkers 390 bomber flown by a crew of four, including pilot Anna Kreisling, the "White Wolf of the Luftwaffe," flew from Norway to Canada, then turned south at 22,000 feet (6,700 meters) to arrive within 25 miles (40 kilometers) of New York City. After taking photographs, it flew unopposed over the Atlantic to a

A rare photo showing the inside works of Little Boy, the atomic bomb that would be dropped on Hiroshima in 1945. Though U.S. built, the science behind the bomb stemmed from Germany.

landing site outside Paris. German airmen taken into captivity at a giant air base in Norway that housed some JU-390 bombers told their captors they were preparing for "a New York mission."

So why didn't the Nazis drop a nuclear bomb on their enemies? It would appear they had no adequate delivery system. Their Norway air base was not complete when the war ended; the three-stage A-10 rocket did not have a reliable guidance system; but mainly, with the allies fighting their way to Berlin and the Russians pouring into East Germany, Nazi leaders realized that the war was over for them and that launching an atomic attack would have brought unthinkable retaliation onto Germany, a likelihood no one wanted. And through all this, Hans Kammler became the last SS officer to gain the rank of *SS-Obergruppenführer* (Senior Group Leader, equivalent to a U.S. Army lieutenant general). Until after April 1942, it was the highest possible SS rank, second only to Reichsführer-SS Heinrich Himmler himself. The man in charge of Nazi super weapons—rockets, jet planes, flying saucers, atomic weapons, and the Bell—disappeared after telling rocket scientist Wernher von Braun he was planning to bargain with the Americans by trading Nazi secrets for his life. The more notorious Nazi leaders either escaped, committed suicide, or were tried as war criminals. General Hans Kammler, however, was largely unknown to the public though he undoubtedly was high on the list of wanted Nazi war criminals considering his involvement in the construction of concentration camps and their gas chambers as well as his participation in the leveling of the Warsaw ghetto. "Unlike Himmler," noted Nick Cook, a former aviation editor and aerospace consultant to *Jane's Defence Weekly*, "Kammler had something of value to deal—something tangible. By early April [1945], Hitler and Himmler had placed under his direct control every secret weapon system of any consequence within the Third Reich—weapons that had no counterpart in the inventories of the three powers that were now bearing down on central Germany from the east and the west."

With secret projects in the hands of the fanatical SS and with factories and research facilities scattered over—and under—the countryside, it is entirely conceivable that an atomic device or a flying saucer utilizing exotic new propulsion systems could have been developed without the knowledge of anyone except Himmler, who committed suicide by poison capsule on May 23, 1945, after being caught trying to sneak through British lines disguised as a German Army private. Perhaps after the war, certain right-wing circles with SS connections did know more about German saucers than Speer or other ranking Nazi leaders.

As the war drew to a close, Kammler made no secret of the fact that he intended to use both the V-2 scientists and rockets under his control as leverage for a deal with the Allies. On April 2, 1945, on Kammler's orders, a special train carried rockets and 500 technicians and engineers escorted by 100 SS troopers to an Alpine redoubt in Bavaria. According to von Braun and Dornberger, Kammler planned to "bargain with the Americans or one of the other Allies for his own life in exchange for the leading German rocket specialists."

Yet on April 4, 1945, when von Braun pressed Kammler for permission to resume rocket research, the SS officer quietly announced that he was about to disappear for "an indefinite length of time." True to his word, no one saw Kammler again. As everyone knows, von Braun, Dornberger, and other scientists as well as many of the V-2 rockets were taken into custody by the Americans, who brought them to the United States to become the foundation of the modern space program.

Perhaps after the war, certain right-wing circles with SS connections did know more about German saucers than Speer or other ranking Nazi leaders.

Author Jean Michel, himself an inmate of Concentration Camp Dora, which provided slave labor for Kammler's rocket program, wrote of Kammler, "The chief of the SS secret weapon empire, the man in Himmler's confidence, disappeared without a trace. Even more disturbing is the fact that the architect of the concentration camps, builder of the gas chambers, executioner of Dora, overall chief of all the SS missiles has sunk into oblivion. There is the Bormann mystery, the [Dr. Josef] Mengele enigma; as far as I know, no one, to this day, has taken much interest in the fate of *Obergruppenfuehrer* SS Hans Kammler." Michel, along with others, wondered "why had the 'cold and brutal calculator' described by Speer, so abruptly discarded the trump cards he had so patiently accumulated?" Did Kammler escape with weapons plans even more technologically advanced and secret than the V-2 rocket? Did the Reich, or an extension of it, have the capability to produce a UFO or an anti-gravity device so as to deal from a position of strength with one of the Allied nations? And did any of this exotic technology stem from the knowledge of the ancient astronauts?

Information, principally from Dornberger, suggested that Kammler committed suicide when the Czech resistance overcame SS troops in Prague. However, there was no proof of this and the issue remains unresolved.

British researcher Mark Birdsall, after an intensive study of Nazi secret weapons, concluded, "Without question, nearly all Foo-Fighter and Ghost Rocket reports can be categorized as advanced technology channeled from these various secret German WWII scientific facilities."

Authors Renato Vesco and David Hatcher Childress, citing Italian Ministry of Aeronautics documents dated September 16, 1946, claim the British may have been the benefactors of such devices. They said that in August 1946, the BBC reported that a new aeronautical research center was to be built in Bedfordshire that would produce "machines that it is hoped will be able to reach at least 1,500 mph." The report added, "According to some experts, these planes have already been built and tested and it is probable that in the near future they will be flying over Great Britain. If necessary, such planes could fly nonstop around the world many times, because they need fuel only for takeoff and landing. Great Britain has already astonished the world with its excellent turbojet engines, but this new development of British scientists is the greatest step that aeronautics has taken since man began to fly."

Since no such craft were ever flown in England, Vesco and Childress concluded that testing must have been carried out elsewhere—perhaps in the wilds of southwest Canada.

They cited a report in the *Toronto Star*, in which Minister of Defense Production C. D. Howe told the House of Commons that a new type of aircraft was being built by the Royal Canadian Air Force and A. V. Roe Ltd. (AVRO) at facilities near Malton, Ontario. The newspaper commented that Howe's words were "adding weight to reports that AVRO is even now working on a mockup model of a 'flying saucer' capable of flying 1,500 miles per hour and climbing straight up in the air."

The United States may have shared in this new technology, as suggested by another Toronto news story, which stated, "A mockup of the Canadian flying saucer, the highly secret aircraft in whose existence few believe, was yesterday shown to a group of 25 American experts, including military officers and scientists."

This partnership was confirmed on October 25, 1953, when U.S. Air Force Secretary Donald Quarles released a statement advising, "We are now entering a period of aviation technology in which aircraft of unusual configuration and flight characteristics will begin to appear.... The Air Force will fly the first jet-powered vertical-rising airplane in a matter of days. We have another project under contract with AVRO Ltd. of Canada, which could result in disc-shaped aircraft somewhat similar to the popular concept of a flying saucer.... While some of these may take novel forms, such as the AVRO project, they are direct-line descendants of conventional aircraft and should not be regarded as supra-natural or mysterious...."

By the mid-1950s, other voices were indicating a major technological breakthrough in aircraft propulsion. Aviation pioneer Lawrence D. Bell was quoted in a

An assistant secretary of defense to President Eisenhower, Donald Quarles suggested that modern aircraft design would tend toward disc-shaped aircraft in the future.

1956 article entitled "The G-Engines Are Coming!" as stating, "We're already working on nuclear fuels and equipment to cancel out gravity." George S. Trimble, head of Advanced Programs for Martin Aircraft, said the conquest of gravity "could be done in about the time it took to build the first atomic bomb." Bill Lear, the designer of the Lear Jet, was effusive about anti-gravity, claiming, "All matter within the [Gravity] ship would be influenced by the ship's gravitation alone."

It remains uncertain if the gravity ships these aviation giants were discussing included the AVRO project in Canada or more secret designs. The AVRO saucers—there were at least two versions, the AV-9 and the AZ-9 "AVRO-Car"—were disc-shaped, jet-powered craft, designed by John Frost for AVRO Ltd., which reportedly were first flown in 1959.

When the United States began working with the Canadians, the idea of a circular aircraft was not new. It had produced its own flying saucer in 1942 when Charles H. Zimmerman designed the V-173 "Flying Flapjack" for the U.S. Navy. This experimental, disc-shaped craft was built and test-flown by Chance-Vought Corp. but reportedly was abandoned in 1947 as impractical. An original V-173 was on exhibit in the Smithsonian Institution for several years. Likewise, the AVRO-Car saucer project reportedly was termed a failure and canceled in 1960.

"However," wrote author W. A. Harbinson in 1991, "while the Canadian and U.S. governments have insisted that they are no longer involved with flying saucer construction projects, there are many who believe that they are lying and that the Canadian, British, U.S., and even Soviet governments are continuing to work on highly advanced, saucer-shaped, supersonic aircraft based on the work done in Nazi Germany."

Lending weight to this allegation was a CIA memorandum dated October 19, 1955, which stated, "(AVRO-Car designer) Mr. Frost is reported to have obtained his original idea for the flying machine from a group of Germans just after World War II...."

A stranger variation of this charge came from former U.S. Air Force Lieutenant Colonel George Edwards, who claimed he worked on the AVRO project and came to understand that it was a cover for testing a "real alien space craft." Edwards said, "The VZ-9 was to be a 'cover' so the Pentagon would have an explanation whenever people reported seeing a saucer in flight." This theme was taken up by writer Robert Dorr, an Air Force veteran who claimed to have learned of an alien saucer recovered from a crash on the East Coast in 1953. Dorr said use of the AVRO-Car as a "smoke screen" to shift public attention away from the real UFO answered many questions about the AVRO program—such as why the weapons system was never designed to be armed, why as the current aerospace leader the United States entered business with a secondary power like Canada, and why the AVRO was so publicized when first announced in 1955 but not publicized when it was test flown in 1959.

Recently, both reports and photographs of more sophisticated flying saucers bearing USAF markings have surfaced. It is unclear whether these were used for propulsion or if they remain in the Air Force inventory.

However, it is intriguing to note that America's first highly-publicized UFO sightings—the famous Kenneth Arnold saucer incidents of June 1947—took place in the northwest United States and, in both cases, the UFOs flew off toward Canada.

Could it be that something much more advanced than mere rockets and jet planes had made its way into the U.S. government arsenal, which by the fall of 1947 had come under the control of the National Security Council thanks to President Harry Truman's hurried signing into law of the National Security Act that same year?

Colonel John Alexander, writing about advanced weaponry in his 2003 book *Winning the War*, echoed prevalent thinking both in scientific and military circles when he stated that while serious anti-gravity propulsion research began in the 1950s, a time when many companies and small inventor groups were looking into anomalous couplings between electromagnetic forces and special materials or electromagnetic and gravitational forces (aka electrogravitics), but nothing came from it and the subject was dropped.

Or was it? Did anti-gravity simply sink ever deeper into America's "black" projects, which have come to include electromagnetic pulse weapons, laser technology, weather modification, bio-chemical spraying, and even mind control?

In his 2001 book *The Hunt for Zero Point*, British journalist Nick Cook, aviation editor for *Jane's Defense Weekly*, makes a compelling argument that Kammler and the Nazi experiments with anti-gravity, last located in a top-secret SS facility in Poland, indeed survived the war and were put to secret use by a clandestine element, a "shadow government" that ufologists call Majestic-12 or simply MJ-12. Several hundred documents leaked to the public beginning in the mid-1980s indicate that such a program exists and is ongoing.

Boeing, the world's largest aerospace company, announced in 2003 that it was working on anti-gravity propulsion systems. According to CNN reporter Nick Easen, "GRASP or Gravity Research for Advanced Space Propulsion, was only recently reported in *Jane's Defense Weekly*, but the U.S. military may have had the technology for years."

Some aerospace researchers have claimed that U.S. military craft using anti-gravity technology have been operating since at least the 1980s. Calls have been made for the military to unveil its secret technology for commercial benefit. However, gaining information on the government's black technology is virtually impossible as officially a black program may be classed as "deniable," meaning insiders are able, even encouraged, to deny any knowledge about such research. Unlike other nations that have secret programs, the United States has a carefully constructed, tightly controlled, and well-orga-

Edward Snowden, who is now living in exile after revealing U.S. government surveillance secrets, has also noted that the U.S. spent nearly $53 billion on secret projects in 2012.

nized black technology expenditure program, according to Easen. According to whistleblower Edward Snowden, the U.S. budget for black or classified projects was in excess of $52. 8 billion in 2012.

Could such research of black technology stem from an unsettling combination of Nazi technology and ancient secrets regarding monatomic elements? Could such technology be tied to the continuing search for sub-atomic or zero-point energy? And could obtaining such secrets be an underlying reason for our impetuous invasion of Iraq?

Could all the fabulous technology developed in Nazi Germany have come through secret societies tracing their origins back to the ancient astronauts of legend? As will be seen, the Illuminati were connected to several older secret societies.

But many other questions remain. What happened to David Hudson and his proclaimed intent to bring the benefits of the monatomic gold powder to the public?

Why has the International Monetary Fund been accused of artificially holding down the price of gold so that certain unidentified purchasers can stockpile inexpensive gold? And why have major multinational corporations announced their move to fuel cell energy, when such cells depend on elemental metals? Who controls such metals?

Is the public about to gain unimaginable benefit from the rediscovery of ancient secrets concerning energy manipulation and the manufacture of high-spun gold powder? Or will this discovery, like so many others, be hidden away from the public in order to maintain current monopolies?

Now let us consider some of the better-known and well-documented secret societies that may have had an impact on the theology of the Illuminati.

Gnostics

One of the earliest and least-known of mystical groups was the Gnostics. Gnosticism, derived from the Greek word for knowledge, *Gnosis*, reportedly was founded by Simon the Magician, a contemporary of Jesus's, who was later scorned as the "Father of All Heretics." He advanced the ideas of the Greek philosophers, such as Socrates, who taught that the human soul exists outside the physical body, and therefore has access to universal knowledge, and that wisdom, or *Gnosis*, was brought down to earth from the heavens.

Scattered throughout early civilizations, Gnostics claimed to have an intuitive understanding of the mysteries of God and Earth. They were anti-authoritarian and spurned any need for religious figures to interpret the word of God. Early Christian Gnostics claimed to be the keepers of secret knowledge as found in the Gnostic papyrus books discovered at Nag Hammadi in 1945. It was this discovery that first afforded any view of Gnosticism other than the damning rhetoric of the Catholic Church. "[C]ertain details prove that the Gnostic holy books (from Qumran and Nag Hammadi) must be assigned such an early date that Christianity itself may be seen as no more than a 'branch of Gnosticism,'" wrote Andre Nataf, a researcher into the occult.

Basilides, an early Egyptian Christian Gnostic, founded the Alexandrian Cult in the first century C.E. This group sought to blend the ancient mysteries into Christianity. The Alexandrians believed that strange extraterrestrial beings called "aeons" acted as messengers between the heavens and earth. The Persian Zoroaster began his own form of Gnosticism about 500 years before the time of Jesus. Known as Zoroasterianism, this movement spread widely until pushed out by invading Muslims in the seventh century.

It is claimed that Gnosticism originated in Mesopotamia, first in the area of Iran and then on to Asia Minor, Syria, and Babylon, where it was picked up by the Israelite captives and carried back to Palestine and Egypt.

According to the Masonic philosopher Manly P. Hall, Gnosticism was an integral part of the ancient mysteries since both involved the belief that only personal inner enlightenment could bring understanding and wisdom. "This knowledge of how man's manifold constitution could be most quickly and most completely regenerated to the point of spiritual illumination constituted the secret, or esoteric, doctrine of antiquity," wrote Hall. He added that such spiritual illumination had to be jealously guarded from "profane" or disrespectful persons who might abuse or misuse such knowledge. So lengthy periods of initiation were instituted and the most sensitive ancient knowledge was shrouded in symbols and allegory. "Christianity itself may be cited as an example," Hall wrote. "The entire New Testament is in fact an ingeniously concealed exposition of the secret processes of human regeneration."

Gnosticism, once described as "religious existentialism," flourished until declared a heresy by a council of bish-

> The Alexandrians believed that strange extraterrestrial beings called "aeons" acted as messengers between the heavens and earth.

ops of the Roman Church in 325 C.E. It was later the basic theology of the Cathars, located in southern France, until wiped out by a papal army during the Albigensian Crusade beginning in 1209. Certain Gnostic beliefs eventually found their way into the Bavarian Illuminati.

Cabala

The Cabala, also known as Kabbalah or Qabbalah, is a school of thought of Hebrew origins and means "tradition." The Cabala taught a form of Gnosticism in which practitioners seek to find divinity within themselves. Like the Bible, the Cabala reportedly contains hidden meanings. Similar coded knowledge may be found within the *Torah* and other old Hebraic texts such as the *Sefer Yezirah* (Book of Creation) and the *Sefer HaZohar* (Book of Light).

These books, produced centuries before the time of Jesus, predate the Talmud, a compilation of elder Jewish laws and traditions first written in the fifth century C.E. There are two versions of the *Talmud*, one originating in Babylon and the other from Jerusalem. According to the Book of Light, God gave "mysteries of wisdom" to Adam while still in the fabled Garden of Eden. It may be significant that the Sumerian term *Edin* denoted the first settlement of the Anunnaki in southern Mesopotamia. These elder secrets were then passed on through Adam's sons to Noah and then Abraham long before the Hebraic Semites, or Israelites, existed as a distinct people.

Many researchers, including Jewish scholars, believe the Cabala began as an oral tradition concerning the ancient Egyptian mysteries. Later, they were passed down from Moses to the Israelite leadership.

The idea of Moses holding ancient secrets from the earliest times was strongly supported by Eliphas Levi, a pen name of the nineteenth-century French Bible scholar Alphonse Louis Constant. "There is a tremendous secret which has already turned the world upside down, as shown by the religious traditions of Egypt, which were symbolically resumed by Moses in the early chapters of Genesis," wrote Levi, who claimed that the Cabala contained knowledge carried out of Sumer by Abraham, "the inheritor of the secrets of Enoch and the father of initiation in Israel."

Abraham, earlier called Abram, was said to possess a tablet of symbols representing all of the knowledge of humankind handed down from the time of Noah. Known to the Sumerians as the "Table of Destiny," it was this table of knowledge—known to the early Jews as the "Book of Raziel"—that reportedly provided King Solomon with his vast wisdom. It was said that whomever possessed Cabala also possessed *Ram,* the highest expression of cosmic knowingness. The very name Ab-ram—or Av-ram—means "[He] who possesses *Ram."* This expression was used in India, Tibet, Egypt, and the Celtic world of the Druids, who had emigrated from Mesopotamia, to denote a high degree of universal wisdom. The Sumerian "Table of Destiny" is thought to be the same as the "Tables of Testimony" mentioned in Exodus 31:18. Other Bible verses—Exodus 24:12 and 25:16—make it clear that these tables are not the Ten Commandments. "This ancient archive is directly associated with the Emerald Table of Thoth-Hermes and, as detailed in alchemical records of Egypt, the author of the preserved writings was the biblical Ham," explained author Laurence Gardner, an internationally known genealogist. "He was the essential founder of the esoteric and arcane 'underground stream' which flowed through the ages and his Greek name, Hermes, was directly related to the science of pyramid construction, deriving from the word *herma,* which relates to a 'pile of stones'…. Outside Egypt and Mesopotamia, the Table was known to Greek and Roman masters such as Homer, Virgil, Pythagoras, Plato, and Ovid, while in much later times, the seventeenth-century Stuart Royal Society of Britain was deeply concerned with the analysis and application of the sacred knowledge (in) conjunction with the Knights Templars and the Rosicrucian movement.…"

The first page of the 1558 edition of the *Sefer HaZohar,* which is the main source of the Kabbalah.

Some of the Cabala was drawn from the philosophies of Mesopotamian mystics and much like our understanding of history and religion today, the information within the Cabala became garbled over the centuries through both misinterpretations as well as foreign influences. Pure or tainted, the mystical knowledge of the Cabala passed from Mesopotamia through Palestine into Medieval Europe where it first appeared in writing at the end of the thirteenth century. It was scribed by a Spanish Jew named Moses de Leon, who may have devised the title *HaZohar,* a literary creation that caused critics to accuse him of fabricating the entire work. The legendary Knights Templar brought Cabalistic knowledge back to Europe from the Holy Land at the time of the Crusades and such knowledge was passed along through the stone mason guilds created by the Templars. Masonic historians have acknowledged that the first evidence of "Judeo-Christian mysteries" introduced into Freemasonry came during this very time. It has also been documented that the hidden knowledge within the Cabala has been utilized through the centuries by nearly all secret societies, including Freemasonry, the Rosicrucians, and through the Illuminati on into modern groups. "Since the suppression of the Mysteries … their tradition and teachings have been continued in secret and under various concealments, and to that continuation our present Masonic system is due," confirmed masonic historian Walter L. Wilmshurst.

Grand Master Mason Albert Pike gave great importance to the Cabala as a key to Masonic esotericism. He wrote, "One is filled with admiration, on penetrating into the Sanctuary of the Kabalah, at seeing a doctrine so logical, so simple, and at the same time so absolute. The necessary union of ideas and signs, the consecration of the most fundamental realities by the primitive characters; the Trinity of Words, Letters, and Numbers; a philosophy simple as the alphabet, profound and infinite as the Word; theorems more complete and luminous than those of Pythagoras; a theology summed up by counting on one's fingers; an Infinite which can be held in the hollow of an infant's hand; ten ciphers and twenty-two letters, a triangle, a square, and a circle,—these are all the elements of the Kabalah. These are the elementary principles of the written Word, reflection of that spoken Word that created the world!"

> The legendary Knights Templar brought Cabalistic knowledge back to Europe from the Holy Land at the time of the Crusades and such knowledge was passed along through the stone mason guilds created by the Templars.

The eighteenth-century Jewish philosopher and Bible translator Moses Mendelssohn, known as "the German Socrates," was a student of the Cabala and was a mentor to Adam Weishaupt, founder of the Illuminati. Mendelssohn may have also been a link between Weishaupt and banker Mayer Rothschild. Another link was Mendelssohn follower Michael Hess, the tutor of Jacob Rothschild's children, who later headed the Philanthropist School for needy Jewish children established by Mayer Amschel Rothschild in Frankfurt. The blending of Cabalistic teachings with later secret societies was further confirmed in 1984 when more than 500 papers of British poet John Byrom were discovered in England. Byrom, who lived from 1691 to 1763, was a Freemason, a fellow of the Royal Society, and a leader of the Jacobite movement to restore the Stuart monarchy. He was a member of a group called the "Sun Club," also known as the "Cabala Club," devotees of sacred geometry, architecture, and cabalistic, Masonic, hermetic, and alchemical symbols.

The Mystery Schools

The word "Illuminati," meaning "a person who has been enlightened, or illuminated, by receiving knowledge from a higher source," may well have originated in the ancient Mystery Schools of Greece and Egypt. The term also was used to describe early baptized Christians and higher degrees of initiation in some secret societies. In order to include the Mystery Schools of Egypt and Greece, all the early societies sought to penetrate the secrets of the past. With the occupation of Mesopotamia by the Persians, the cult of Mithra arose and held sway well into the time of the Roman Empire. According to legend, Mithra was the son of Ahura Mazda, the Persian god of light and illumination. Described as one of the Anunnaki, Ahura Mazda was viewed as the highest spirit of worship in Zoroastrianism. Zoroaster was a religious figure who was said to have had an encounter with his god Ahura Mazda, who, like the biblical Ezekiel, appeared to him in a shining light from the sky. Ahura Mazda is usually represented as a figure flying in a winged vehicle. Some researchers believe this god represented lingering knowledge of the Sumerian Anunnaki and may have influenced the later Greek, Roman, and Jewish ideologies. Zoroastrianism led to Mithraism, and Mithra, being a powerful warrior, was appealing to the Roman soldiers who carried his worship back to Rome. Christian emperors generally stamped out Mithraism and many other sects, but some basic knowledge may have passed on into more recent societies such as the Rosicrucians, Freemasons, and Illuminati. Every five years, the ancient Greeks worshipped near Athens in a town named Eleusis. The rites were devoted to Persephone, the daughter of Demeter (known as Ceres to the Romans), the goddess of corn, grain, and fertility; Persephone was reportedly a daughter of their main god Zeus. When Persephone was abducted by Hades and taken to the Underworld, Demeter cursed the world by causing all plants to die. Zeus and Hades reached a compromise, dictating that Persephone would return but spend four months of the year with Hades. Thus were created the winter months. This goddess worship, with its belief in death and resurrection coupled with a strict vow of secrecy by initiates, became known as the Eleusinian Mysteries. It was outlawed in 392 C.E. by Roman emperor Theodosius following the Christianization of the Roman Empire under Constantine.

Mystery School traditions can be traced back even long before ancient Egypt and Greece. The Babylonian Mystery School involved practically everything considered "Illuminati symbolism."

One early secret within the Mystery Schools is that their members believed there are only a few truly mature minds in the world and that they were

The fourth-century B.C.E. Ninnion Tablet shown here depicts Greek gods Demeter, Persephone, and others bearing symbols of various Eleusinian Mysteries.

among these chosen few. They believed that those minds belonged exclusively to them, a common secret-society view of humanity. Initiates of the Mysteries were thought capable of individual reasoning based on facts, while the masses were considered only slightly better than animals and had to be taught using the simplest of terms. Jesus may have exhibited this trait as recorded in Mark 4:33 (*New International*): "With many similar parables [stories] Jesus spoke the word to them, as much as they could understand. He did not say anything to them without using a parable. But when he was alone with his own disciples, he explained everything."

It is said that the initiates of the Mysteries could communicate directly to the gods and they received replies. Only the masses participated in sacrificial rites near mute stone idols. The elect were illuminated with the knowledge of the Mysteries and thus were known as the illluminati or the Illuminated Ones, the guardians of the "Secrets of the Ages." But all such secrets again can be traced back to the earliest known civilization—Sumer. Even Bible stories and aspects such as the Trinity, the cross, resurrection, and Mary worship can all be found in the writings of Babylon and Sumer. For example, the ancient Sumerian cuneiform tablets give an account of the Great Flood that is amazingly similar to that of the Bible, yet at the same time astonishingly different. They state that about 12,000 years ago the Anunnaki leadership realized that severe climatic changes would occur with the imminent return of the planet Nibiru, which they said orbits the Earth every 3,600 years. It was decided to allow nature to wipe out the humans while the Anunnaki waited events out in orbiting evacuation ships.

This account tells how the Anunnaki science officer, the Sumerian deity Enki, passed along this murderous secret to one of his most prized human assistants, identified as the Sumerian Ziusudra or Utnapishtim.

Utnapishtim has been called the "Sumerian Noah" and the biblical account of the flood is obviously an edited version of the original Sumerian account with their several Anunnaki gods compressed into the monotheistic God of the Bible. The Sumerian texts describe how Enki instructed Utnapishtim/Noah to construct an ark, including the use of readily available bitumen to make it waterproof. The *Gilgamesh* version gave some interesting details deleted from the biblical account. Enki also instructed Utnapishtim/Noah, "Aboard ship take thou the seed of all living things...."

This instruction is most fascinating because, since Enki had been the science officer involved in genetic engineering, it would seem more plausible that Utnapishtim/Noah took DNA samples of all living things rather than a boatload of animals, insects, and plants.

The Akkadian account makes it clear the Great Flood was not the result of heavy rains. It described a darkness accompanied by colossal winds, which increased in intensity, destroying buildings and rupturing dikes. Such conditions would be expected by the near passage of a large planetary body. Scattered archeological excavations over many years indicate that what is regarded as the Great Flood was a planet-wide catastrophe, though not every portion of the world went underwater. But even today, most of the original Anunnaki cities in Mesopotamia remain deep under water and silt near the mouths of the Tigris and Euphrates rivers.

In both the Akkadian and biblical accounts, after six days and nights the ark came to rest on a mountaintop, identified as Mount Ararat in eastern

Flood stories pervade cultures throughout the world, such as in India. This 1870 artwork depicts the god Vishnu rescuing Manu (the progenitor of humanity) after the flood.

Turkey. After sending a dove, a swallow, and a raven from the ark, only the raven stayed away, indicating that dry land was nearby.

The teachings of these ancient schools, including those in India, contain parallel legends to explain both history and society. Examples include not only tales of the Great Flood, but also a virgin who produces a son, a deity who dies and then returns, gods who represent celestial beings, new gods derived from older gods, and sky gods who taught humans the basics of culture, law, language, the written word, mathematics, astronomy, and agriculture. The Mystery Schools, guardians of ancient lore, spread their knowledge far and wide. Canadian mystic and ranking Mason Manly P. Hall stated, "Time will reveal that the continent now known as America was actually discovered, and, to a considerable degree, explored more than a thousand years before the beginning of the Christian era. The true story was in the keeping of the Mystery Schools, and passed from them to the Secret Societies of the medieval world. The Esoteric Orders of Europe, Asia, and the Near East were in at least irregular communication with the priesthoods of the more advanced Amerindian nations. Plans for the development of the Western Hemisphere were formulated in Alexandria, Mecca, Delhi, and Lhasa [Tibet] long before most European statesmen were aware of the great Utopian program."

Some have suggested such hidden knowledge was also passed down through Muslim communities such as the Ismaili sect, which has been closely connected to the Knights Templar, known to have brought Illuminati ideals to Europe. According to an Ismaili website, "As Muslims, the Ismailis affirm the fundamental Islamic testimony of truth, the Shahada, that there is no God but Allah and that Muhammad (peace be upon him and his family) is His Messenger. They believe that Muhammad was the last and final Prophet of Allah, and that the Holy Quran, Allah's final message to mankind, was revealed through him. Muslims hold this revelation to be the culmination of the message that had been revealed through other Prophets of the Abrahamic tradition before Muhammad, including Abraham, Moses and Jesus, all of whom Muslims revere as Prophets of Allah."

Again, we see that it was Abraham, or Abram, the patriarch of both the Israelites and the Muslims, who brought the ancient knowledge of the Anunnaki to Palestine and Egypt from his home in the Mesopotamian city of Ur. The Old Testament (Genesis 12:1–2) tells how Abraham was encouraged to make this move by an actual conversation with his god, who told him, "Get thee out of thy country, from your kindred and from thy father's house, unto a land that I will show thee: And I will make of thee a great nation, and I will bless thee, and make thy name great, and thou shalt be blessing...."

And since it has been calculated that Abraham lived about 4,000 years ago, reaching the age of 175 (Genesis 25:7), and the Sumerian civilization did not become established until about 3,000 years ago, it can be surmised that

Abraham, during his early life in Ur, located on the Euphrates River near the Persian Gulf, may have had access to first-hand information concerning Anunnaki technology and knowledge. It has been speculated that knowledge brought by Abraham may have helped create the miraculous empire than sprang up in Egypt after 3100 C.E.

Essenes

Gnosticism and the mystic teachings of the Cabala played an important role in an early Jewish ascetic sect known as the Essenes. The Essenes provoked such conflict with religious leaders of the other two major Jewish sects—the Pharisees and Sadducees—that the sect finally moved out of Jerusalem and established a monastery at Qumran on the north end of the Dead Sea, which they called "the Wilderness." The word "Essenes" was derived from the Greek words *essaios*, meaning "secret" or "mystic," and *essenoi*, indicating healing or physician. The Essenes have been connected to a later branch of an Egyptian Mystery School called the Great White Brotherhood of Therapy, which practiced esoteric healing traditions. It has been proposed that the Essenes, the custodians of ancient and esoteric knowledge, were also the initiators and educators of Jesus. British author Laurence Gardner noted, "It was into this White Brotherhood of wise therapeutics and healers—the original Rosicrucians—that Jesus was later initiated to progress through the degrees and it was his high standing in this regard which gained him the so often used designation of 'Master.'"

Other authors also claim Jesus was an Essene along with his parents, Mary and Joseph, and his brother James. Most modern fundamentalists tend to dismiss this connection because tying Jesus to Gnosticism and the Essenes disturbs their rigid dogma. It is noticeable, however, that in the New Testament, Jesus disparages both the Pharisees and Sadducees, but oddly there is no mention of the Essenes, indicating he either was a member and had no call to rebuke them or all references to that group have been excised.

The Bible tends to confirm that Jesus may have studied in the same temple of Melchizedek where Pythagoras had studied six centuries before. Hebrews 6:20 states that "where Jesus has gone as a forerunner on our behalf, having become a high priest forever after the order of Melchizedek."

> **I**t has been proposed that the Essenes, the custodians of ancient and esoteric knowledge, were also the initiators and educators of Jesus.

Melchizedek is one of the most mysterious and least understood characters in the Bible.

Gardner claimed the name Melchizedek was an Essene-created composite of the archangel Michael and the Hebrew high priest Zadok, hence Michael-Zadok. Others believe this "king of Salem," an early name for the future Jerusalem, was a pre-incarnation of Jesus, while some have suggested that Melchizedek actually was the Sumerian deity Enki. Of course, by the time of Jesus, awareness of the Anunnaki and their technology had been largely lost. The Essenes, active at the time of Christ, have been referred to as the protectors of "mystic Christianity" based on the earlier mysteries. Although certainly known to their neighbors, their presence was either not recorded in the New Testament or later excised.

In fact, little to nothing was known regarding the Essenes until the discovery of the Dead Sea Scrolls in 1947, just two years after a Gnostic library was found in the Egyptian town of Nag Hammadi. Apparently, as the Roman armies advanced during the Jewish Revolt of 70 C.E., the Essenes fled from Qumran after hiding their sacred scrolls in earthen jars buried in nearby caves. Eventually word of the discovery reached the ears of Hebrew University archeologist Yigael Yadin, who mortgaged his home and traveled into dangerous Arab areas seeking the scrolls. He managed to secure seven of them for his university, which promptly published them.

"Not so for the remaining scrolls," reported Bible scholar and former intelligence analyst Patricia Eddy. "The Rockefeller Archaeological Museum in Palestine soon became involved and managed to acquire the rest of the scrolls from the government of Jordan ... who stipulated that no Jewish scholars be allowed access to the ancient Jewish texts. Today, Israel controls the scrolls as a result of overrunning the place where they were stored during the Six Day War of 1967 ... these scrolls are largely unpublished today (and) no one knows if all of them have been obtained. There is the possibility that others are in the possession of, or have been destroyed by, the [Arab] Bedouins."

The Essene authors of the Dead Sea Scrolls had a profound effect on the first Christians in Jerusalem, who soon differed in theology from Paul and his followers outside Palestine. This is evidenced by the fact that the interpretations of the Old Testament found in the scrolls are similar to the interpretations of Jesus's brother James and the Jerusalem Christians.

The conflicts both within and without Christianity were settled by the Roman Emperor Constantine in what Gardner described as "a strategic buyout by the enemy." "Apart from various cultic beliefs, the Romans had worshipped the Emperors in their capacity as gods descended from others like Neptune and Jupiter," Gardner explained. "At the Council of Arles in 314, Constantine retained his own divine status by introducing the omnipotent God of the Christians as his personal sponsor. He then dealt with the anom-

A circa 1500 painting depicting the baptism of Emperor Constantine. The Roman emperor converted to Christianity, but he still asserted his divine status and also replaced some Christian rituals with those of the Roman gods.

alies of doctrine by replacing certain aspects of Christian ritual with the familiar pagan traditions of sun worship, together with other teachings of Syrian and Persian origin. In short, the new religion of the Roman Church was constructed as a 'hybrid' to appease all influential factions. By this means, Constantine looked towards a common and unified 'world' religion—Catholic meaning *universal*—with himself at its head."

This attempt to co-opt Christianity was sealed at the Council of Nicaea in 325 C.E. and one year later, Constantine ordered the confiscation and destruction of all works that questioned the newly constructed orthodoxy. He also opened the Lateran Palace to the bishop of Rome, creating an early Vatican of sorts. In 331 C.E., the emperor ordered new copies made of Christian texts, most of which had been lost or destroyed during the previous persecutions. "It was at this point that most of the crucial alterations in the New Testament were probably made and Jesus assumed the unique status he has enjoyed ever since," noted authors Michael Baigent, Richard Leigh, and Henry Lincoln in *Holy Blood, Holy Grail*.

The Essenes played a big role in the time of Jesus. They carried on the hermetic traditions of the Greeks. In the early 1900s, a Russian-born train engineer named Georgi Ivanovich Gurdjieff claimed to have found the intact manuscript of an Essene Master in an Indian monastery, which explained the relationship of musical rhythms to the human body as taught by the sixth-century B.C.E. Greek philosopher Pythagoras, a great influence on Plato, Freemasonry, and the Illuminati.

It was Pythagoras, well known for his accurate prophecies, who may have been the first to predict a "New World Order," at that time thought to mean the arrival of the Messiah.

It has been noted that the followers of Pythagoras as well as the later Freemasons used the mason's trowel, a prominent Essene symbol, in their ceremonies and literature. And like the Masons and subsequent Illuminati, the Essenes used intricate codes and allegories to protect their knowledge from the uninitiated as well as from the Roman authorities. "The fact that so many artificers [craftsmen] were listed among their number is responsible for the order's being considered as a progenitor of modern Freemasonry," wrote Hall.

The Essenes also were one of the most effective of the ancient secret societies. Some researchers have referred to the Essenes as the protectors of "Mystic Christianity," the earliest form of Christianity based on the Ancient Mysteries.

Based on the recent discoveries that made available such ancient texts as *The Gospel of Truth*, *The Gospel of Thomas*, *The Testimony of Truth*, *The Gospel of Mary* and *The Interpretation of Knowledge*, researchers today have a much broader and more complete knowledge of biblical times than ever before in history, despite the fact that much of this new information has still not reached a general audience.

Author Nesta Webster, a passionate Christian writing in 1924, long before the recent finds, deplored the connection between Jesus and the Essenes as well as their source of knowledge. "The Essenes were therefore not Christians, but a secret society ... bound by terrible oaths not to divulge the sacred mysteries confided to them," she declared. "And what were those mysteries but those of the Jewish secret tradition which we now know as the Cabala.... The truth is clearly that the Essenes were Cabalists, though doubtless Cabalists of a superior kind.... The Essenes are of importance ... as the first of the secret societies from which a direct line of tradition can be traced up to the present day."

Others argue that today's recently acquired knowledge in astronomy and philosophy may have been commonplace to the Gnostic Essenes of Jesus's time. Furthermore, Gardner observed, "Entirely divorced from the fabricated Christianity of the Roman Empire, their faith was closer to the original teachings of Jesus than any other...."

> **S**ome researchers have referred to the Essenes as the protectors of "Mystic Christianity," the earliest form of Christianity based on the Ancient Mysteries.

Of all the Christian factions, the Essenes may indeed have had the purest of the ancient traditions at that time, as acknowledged by both supporters and critics. The secrets of these early groups must have been most profound and compelling to have caused members over the centuries to persevere in their effort to protect and propagate their knowledge against official and clerical censure and oppression. It is abundantly clear that this knowledge, passed down largely through ritual allegory and symbols, predates the ancient Egyptians.

One mystical society said to have influenced, if not created, both the Knights Templar and the Illuminati is the Prieuré de Sion, or Priory of Sion, a highly controversial group made popular by the publishing success of author Dan Brown's 2003 book *The Da Vinci Code* and a previous work entitled *Holy Blood, Holy Grail*, which posited that the Priory protected the secret lineage of Jesus and Mary Magdalene. Most today believe accounts of the Priory to be a hoax contrived by Pierre Plantard, a Frenchman who claimed to be a direct descendant of the French Merovingian royal line, the servant kings, and who was connected to right-wing occult circles. According to Plantard, the Priory was founded by Godfrey of Bouillon on Mount Zion in the Kingdom of Jerusalem in 1099 prior to the Templar Order. Reportedly, its Grand Masters included Leonardo da Vinci and Isaac Newton and its primary goal was to restore the Merovingian line. The Priory was also said to have created the Knights Templar as a military arm and financial branch.

In court cases involving book royalties in the 1980s, Plantard was forced to confess that he had fabricated the Priory documents. Researcher Terry Melanson in 2009 wrote, "For conspiracy theorists who've concocted an entire edifice (books, DVDs, lectures, etc.) based on the notion of a tangible secret society called the Priory of Sion, it is a hard pill to swallow. Sorry, but the fact is that the authors [who perpetuated the Priory story] were duped. The whole thing is a fairy tale, a scam—beginning to end."

Nevertheless, it is highly significant that so many esoteric beliefs can be traced back to Egypt, Palestine, and, more specifically, the ancient cultures of Mesopotamia.

Roshaniya

One elder sect that may have been a forerunner of the Illuminati was the Roshaniya of Afghanistan, referred to as the "enlightened ones." This group conducted rites and rituals similar to the later Illuminati. A leading luminary of this cult was Bayazid Ansari, who claimed his family was descended from the Ansar, those "helpers" who aided Mohammed in his flight from Mecca. Not only did Roshaniya practices parallel those of the Illuminati—such as indulging oneself, gaining power, the use of subterfuge, allegiance only to their cult, and a fight against the established order (at that time, the Imperial Mogul)—but the number and types of earned degrees were eerily similar to those of the Illuminati. "Like the Roshaniya, the Illuminati stated that they had the objective of gaining important converts for the purpose of improving the state of the world," wrote Idries Shah, the son of an Afghan noble family, who used the pen name Arkon Daraul.

The House of Wisdom, founded during the Golden Age of Islam (approximately the eighth century to the thirteenth century), was a center of learning located in Baghdad that taught science, medicine, alchemy, geography, zoology, and astronomy and included both Christians and Jews. At one time, it housed the greatest collections of books in the world and had its own astronomical observatories. It was destroyed in 1258 during the sack of Baghdad by the Mongols. Within the House were records of the Roshaniya. The

This 1430 manuscript illustration shows the 1258 siege of Baghdad by Mongol hordes. The destruction of the House of Wisdom in that city destroyed an invaluable repository of scientific books.

major tenets of the Roshaniya were: the abolition of private property; the elimination of religion; the elimination of nation states; the belief that illumination emanated from the Supreme Being, who desired a class of perfect men and women to carry out the organization and direction of the world; belief in a plan to reshape the social system of the world by first taking control of individual countries one by one; and the belief that after reaching the fourth degree one could communicate directly with the unknown supervisors who had imparted knowledge to initiates throughout the ages. They believed wise men would again recognize this Brotherhood.

The ideals of this cult, which sound surprisingly like the later agenda of the Illuminati, can still be found in the political philosophies of today. The Roshaniya, like the later agenda of the Illuminati, gave allegiance to no particular nation, although they used nationalism to further their aims. This ancient Brotherhood's only goal was to gain economic and political power over their entire world. They also were determined to eliminate all Christians, Jews, and atheists.

> The incontestable fact here is that there are significant prehistorical overtones to the doctrines of both Freemasonry and Rosicrucianism.

The Roshaniya even called themselves the Order. Like the later Illuminati, initiates took an oath that absolved them of all allegiance except to the Order and pledged, "I bind myself to perpetual silence and unshaken loyalty and submission to the Order.... All humanity which cannot identify itself by our secret sign is our lawful prey." This oath remains essentially the same to this day in many secret societies. Another rule of the Roshaniya, copied later by the Illuminati, was never to use the same name and never mention the name of their order or utter the name "Illuminati." Some feel this rule is still in effect today and that it may well have been the breaking of this rule, at the time the Bavarian authorities became aware of the Order, that resulted in Adam Weishaupt's downfall.

The Roshaniya cult preached that there was a spirit world apart from our material world. Spirits after death could continue to be powerful on earth but only through a member of the Order and only if the spirit had been itself a member of the Order before its death. The Roshaniya believed members of the Order gained power from the spirits of dead members.

Another similarity with the later Illuminati was the Roshaniya procedure of recruiting travelers as initiates and then sending them out to establish new chapters of the Order. Some researchers believe the Assassins were a branch of the Roshaniya cult. Some claim branches of the Roshaniya still exist.

However, any discussion concerning philosophies, magic, and religion is quickly enmeshed in a quagmire of definitions, interpretations, and personal beliefs. The incontestable fact here is that there are significant prehistorical overtones to the doctrines of both Freemasonry and Rosicrucianism.

Consider how the various threads of ancient knowledge were brought into focus within modern secret societies. A major source of those ancient secrets was through the discoveries of a group of medieval knights—the legendary Knights Templar.

Knights Templar

Even before being outlawed in 1307, the Illuminati had insinuated their doctrinal theology (termed Illuminism) into Freemasonry, itself a direct descendent of the legendary Knights Templar.

It has long been said the Knights Templar brought ancient knowledge from the Cabala and the Mystery Schools back to Europe from the Holy Land at the time of the Crusades and that this knowledge was passed along through the stonemason guilds formed by the Templars. Masonic historians have acknowledged that the first evidence of "Judeo-Christian mysteries" introduced into Freemasonry came during this very time. It has also been documented that the hidden knowledge within the Cabala has been utilized through the centuries by nearly all secret societies, including Freemasonry, the Rosicrucians, and through the Illuminati into modern groups.

So, it is incumbent on any serious researcher of the Illuminati to delve into the background and beliefs of these warrior knights. Until the fall of Constantinople in 1453, the Roman church stood supreme as the authority in the Western world. Through the lending of both its money and blessings, the Vatican dominated kings and queens and controlled the lives of ordinary citizens through fear of excommunication and its infamous Inquisition.

Following repeated attempts at invasion by Islamic armies, Christian Europe launched crusade after crusade against the Muslims, particularly those holding the Holy Land (Palestine) in the Middle East. In southern France, certain families held doctrinal beliefs dating back to the suppression of the Cathars. These beliefs concerned a more human Jesus, his wife Mary Magdalene, and their descendants. This, of course, ran counter to the teachings of the Church. The Crusades presented a convenient excuse to take the Holy Land and search for verification of these traditions. Some researchers even suggest that the Crusades may have been fomented by this search for hidden knowledge. Peter the Hermit, along with St. Bernard, a personal tutor to the Crusade's leader, Godfrey de Bouillon, were instrumental in promoting the First Crusade. De Bouillon was later associated with the creation of the Knights Templar.

Following the fall of Jerusalem during the First Crusade in 1099, Crusaders apparently found some verification of the heretical ideas that supported elder traditions, principally those originating in southern France. It was this conflict that led to the creation of societies that used secrecy as protection from the Roman Church.

The Knights Templar brought back more than just heretical hearsay—they reportedly returned to Europe with hard evidence of error and duplicity in Church dogma. Over time, they became known as heretics and blasphemers and an attempt was made by the Church to exterminate them. However, Templar traditions live on today within Freemasonry.

The Templars, originally a religious-military knighthood called The Order of the Poor Knights of Christ and of the Temple of Solomon were formed in 1118 when nine French Crusaders appeared before King Baldwin of Jerusalem and asked to be

The Templars comprised three classes: Brethren (left), who were wealthy men that were not from the nobility; Knights (center), who were from noble families and remained unmarried; and Chaplains.

allowed to protect pilgrims traveling to the Holy Land. They also asked permission to stay in the east wing of his palace, which was adjacent to the recently captured Al-Aqsa Mosque, former site of King Solomon's Temple. Their requests were granted and the Order became known as the Knights of the Temple, soon shortened to Knights Templar.

As the Templars grew in numbers and power, their order took on an increasing number of rites, many of which were reflected in the later Freemasons and Illuminati. Initially there were three classes—the Knights, composed of unmarried men from noble families; the Chaplains, who took vows of poverty, chastity, and obedient service; and the Brethren, which included talented and wealthy men who lacked noble birth. All Knights and Chaplains were required to undergo strict initiation ceremonies. Scant attention has been paid to the Knights in traditional history books, and their role in shaping future events has been mostly relegated to footnotes. It is known that the Order flourished, becoming extraordinarily wealthy and powerful, until 1307, when they were crushed by an envious French king and a pope fearful of their secrets. With the destruction of the Templars, the Church attempted to wipe out all evidence of the Order and their secrets, which involved the innermost mysteries of Christianity—issues so volatile that the Templars had to be destroyed by the very church that ordained them.

Thanks to the effort of a number of scholars, today the record of Templar origins and contributions has been reassembled and reappraised. These knights were led by Hugh de Payens, a nobleman in the service of André de Montbard, the uncle of Bernard of Clairvaux, later known as the Cistercian Saint Bernard. Montbard also was a vassal of the Count of Champagne. "… Payens and his nine companions all came from either Champagne or the Languedoc [regions of France], and included the Count of Provence, and it is quite apparent that they went to the Holy Land with a specific mission in mind," wrote authors Lynn Picknett and Clive Prince. Provence lies adjacent to the Languedoc and includes Marseilles, where Mary Magdalene reportedly arrived in Europe after the crucifixion of Jesus Christ.

Saint Bernard continued to support the Templars as he rose to prominence.

During the first nine years of their existence, the Templars recruited no new members and did little to protect the roads to Jerusalem. The protection of pilgrims was undertaken by another order, the Knights of the Hospital of St. John of Jerusalem, also known as the Hospitallers. Leaving such protection to the Hospitallers, the Templars kept close to their quarters and excavated for treasure deep under the ruins of the first permanent Hebrew sanctuary, Solomon's Temple. Initially constructed some 3,000 years ago on Mount Moriah in Jerusalem, Solomon's Temple was planned by his father, the biblical King David, and was a carbon copy of a Sumerian temple constructed almost 1,000 years earlier and dedicated to Ninurta, the foremost son of the Anunnaki leader Enlil. Many researchers believe Enlil to be the vengeful god of the Old Testament. Solomon's Temple was destroyed during the Babylonian conquest about 586 B.C.E., then rebuilt by King Zerubbabel after the Jews returned from captivity. Much of the new design was based on a vision by the prophet Ezekiel, who in the Old Testament described his experiences with flying devices. In the time of Jesus, Zerubbabel's temple was greatly reworked to become the palace of King Herod the Great. It was destroyed only four years after its completion in 70 C.E. during the Jewish revolt against the Romans. Knowing that the Romans intended to conquer Jerusalem, the Israelites hid Solomon's Treasure—gathered during their sojourn in the wilderness and consisting of gold, silver, and jewels as well as documents of ancient knowledge—beneath the temple by sealing off passageways and rooms. Today, remnants of the Jewish temples are enclosed within the Dome of the Rock mosque, an Islamic holy shrine second only to Mecca and Medina.

There is no question that Templar excavations under Herod's Temple were extensive. In 1894, a group of British Royal Engineers led by Lieutenant Charles Wilson discovered evidence of the Templars while mapping vaults under Mount Moriah. They found vaulted passageways with keystone arches, typical of Templar handiwork. They also found artifacts consisting of a spur, parts of a sword and lance, and a small Templar cross, which are still on display in Scotland. It was during their excavations, according to several accounts, that the Templars acquired scrolls of hidden knowledge, again most probably dealing with the life of Jesus and his associations with the Essenes and Gnostics. They also reportedly acquired the legendary Tables of Testimony given to Moses as well as other holy relics—perhaps even the legendary Ark of the Covenant and the Spear of Longinus—which could have been used to validate their claims as an alternative religious authority to the Roman church. Author Laurence Gardner confirmed that, in addition to treasure, the Templar excavators also recovered "a wealth of ancient manuscript books in Hebrew and Syriac … many of these predated the Gospels, providing first-hand accounts that had not been edited by any ecclesiastical authority. It was widely accepted that the Knights possessed an insight which eclipsed orthodox Christianity, an insight that permitted them the certainty that the Church had misinterpreted both the Virgin Birth and the Resurrection."

Such reports were well supported by the discovery of a document etched on copper among the Dead Sea Scrolls found at Qumran on the northwest shore of the Dead Sea in 1947. This "Copper Scroll," translated in the mid-1950s at Manchester University, not only mentioned a vast treasure of both gold and literature but actually described the treasure's hiding place—the site of the Templar excavations beneath Solomon's Temple.

It apparently was one of several copies, another of which may have come into the hands of the Templars. With its detailed directions to hidden Hebrew valuables, the "Copper Scroll" was literally a treasure map.

Their newfound wealth as well as their possession of lost documents also could explain the rapid acceptance of the Templars by awe-struck Church leaders. With this knowledge, the Templar leaders, either directly or by implication, must have greatly intimidated Church officials and resulted in growing wealth and power.

Claiming to be poor even though most of the Templars were members of or connected to royal families—their original seal depicted two knights sharing one horse—the Order's fortunes suddenly soared. Their leaders began traveling, recruiting members, and gaining acceptance from both the Church and European royalty.

A reproduction of part of the "Copper Scroll," one of the Dead Sea Scrolls found in Qumran.

On January 31, 1128, Templar Masters traveled to the Council of Troyes about 75 miles (120 kilometers) southeast of Paris. This council was composed of Catholic archbishops, bishops, and abbots, including St. Bernard, by then the head of the powerful Cistercian Order. With the added endorsement of King Baldwin, the council approved the Templars as an official military and religious order. This resulted in Pope Honorius II approving a "Rule" or constitution for the Knights Templar, which sanctioned contributions to the Order.

This "Rule" was prepared by St. Bernard and copied the structure of his Cistercian Order. To support the religious side of the Order, the "Rule," among other things, ordered all new Templars to make a vow of chastity and poverty, which included turning over all their property to the Order. On the military side, Templars were forbidden to retreat in combat unless their opponents outnumbered them more than three to one and their commander approved of a withdrawal.

The structure of the Order was a forerunner of Freemasonry. Each local branch was called a "Temple" and its ruling commander reported to and pledged obedience to the Grand Master. Within the ranks there were four classifications—knights, sergeants, chaplains, and servants. As in later Freemasonry, there was great emphasis on keeping secrets from both the public and their fellow Templars.

The power and prestige of the Order increased rapidly and at the zenith of its popularity counted a membership of about 20,000 knights. The distinctive white surcoat emblazoned with a red cross worn only by the Knights Templar was always seen in the thick of battle. By the mid-twelfth century, the Knights Templar had established itself as the single most wealthy and powerful institution in Christendom, except for the Vatican.

Contributions from royalty and the nobles were not just in coin or land. Members received lordships, baronies, landlord status, and castles. Grand Master Payens had many high-level connections. He was married to Catherine de St. Clair, a member of a prominent Scottish family who donated land south of Edinburgh where the first Templar study center or preceptory was built outside the Holy Land. St. Bernard, who had supported the Templars so well at Troyes, and his Cistercian Order also prospered. In 1139, Pope Innocent II, a protégé of St. Bernard, proclaimed that the Templars would answer to no other authority than the pope. This license to operate outside any local control meant an exemption from taxes, which considerably increased the wealth of the Order. The pope also granted the Templars the most unusual right to build their own churches. It was to advance such construction that the Templars originated the first stonemason guilds. Stonemasons became lay members of the Templar Order and received all their advantages, such as exemption from paying tax.

By the 1200s, the Templars owned about 9,000 castles and manors throughout Europe, yet as a religious order paid no taxes. Their investments included basic industries, particularly in the building trades. They owned more than 5,000 properties in England and Wales alone. Their empire stretched from Denmark to Palestine. They used the revenue from these holdings to build a huge fleet of ships and underwrite a vast banking system. The concept of using money to produce more money was coming into focus. Although conventional history traces the development of modern banking to early Jewish and Italian lending institutions, it was the Knights Templars who predated the famous Rothschilds and Medicis. Drawing on the ancient financial knowledge of the earlier Mystery Schools, the Templars learned to perform the same functions as a modern bank—wealth storage, loans, and even a system of credit. In the Middle Ages, Christians were prohibited from the practice of usury, charging interest on loans. It was considered sinful. The Templars avoided this restriction by emphasizing the military rather than the religious aspects of their Order. In one case, old documents revealed the Templars charged as much as 60 percent interest per year, a much higher rate than other money lenders of their time. Like Swiss banks today, the Templars held long-term private trust funds, accessible only by the originators of the account.

Although conventional history traces the development of modern banking to early Jewish and Italian lending institutions, it was the Knights Templars who predated the famous Rothschilds and Medicis.

It also appears as though they first introduced the credit card and packaged tours as they developed fund transfers by note, a Muslim technique most probably obtained from the Assassins and other contacts in the Middle East. Pilgrims to the Holy Land faced many hazards and obstacles. They were prey for ferrymen, toll collectors, innkeepers, and even Church authorities demanding alms, not to mention highway robbers and thieves. For protection against such misfortunes, the Templars developed a system whereby the traveler could deposit funds with the commander of the local temple and receive a specially coded receipt. This receipt was issued in the form of a letter of credit, redeemable from any temple. At the end of his journey, the traveler would receive either a cash refund of his account balance or a bill to cover any overdraft. It was a system that closely resembled both a bank check and the modern credit card. Often, the Templars even performed the duties of tax collectors. They collected papal taxes, tithes, and donations for the Church as well as taxes and revenues for the English king. They also mediated in disputes involving ransom payments, dowries, and pensions. At the peak of their power, the Templars handled most of the available capital in Western Europe.

Along with banking practices, the Templars brought to Europe their acquired knowledge of architecture, astronomy, mathematics, medicine, and medical techniques. In less than one hundred years after formation of the Order, the Knights Templar had evolved into the medieval equivalent of today's multinational corporation. Their control over industry and finance was tremendous and they had grown into a fearful military power, complete with their own naval fleet based in the French Atlantic port of La Rochelle. Their fleet's ensign was a black flag displaying a white skull and cross bones. Early sea battles pitted remnants of the Templar fleet against the Catholic countries of France and Spain. Only centuries later did buccaneers attack British ships and the age of piracy begin, the symbolic and spiritual origins of the black banner forgotten. There are even reports of Templars, led by Henry St. Clair of Rosslyn in Scotland, sailing to North America in 1396, almost a century before Columbus. This little-known Templar presence in the New World was convincingly detailed in the 2004 book *Templars in America* by Tim Wallace-Murphy and Marilyn Hopkins.

The Templars were not content to simply acquire existing castles and other structures. They were avid builders, constructing immense fortified estates, particularly in southern France and the Holy Land. Many were built on peninsulas or mountain tops making them practically impregnable. Granted the privilege to build their own churches, the Templars became the prime movers behind the construction of the great Gothic cathedrals of Europe.

The Convent of Christ Castle in Tomar, Portugal, was built by the Knights Templar in 1160 as one of their many fortifications in Europe.

The name "Gothic" is believed to have been derived from the Germanic tribes of Goths that overran the Roman Empire. However, Gardner and others argue that, at least when pertaining to architecture, the name may have come from the Greek *goetik*, meaning something magical. And the Goths certainly had nothing to do with the magical architecture of an amazing number of cathedrals constructed during the twelfth century—just after the Templars brought their secrets back to Europe.

The people of the time were astounded by the impossibly high vaulted ceilings and flying buttresses of the new cathedrals. Pointed arches and vaulting coupled with magnificent stained glass windows reflected new techniques inspired by Templar knowledge of sacred geometry and metallurgy techniques. One of those who perfected the Gothic stained glass was Omar Khayyam, again connecting the Templar builders to the Eastern knowledge of the Assassins. St. Bernard once defined God as "length, width, height and depth," a clear evocation of the Masonic geometrical knowledge of Pythagoras, Plato, and the ancient Mystery Schools.

Another clear connection between the Templars and their work within Solomon's Temple can be found in Rosslyn Chapel, a miniature cathedral in the small Scottish town of Roslin, south of Edinburgh. William Sinclair, a descendant of the prominent St. Clair family and connected by marriage to Grand Master Payens, founded the chapel in 1446, but it was finished in 1486 by his son, Oliver. It was intended to be the first part of a larger church but that was never completed.

Rosslyn Chapel reflects Egyptian, Celtic, Jewish, Templar, and Masonic symbolism. The only certain Christian imagery was in later Victorian alterations. The chapel's floor plan is an exact match of Solomon's Temple in Jerusalem, even including two important columns at the entrance. These columns are called Jachin and Boaz, names tied to the Ancient Mysteries that still carry mythical and mystical significance for both Jews and Freemasons. It is interesting to note that at the time the Templars built their first Gothic cathedrals, not one carried a depiction of the Crucifixion, a most strange anomaly for a Christian order but strong evidence that the Templars indeed denied the orthodoxy of the Church. The seeds of Templar heresy spread through the Cistercians of St. Bernard and were reflected in the symbolic architecture of the Gothic cathedrals. As the Templars thrived, the Church became ever more antagonistic, as the clergy began to realize the threat posed by their knowledge. The Templars, in their turn, grew antagonistic toward the Church, believing the true church, one of mysticism, reincarnation, and good works, had been taken over by dark forces. Templar leaders saw the Church, "the one true faith," as an irresistible attraction to corrupt officials, scalawags, and con men, as well as the pious, and that often instigated bloody massacres against its enemies, which eventually came to mean anyone who failed to acquiesce to its authority.

As the Templar's power and wealth grew, so did their pride and arrogance. In 1215, England's King John was residing part time in the London Temple when an alliance of noblemen—many of them Templars—forced him to sign the Magna Carta, or Great Charter, insuring a constitutional monarchy in that nation.

In the late 1200s, the Templars contributed to the creation of another military order—the formidable Teutonic Knights, those childhood heroes of Adolf Hitler. The Teutonic Knights had created a gigantic principality of their own called the *Ordenstaat*, which extended from Prussia through the Baltic to the Gulf of Finland. France's King Philip IV grew ever more envious of the Templar's wealth and fearful of their military strength. At one time, Philip sought refuge in the Paris Temple to escape a rebellious mob. He knew from personal experience the wealth of the Templars and was heavily in debt to them. Adding to his rage against the Templars was the fact that he had been turned down as a member of the Order.

> The Templars, in their turn, grew antagonistic toward the Church, believing the true church, one of mysticism, reincarnation, and good works, had been taken over by dark forces.

In 1305, Philip journeyed to Rome and convinced Pope Clement V that the Templars were actually plotting the destruction of the Roman church. The pope accepted Philip's word as the French king had been the power behind his own ascension to the papacy. According to Masonic author Albert Mackey, Philip had agreed to support Clement's bid for the papacy in return for a secret commitment to crush the Knights Templar.

Furthermore, since it was widely whispered that the Templars were attempting to restore the ancient Merovingian kings both in France and other states, Philip's charges fell on receptive ears. The Merovingians were said to trace their bloodline back to Jesus, which presented a grave challenge to Rome's authority and supported the idea that the Templars had gained secret knowledge regarding the biblical accounts of Christ.

With the blessing of the pope, King Philip returned to France and drew up a list of charges against the Templars, ranging from subversion to heresy. Philip issued secret orders to officers throughout the country, which were not to be opened until a predetermined time. This came at dawn on Friday, October 13, 1307, a date that from that time onward brought a sinister connotation to any Friday the thirteenth. Authorities spread out over France and quickly rounded up all the Templars at hand. Charged with a number of practices, including necromancy, homosexuality, abortion, blasphemy, and practice of the black arts, captured knights were imprisoned, interrogated, tortured, and burned. Paid witnesses gave evidence against the Order and quickly disappeared. It is apparent that many of the charges against this erstwhile Christian order were spurious and contrived. But there is also evidence that the inner circles of the Templars were sympathetic to, if not adherents of, the heresies dealing with Mary Magdalene, John the Baptist, and the crucifixion and resurrection of Jesus. Some researchers have even speculated that the Templar skull and crossbones flag may have pertained to the remains of Mary, John the Baptist, or both.

Despite the suddenness of the arrests and secrecy of Philip's orders, many Templars were forewarned. For example, Jacques de Molay, the Templars' last grand master, gathered many of the Order's books and extant rules and had them burned. Many Templars fled France leaving behind a great mystery regarding both the disappearance of the Templar fleet and the accumulated treasure from the Paris Temple. Most researchers believe the fleet left with the missing treasure for the sanctuary of Protestant Scotland, the location of Rosslyn Chapel. Robert

In the early fourteenth century, the Knights Templar were accused of various heresies, and many were tortured and burned to death.

the Bruce, king of the Scots, offered refuge from the persecution of the Order, which soon spread outside France. King Robert, himself a Templar by birth, was at war with England's King Edward II and had been excommunicated by the Roman Church for warring with Edward, France's King Philip's son-in-law. Cut off from both the Church and the neighboring English, Robert welcomed fleeing Templars.

Some Masonic writers even credit Robert's victory over the English at the Battle of Bannockburn to the late arrival of Templars on the field. This battle, which secured Scotland's independence from England, was fought on June 24, 1314, St. John's Day, one of the most significant days of the year for Templars, who venerated the saint.

By the time of the Battle of Bannockburn, the Templars supposedly no longer existed. In 1312, the Order had been officially dissolved by the pope at the insistence of King Philip and in 1314, the Order's last official grand master, Jacques de Molay, was burned at the stake in Paris. Despite his efforts, King Philip obviously failed to exterminate all the Templars. Those in Scotland, Portugal, and a few other locations escaped the persecution while many Templars simply doffed their very visible surcoats emblazoned with a large red Maltese cross and blended into other organizations descended from the Templars. They just joined other groups such as the Hospitallers, Knights of Malta,

Knights of St. John, Freemasonry, and the Rosicrucians. The lines of membership in these groups blurred as they became more intertwined with the Templars and each other.

In his 2006 book *Secret Societies: Their Mysteries Revealed*, award-winning author John Lawrence Reynolds explained, "Masonic records trace the Templar-Mason connection back to an oration delivered in 1737 in the Grand Lodge of France by a Mason named Chevalier Ramsey. Ramsey claimed Freemasonry dated from 'the close association of the order with the Knights of St. John in Jerusalem' during the Crusades, and that the 'old lodges of Scotland' preserved the genuine Masonry abandoned by the English. From this rather dubious historical connection spun the Scottish Rite...."

> **Composed of the best and brightest of men, the Jesuits began to resist the authority of the Roman Church and its power over governments....**

Another order created specifically to combat the Vatican's enemies and to protect the secrets of the church was the Jesuits. This order, officially known as the Society of Jesus, was formed in 1540 by Ignatius of Loyola, a soldier-turned-priest who swiftly turned the organization into an aggressive militant force against both heretics and Protestants alike. It was the structure of the Jesuits that Adam Weishaupt used as a template for his Illuminati.

But even the militant Jesuits proved susceptible to the lure of the secret knowledge of the Templars, having gotten too close to their heresies. Composed of the best and brightest of men, the Jesuits began to resist the authority of the Roman Church and its power over governments, resulting in a ban against the Order by Pope Clement XIV in 1773. But the imperative of protecting the church forced a reinstatement of the Jesuits, including all former rights and privileges, by Pope Pius VII in 1814. Perhaps due to the unreliability of the Jesuits, the persecution of enemies of the Church fell to the infamous Inquisition, which lasted until 1820. The late Laurence Gardner, an internationally known sovereign and chivalric genealogist, with insider access to the records of a number of European royal households, served as a prior of the Celtic Church and was presidential attaché to the European Council of Princes. "Meanwhile, those of the privileged class who possessed true esoteric skills and Hermetic knowledge were obliged to conduct their business in the secrecy of their lodges and underground clubs," noted Gardner, adding: "[T]he once revered knowledge of the Templars caused their persecution by the savage Dominicans of the 14th century Inquisition. It was at that point in the history of Christianity that the last vestige of free thinking disappeared."

Gardner asserted that the Templars indeed survived by going underground and fusing with other secret societies, specifically the Rosicrucians and the Freemasons. "These days, history books and encyclopedias are almost unanimous in declaring that the Knights Templar became extinct in the 1300s. They are quite wrong," declared Gardner. "The Chivalric Military Order of the Temple of Jerusalem [an updated title for the Knights Templars]—as distinct from the later contrived Masonic Templars—is still flourishing in continental Europe and Scotland."

Much of the inner lore of both the Freemasons and the Illuminati may have stemmed from the Knights Templars' close association with a fanatical Islamic sect during the crusades for the Holy Land.

Assassins

The sect known as the Assassins developed a dictatorial pyramid command structure copied by nearly all subsequent secret societies, including the Illuminati. These killers were so infamous that even today their very name is synonymous with terror and sudden death.

The name reportedly was derived from the cannabis drug hashish, which members smoked in preparation for killing. Sect killers, who were taught that murder was a religious duty, became known as *hashshasin* (Arabic for "hashish smoker"), which over time became simply "assassin." This is the popular origin of the name. However, some researchers suggest the name may have stemmed from the Arabic word *assasseen*, meaning "guardians of the secrets."

Assassin founder Hasan bin Sabah was a schoolmate of the Persian poet laureate Omar Khayyam and Nizam ul-Mulk, who later became the Grand Vizier to the Turkish sultan of Persia. Hasan had his own secrets to guard. He had gained esoteric knowledge from the former and royal privileges from the latter. After being caught in a money-pilfering scandal, Hasan was forced to flee Persia for Egypt, where he was further indoctrinated in ancient secrets, including intimate knowledge of the Hebrew Cabala.

While in Egypt Hasan may have laid his plans for the formation of his Assassin sect while studying the organization and practices of the *Dar ul Hikmat* (House of Knowledge) or Grand Lodge of Cairo created in 1004. This lodge was a repository for the ancient knowledge and wisdom brought forward from the days of Adam, Noah, Abraham, and Moses. Lodge members perfected the techniques used centuries later by Weishaupt to organize the Illuminati. It was here Hasan learned duplicitous tactics, as members claimed to be both Muslims and Christians at the same time, and recognition signs, some of which can still be found in Grand Orient Freemasonry. As in all secret societies, while most members were simply fervent worshippers, the top leadership had other agendas.

Hasan bin Sabah (or Hassan I Sabbah) was a missionary who founded the *hashshasin* (assassins), an offshoot of Ismailism. Lacking their own army, the *hashshasin* attacked their enemies one by one.

Hasan's killer cult came into existence about 1094 when he and some Persian allies took the mountain fortress of Alamut on the Caspian Sea in Iran. He created his own Shia Ismaili sect, which came to be known as the Assassins. Hasan, known as the "Old Man of the Mountain," forged a personality cult centered on himself and struck fear due to his sect's lethal violence.

The higher initiates were taught the Assassin secret doctrines, one of which was "Nothing is true and all is allowed," a phrase eerily reminiscent of the Law of Thelema, expressed as "Do what thou wilt shall be the whole of the Law." This law was passed through the Illuminati to Aleister Crowley's Ordo Templi Orientis (OTO), or Order of Oriental Templars.

The Assassins also believed there is only one God and everything in creation, including humankind, is part of a universal whole, a concept along the lines of Albert Einstein's Unified Field Theory, which continues to be seriously studied by modern scientists. Finally, the Assassin dogma that the end justifies the means may well have been a precursor of that same philosophy that passed into the Illuminati and then into "Illuminized" Freemasonry.

The power of the Assassins increased through the mid-twelfth century when the cult boasted a string of strongholds stretching throughout Persia and Iraq. Their influence may have even reached to the secret society of Thugs in India, who were known to use recognition signs similar to the Assassins.

As grand master, Hasan created a system of apprentices, fellows of the Craft and Masters, which has been compared with the later Masonic degrees. Masonic historian Mackey admitted the Assassins' "connection with the Templars, as historically proved, may have had some influence over that Order in molding, or at least in suggesting, some of its esoteric dogmas and ceremonies."

The system of grand masters, grand priors, religious devotees, and their degrees of initiation were mimicked later by the Templars, Freemasons, and Illuminati. In 1129, Jerusalem's King Baldwin II asked Payens and his Templars to aid in an ill-fated attack on the Muslim city of Damascas. This somewhat hasty and ill-conceived operation brought the Templars into contact with the notorious Assassins. By several accounts, it was here the Templars joined with the Assassins in joint operations during the Crusades, providing the opportunity for the Templars to learn their esoteric ancient knowledge. It must be noted that there were only slight differences between the average fighting man of both the Templars and the Assassins. Both groups were filled with brutish, ignorant, and bloodthirsty men who merely did what they were told. As with the future Illuminati, only their leaders knew the underlying truths of their order.

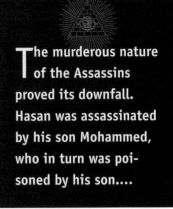

The murderous nature of the Assassins proved its downfall. Hasan was assassinated by his son Mohammed, who in turn was poisoned by his son....

The murderous nature of the Assassins proved its downfall. Hasan was assassinated by his son Mohammed, who in turn was poisoned by his son, who had learned of Mohammed's plan to also kill him. By 1250, invading Mongol hordes had captured the last Assassin stronghold, effectively eliminating the order. According to some researchers, however, pockets of Assassins may still exist in the Middle East today.

Rosicrucians

The Rosicrucians are another of the secret brotherhoods that many consider the progenitors of Freemasonry and the Illuminati. This group also reportedly has knowledge and secret traditions reaching back into antiquity. The Order of the Rosy Cross was founded in 1188 by a pre-Masonic Templar named Jean de Gisors, a vassal of English King Henry II. Some recent writers, however, believe that Rosicrucianism and Freemasonry were separate philosophies that only merged in the late eighteenth century along with Illuminati influence. Whatever the truth, the fact remains, as acknowledged by Masonic historian Mackey, that "a Rosicrucian element was very largely diffused in the *Hautes Grades* or High Degrees [of Freemasonry coming from] the continent of Europe about the middle of the 18th century."

Although the Rosicrucians claim to trace a lineage back to ancient Egypt and beyond, the name only became public between 1614 and 1615 with the publication of two tracts. One, entitled *Fama Fraternitatis Rosae Crusis*, or *Report of the Rosicrucian Brotherhood*, was supposed to have been written by Christian Rosenkreutz (translated literally as Rosy Cross) and detailed his journeys through the Holy Land and the Mediterranean area as he gained esoteric Eastern knowledge. After studying with the illuminated Alumbrados of Spain, Rosenkreutz returned to Germany where he formed the Order of the Rosy Cross.

The name has variously been interpreted as a play on the name Rosenkreutz; derived from the Latin *ros*, or dew, and *crux*, or cross; a chemical symbol for "light"—hence, knowledge; a reference to the blood-covered cross of Jesus; or the red cross on the shields of the Knights Templar. Count Mirabeau, the Freemason French Revolution leader, claimed the Rosicrucians were, in fact, nothing more than the outlawed Knights Templar under another name.

The fictional tracts, known as the "Rosicrucian Manifestos," disclosed the existence of this secret brotherhood and promised a coming age of enlightenment along with the revelation of ancient secrets. They most probably were written by Johann Valentin Andreae, a German Lutheran cleric who traveled extensively through Europe before becoming spiritual counselor to the Illuminist Duke of Brunswick, chairman of the Freemason Convention of Wilhelmsbad, and the Freemason leader connected to William of Hesse and the Rothschilds.

Title page of the *Fama Fraternitatis Rosae Crusis*, published in 1614, which was key to establishing the secret society of Rosicrucians.

A third Rosicrucian publication, the fantasy *Chemische Hochzeit* ("The Chemical Wedding"), by Christian Rosenkreutz, was so filled with symbolic references to the outlawed Knights Templar that the Catholic Church condemned it along with the Rosicrucian Manifestos. One early German Rosicrucian society called the Order of the Gold and Rosy Cross became the basis of the Freemason Strict Observance Lodge, which many years later was taken over by the Illuminati.

Rosicrucians were seen by the Church as Satanists and accused of making compacts with the devil and sacrificing children. Others saw them as the progenitors of today's scientific inquiry as well as protectors of ancient secrets. It seems apparent that the Rosicrucians—like the Cathars and Templars before them—had access to an ancient knowledge that held more substance than anything promulgated by Rome.

But the rise of the Protestant orders did little to decrease the violence aimed at anyone diverting from Catholicism. Ironically, Rosicrucian scientists, astronomers, mathematicians, navigators, and architects also became religious victims. Like the Roman

Church, Anglican clerics called them pagans and heretics. The rational humanist Rosicrucians were forced underground by the church and Rosicrucian leaders such as Christopher Wren and Elias Ashmole established Rosicrucian-based Speculative Masonry at the formation of the Grand Mother Lodge of Freemasonry in 1717. Nineteenth-century Masonic author J. M. Ragon noted that the Rosicrucians and Freemasons merged during this time, even meeting in the same room at Masons' Hall in London.

By 1750, the previous distinctions between Freemasons, Rosicrucians, and other organizations that claimed Templar origins had blurred to the point that they all appeared virtually the same. Rosicrucian theology today indeed indicates knowledge that can be traced through Plato and Pythagoras to the Egyptian Mystery School of Pharaoh Tuthmosis III, some 1,500 years before Christ. Nesta Webster wrote, "Rosicrucianism was a combination of the ancient secret tradition handed down from the patriarchs through the philosophers of Greece and of the first Cabala of the Jews."

Two competing orders of Rosicrucians are still active in the United States today. Both claim to hold secrets handed down from ancient Egypt and both are the object of scorn and derision by religious fundamentalists.

> **B**y 1750, the previous distinctions between Freemasons, Rosicrucians, and other organizations that claimed Templar origins had blurred to the point that they all appeared virtually the same.

Recent Societies

Today there is a multitude of secret societies in the world, some well-known and some not so. A few of the better-known ones include:

- The Ancient Order of Hibernians, organized in 1890 to protect Catholics from anti-Catholic forces and to assist Irish Catholic immigrants.
- The Knights of Columbus, the largest network of Catholic men and their families in the world, was founded in 1882 and primarily modeled after Freemasonry.
- The Prelature of the Holy Cross and Opus Dei, known simply as Opus Dei, is a Catholic society formed in 1928 by Saint Josemaría Escrivá de Balaguer in Spain and now operating in eighty nations. The society asserts its aim is to "contribute to that evangelizing mission of the Church, by promoting among Christians of all social classes a life

fully consistent with their faith" during their daily lives. The Opus Dei Awareness Network (ODAN) claims the society is "the most controversial group in the Catholic Church today" having become the "personal prelature" of Pope John Paul II, who in 1982 freed it from local control by priests and church officials. "As a religious order free from the control of local bishops, Opus Dei has become a target for the same pressures that once focused on the Knights Templar and Jesuits, two older orders that once possessed the same independence," explained author John Michael Greer.

- The National Grange, formed in 1867 as a secret society of both men and women based largely on Freemasonry to promote rural life, particularly in the war-ravaged South.

- The Ancient Order of Druids (AOD), a fraternal organization founded in London in 1781 to perpetuate the beliefs of the druids, ancient shaman priests of the Iron Age Celts.

- The Mystic Order of Veiled Prophets of the Enchanted Realm (M.O.V.P.E.R), sometimes referred to as The Grotto, a fraternal organization within Freemasonry to solicit funds to aid cerebral palsy research.

- The Hermetic Order of the Golden Dawn, also known as the Golden Dawn, was founded in 1887 by three Freemasons steeped in Rosicrucian lore. The order, dedicated to the study of metaphysics, paranormal, and occult "Magick," was active in the United Kingdom during both the nineteenth and twentieth centuries and has been a great influence on Western occultism.

- The Knights of Pythias was founded in 1864 in Washington, D.C., by Justus H. Rathbone, who had been inspired by a play by the Irish poet John Banim concerning the legend of Damon and Pythias. It was the first fraternal organization to receive a charter under an act of the United States Congress.

- The Loyal Order of Moose was founded in 1888 and is dedicated to providing health benefits to its members who today are active in a thriving network of Moose Lodges throughout the United States.

- The Ku Klux Klan (KKK), or the Klan, is the name of separate past and present right-wing organizations in the United States which have advocated extremist views on white supremacy, white nationalism, and anti-immigration. It was most active in the early twentieth century.

- The Knights of the Golden Eagle, a fraternal society founded in Baltimore in 1873, was active in twenty states until its decline between 1943 and 1944, during World War II.

Another more recent order with a heritage reaching back to the medieval Teutonic Knights is the Thule-Gesellschaft, or Thule Society, named after a legendary northern country from Greek mythology. The Teutonic Knights were a twelfth-century offshoot of the Knights Templar that used the swastika as their emblem. The Thule Society was formed in 1918 in Munich to seek a return of power to Germany following its defeat in World War I and the failure of the Treaty of Versailles. Many prominent members of the Thule Society became leaders in an off-shoot political party, the National Socialist German Workers Party (Nazis). It is also believed that the Illuminati theology, spreading among the Freemasons, laid the groundwork for other more mystical societies such as the Ordo Templi Orientis (OTO), or the Order of the Temple of the East. The OTO was founded at the beginning of the twentieth century as an international fraternal and religious organization dedicated to having the Law of Thelma ("Do what thou

The symbol of the Thule Society employed a swastika, which would, of course, be used in the German Workers Party, or Nazis.

wilt shall be the whole of the Law") as its guiding principle. Like Freemasonry and the Illuminati, the OTO prescribes an initiatory system followed by a series of secret ritual dramas to introduce esoteric teachings.

Many modern secret societies, such as the ones listed here, have drawn their rituals and beliefs from earlier orders. One is the International Order of St. Hubertus, which came to public attention in February 2016 when Supreme Court justice Antonin Scalia was found dead at the hunting ranch of one of the order's members in Texas.

The order, rooted in Catholicism and whose insignia is the Maltese Cross of the Knights Templar, is named after Hubert, the patron saint of hunters and fishermen. The group's grand master is Istvan von Habsburg-Lothringen, archduke of Austria, and includes prominent persons in both Europe and America. The "grand master" title and the structure of the order, along with its European royalty members, link the order to Illuminized Freemasonry. In 1726, the founder of St. Hubertus, Count Franz Anton von Sporck, established a Freemason lodge in Prague. The U.S. chapter of this order was formed in 1966 at a meeting of the Bohemian Club in San Francisco, which is connected to the very secretive and exclusive Bohemian Grove group that meets every July and has included very high-ranking American corporate and political leaders such as U.S. presidents Ronald Reagan, George H. W. Bush, and Richard Nixon. It might be noted that the symbol of Bohemian Grove is the owl, just like the original Illuminati.

Another modern-day secret society credited with great power is known as the Bilderberg Club, or Group or Conference or Meetings. Though there are no documented links to earlier societies, this society is composed of some of the most influential men and women in the world, including prime ministers, presidents, and international bankers They meet once a year under heavy security and secrecy. It is so secretive it does not have an official title. The group was first discovered meeting in 1954 at the Bilderberg Hotel in Holland from which it took the name. Adding to its secrecy and exclusivity, only its steering committee decides who can be a member. It is believed that the Bilderbergers provide a meeting place for world leaders to air plans and grievances and to synchronize their activities.

In its 1987 Christmas edition, *The Economist* described Bilderberg as "the most powerful private club in the world. Its power has certainly not diminished as the decades have rolled by and neither has its secrecy. Although it began with trade unionists and powerful people it wanted to persuade, ... [today] Bilderberg has boiled down to a rotten core of bankers, royalty, arms industry, oil and media barons and Rory Stuart [British] MP, in the tradition of Kissinger, Blair, Cameron, Osborne and Balls, has thrown his lot in with them."

Edward Mandell House was a top political advisor to President Wilson during World War I. He predicted the creation of a central bank and graduated income tax.

Bilderberg is comprised of many of the inner core leaders of other modern societies—the Council on Foreign Relations and its sister organization in Britain, the Royal Institute of International Affairs, and a more recent group, the Trilateral Commission. The Council on Foreign Relations, which according to some has directed U.S. foreign policy since before World War II, was formed following the failure to establish a one-world government during the Paris Peace Conference of 1919. Attending the Paris peace conference were President Woodrow Wilson and his closest advisers, Colonel Edward Mandell House (the title was honorary as House never served in the military), bankers Paul Warburg and Barnard Baruch, and almost two dozen others. Conference attendees embraced Wilson's plan for peace, which included the formation of a League of Nations. However, under American law, the covenant had to be ratified by the U.S. Senate, which failed to do so.

It was House, a self-described Marxist socialist, who in 1921 authored a book entitled *Philip Drew: Administrator* in which he described a "conspiracy" within the United States to establish a central bank and a graduated income tax and a plan to control both political parties. Two years after the publication of his book, two, if not all three, of his stated goals had been met in reality.

Undeterred by the Senate's vote, Colonel House, along with both British and American peace conference delegates, met in Paris's Majestic Hotel on May 30, 1919, and resolved to form an "Institute of International Affairs," with one branch in the United States and one in England. The English branch became the Royal Institute of International Affairs with a sister organization in America. The stated purpose of these organizations was to guide public opinion toward acceptance of a one-world government or globalism.

The U.S. branch was incorporated on July 21, 1921, as the Council on Foreign Relations (CFR). It was built upon an existing, but lackluster, New York dinner club of the same name, which had been created in 1918 by prominent bankers and lawyers for discussions on trade and international finance. Article II of the new CFR's by-laws stated that all meetings were secret and anyone revealing details of CFR discussions in contravention of CFR rules and regulations would be dropped from membership. Initial funding for the CFR came from bankers and financiers such as J. P. Morgan, John D. Rockefeller, Bernard Baruch, Jacob Schiff, Otto Kahn, and Paul Warburg. Today, funding for the CFR comes from major corporations such as Xerox, General Motors, Bristol-Meyers Squibb, Texaco, and others as well as the German Marshall Fund, McKnight Foundation, Dillon Fund, Ford Foundation, Andrew W. Mellon Foundation, Rockefeller Brothers Fund, Starr Foundation, and the Pew Charitable Trusts. The CFR is at the center of corporate America.

Many CFR members belong to upper-crust social register groups such as the Century Association, the Links Club, the University Club, and Washington's Metropolitan Club. In an effort to avoid the designation as a corporate-run "Old Boys" club, in recent years the CFR has extended its membership to include a few blacks and more than a dozen women. To broaden its influence beyond the eastern seaboard, the CFR created Committees on Foreign Relations composed of local leaders in cities across the nation. More than thirty-seven such committees comprising about 4,000 members existed by the early 1980s.

Admission to the CFR is a very discriminating and painful process. Candidates must be proposed by a member, seconded by another member, approved by a membership committee, screened by the professional staff, and finally approved by the board of directors.

Critics, noting that the CFR has had its hand in every major twentieth-century conflict, view the CFR as a group set on world domination through multinational business, international treaties, and world government. Former

U.S. Navy judge advocate general Admiral Chester Ward, a longtime CFR member, once stated, "CFR, as such, does not write the platforms of both political parties or select their respective presidential candidates, or control U.S. defense and foreign policies. But CFR members, as individuals, acting in concert with other individual CFR members, do."

"Once the ruling members of the CFR have decided that the U.S. Government should adopt a particular policy, the very substantial research facilities of CFR are put to work to develop arguments, intellectual and emotional, to support the new policy, and to confound and discredit, intellectually and politically, any opposition," Ward explained.

Critics, noting that the CFR has had its hand in every major twentieth-century conflict, view the CFR as a group set on world domination....

The CFR wields power far outside itself. According to the Capital Research Center's *Guide to Nonprofit Advocacy and Policy Groups*, CFR board members are associated with such influential organizations as the Committee for Economic Development, the Peterson Institute for International Economics, the Committee for a Responsible Federal Budget, the Business Enterprise Trust, the Urban Institute, the Business Roundtable, the U.S. Council on Competitiveness, the U.S. Chamber of Commerce, the now defunct National Alliance of Business, the Brookings Institution, the Business-Higher Education Forum, the Washington Institute for Near East Policy, the Ethics and Public Policy Center, the Hoover Institution, the Center for Strategic and International Studies, the Wilderness Society, and the American Council for Capital Formation.

The public presence of the CFR is its publication *Foreign Affairs*, termed "informally, the voice of the U.S. foreign-policy establishment." Even the establishment-orientated *Encyclopedia Britannica* admitted, "Ideas put forward tentatively in this journal often, if well received by the *Foreign Affairs* community, appear later as U.S. government policy or legislation; prospective policies that fail this test usually disappear."

Since before World War II, CFR members have been a core of U.S. foreign policy. Pulitzer Prize-winning journalist J. Anthony Lukas once noted, "From 1945 well into the sixties, Council members were in the forefront of America's globalist activism." The council once even suggested revamping the U.S. State Department. In February 2001, seven months before the attacks of 9/11, the CFR released a report calling for reforms within the State Department, which it accused of being "in a profound state of disrepair, suffering from long-term mismanagement, antiquated equipment, and dilapidated and insecure facilities."

Rockefeller family biographer Alvin Moscow has written, "So august has been the membership of the Council that it has been seen in some quarters as the heart of the eastern Establishment. When it comes to foreign affairs, it *is* [emphasis in the original] the eastern Establishment. In fact, it is difficult to point to a single major policy in U.S. foreign affairs that has been established since [Woodrow] Wilson which was diametrically opposed to then current thinking in the Council on Foreign Relations."

However, journalist Lukas rejected the "simple-minded" notion of direct dictatorial control from within the CFR by noting, "one must also recognize that influence flows as well through more intricate channels: the personal ties forged among men whose paths have crossed time and again in locker rooms, officers' messes, faculty clubs, embassy conference rooms, garden parties, squash courts and board rooms. If the Council has influence—and the evidence suggests that it does—then it is the influence its members bring to bear through such channels."

Several researchers have accused the CIA of serving as a security force not only for corporate America but also for friends, relatives, and fraternity brothers of CFR members. Chase Bank officer and former CFR chairman John J. McCloy, who served as foreign policy adviser to six U.S. presidents, once commented, "Whenever we needed a new man [for a government position], we just thumbed through the roll of council members and put through a call to New York."

Because critics have viewed the CFR as an instrument of control by the "liberal Eastern Establishment," it was expedient to expand its activities. This

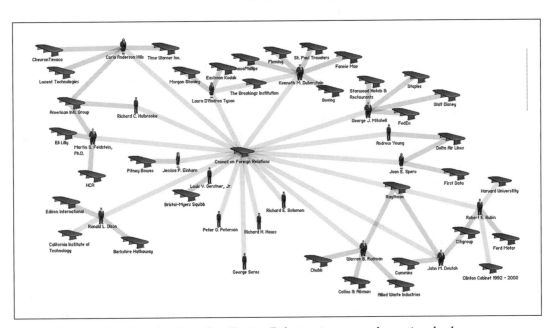

A 2004 diagram shows how the Council on Foreign Relations is connected to various banks and other large corporations.

was accomplished in July 1973 when the Trilateral Commission was founded by CFR luminaries David Rockefeller and former U.S. national security advisor Zbigniew Brzezinski.

Initially the stated purpose of the Trilateral Commission was to create a "New International Economic Order." However, in recent materials, this has been changed to merely fostering a "closer cooperation among these core democratic industrialized areas of the world with shared leadership responsibilities in the wider international system."

In 1970, Brzezinski wrote in the CFR publication *Foreign Affairs*, "A new and broader approach is needed—creation of a community of the developed nations which can effectively address itself to the larger concerns confronting mankind.... A council representing the United States, Western Europe and Japan, with regular meetings of the heads of governments as well as some small standing machinery, would be a good start." Later that year, in his book *Between Two Ages: America's Role in the Technetronic Era*, Brzezinski declared, "national sovereignty is no longer a viable concept," and prophetically foresaw a society "... that is shaped culturally, psychologically, socially and economically by the impact of technology and electronics—particularly in the area of computers and communication."

Plans for a commission of trilateral nations were first presented by Brzezinski during a meeting of the ultra-secret Bilderberg group in April 1972 in the small town of Knokke, Belgium. With the blessing of the Bilderbergers and the CFR, the Trilateral Commission began organizing on July 23–24, 1972, at the 3,500-acre Rockefeller estate at Pocantico Hills, a subdivision of Tarrytown, New York.

Commission members publish publicly available "Task Force Reports," or "Triangle Papers," as well as a newsletter, *Trialogue*. "Many of the original members of the Trilateral Commission are now in positions of power where they are able to implement policy recommendations of the Commission; recommendations that they, themselves, prepared on behalf of the Commission," noted journalist and Trilateral Commission researcher Robert Eringer. "It is for this reason that the Commission has acquired a reputation for being the Shadow Government of the West."

Noting the similarities of Trilateral and Illuminati agendas, the late senator and presidential candidate Barry Goldwater wrote, "What the Trilaterals truly intend is the creation of a worldwide economic power superior to the political government of the nation-states involved. As managers and creators of the system they will rule the world."

Commission spokespersons like to point out that the group does not receive any government funding. Early funding in the 1970s came from tax-exempt foundations such as the Rockefeller Brothers Fund, which in 1977 alone put up $120,000. Donations also came from the Ford Foundation, the

Lilly Endowment, the German Marshall Fund, and corporations such as Time, Bechtel, Exxon, General Motors, Wells Fargo, and Texas Instruments.

Although not given to hidden symbols and occult practices, both the CFR and the Trilateral Commission qualify as secret societies because no member of the public can apply to join. New members are carefully screened for their globalist views and must be approved by a membership committee. Additionally, no one is allowed to make public what transpires in their meetings. It is easy to see why so many people believe that U.S. government policy has been directed from these Rockefeller-dominated and secretive organizations. One such person is Texe Marrs [no relation to this author], a former U.S. Air Force officer and University of Texas faculty member who operates two Christian ministries from Austin, Texas. "Among the evil culprits I fingered over the years were such anti-American globalist groups as the Council on Foreign Relations, The Trilateral Commission, the Freemasons and the Bilderbergs. All play important roles in the on-going conspiracy. But behind them all is the satanic influence and power of Zionists. Zionists, in fact, are the real, but, so often, unheralded authors of the globalist plot," he stated. Marrs, along with many others, believes that the one-world objectives of the illuminized Freemasons, having failed to achieve success through political organizations such as the League of Nations and the United Nations, are today working through controversial corporate international trade agreements, such as the North American Free Trade Agreement (NAFTA), the Security and Prosperity Partnership (SPP), and the proposed Trans-Pacific Partnership (TPP, which was rejected by the Trump administration).

> Marrs ... believes that the one-world objectives of the illuminized Freemasons, having failed to achieve success through political organizations ..., are today working through controversial corporate international trade agreements....

"Now, finally, this traitorous clique of elitists has stepped out of the shadows into the light. No longer need they fear public disapproval. So effective has been their psychological brainwashing campaign and their dumbing down of the citizenry, the arrogant plotters believe they can finally come out and defiantly show themselves. Evidently, they think that no one is able to stop or even delay their bold plot to murder—yes, murder—America," Marrs warned.

In addition to its newsletter *Trialogue*, the Trilateral Commission regularly issues a number of publicly available "Task Force Reports," or "Triangle Papers." For some time, conspiracy newsletters and blogs of both the right and left have used these to reveal Trilateral "secrets." Since such secrets are largely gained directly from the commission publications, it seems apparent that these publications don't contain any true inner secrets.

One worrisome paper issued in 1975 by the CFR is entitled *The Crisis of Democracy*. One of its authors, Harvard political scientist Samuel P. Huntington, asserted that America needed "a greater degree of moderation in democracy." He argued that democratic institutions were incapable of responding to escalating crises and that leaders with "expertise, seniority, experiences and special talents" were needed to "override the claims of democracy."

Huntington should know about how those espousing Trilateralist policies often end up implementing those same policies in the government, as just three years after his paper was published, he was named coordinator of security planning for President Jimmy Carter's National Security Council. In this capacity, Huntington in 1979 prepared Presidential Review Memorandum 32, which led to the 1979 Presidential Order creating the Federal Emergency Management Agency (FEMA), a civilian organization with the power to take totalitarian control of government functions in the event of a national "emergency."

Another Trilateralist, the late Nature Conservancy CEO John Sawhill, authored an early commission report entitled *Energy: Managing the Transition*, which made recommendations on how to manage a movement to higher costing energy. Sawhill was appointed deputy secretary of the Department of Energy. Trilateralist C. Fred Bergsten participated in the preparation of a commission report called *The Reform of International Institutions*, then went on to become assistant secretary of the Treasury for International Affairs.

Eyebrows were raised when President Jimmy Carter, reportedly on instructions from David Rockefeller, appointed banker Paul Volcker to head America's powerful central bank—the Federal Reserve. Volcker had been a founding member of the Trilateral Commission and chairman emeritus of the secretive Council on Foreign Relations, as well as a long-time member of the Bilderbergers. He was replaced as the leader of the Federal Reserve during the Reagan administration by Alan Greenspan, also a member of the Trilateral Commission, the CFR, and the Bilderbergers. In 2006, President George W. Bush replaced Greenspan with Ben Bernanke, a Bilderberg attendee, and in 2014, Janet Yellen, Greenspan's protégá and a CFR member, took his place. With many such connections between the corporate world and government service, it is no wonder that the Trilateral Commission has been called the Shadow Government of the West. Many researchers see this organization as a modern embodiment of the central command and control sought by the Bavarian Illuminati.

It would appear that the Trilateral Commission may be following in the steps of Weishaupt and his original Illuminati. Barry Goldwater observed, "What the Trilaterals truly intend is the creation of a worldwide economic power superior to the political government of the nation-states involved. As managers and creators of the system they will rule the world."

The indisputable connections between America's leadership and the Trilateral Commission, as well as the CFR, coupled with the fact that globalist banker David Rockefeller has been a leading luminary in both groups, has

Former Federal Reserve chairmen Paul Volcker (left) and Alan Greenspan both had connections to the Council on Foreign Relations and the Bilderbergers.

prompted concern among conspiracy writers on both the left and right. It is easy to see why so many people believe that U.S. government policy has been directed from these Rockefeller-dominated organizations.

Don't think that all this belongs in some distant past. Within his first ten days in office, President Barack Obama had appointed eleven Trilateral Commission members to key positions in his administration. David Rockefeller was Obama's principal foreign policy advisor. Since the official commission membership list names only eighty-seven members from the United States, this means Obama appointed more than 12 percent of the commission's U.S. membership to top-level government positions. In fact, since the Carter administration but prior to Obama's second term, all U.S. presidents and vice presidents—except for Obama and Joe Biden—along with six of the last eight World Bank presidents and more than half of all U.S. secretaries of state and three-quarters of the secretaries of defense have been Trilateralists.

This situation was called "undue influence," as these commission members within the Obama administration controlled some of the nation's most important needs: financial and economic crisis, national security, and foreign policy.

According to an CFR article published in 2017, members were not happy with the prospect of a Donald Trump presidency. "The Trump administration seems determined to muddle through its foreign policy without initial guiding principles, benchmarks for progress, or the means of adjudicating between competing objectives, and with a wildly improvisational leadership style that has no precedent in recent history. Such an approach is dangerously nearsighted and presents an exceptionally high risk of failure—not only in achieving his few stated foreign-policy goals, from the defeat of the Islamic State to the containment of China, but also in assuring basic peace and prosperity for the American people," wrote Micah Zenko, and Rebecca Friedman Lissner.

The global banks and corporations now dominate the nation states, including the United States, with no regard for due process, Congress, or the will of the people. Adam Weishaupt would no doubt approve.

Freemasonry

Since the philosophies of the Illuminati became so intertwined with Freemasonry, it is incumbent to make a close study of that order. Most conspiracy theories today eventually circle back to the Freemasons, one of the largest and most familiar of the secret societies. Freemasonry is a fraternal organization established between the sixteenth and seventeenth centuries as an outgrowth of the outlawed Knights Templar Order. Other secretive groups whose memberships were mixed with those of the Templars included the Hospitallers, the Knights of Christ, the Knights of Saint John, the Teutonic Knights, and the powerful Knights of Malta, which still exists today

With more than six million members worldwide, primarily in Europe, the United Kingdom, and America, and openly engaged in charitable works, the Brotherhood traces its ancestry back to the Mystery Schools of Greece and Egypt and provides the connective tissue between ancient and modern secret societies. It was a formidable organization even before certain lodges, originally called "Mysteries," became "illuminized" in the late eighteenth century. Poking fun at the ubiquitous presence of the Masons, American journalist and author Ambrose Bierce in his book *The Devil's Dictionary* described Freemasonry as "An order with secret rites, grotesque ceremonies and fantastic costumes, which, originating in the reign of Charles II, among working artisans of London, has been joined successively by the dead of past centuries in unbroken retrogression until now it embraces all the generations of man on the hither side of Adam and is drumming up distinguished recruits among the pre-Creational inhabitants of Chaos and Formless Void. The order was founded at different times by Charlemagne, Julius Caesar, Cyrus, Solomon, Zoroaster, Confucius, Thothmes, and Buddha. Its emblems and symbols have been found in the Catacombs of Paris and Rome, on the stones of the Parthenon and the

Chinese Great Wall, among the temples of Karnak and Palmyra and in the Egyptian Pyramids—always by a Freemason."

It is clear that secret societies—both then and now—were concerned not only with political and commercial issues but also with matters pertaining to royal bloodlines, ancient religions, and spiritualism. Hidden knowledge involved secrets from the distant past that provided a basis for secret society theologies. These secrets continue to attract the attention of corporate leaders, high-level society members, European royalty, and even intelligence agencies. Much more will be said later about the merger of Freemasonry and the notorious Illuminati, the secret order that has garnered more myths, misinformation, and scrutiny by conspiracy theorists and the media than any other, with the possible exception of Freemasonry itself.

> **M**ost conspiracy theories today eventually circle back to the Freemasons, one of the largest and most familiar of the secret societies.

The most famous of the Masonic symbols—the letter "G" inside a square and compass—stands for geometry, according to Masonic historian Albert Mackey, who added that Masons have been taught that masonry and geometry are synonymous terms. The geometrical symbols found in modern Freemasonry pertain to the geometrical secrets of the Medieval Masons, now admitted to be lost. Occult geometry, sometimes called "sacred geometry," long has utilized geometrical symbols, such as the circle, the triangle, and the pentagram, as symbols for metaphysical and philosophical concepts. Others have claimed the "G" stands for the Greek word *Gnosis*, meaning knowledge or mystical enlightenment. Authors Christopher Knight and Robert Lomas had an interesting take on the well-known Masonic symbol of the square and compass. They claimed it originated as a stylized form of the ancient symbol for a king's power—a pyramid with its base at the bottom representing earthly power—superimposed with a reversed pyramid representing the heavenly power of the priest. Together, these pyramids of power create the symbol that has come to be known as the Star of David. "It first came into popular use on a large number of Christian churches in the Middle Ages," they wrote, "and the earliest examples were, we were amazed to find, on buildings erected by the Knights Templar. Its use in synagogues came very much later."

Critics of Freemasonry have claimed the prominent "G" stands for Gnosticism, a philosophy of Gnostic sects such as the previously mentioned Spanish Alumbrados, outlawed by the early Church.

One Masonic tradition claimed that Abraham, the patriarch of the Hebrews, taught the Egyptians special knowledge of building construction predating the Great Flood. Later, this knowledge—reported as the work of the legendary Hermes Trismegistus—was collected by Greek philosopher Euclid, who studied the work under the name geometry. The Greeks, and later the Romans, called this discipline architecture.

The symbol of the Freemasons.

While authorities disagree as to the actual origin of Freemasonry, all acknowledge that it predates Ancient Egypt. Masonic lore traces the origins back to the construction of the biblical Tower of Babel and King Solomon's Temple at Jerusalem. The Masons, the direct descendants of the earlier Egyptian and Greek guilds of masons, utilized esoteric construction techniques that had been passed down through the sects and Mystery Schools, some of which continue to confound modern builders.

During the late Middle Ages, opposition to the Holy Roman Universal (Catholic) Church was forced deep underground. Among the only organized groups able to move freely throughout Europe were the guilds of stonemasons, who maintained meeting halls or "lodges" in every major city and were the major force behind the construction of Europe's churches and cathedrals. Masons proved an ideal vehicle for the flow of information and the covert distribution of anti-clerical teachings.

Most writers trace Masonic secrets through the Knights Templar, those warrior priests of the Crusades. One eighteenth-century writer claimed modern Freemasonry was founded by Godfrey de Bouillon, leader of the First Crusade that captured Jerusalem.

The secrets of the origins of Freemasonry have been tightly held despite the publication of numerous books and literature on the subject. Walter Wilmshurst, a ranking Mason and author of *The Meaning of Masonry*, wrote that "the true, inner history of Masonry has never yet been given forth even to the Craft itself." Many researchers believe that even most Masons themselves have lost sight of Masonry's true origin and purpose.

Much of the confusion over Freemasonry's origins and growth dates from the rift between the Roman Catholic Church and the Protestant Church of England when many Masonic records were lost. Wars and revolutions took their toll on Masonic libraries in all nations. King Henry VIII, in breaking with Rome, not only discontinued the church's building programs in England causing widespread unemployment, but looted the assets of the Masons under the guise of taxes and tribute. To survive, the lodges began opening their memberships to non-Masons. These outsider merchants, landowners, and others—many with Templar backgrounds—became known as "Speculative" Masons. They embraced a mystical and esoteric doctrine based on traditions predating Freemasonry and brought to the Order by Knights Templar members fleeing persecution by the Church. By the time four London lodges formed a United Grand Lodge in 1717, Speculative Freemasonry completely dominated the original guild stonemasons or "Operative" Masons. It is primarily from Speculative Masonry that the Order derived its esoteric knowledge. Explained Nesta Webster:

> Speculative Masonry may have derived from the [biblical] patri-archs and the mysteries of the pagans. But the source of inspira-tion which admits of no denial is the Jewish Cabala.... The fact remains that when the ritual and constitutions of Masonry were drawn up in 1717, although certain fragments of the ancient Egyptian and Pythagorean doctrines were retained, the Judaic version of the secret tradition was the one selected by the founders of the Grand Lodge on which to build up their system.

German Mason Karl Gotthelf, Baron von Hund und Altengrotkau, a member of the Frankfurt Lodge, admitted carrying on the traditions of Knights Templar forced into exile in Scotland in the early 1300s. Other Order mem-bers openly proclaimed themselves "Knights of the Temple." In 1751, Hund formed an extension of the Scottish Rite called the Order of the Strict Obser-vance after its oath of unquestioning obedience to mysteri-ous and unseen "superiors." He claimed to be carrying out the orders of these unknown superiors, who were never identified or located. This Order ended with the fusion of the Illuminati and German Freemasonry during the Con-gress of Wilhelmsbad in 1782, as will be detailed later.

The vast majority of American Freemasons look upon their brotherhood as little different from that of the Lion's Club, the Optimists, or the Chamber of Commerce. And from their standpoint, this is true. Masonic literature makes clear that only those initiates who progress beyond thirty-three-degree status are educated in the group's true goals and secrets.

Masonic author and Past Provincial Grand Registrar Walter Wilmshurst explained, "There has always existed an external, elementary, popular doctrine which has served for the instruction of the masses who are insufficiently prepared for deeper teach-ing. There has been an interior, advanced doctrine, a more secret knowledge, which has been reserved for riper minds and into which only proficient and properly prepared candidates, who voluntarily sought to participate in it, were initiated." The Thirty-third Degree Mason Manly P. Hall gave more details:

> **B**y the time four London lodges formed a United Grand Lodge in 1717, Specu-lative Freemasonry completely dominated the original guild stonemasons or "Operative" Masons.

> Freemasonry is a fraternity within a fraternity—an outer organi-zation concealing an inner brotherhood of the elect ... the one visible and the other invisible. The visible society is a splendid

camaraderie of 'free and accepted' men enjoined to devote them-selves to ethical, educational, fraternal, patriotic and humanitar-ian concerns. The invisible society is a secret and most august fraternity whose members are dedicated to the service of a ... *arcanum arcandrum* [a sacred secret].

Mason Albert Pike, who was prominent in the nineteenth century, conceded that Freemasonry has "two doctrines, one concealed and reserved for the Masters, ... the other public...." Wilmshurst confirmed that the "first stage" or initial degrees of Masonry are "concerned merely with the surface-value of the doctrine" and that "beyond this stage the vast majority of Masons, it is to be feared, never passes."

Author A. Ralph Epperson made the interesting observation that every Mason will deny that there exists an inner and outer circle to the Order because the "average Mason" is truly unaware of this system while the "illumi-nated Mason" is pledged not to reveal it. "[T]his second layer is protected by an oath of secrecy, which means that if you knew about its existence, you would be obligated by an oath not to tell anyone," he explained.

Linking both the Freemasons and the Illuminati with a similar duality, Epperson saw that deception was accomplished by providing both initiate Masons and the inquiring public alike with such a mass of contradictory and confusing information, traditions, and history that even Masonic scholars can-not agree on many issues. Author Mackey acknowledges that Masonic records are "replete with historical inaccuracies, with anachronisms, and even with absurdities."

Wilmshurst explained the reason for such obfuscation by writing, "The growth [of Freemasonry] synchronizes with a corresponding defection of inter-est in orthodox religion and public worship ... the simple principles of faith and the humanitarian ideals of Masonry are with some men taking the place of the theology offered in the various Churches...."

So Freemasonry, though disclaimed to be a religion, nevertheless offers a substitute for religion. No wonder it had to be circumspect in its teachings. Up to within living memory, anyone speaking concepts popularly believed to be sacrilegious or blasphemous risked serious community censure, bodily injury, or even death.

The transition from ancient secret societies to more modern secret orga-nizations was invigorated by the introduction of "Illuminized" Freemasonry in the late 1700s, itself a blending of elder esoteric lore with Cabalistic traditions. These secrets continue to lurk at the inner core of Freemasonry even as its unknowing millions of members enjoy its outward philanthropy and fellowship.

Several modern organizations, while not officially Masonic, nevertheless draw from Masonic lore. These include such social or "fun" organizations as Ancient Arabic Order of the Nobles of the Mystic Shrine (Shriners) and the

Orders of the Eastern Star, DeMolay, Builders, and Rainbow. These groups are predominately American as British Masons are expressly forbidden to join such affiliates.

This brings up a very important point to remember—in the early nineteenth century, a major split developed between European and American Freemasonry. Today, the beliefs and activities of one cannot be ascribed to the other.

Since the late eighteenth century, there has been continuing concern and speculation regarding the role of the Freemasons in world affairs, beginning with the American and French Revolutions and continuing up to today. To understand this suspicion, just consider this brief list of significant Masons, beginning with American presidents George Washington, James Monroe, Andrew Jackson, James K. Polk, James Buchanan, Andrew Johnson, James Garfield, William Howard Taft, Warren G. Harding, Harry S. Truman, Gerald Ford, and both Theodore and Franklin Roosevelt. Other famous American

Many prominent U.S. leaders were Freemasons, including President George Washington.

Masons include John Hancock, Benjamin Franklin, Paul Revere, Sam Houston, Davy Crockett, Jim Bowie, Douglas MacArthur, J. Edgar Hoover, and Hubert Humphrey. Historical foreign Masons include Winston Churchill, Cecil Rhodes, Horatio Nelson, Duke Arthur Wellington, Sir John Moore, Simón Bolívar, Giuseppe Garibaldi, Franz Joseph Haydn (who provided the melody to *Deutschland über Alles*), Wolfgang Amadeus Mozart, Johann Wolfgang von Goethe, Voltaire (François-Marie Arouet), Giuseppe Mazzini, Mikhail Bakunin, Alexander Kerensky, Alexander Pushkin, Benito Juárez, and José de San Martin.

This wide range of personalities could allow the argument that any consistency in Masonic political and social theology is impossible. But consider the odds that so many diverse world leaders and artists could all come from the same secretive fraternity. To deny any relationship between Freemasonry and world events, one also must ignore the infusion of Illuminati doctrine into Freemasonry in the late 1700s. Such infusion included the philosophies of Georg Wilhelm Friedrich Hegel and Weishaupt, which included "the end justifies the means" and "to achieve synthesis requires two opposing forces." It is clear that Illuminized Freemasons have used any and every opportunity to advance their cause regardless of which side they may support at the moment.

The famous Masonic slogan *Ordo ab Chao* (Order out of Chaos) is generally regarded as referring to the Order's attempt to bring an order of knowledge to the chaos of the various human beliefs and philosophies in the world—a new world order.

Author Texe Marrs offered a more sinister interpretation, writing that *Ordo ab Chao* is a "Secret Doctrine of the Illuminati" based on German philosopher Georg Hegel's concept that "crisis leads to opportunity," usually practiced as "problem, reaction, solution." They work to invent chaos, to generate anger and frustration on the part of humans and thus, take advantage of peoples' desperate need for order," Marrs explained.

In 1826, Freemasonry was flourishing in the new United States with an estimated 50,000 members, mostly educated and professional men. But one Mason broke ranks.

Captain William Morgan of Batavia, New York, a thirty-year defector from Masonry, announced he planned to publish a book exposing Masonic secrets, claiming the order was "the bane of our civil institutions." But before publication, both Morgan and his publisher were kidnapped. The publisher was eventually rescued, but Morgan was never seen again. Rumors that Morgan had been abducted and murdered by the Masons spread through New York and on into the New England and Mid-Atlantic states, and a major scandal erupted.

Rumors that Morgan had been abducted and murdered by the Masons spread through New York and on into the New England and Mid-Atlantic states, and a major scandal erupted.

A public backlash against Masonic secrecy and exclusivity resulted. More than 45,000 members left the order and more than 2,000 lodges closed. In 1829, a New York state senate committee investigated Freemasonry and reported that wealthy and powerful Masons were found at every level of government and that the news media, "this self-proclaimed sentinel of freedom," was silent, having "felt the force of Masonic influence...." This was later confirmed by a Massachusetts state committee resolution stating, "Resolved, on the report of the Committee appointed to inquire how far Freemasonry and French Illuminism are connected, that there is evidence of an intimate connection between the high orders of Masonry and French Illuminism."

Opponents of President Andrew Jackson—himself a Freemason—took advantage of the scandal to form the Anti-Masonic Party, the first time a third party was created in the United States. A serious blow had been delivered against Masonry, which lasted for decades. As American Masonry recovered, it evolved into a different form from its European brothers, who kept the more traditional rites and beliefs.

But even in Europe, wars, revolutions, and social change caused damage to the original Masonic lore. In fact, according to the late Laurence Gardner, a past Master Mason of the United Grand Lodge of England, "… it is fair to say that modern Freemasonry's best kept secret is that it actually holds no secrets of any genuine substance."

Gardner explained that when England's King James II went into exile in France in 1688, with him went the traditional Masonic knowledge of the Scots, beneficiaries of the Knights Templar teachings. His followers were known as Jacobites. "Even though all the relevant documentation was not carried to France by King James' supporters, a good deal was burnt and destroyed," noted Gardner. "Intellectuals of the era, such as Sir Christopher Wren (b. 1632) and Sir Isaac Newton (b. 1642) did their best to work with the information at hand. They knew that masonic lore was connected with Cabala wisdom philosophy.... They also knew that it was related to the culture of the biblical kings and were aware of a scholarly existence before the days of the Roman Empire. They researched the technology of the ancient Babylonians, the philosophies of Pythagoras and Plato, and the mystery traditions of old Egypt, becoming thoroughly absorbed in history beyond the bounds of biblical scripture. But for all that, and despite their own considerable scientific achievements, they also knew that they lived only in the shadow of King Solomon."

Three years after George, the Elector of Hanover, Germany, was brought to England in 1714 and installed as King George I, the Grand Lodge of London was formed and from there sprang most modern Masonry, mixed with Rosicrucian theology. Rosicrucian leaders Christopher Wren and Elias Ashmole had firmly established Rosicrucian-based Speculative Masonry deep within the Order. It was the avowed Rosicrucian Ashmole who drew up the three basic Masonic degrees adopted by the Grand Lodge. Nineteenth-century Masonic author J. M. Ragon asserted that the Rosicrucians and Freemasons merged during this time, as demonstrated by the fact both groups met in the same room at Masons' Hall in London.

"Following the death of Sir Christopher Wren in 1723, those at the forefront of Hanoverian Freemasonry began to formulate an historical back-drop for their evolving, non-operative Craft," noted Gardner. "Such things as tolerance and benevolence were cemented as objectives, while signs and tokens were established, along with the aim of building a socially aware community." It was not until 1762 that the first mention was made of the well-known Masonic story of the two pillars of Solomon's Temple.

"[M]asonic rituals were constructed, and are still performed as plays," said Gardner. "But their scripts have been amended and modified. Thus, although the staging (whether the death of Hiram Abiff [the Widow's Son, whom Masons say was the chief architect of Solomon's Temple] or something else) is superficially preserved, the intended deeper meanings have been ignored and forgotten, if not lost altogether." He said Masonic texts from 1717 most likely were produced by Sir Francis Bacon, believed by some to be the real author of the Shakespeare material as well as the person who masterminded and oversaw production of the King James Version (KJV) of the Bible. Bacon was in charge of forty-five scholars who translated and collated the KJV, making him the forty-sixth. For a coded clue as to Bacon's contributions, see Psalms 46—count forty-six letters from the beginning to get the word "shake" and forty-six words from the end to get the word "spear." The number forty-six was Bacon's cypher.

With so much of Masonic lore newly derived, it would appear the only true Masonic secret is the awareness of prehistoric "gods" who illuminized certain individuals with their knowledge. This knowledge was passed down through ancient Mystery Schools to the founders of both the Jewish and Christian religions, whose traditions were brought to the inner core of modern Freemasonry by the Knights Templar and the later Illuminati.

Illuminati

The name "Illuminati" means the enlightened ones and usually refers to a person who has been enlightened, or illuminated, by receiving knowledge from a higher or esoteric source.

Some believe this name came from a small splinter group of Gnostics in Spain called the "Alumbrados" (enlightened or illuminated). It was founded by a Spanish Jesuit, Ignatius of Loyola. The Alumbrados taught a form of Gnosticism, believing that the human spirit could attain direct knowledge of God and that the trappings of formal religion were unnecessary for those who found the "light." It is no wonder that the Spanish Inquisition instituted by the Catholic Church issued edicts against this group in 1568, 1574, and 1623.

Others, such as the Polish philosopher Józef Maria Hoene-Wronski, writing in the 1800s, believed the Illuminati's history went much further back. "The name Illuminati ... appears to have been introduced only about 1775 by the secret society which was founded by Weishaupt, and developed, it is said, by Baron Knigge," he wrote. "But, ... it must have existed from the greatest antiquity. And actually the mystic affiliations under the Pyramids of Egypt, the esoteric sect of Pythagoras, the astrologers or mathemati-

> Some believe this name [Illuminati] came from a small splinter group of Gnostic in Spain called the "Alumbrados" (enlightened or illuminated).

cians of Rome in the time of Domitian, the House of Wisdom of Cairo, the Ismailis or Assassins, Companions of the Old Man of the Mountain, the Templars, the Rose-Croix … appear to form but an uninterrupted chain of these superior affiliations … under the name of Illumines."

Adam Weishaupt, founder of the Bavarian Illuminati, was greatly influenced by older philosophies and particularly by a merchant known only as Kolmer, a man linked to Gnosticism. He was suspected by some researchers to be the same man called Altotas, who was admired and mentioned by the French court magician and revolutionary Alessandro Cagliostro. Both were steeped in the esoteric knowledge of Egypt and Persia. Kolmer preached a secret doctrine based on an ancient form of Gnosticism called Manicheism, or Mandaeanism, that had used the word "Illuminated" prior to the third century. Kolmer reportedly met Cagliostro on the Island of Malta, the old Knights Templar stronghold, while on his way to France and Germany in the early 1770s. Cagliostro, the future French revolutionary, then became involved in Masonic activities with the famed Venician lover Giovanni Giacomo Casanova, as well as the mysterious Count of Saint-Germain. In Germany, Kolmer passed his secrets along to Weishaupt, who then spent several years determining how to consolidate all occult systems into his new "Illuminated" order. Weishaupt's devotion to the ancient mysteries of Mesopotamia is evidenced by the fact that the Illuminati adopted the old Persian calendar.

Although some believe the name "Illuminati" may have originated in the ancient Mystery Schools of Egypt and Greece, it also came to describe early baptized Christians. The Rosicrucians used the term to mean higher levels of initiation. Originally, the stated goals of the Illuminati Order appeared benevolent. They were to oppose and try to stop superstition, prejudice, religious influence over the masses, abuses of government power, and gender inequality. Others, however, saw members of the Order as anarchists or descendants of the Knights Templar and the Assassins of Hasan bin Sabah and some as nothing less than worshippers of Satan intent on dominating the world.

Due to Weishaupt's outspoken views against the Church and royalty and his support of equality and justice, some researchers have suspected that the Illuminati was some sort of proto-communistic organization dedicated to bringing about a proletarian revolution. No one knows their objectives for certain because any true goal of the Illuminati was hidden due to their extreme secrecy and the compartmentalization of the Order.

Less than a half dozen people were present at the first meeting of the Order, but it grew rapidly and only a few years later it had chapterhouses all over Germany, Austria, France, Italy, Hungary, and Switzerland. Many influ-

> In Germany, Kolmer passed his secrets along to Weishaupt, who then spent several years determining how to consolidate all occult systems.

ential men became members, including noblemen, intellectuals, and progressive politicians.

During its life, the Bavarian Illuminati counted among its members many prominent men, including literary giants such as Johann Wolfgang von Goethe and Johann Gottfried Herder and even nobles such as the reigning dukes of Brunswick, Gotha, and Weimar.

Other prominent Illuminati included the Grand Duke of Saxe-Weimar-Eisenach Karl August; Duke of Saxe-Gotha-Altenburg Ernest II, along with his brother and successor Augustus; the Grand Duke of Frankfurt Karl Theodor Anton Maria von Dalberg; Duke Ferdinand of Brunswick-Wolfenbüttel; the Duke's assistant, Johann Friedrich von Schwartz; Count Franz Georg Karl von Metternich, Imperial Ambassador at Koblenz; the governor of Galicia, Count Joseph Brigido; the chancellor of Bohemia, Baron Franz Karl Sales Kressel, with his vice chancellor, Count Leopold Kolowrat, a Masonic grand master; the chancellor of Hungary and Transylvania, Count George Bánffy von Losoncz; the ambassador to London, Count Johann Philipp Karl Joseph von Stadion-Warthausen; and the ambassador to Paris, Warsaw, and England, Baron Gottfried von Swieten. These names mean little to the modern reader, but just know that they were the most educated thinkers of their time and are the ancestors of many of today's European leaders, whose bloodlines also reach deep into American society.

Membership in the Illuminati grew quickly, especially with the Order's fusion with a group within Freemasonry called the Order of Strict Observance. Also, as the Church and remaining Jesuits moved to restore pre-Enlightenment restrictions on speech and thought, the disaffected among the population proved easy targets for Illuminati recruiters. It was only in the last stages of the Age of Enlightenment that the philosophies and practices of the past societies, especially those begun in ancient times, came together in the Illuminati. Although the printing press had been around since the mid-fifteenth century, only the educated elite could read and write. Since only the wealthy aristocrats and professionals could afford an education, the great mass of the public was illiterate and susceptible to superstition and manipulation by both church and state.

Famed German author Johann Wolfgang von Goethe, whose works gave rise to Romantic literature, is among the prominent literary figures in history who were part of the Illuminati.

It was left to the educated members of the Rosicrucians and Freemasons to form secret societies for the study of material and knowledge banned by the church and state. Some recent writers, however, argue that Rosicrucianism and Freemasonry began as separate philosophies but only merged in the late eighteenth century with the advent of the Illuminati.

Summary

Humans are herd animals and, as such, naturally bunch together for safety and companionship. As the population grew and evolved, individuals within communities formed societies based on mutual interests.

To feel superior to their fellows and to hide from any conflict with authorities, these societies developed and kept secret their knowledge and rituals.

Such societies grew up in the world's oldest western civilizations—in Babylon, Akkadia, Phoenicia, and Assyria. Often viewed as separate civilizations, these cultures were instead merely degraded versions of the first-known great civilization established in Mesopotamia more than 7,000 years ago—Sumer.

The Sumerians wrote their history in cuneiform on clay tablets, which were then baked and turned to stone. More than a half million still exist but only about 20 percent have been translated. Most are stored away from the public in various museums around the world.

Their accounts of history always began with the idea that thousands of years ago spacefarers called Anunnaki came from the sky and brought the people knowledge of astronomy, language, writing, law, and governance. Their tablets stated that 432,000 years before the Great Flood, the Anunnaki came from their home on Nibiru (a planet that revolves around our sun in an elliptical orbit every 3,600 years) through the Great Bracelet (generally considered the Asteroid Belt) to the Earth. Here they landed in the Persian Gulf and began to colonize and search for gold. Strikes arose over the hard work and it was decided to engineer a slave race by manipulating the DNA of Earth primitives. Over long centuries, royal dynasties arose and when the various kings opposed each other, warfare (there is evidence it was atomic) broke out causing widespread destruction.

The story of how a hybrid was produced is detailed in the Sumerian literature. It is written that science officer Enki and his assistant Ninhursag took the reproductive cell or egg from a primitive African female hominoid (shall we call her Lucy?) and fertilized it with the sperm of a young Anunnaki male. The fertilized ovum was then placed inside an Anunnaki woman—reportedly Enki's own wife, Ninki—who carried the child to term.

Although a Caesarean section was required at birth, a healthy young male *Adama* hybrid, combining the DNA of both Anunnaki and Earth primitive, was produced for the first time, bypassing natural evolution by millions of years. Others were produced but they had a long way to go. According to an

It is written that science officer Enki and his assistant Ninhursag took the reproductive cell or egg from a primitive African female hominoid ... and fertilized it with the sperm of a young Anunnaki male.

ancient Sumerian text translated as *The Myth of Cattle and Grain*, "When Mankind was first created, they knew not the eating of bread, knew not the dressing with garments, ate plants with their mouth like sheep, drank water from the ditch...."

There is little controversy over the translations of these tablets, only the interpretation. When first translated in the mid-1800s, the most erudite scholar had no concept of spaceships, atoms, genetics, DNA, or even heavier-than-air flight. They simply wrote off the Sumerian accounts as stories of their gods. It was all mythology. This continues to be taught in conventional histories today. But a growing number of researchers now have come to believe that these accounts of extraterrestrials visiting the Earth and bestowing their wisdom may represent historical knowledge rather than mythical tales.

The accounts of the Sumerian tablets even correlate well with Bible stories, such as the account of a human taught by his god to build an ark to escape the flood (the story of Noah is also given in the Sumerian tablets but the primary figure's name is Utnapishtim), Ezekiel being carried away in a fiery wheel, and the two faces of the Old Testament god Yahweh, who would be angry and vengeful one moment, but loving and caring the next. It is also clear in the Old Testament that King Nebuchadnezzar II of Babylon had access to unknown technology with his structure of gold that apparently could create some sort of energy field. The Anunnaki established the dominance of priesthoods along with the divine right of kings to control the earliest civilizations. Such priesthoods quickly learned to control their followers through the management and lending of money and they were loath to give it up when their gods withdrew from the human world.

It was through these alien overlords that humans first learned advanced technology. Bits and pieces of this knowledge were passed down through secret societies and Mystery Schools. Some such knowledge is just now being rediscovered, such as the amazing properties of monatomic elements, which may bring about a cure for disease and even aging. The use of Orbitally Rearranged Monatomic Elements (ORME) to manipulate basic energy might even open the door to space flight though wormholes, abundant free energy, and even interdimensional or time travel.

It seems probable that the "manna" used by Moses to feed the Israelites in the desert was actually the same white powder of gold, or ORME, used by the Egyptian pharaohs in rituals on their journey to the afterlife. Moses, who may have actually been Akhenaten, was well schooled in the Egyptian mysteries handed down from Sumer.

The names of the gods changed as the languages of the civilizations changed but their characteristics remained the same. This has led some researchers to conclude that gods such as Enlil, Ra, Zeus, and Jupiter may have referred to real individuals.

It is suspected that America's precipitous invasion of Iraq in 2003 might have been in response to new archeological discoveries there rather than oil or non-existent weapons of mass destruction. After all, ignoring warnings from around the world, U.S. forces stood idly by as the Iraqi National Museum in Baghdad was looted. A later investigation determined that the looting was an inside job designed to seize newly found artifacts, probably relating to ancient alien technology.

This advance technology from the past has been sought throughout history, from the alchemists of the Middle Ages to military and intelligence operatives of today. Even the German Nazis traveled far and wide in an effort to gain occult knowledge.

Nazi super science came under the control of SS General Hans Kammler, who disappeared after the war and may have traded the Nazi secrets of jet flight, rockets, the atom bomb, the mysterious "Bell" and even flying saucers to the western allies in exchange for his life. It is well documented that thousands of unreconstructed Nazis were brought to the United States and rolled into the military-industrial complex to aid in the Cold War against the old Soviet Union. In addition to their scientific and military knowledge, we unfortunately also became infused with their fascist and Illuminati doctrines.

The search for such technology—to include the truth of human origins—began with the Gnostics, people who felt they had a direct relationship with the spiritual and did not need religious leaders to interpret God's will. Their philosophy grew from the knowledge dating back to Sumer and passed along through occult texts such as the Jewish Cabala. The free-thinking Gnostics were hunted down and massacred by the early Roman Church as heretics.

The elder secrets from Sumer were passed down through Adam's sons to Noah and on to Abraham, long before the Hebraic Semites, or Israelites, existed as a distinct people. It may also have been the biblical Abraham, who was a chief Sumerian and the patriarch of both the Semitic Jews and Palestinian Arabs, who brought remnants of the Anunnaki knowledge to Egypt, resulting in the first great Egyptian empires.

Both Gnosticism and the mystic teachings of the Cabala buttressed the beliefs of an early Jewish ascetic sect known as the Essenes. In the New Testament, Jesus preaches against the two dominant Jewish religious sects—the Pharisees and Sadducees. The fact that he never attacked the Essenes has prompted some Bible researchers to believe that

Moses, who may have actually been Akhenaten, was well schooled in the Egyptian mysteries handed down from Sumer.

Jesus himself was an Essene. Much knowledge of the Essenes, thought to be the protectors of "Mystic Christianity," was not known until after the discovery of the Dead Sea Scrolls in 1947. Apparently mention of the Essenes in the Bible had been long ago removed.

Other secret societies also carried the fragmented knowledge of the old sky gods. One such was the Roshaniya of Afghanistan. Their ideology—the abolishment of private property; the elimination of religion; the elimination of nation states; the belief in a plan to reshape the social system of the world; and the belief that one could communicate directly with the unknown supervisors who had imparted knowledge to initiates throughout the ages—was surprisingly close to that of the later Bavarian Illuminati. The knowledge of these earlier sects and societies later was passed to the legendary Knights Templar during their sojourn in the Middle East. Officially, the Templars were to guard the roads to Jerusalem protecting pilgrims. However, following the Crusaders' capture of Jerusalem in 1099, they spent more than a decade excavating under the Palace of King Herod, which had been constructed over the old Temple of Solomon, the site where a vast treasure of both wealth and knowledge had been hidden from the Romans when they sacked the city in 70 C.E. Templars later brought their knowledge and skills back to Europe, prompting a new era of culture and enlightenment.

Some of the knowledge gained by the Templars in the Holy Land came through an Arab secret society called the Assassins, named for their murderous ways after ingesting hashish. The Assassin doctrine that the end justifies the means may have been a precursor of that same philosophy found in the Illuminati and later within "Illuminized" Freemasonry. The Assassin system of grand masters, grand priors, religious devotees, and their degrees of initiation were later copied by the Templars, Freemasons, and Illuminati.

Templars brought to Europe the methods of resuscitation, the use of magnetic compasses for guidance at sea, and the secrets of architecture, which resulted in the magnificent Gothic cathedrals. With their own fleet of ships, they traveled far and wide, apparently even reaching North America long before Columbus sailed. The Templars were the progenitors of several other secret societies, such as the Teutonic Knights, Knights of St. John, Knights of Malta, and the stone mason guilds that in time evolved into Freemasonry.

Much knowledge of the Essenes, thought to be the protectors of "Mystic Christianity," was not known until after the discovery of the Dead Sea Scrolls in 1947.

The Templars also greatly influenced the Society of Jesus, members of which are called Jesuits. The Jesuits are a secret society formed within the Catholic Church to protect its dogma. Peeved at their growing power and influence, the Jesuit Order was temporarily dissolved by papal command in 1773 but later reinstated. The Templars became so wealthy and powerful due to their esoteric knowledges that a jealous king of France along with the pope felt they must move against them. On October 13, 1307, which was a Friday, Templars across Europe were rounded up, tortured, and punished. Yet many simply hid within the crowd or fled to Scotland where Robert the Bruce gave them sanctuary, as he previously had been excommunicated by the Church. Thus, Templar doctrines continued to flourish within the masonic organizations.

> **L**ike other societies, the Rosicrucians claim to hold knowledge from the Ancient Mysteries. And, like other societies, the Rosicrusians were attacked as heretics by the Church.

In 1188, a Templar named Jean de Gisors, a bonds-man of English King Henry II, formed yet another esoteric society called the Order of the Rosy Cross, which evolved into the Rosicrucian Society. Like other societies, the Rosi-crucians claim to hold knowledge from the Ancient Mys-teries. And, like other societies, the Rosicrusians were attacked as heretics by the Church. By the mid-1700s, the distinctions between Freemasons, Rosicrusians, and other organizations that claimed Templar origins had blurred to the point that they appeared virtually identical. Today, numerous secret societies operate around the world. They range from the beneficial and benign to the occult and satanic. It is thought by many that Illuminati theology, spread among Freemasonry, laid the ground-work for even more mystical societies such as the infamous *Ordo Templi Orientis* (OTO) or the Order of the Temple of the East made notorious by Aleister Crowley. Some societies, such as the Ku Klux Klan, have been accused of preaching hate and violence. More benevolent societies, such as the Order of the Moose, Knights of Pythias, and the Grange, are largely social clubs work-ing for charitable causes. Then there are the organizations that, while not so secretive, nevertheless wield considerable power in the world today with little oversight by the public. These include the Council on Foreign Relations (CFR), the Trilateral Commission, and the notorious Bilderberg Group, creat-ed by globalists after World War II and comprised of European royalty along with political and corporate world leaders who meet secretly each year to dis-cuss world affairs.

One Freemason lodge founded in 1726 in Prague is the basis for the Bohemia Club founded in 1966 in San Francisco. This club, in turn, created the very secretive and exclusive Bohemian Grove group, which meets yearly and has included important American corporate and government leaders, including Presidents Nixon, Reagan, and George H. W. Bush. The symbol of Bohemian Grove is the Minerval owl and their strange ceremonies, including a pretend human sacrifice, mimic older Illuminati rituals.

Although not given to hidden symbols and occult practices, both the CFR and the Trilateral Commission qualify as secret societies because no

> The idea of a wealthy corporate elite trying to run the world has given rise to the notion of their attempt to instill a global socialist system of governance and finance—a New World Order.

member of the public can apply to join. New members are carefully screened for their globalist views and must be approved by a membership committee. Additionally, no one is allowed to make public what transpires in their meetings. Many researchers, noting the predominance of powerful government and corporate leaders in these secret societies, see collusion and conspiracy. They see evidence that world events are guided or controlled by these society members. The idea of a wealthy corporate elite trying to run the world has given rise to the notion of their attempt to instill a global socialist system of governance and finance—a New World Order.

But any attempt to dissect the secrets of the secret societies eventually circles back to Freemasonry, the largest such society in the world with more than six million members, primarily in Europe, the United Kingdom and America.

Freemasons claim knowledge and rituals brought from the Holy Land by the Knights Templars that date back to the prehistoric gods and the earliest Mystery Schools, even to the Tower of Babel, the time of the Anunnaki.

Almost all facets of Freemasonry are steeped in controversy, even among themselves. Critics of Freemasonry have claimed the prominent Masonic symbol of a "G" within a square and compass stands for Gnosticism, while others say it stands for "God," and yet others maintain it represents the science of geometry, the foundation of architecture and stonemasonry. Furthermore, Masonic authors have revealed that within Freemasonry there are two circles— one the large, outer circle of members who only know what they have been taught and an elite, inner circle of initiates who have learned the inner secrets of the Order. In the late 1700s, Illuminati doctrines were infused in many Masonic lodges, creating what is known as "Illuminized" Freemasonry, a blending of masonic structure and older esoteric Templar lore with Cabalistic traditions. These secrets continue to lurk at the inner core of Freemasonry even as its unknowing millions of members enjoy its outward philanthropy and fellowship. They have forgotten that the first viable third political party in the United States was the Anti-Masonic Party, formed by people angered over the far-reaching power of the order in politics, government, and the judicial system. In reestablishing Freemasonry in the United States, the lodges there grew apart from the lodges of Europe, which still carry the more esoteric and Illuminized versions of masonry. The U.S. lodges became largely centers for social and business contacts along with charity work such as the Shriners Orthopaedic and Burn Center Hospitals, which give free care to children. The ancient knowledge of the Anunnaki was passed through the Sumerians, Babylonians, Assyrians, and Egyptians down to the Mystery Schools of the Greeks and Romans, then on through the Knights Templar, Assassins, and Rosicrusians to Freemasonry until it was collected together by a group of German intellectuals in the late 1700s—the Bavarian Illuminati. Founded by a Jesuit-trained academic named Adam Weishaupt in 1776, the Illuminati quickly gained a sizeable membership that spread to Austria, France, England, and even to the new nation of the United States. Both Founding Fathers George Washington and Thomas Jefferson revealed their awareness of the Illuminati in their writings and correspondence. The Illuminati proved a melting pot for the various cults, sects, and secret societies, all of which claimed to hold secrets passed down from the sky gods of old. Members combining ancient and arcane wisdom with more modern scientific knowledge were further stimulated by the consciousness raising taking place during the Age of Enlightenment. Apart from the structure and rituals of the Illuminati are the doctrines and theology that precipitated men within such modern movements as the French and American Revolutions, the Russian Revolution, and the rise of communism right through Adolf Hitler and his Third Reich. Manifestations of Illuminati doctrine can even be detected in the divisive politics within the United States today.

It all began in Germany.

GERMANY

In 1776, the year the British colonists in North America began to form the United States by issuing the Declaration of Independence, five university students in Germany met to form their own fraternity, one that would cast a shadow across history beyond anything they could have imagined—the infamous Bavarian Order of the Illuminati. Students of conspiracy have long viewed the Illuminati as one of the first public exposures of ideals that have long permeated various secret societies. Since so many groups and individuals have claimed to be a member or have some connection with the Illuminati, it is incumbent on the serious student to study the Order in depth. To begin to understand the mysterious and elusive Illuminati, one must first consider its historical predecessors as presented previously, and then turn to Germany in the eighteenth century.

The period between 1730 and 1780 has been called the High Enlightenment, the latter part of the Age of Enlightenment. It was a time when many different men from many different countries conceived a wide array of ideas concerning the meaning of enlightenment. Though differing in many ways, they generally agreed with the era's major theme of human progress through rational questioning and intelligent discourse. This was the time of English philosopher and political theorist John Locke, Scottish philosopher and essayist David Hume, French philosophers Jean-Jacques Rousseau and François-Marie Arouet (better known as Voltaire), and American philosophers and Founding Fathers Thomas Jefferson and Thomas Paine. By the mid-eighteenth century, various groups and movements began to exchange ideas that eventually coalesced into a loose organization of intellectuals who called themselves the "Philosophes." These men of letters sought to free the world from the restrictions of both church and state, in fact all of Christian civilization. "The Bavarian Illuminati originated during this age which also bred the growing belief in the acquisition of truth through observation and experience. The Age of Enlightenment was in full swing and by the end of the Eighteenth Century an explosion of natural philosophy, science, the resurgence of hermeticism and occult experimentation, all competed directly with the traditional teachings of the Church and the Jesuit monopoly in the Universities and Colleges," wrote *Illuminati Conspiracy Archive* site owner Terry Melanson.

In Germany, which had yet to become a unified nation, the disparate principalities and states experienced their own Enlightenment, or *Aufklärung,* even as Frederick the Great began to bring Prussia out of years of war into some sort of unity. In 1738, Frederick became a Freemason and supported initiatives of the Enlightenment. German philosopher Immanuel Kant explained enlightenment thusly:

> This enlightenment requires nothing but *freedom* [emphasis in the original]—and the most innocent of all that may be called "freedom": freedom to make public use of one's reason in all matters. Now I hear the cry from all sides: "Do not argue!" The officer says: "Do not argue—drill!" The tax collector: "Do not argue—pay!" The pastor: "Do not argue—believe!" Only one ruler in the world says: "Argue as much as you please, but obey!" We find restrictions on freedom everywhere. But which restriction is harmful to enlightenment? Which restriction is innocent, and which advances enlightenment? I reply: the public use of one's reason must be free at all times, and this alone can bring enlightenment to mankind.

Kant summed it all up in a 1784 essay entitled "What Is Enlightenment?" by citing the era's philosophic motto, "Dare to know! Have courage to use your own reason!"

It also was a time of religious innovation. Both Catholics and Protestants sought to realign their faith along more rational lines while humanists questioned God's involvement in worldly affairs. It was a halcyon age for secret societies such as the Freemasons, the Rosicrucians, and the Bavarian Illuminati. Europeans, including some women, discovered new forms of fellowship, while coffeehouses, newspapers, and literary gatherings provided venues for the circulation of such innovative concepts.

But while Enlightenment ideals spread in England, France, and even America, the situation was much different in the southern German electorate of Bavaria. Religious statutes and holy relics were abundant and supplicating oneself to the priests and nuns was the order of the day for the common people.

The Society of Jesus had been created by the Vatican to check the progress of Martin Luther's Reformation, which came in 1517. While the

Jesuits failed to eliminate Protestantism, they did succeed in stopping the growth of the movement in southern Germany and other countries of Europe.

Bavaria had long been a bastion of Catholicism and was tightly controlled by the Jesuits, who were determined to eradicate Protestantism, both through the mechanism of confession as well as control over both the government and education system. Most of the Bavarian colleges and secondary schools were founded and administered by Jesuits. Any curriculum or book displaying the slightest suggestion of liberal free thinking was forbidden. The small number of educated and thoughtful persons found such clericalism insufferable. It was into this enlightened age of new thinking and radical ideals clashing with the old establishments of church and state that the Illuminati, a focal point for mystical thinking going back into the near-forgotten past,

Frederick the Great, who was King of Prussia, was a Freemason who helped unite his people and supported the ideas behind the Enlightenment.

came into being. As has been shown, while Illuminati concepts can be traced back through history to the earliest sects claiming ancient and esoteric knowledge, the Order was first publicly identified in 1776. On May 1 of that year—a pre-Christian festival day long established to honor spring and today celebrated by socialists and communists—the Bavarian Illuminati was formed by Johann Adam Weishaupt, a professor of canon law at the University of Ingolstadt of Bavaria, Germany.

Weishaupt was born on February 6, 1748, in Ingolstadt, today part of Munich, then capital of the German state of Bavaria. At the time of his birth, there was no German nation, only a collection of principalities, duchies, religious providences, and states ruled by the Emperor Francis I. Southern Germany was dominated by the Catholic Church, and specifically, the Jesuits, and the Inquisition was still very active. No one at that time contemplated concepts such as freedom of religion and speech.

Weishaupt's parents were Jewish. Some even say his father, Johann Georg Weishaupt, was a Cabalist rabbi. Following the death of his father in 1753, five-year-old Adam was placed in the charge of his godfather, Baron Johann Adam Freiherr von Ickstatt. At least one researcher has claimed the baron was young Adam's grandfather, who had changed his name from Weishaupt to Ickstatt upon renouncing Judaism. Ickstatt was a professor of law at the University of Ingolstadt. Labeled a radical by some, in 1745 the baron was selected by the Bavarian elector Maximilian Joseph to reorganize the nearly 300-year-old university along more liberal lines. A supporter of the Age of Enlightenment, Ickstatt gave Weishaupt access to his private library. It was here the young Weishaupt was introduced to the works of radical French writers such as Rousseau and Voltaire and inculcated with idealism and rationalism. At age seven, Adam was enrolled in a Jesuit school, where he often got in trouble with his teachers because of his youthful ideals and love of free expression.

In 1768, at age twenty he graduated from the University of Ingolstadt with a doctorate in law. About this time he converted to Protestantism, despite his Catholic training. Thanks to his godfather's position, young Weishaupt also had access to books in the university's library that were generally banned by the Jesuits, who tightly controlled Bavaria at that time. These forbidden tomes of ancient mysteries, cults, and paganism greatly influenced Weishaupt. He became a free thinker studying the works of prominent Age of Enlightenment thinkers, such as French philosopher Denis Diderot, who wrote such lines as "Man will never be free until the last king is strangled with the entrails of the last priest" and "The philosopher has never killed any priests, whereas the priest has killed a great many philosophers."

After graduation, Weishaupt's education allowed him to become a tutor and in 1772, at the young age of twenty-four, he became a professor of law. A year later, he married Afra Sausenhofer of Eichstätt.

In 1775, he was named to the lofty position of professor of natural and canon law, an office previously filled only by a member of the Jesuits. Although the Jesuit Order had been dissolved two years previously by Pope Clement XIV, who had become wary of its power, it still held the local purse strings and so retained control of the university. Weishaupt was the only non-cleric at the university and often came under criticism, especially if the faculty thought he was presenting liberal or Protestant material.

Both Weishaupt's Protestantism and his promotion further enraged the authorities and pitted the young idealist against the more traditional faculty members, many of them Jesuits. However, despite his outspokenness and his contempt for the restrictions on political and religious thought of the day, Weishaupt drew supporters both from the Lodge and from some students and faculty at the university. They respected Weishaupt for his open-mindedness. They would meet periodically in his quarters to discuss religion, philosophy, and the issues of the day.

Topics included classic religion and theology along with ancient mysteries of the Greek Eleusis and Roman Mithriac cults. They also studied the works of

Pythagoras, the Greek philosopher and mathematician whose work greatly influenced the study of geometry. By some reports, these gatherings were similar to modern-day university student activities in that, along with deep discussions, there was drinking, music, and even the consumption of cannabis. A 1969 magazine article stated that Weishaupt noted that he had studied the teachings of Hassan bin Sabbah, founder of the infamous Muslim Assassins (Hashshashin) and that he achieved "illumination" by ingesting homegrown marijuana. A slogan later adopted by the Illuminati, *Ewige Blumenkraft,* or "Eternal Flower Power," was a harbinger of the psychedelic 1960s slogan.

Initiated into Freemasonry, Weishaupt, that student of ancient esoteric knowledge, found that no one in his lodge seemed to truly understand the occult significance of their own ceremonies. Frustrated with both the Masons and the hidebound faculty at Ingolstadt, Weishaupt decided to form his own organization, based loosely on the structures of both the Freemasons and the Jesuits.

Bavarian Illuminati founder Adam Weishaupt was influenced by Gnosticism and the esoteric knowledge of the ancient Persians and Egyptians.

"From this, original intention, however, he was soon diverted, in part because of the difficulty he experienced in commanding sufficient funds to gain admission to a lodge of Masons, in part because his study of such Masonic books as came into his hands persuaded him that the 'mysteries' of Freemasonry were too puerile and too readily accessible to the general public to make them worthwhile," noted Dr. Vernon L. Stauffer, a former professor at Columbia University. "He deemed it necessary, therefore, to launch out on independent lines. He would form a model secret organization, comprising 'schools of wisdom,' concealed from the gaze of the world behind walls of seclusion and mystery, wherein those truths which the folly and egotism of the priests banned from the public chairs of education might be taught with perfect freedom to susceptible youths. By the constitution of an Order whose chief function should be that of teaching, an instrument would be at hand for attaining the goal of human progress, the perfection of morals and the felicity of the race."

Weishaupt's Bavarian Illuminati began with only five members—Weishaupt and law students Franz Anton von Massenhausen, Max Edler von Merz, Andreas Suto, and a man named Bauhof or Bauhoff.

These university men, imbued with privilege, education, and the youthful zealousness of the Age of Enlightenment, attempted to create a fraternity of progressive, even radical, thinkers who could change the old conventions of their world. The Order initially was known as *Bund der Perfektibilisten*, "The Order of Perfectibilists" or Perfectibilists. But this awkward name was replaced in April 1778 with "Ordo Illuminati Bavarensis," or the Order of the Bavarian Illuminati. The goal of the Order was the abolition of all monarchical governments and state religions in Europe and its colonies and a return to humanistic rational thinking and reason.

Less than a year after forming the Illuminati and despite his previous misgivings about the effectiveness of Freemasonry, Weishaupt further angered the Jesuits when he joined the Lodge Prudence, *Theodor zum guten Rath* (Theodore of Good Counsel) in Munich. This was a Masonic group that deviated from conventional Freemasonry by delving deeply into both science and mysticism. Weishaupt was admitted in February 1777. Some researchers today have voiced the suspicion that Weishaupt may have been a pawn of the Jesuits and that his Illuminati was secretly encouraged by them as a ploy to learn what their opponents were doing.

Weishaupt's Munich lodge was one that practiced the "Rite of Strict Observance." This rite was first initiated in 1751 by German Mason Baron Karl Gotthelf von Hund as an extension of the Scottish Rite. This offered Weishaupt a great opportunity for expanding Illuminati theology as Hund concurrently was serving as grand master of the Teutonic Knights and an adviser to the Hapsburg emperor. Some writers believe Weishaupt may have joined the Freemasons in an effort to acquire rites that he might copy.

Having been told by a priest named Abbé Marotti that the Freemason secrets came from the knowledge of older religions, Weishaupt was encouraged to work more closely with the Freemasons and insinuate his own order into the lodges. But as Weishaupt attempted to blend his Illuminism into masonry, he soon became frustrated with the Munich lodge, thinking the members did not understand the hidden and occult meanings behind their order. His own progress through the three degrees of "Blue Lodge" masonry was slow and he did not think he was learning the innermost Freemason secrets. The Masons and the Jesuits both may have been leery of this new member; in fact, Weishaupt felt he was under surveillance. He was quoted as saying, "I believed that I was under the strictest observation of many persons not known to me; toward this end I sought to fulfil my duties most accurately, because nothing seemed as certain to me as that none of my actions went unnoticed."

Meanwhile studying in Munich, Illuminati member Massenhausen was actively recruiting for the Order. One month after the founding of the Illuminati, Massenhausen enlisted Franz Xaver von Zwack, a scion of German nobility and a former student of Weishaupt. Massenhausen lost favor with Weishaupt when he learned his friend had intercepted correspondence between himself and Zwack and may have misappropriated Order funds. For Weishaupt's part, he came to believe that Massenhausen's recruits were substandard. Weishaupt thought certain secret traditions were "above the comprehension of common minds." In a letter to Zwack, he espoused his desire to mold Illuminati members to his will by writing, "We cannot use people as they are, but begin by making them over."

Zwack, whose Illuminati code name was Cato, soon became Weishaupt's right-hand man and later held a powerful position serving as secretary of the Bavarian National Lottery. In 1778, possibly with the aid of Weishaupt, Zwack also joined Munich's Theodore of Good Counsel Masonic Lodge and soon rose in rank to "Keeper of the Seals." That same year, Massenhausen graduated from Ingolstadt, moved out of Bavaria, and played no further role in the Illuminati, which by then had grown to twelve members.

Weishaupt's right-hand man was Franz Xaver von Zwack, a Munich councilor who went by the code name "Cato."

Zwack, a man of noble birth, took on recruiting duties and soon both the quantity and quality of the Order's membership began to grow. One of his prize recruits was Jakob Anton Hertle (code name Marius), a professor at Ingolstadt, a canon in Munich, and later one of the most ranking Illuminati. By the end of 1778 the Order counted more than two dozen members scattered in the German cities of Munich, Ingolstadt, Ravensberg, Freising, and Eichstätt.

In 1779, two years after Weishaupt's initiation into Freemasonry, he wrote to Zwack and Hertel suggesting the Order be renamed the Society of Bees. The bee connection again demonstrates the close ties of the Illuminati to Masonry, as the beehive has long been an important Freemason symbol. Today's Masonic Lodges were once referred to as "Hives" and any internal disputes are called "Swarming." One eighteenth-century Masonic ritual stated, "The Beehive teaches us that as we are born into the world rational and intelligent beings, so ought we also to be industrious ones and not stand idly by or gaze with listless indifference on even the meanest of our fellow creatures in a state of distress if it is in our power to help them without detriment to ourselves or our connections...."

The symbol of bees also connects to the aforementioned ancient Greek Eleusinan Mysteries, in which honey was thought to be a divine product from the gods and Eleusinian priestesses were called *elissa,* or bees.

One particularly important recruit for the Illuminati was Count Thaddäus von Thurn und Taxis, whose family had been named by Emperor Maximilian I to run the imperial postal system in the Habsburg's Holy Roman Empire. The count served as general postmaster and, as such, was privy to all correspondence, as by the late eighteenth century all mail was ordered opened and inspected before delivery. "The Thurn und Taxis family had the advantage of foreknowledge about politics and business that no other ruling house had been privy to," noted Melanson. "This allowed the family unprecedented insider knowledge [of which] the Rothschilds were keen to exploit...."

By the end of 1779, Weishaupt's Illuminati had gained complete control over Munich's Masonic Lodge and recruits were growing within other lodges. The public had not heard of the Order, which had attained an aura of mystery and myth within Masonic circles, especially among the uninitiated. "In November, not knowing that Constantine Marquis de Costanzo was indeed a member of the Illuminati, ... a Master of the Chair for the Royal York Lodge in Munich, had asked the former if he was aware of a 'Society of the Illuminati,' whose ambition was the domination of Freemasonry," wrote Melanson.

In 1780, two events greatly impacted Weishaupt's life. His wife, Afra, died in February and in July he initiated the Nobleman Adolph Franz Friedrich Ludwig Knigge, a leading Strict Observance Freemason and a man well connected to the court of Hesse-Kassel and Weimar. Knigge soon became a prominent Illuminati member and even began fashioning some of the lower degrees of Masonry into Illuminati rites. He also became particularly effective in recruiting for the Illuminati as he traveled widely, adding members to the Order of Strict Observance.

Knigge, long fascinated with the subjects of theosophy, magic, alchemy, and the Rosicrucians, recruited enthusiastically for Strict Observance Freemasonry, the members of which claimed direct descent from the Knights Templar and the Rosicrucians. They too swore allegiance to "unknown

German author Adolph Franz Friedrich Ludwig Knigge was a leader within the ranks of the Illuminati. He adapted some Freemason rites for the Illuminati.

superiors," believed to be anonymous benefactors, controlling mystics, or even nonhuman entities. Such beliefs were sustained by rites said to predate the modern era. Knigge and the Strict Observance lodges found that claiming continuous, ancient descent from elder secret societies was much more appealing than the more recent societies. Weishaupt understood this well, having concocted a mythical genealogy of his own based on his earlier occult studies. Weishaupt admitted as much to Knigge from the start and Knigge proceeded to add to the myths, even including some of his own design, such as the claim that Illuminati knowledge dated back to the time of Noah. He also set about mounting a recruitment effort with great vigor. Knigge had long been unsuccessfully proposing reforms in Freemasonry. When he discovered the strength of Weishaupt's Illuminati, he joined and took up their cause. According to Vernon L. Stauffer, author of *New England and the Bavarian Illuminati,* the enrollment of the North German diplomat Knigge provided the new order not only with entre to higher levels of German society but presented it with a "genus for organization."

"Two weighty consequences promptly followed as the result of Knigge's entry into the order. The long-sought higher grades were worked out, and an alliance between the Illuminati and Freemasonry was effected," noted Stauffer.

It was Knigge's new marketing plan for the Illuminati—one that bypassed young impressionable students for established professional men of substance—that molded the Order into a much more formidable force.

Some prominent Illuminati members included Duke Ferdinand of Brunswick, Duke Ernst II or Gotha, and noted German writer and poet Johann Wolfgang Goethe, who was an adviser and close confidant to Duke Karl August of Saxe-Weimar-Eisenach. Ernst II's descendants include the royal Windsor family of England, whose German name Saxe-Coburg und Gotha was changed by King George V in 1917 due to World War I, which pitted England against Germany. Quite popular initially, the Order soon had enrolled about 2,000, including some of the most distinguished men of Germany. Recruiting among the wealthy elite resulted in the Order's rapid expansion into other countries. Soon, lodges were to be found in France, Belgium, Holland, Denmark, Sweden, Poland, Hungary, and Italy.

Knigge's prominence enhanced the Illuminati's pubic image and the Order grew. By the year 1788, nearly all Masonic lodges in Europe, as well as most courts and governments, had been infiltrated by men who subscribed to Illuminism.

Weishaupt encouraged rational and enlightening communications among the Order's membership, thus inadvertently creating the first full-fledged correspondence course. The literate members of the Order contributed many books, learned letters, and pamphlets of the day.

Knigge may be best remembered for a book written after he left the Illuminati. In 1788, four years after leaving the Order, Knigge published *Über den*

Umgang mit Menschen (*On Human Relations*), a book on the fundamental principles of human relations, not necessarily etiquette but simply good manners. In fact, today, the German word *Knigge* has come to mean good manners.

One of Weishaupt's early recruits who connected the Illuminati to the Rothschild family reportedly was William IX. William employed Mayer Amschel Bauer Rothschild as his general agent and banker.

Mayer Amschel Bauer, a German Jew, was born on February 23, 1744, in Frankfurt, then a hotbed of anti-Semitism stemming from the widely publicized philosophies of Immanuel Kant and Johann Fichte. His father dealt in fine silk cloth despite ordinances prohibiting Jews from the practice.

Young Mayer studied to become a rabbi. He was particularly schooled in *Hashanah*, a blending of religion, Hebrew law, and reason said to contain secrets handed down from the mystical Cabala, a study that had become popular during the "Age of Enlightenment." The death of his parents forced Mayer to leave rabbinical school and become an apprentice at a banking house.

> By the year 1788, nearly all Masonic lodges in Europe, as well as most courts and governments, had been infiltrated by men who subscribed to Illuminism.

Quickly learning the trade, he became financial agent to William IX, royal elector or administrator of the Hesse-Kassel region, and a prominent Freemason. Mayer ingratiated himself to William, who was only one year older than himself, by mirroring his interest in Freemasonry and antiquities. Mayer would locate ancient coins and sell them to his benefactor. He also traded in works of art and various antiquities. Mayer would sell ancient coins and artifacts to William at greatly reduced prices. Considering his rabbinical training coupled with his serious searches for antiquities, he surely developed a deep understanding of the ancient mysteries, particularly those of the Jewish Cabala. It was during this period that the metaphysics of the Cabala began to fuse with the traditions of Freemasonry.

Young Mayer also added to his client list the royal German family of Thurn und Taxis, a descendant of which would be executed as a member of the secret Thule society that created Adolf Hitler. The prominent Thurn und Taxis family administered a courier service throughout the Holy Roman Empire. "They prospered because they received before their rivals news of market trends, commodity prices and major political events," noted Rothschild biographer Derek Wilson. Mayer saw firsthand that information, especially obtained quickly, often meant great wealth. Today, the axiom has become "time equals money." To prevent prying eyes from "reading their mail," the family wrote all correspondence in *Judendeutsch*, German written in Hebrew characters. This code has prevented most researchers from any clear understanding of their methods and intentions.

During this time, according to *The New Encyclopedia Britannica*, "Mayer set the pattern that his family was to follow so successfully—to do business with reigning houses by preference and to father as many sons as possible who could take care of the family's many business affairs abroad."

According to several sources, the Rothschild family fortune was built upon money embezzled from William IX, who was paid an enormous sum by the British government to provide Hessian soldiers to fight American colonists during the Revolutionary War. William handed over this money to Mayer for investment but instead it reportedly was used to establish his son Nathan as head of the London branch of the family banking house. Mayer eventually repaid the money but by then Nathan had gained control over the Bank of England

The Rothschild's coat of arms. The Jewish family overcame odds in Christian Europe to establish a bank in 1760 and create a family fortune and legacy that remains powerful to this day.

and this became the origin of the enormous Rothschild fortune. Biographer Derek Wilson acknowledged this by writing, "… it was the temporary diversion of the immense sums of money originating in Hesse-Kassel which enabled N. M. (as Nathan liked to be called) to launch his banking operation, providing him with both liquidity and prestige."

Rothschild biographer Niall Ferguson wrote, "From the earliest days, the Rothschilds appreciated the importance of proximity to politicians, the men who determined not only the extent of budget deficits but also the domestic and foreign policies…. Rothschild influence extended to royalty as well. Nathan first came into contact with British royalty thanks to his father's purchase of outstanding debts owed by George, Prince Regent—later King George IV—and his brothers."

Meanwhile, Mayer's other four sons had been sent to become the central bankers in Europe—Amschel Mayer in Germany, James in France, Solomon Mayer in Austria, and Karl Mayer in Italy. Acting together, the Rothschild dynasty promoted financial booms and busts and even wars to continually gain immense profits and control.

But it was Nathan who later exerted considerable influence on British Queen Victoria, Prince Consort Albert, and their son. The British Rothschilds also were quite close to most prominent Victorian politicians such as Lord John Russell, Lord William Gladstone, Benjamin Disraeli, Arthur Balfour, Joseph Chamberlain, and Sir Randolph Churchill, Winston's father.

The world's wealthiest man, John D. Rockefeller, was indebted to a Rotchschild bank for the loan that allowed him to invest in the oil industry.

It was also about the time of Nathan's arrival in London that Mayer Bauer changed his name to Rothschild (literally "red shield"), taken from a red shield emblem on the ghetto home of his ancestors. This name change undoubtedly was an attempt to separate his family from the raging anti-Semitism prevalent in Germany at the time. To further insulate the family from such discrimination, the Rothschilds used a stable of registered agents and front men to operate their far-flung business dealings. In North America, in the mid-1800s, as petroleum was becoming recognized as a major requirement to fuel and lubricate the machines of the Industrial Revolution, it was the Bank of Cleveland, a registered Rothschild bank, that loaned the money necessary for John D. Rockefeller to eventually buy up almost the entire oil industry, becoming the world's first known millionaire.

William IX, upon the death of his father, inherited the largest private fortune in Europe. It has been established that the Rothschilds and German royalty were also connected through Freemasonry to the Illuminati. Rothschild biographer Niall Ferguson wrote that Rothschild's son, Salomon, was a member of the same Masonic Lodge as Mayer's bookkeeper, Seligmann Geisenheimer.

Many conspiracy writers link Weishaupt and his Illuminati to Rothschild. Some even claim the creation of the Order was a Rothschild-directed project. According to conspiracy writer Johnny Silver Bear (his adopted Indian name), of *The Silver Bear Café* website, Weishaupt was an admirer of French philosopher and revolutionary leader Voltaire. "It is believed that, as a result of Voltaire's writings, Weishaupt formulated his ideas concerning the destruction of the Church. In 1775, when summoned by the House of Rothschild, he immediately defected [from the Church] and, at the behest of Mayer, began to organize the Illuminati. The first chapter of the order started in his home town of Ingolstadt," wrote Silver Bear.

Such a claim was supported by David Livingston, who wrote: "In 1773, Mayer Rothschild had invited twelve other wealthy and influential men, representing in all the thirteen bloodlines of the Illuminati, to convince them to pool their resources in a plot to bring about a new world order. Thus was Adam Weishaupt commissioned to establish the Illuminati."

According to Canadian naval commander William Guy Carr, Adam Weishaupt defected from Christianity and embraced the Luciferian ideology while teaching in Ingolstadt. He further explained, "In 1770 the money lenders (who had recently organized the House of Rothschild) retained him to revise and modernize the age-old 'protocols' designed to give the Synagogue of Satan ultimate world domination so they can impose the Luciferian ideology upon what remains of the Human Race, after the final social cataclysm, by use of satanic despotism. Weishaupt completed his task May 1st, 1776. The plan required the destruction of ALL [emphasis in the original] existing governments and religions. This objective was to be reached by dividing the masses, whom he termed Goyim (meaning human cattle) into opposing camps in ever increasing numbers on political, racial, social, economic and other issues. The opposing sides were then to be armed and an 'incident' provided which would cause them to fight and weaken themselves as they destroyed National Governments and Religious Institutions."

> The plan required the destruction of ALL [emphasis in the original] existing governments and religions. This objective was to be reached by dividing the masses....

Another link between the Illuminati and the Rothschilds was Michael Hess, the tutor of Jacob Rothschild's children, who was an avid follower of Moses Mendelssohn, the Jewish Cabalist who inspired and mentored Weishaupt.

Masonic historian Albert G. Mackey, however, found it difficult to believe Knigge supported the anti-Christian efforts attributed to the Illuminati as it was initially believed the goal of Illuminism was the elevation of the human race. "Knigge, who was one of its most prominent working members, and the author of several of its Degrees, was a religious man, and would never have united with it had its object been, as has been charged, to abolish Christianity," argued Mackey, who cautiously added, "But it cannot be denied, that in the process of time, abuses had crept into the Institution and that by the influence of unworthy men, the system became corrupted...."

Fundamentalist Christian evangelist Dr. Gerald Burton Winrod, editor of *The Defender*, a right-wing magazine published in Kansas, which during the 1930s grew to a circulation of more than 120,000, published a book in 1935 entitled *Adam Weishaupt—A Human Devil*.

"Secret societies, sometimes founded upon high ideals and lofty precepts, are frequently prostituted by men of evil genius who get control of them for their own private gain and selfish use. Because there is always an element of mystery associated with a lodge, it becomes a convenient cloak and an ideal means for secret operations, when taken over by subversive influences," wrote Winrod.

But what about Adam Weishaupt as a person? "It is, of course, to the advantage of those who are today unloading Weishaupt's schemes upon the

> Knigge and Weishaupt argued constantly. The result of this infighting was quarrels between the founder and the members, which prompted some insubordination.

world to keep his name and his principles away from the public view. It is remarkable how his followers have succeeded in keeping him out of sight," noted Winrod. "In his personal life, this man was a moral pervert. He lived in incestuous relationship with his sister-in-law. When it was discovered that she was to give birth to a child he became seized with fear and planned an abortion. From documents which fell into the hands of the German government it has been discovered that his organization possessed dreadful poisons and had no hesitation about using them when to do so might serve to silence an enemy or advance their cause in other ways."

Winrod said Weishaupt wrote in a letter to a doctor and fellow Illuminist: "We have already tried several things to get rid of the child. She herself is willing to undertake everything. But Euriphon [an ancient Greek physician but here most likely indicating a compliant doctor] is too timid." The abortion failed and the child, a male, was born January 30, 1784.

Knigge founded the upper ranks of the Order, known as Areopagites, who acted as a judicial council. They became critical of Weishaupt's dictatorial management style. The name Areopagites came from a low hill northwest of Athens where Greek leaders met to dispense justice. The Apostle Paul was said to have spoken from the Areopagus.

Many of the Areopagites agreed with many of Knigge's proposed changes within the Order, which while welcomed by the members, were resented by Weishaupt. Knigge and Weishaupt argued constantly. The result of this infighting was quarrels between the founder and the members, which prompted some insubordination. The constant lack of funds, due largely to the altruistic view that the Illuminati was not created to make money, proved another setback to the Order's growth. Many proposed projects, including recruitment incentives, were stymied for lack of funds. The dissention brewing within Illuminati ranks and increasing tensions caused by the Illuminati infiltration of the Freemasons finally resulted in calls for a major convention to clear the air. Thus was convened the Congress of Wilhelmsbad, held in July 1782 in the summer home of William I of Hanau, who later became King William IX, Landgrave [a German title that ranks above a Count] of Hesse-Kassel in 1785. The Wilhelmsbad Congress was "probably the most significant event of the era as far as any official coalition between secret society factions," noted Melanson. This important convention will be discussed later.

It was at the Wilhelmsbad Congress that the Order of Strict Observance was banished from the rites of Freemasonry, and the Illuminati wasted no time in recruiting disgruntled members of that order. Illuminati membership increased significantly, but so did both public suspicion and wariness on the part of officialdom. One of the first public warnings about the Illuminati came from the Rosicrucians who in 1783 issued a pamphlet entitled *The Illuminati Unmasked,* which advised the Order was using Freemasonry to undermine Christian faith and advance a secular philosophy.

Later that year, three professors of the Marianum Academy, a Catholic institution, defected from the Order and sent a letter to the sister-in-law of Bavarian elector Karl Theodor warning of the Illuminati. They said the Order was teaching against both religion and patriotism and even that suicide and the poisoning of one's enemies was acceptable. More seriously, they said the Illuminati was in league with the government of Austria, which at that time was trying to gain control over Bavaria, creating anxiety in the population.

One Berlin Masonic lodge declared its opposition to the Order and described the Illuminati as a "masonic sect that undermines the Christian religion and turns Freemasonry into a political system." Armed with such public declarations, the reaction of the Bavarian government was both immediate and serious. Karl Theodor began drawing up an edict against all secret societies. Originally a supporter of the Enlightenment, Theodor became Duke of Bavaria in 1777, a year after the Illuminati was formed. But the power of Theodor's courtiers and the clergy influenced Theodor to reinstate prosecution against any liberal thinking or activities. Educated men resented the reclaimed restrictions and many became especially susceptible to Illuminati recruitment.

By the spring of 1784, Illuminati membership had grown to almost 3,000, thanks primarily to the influence and connections of Knigge's friends. And with the recruitment of two of the most important figures in German Freemasonry—Duke Ferdinand of Brunswick- Lüneburg and Prince Karl of Hesse, it appeared the complete takeover of Masonry was almost assured. But the conflict between Knigge and Weishaupt, caused by differences of opinion and even possibly by mutual jealousy and distrust, came to a head. Weishaupt, who so humbly sought the assistance of Knigge at the start of the Order, increasingly opposed his innovations and management. Knigge,

Karl Theodor, the Duke of Bavaria, signed an edict outlawing secret societies, including the Masons.

irritated by Weishaupt's authoritarian and secretive leadership, even accused the founder of being a latent Jesuit." "God, what a man!" exclaimed Knigge. "Where does his unrestrained passion lead? Had I ever believed this man capable of such low and ungrateful behavior? And it was under his banner that I was to work for mankind! That is to say, under the yoke of such a pig-headed man! Never again!"

In April 1784, Knigge resigned from the Order and a few months later signed an agreement to return all property, rituals, and initiations belonging to the Order. But he also pledged not to divulge Illuminati secrets. With Knigge's departure the power of the Illuminati began to swiftly decline. On June 22, Karl Theodor, apparently fed up with reports of secret society plots and machinations, issued the first of several edicts banning all such societies.

Summary

On May 1, 1776, a date long celebrated as "International Workers Day" by socialists and communists, four university students at the University of Ingolstadt in Germany, encouraged by Professor Adam Weishaupt, formed a secret fraternity.

Originally the group was called the "The Order of Perfectibilists," meaning those who have reached perfection. But this unwieldy name was soon replaced by the Order of the Bavarian Illuminati.

These well-educated young men—the Jesuit-raised Weishaupt had graduated with a doctorate in law at the age of twenty—were imbued with the utopian ideals of the Enlightenment Age and were well versed in classic literature and mythologies of the Greeks and Romans. They truly believed in a new world order not subservient to the whims of omnipotent monarchs and pompously pious clerics.

These erudite men of the Illuminati may have been the first persons to collect, study, and internalize the beliefs and practices that have long permeated secret societies, carrying fragments of the ancient knowledge down through the ages. Though they differed from others in their understanding and rituals, they generally agreed with the Enlightenment's major theme of human progress through rational questioning and intelligent discourse. Knowledgeable of true history, the marriage and teachings of Jesus and the information, fragmented though it was, handed down from olden gods, the self-proclaimed Illumined ones eschewed the current teaching of the Church. Their jaundiced attitude grew to include the restrictive edicts handed down by the royalty leading the State.

Illuminati theology fell on receptive ears at the time when both men and women, chaffing under the societal restrictions, were whispering dissension in literary meetings, coffee houses, and in alternative, and often subversive, newsletters—an early-day Internet.

Adam Weishaupt was the perfect catalyst to promote these new and radical ideals. Born to Jewish parents, the youngster was sent to live with his godfather, Baron Johann Adam Freiherr von Ickstatt, a professor of law at the University of Ingolstadt, whose extensive library contained many books banned from the public by the Jesuit authorities. Young Weishaupt also had access to the university's vast library, which also contained forbidden works. It was during his time at the university, where he seemed to always be in trouble with the Jesuit authorities upset by his conversion to Protestantism, that the young Weishaupt, filled with the desire to change the world for the better, was considered a radical. The fact that in 1777, Weishaupt joined a Masonic lodge which, unlike others, delved into both science and mysticism also disturbed his Jesuit superiors.

> **Weishaupt believed the Freemasons had largely lost the true meanings of their teachings and rituals....**

He and his followers would spend their nights in his apartments discussing the ancient mysteries of the Greek Eleusis and Roman Mithriac cults along with the works of Pythagoras, the Greek philosopher and mathematician whose work greatly influenced the study of geometry. By some reports, these gatherings included heavy drinking, music, and even the consumption of cannabis. In a foretaste of the 1960s hippies, the Illuminati once adopted the slogan *Ewige Blumenkraft*, or Eternal Flower Power.

Weishaupt soon became disenchanted with his Masonic membership in the Theodore of Good Counsel lodge in Munich, which practiced a custom called the Rite of Strict Observance. This rite, an extension of the Scottish Rite, formed when the Templars fled with their intimate knowledge to Scotland, was initiated in 1751 by German Freemason Baron Karl Gotthelf von Hund. He taught that the rite descended from the knowledge of the Knights Templar and had been handed down from "invisible masters," possibly meaning the ancient sky gods, although the knowledge and understanding of such had long since been lost.

Weishaupt believed the Freemasons had largely lost the true meanings of their teachings and rituals and sought to infuse his knowledge and beliefs of the ancient mysteries into masonry but met some resistance. He also felt the Freemasons were not radical enough in their efforts to educate and elevate the public. His efforts began to bear fruit when Franz Xaver Carl Wolfgang von Zwack, a scion of German nobility and a former student of Weishaupt, was recruited into the Illuminati. Zwack was a well-known official within the Bavarian government and a capable recruiter. He began to recruit ranking members of society into the Order as well as streamlining and even innovating some of the rituals and grades. By 1779, the Order had gained control over the Munich Masonic lodge and its doctrine was becoming more widespread although still largely unknown to the public.

Events moved rapidly. In 1780, Weishaupt's wife, Afra Sausenhofer, died, releasing him to fully concentrate on his work, and he initiated the nobleman Freiherr Adolph Franz Friedrich Ludwig Knigge, a leading Strict Observance Freemason and a man well connected to the court of Hesse-Kassel and Weimar, into the Illuminati. Knigge, a longtime student of theosophy, magic, alchemy, and the Rosicrucians, was well placed in society and proved an enthusiastic recruiter for both the Illuminati and Strict Observance Freemasonry. It was Knigge who cemented the blending of Illuminism with the tenets of Freemasonry. By the early 1780s, Illuminati membership had swelled to more than 2,000 men, many with professional or government positions, including some open-minded royalty. One of the royals associated with the Illuminati was William IX, royal administrator of the Hesse-Kassel region and a prominent Freemason, who through his financial adviser Mayer Amschel Rothschild, leased Hessian soldiers to England to fight the colonials in the American Revolution. Rothschild used embezzled money from William to place his five sons as Europe's most prominent central bankers. Also involved with the Illuminati was Mayer Rothschild's bookkeeper, Seligmann Geisenheimer.

With the funding of the Rothschild banking empire behind him and a host of educated and progressive-thinking Illuminati working for him, Weishaupt's dream of a world free of state and church control seemed to be coming true. This achievement came despite a turbulent personal life in which he impregnated his sister-in-law and then tried to chemically abort the fetus.

In time, Weishaupt and Knigge fell out, constantly arguing over philosophy, management style, and the perennial lack of funds. Although Knigge well represented the absent Weishaupt at the 1782 Congress of Wilhelmsbad, termed "the most significant event of the era as far as any official coalition between secret society factions," his conflict with Weishaupt reached a climax in 1784 when Knigge resigned from the Order. He felt Weishaupt had been ungrateful toward this work and dictatorial in his leadership. That same year, fate turned against Weishaupt and his Illuminati when Prince Elector of Bavaria Karl Theodor, persuaded by accusations against the Illuminati by the Jesuits and others, issued an edict banning such secret societies.

The existence of the Bavarian Illuminati was drawing to an end.

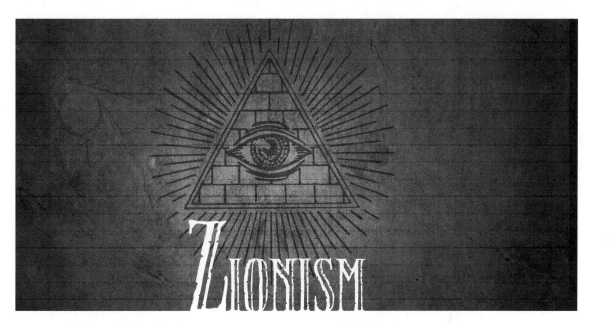

ZIONISM

As if the mixture of Catholicism, Protestantism, and ancient occult mysticism within the Illuminati was not enough to create conflict and confusion, a solid thread of radical Judaism, or more specifically Zionism, may have played a large part in both the Order's creation, theology, and subsequent activities. Zionism is a touchy subject because leaders of the Zionist movement, both Jews and gentiles, have long used the smear of anti-Semitism against anyone questioning the Zionist agenda. Today, even fact-based rational opinions can be labeled "hate speech." So, let's be clear. There are three separate aspects to this subject: Hebrews—technically, Hebrew is the language of the Semitic race that originally inhabited the area of Palestine, but Hebrews came to mean Jewish Semites (ironically, the indigenous Palestinian Arabs are Semites); Jews—those who embrace the religion of Judaism; and Zionists—those who support a political movement begun by people far from Palestine.

While most agree that it is improper to discriminate against anyone because of their race or religion, any political undertaking should be open to examination and criticism. In the realm of politics, much confusion has been sewn on this issue. Supporters of Zionism for years have skillfully attacked their opponents as "anti-Jewish" to the extent that many Americans, Jews and gentiles alike, and especially the media are loath to even question the policies of Zionist-led Israel no matter how odious. But, as will be seen, the Jews as a whole have been the foremost victims of an Illuminati plot rather than the instigators.

To understand Zionism and its relationship to the Illuminati, one must look back into little-known periods in Jewish history. Between the years 652 and 1016 the kingdom of Khazaria existed in the area between the Black and Caspian Seas in what is today mostly Georgia. In 740, the king of Khazaria converted to Judaism and, like the Romans under Emperor Constantine, his subjects followed. Many Khazars fled west into Europe when in 969 Khazaria was overrun by Scandinavian migrants called the Rus. The area came to be called Russia. Displaced descendants of the Khazarian Empire migrated into Western Europe. In the Netherlands, the Khazars, or Ashkenazi Jews as they came to call themselves, prospered and began to spread across Europe and then to America. It should be noted that while at no time were these people connected to the Hebrews of Palestine, they nevertheless were the originators of Zionism. Arthur Koestler, Jewish author of *The Thirteenth Tribe*, explained, "In the twelfth century there arose in Khazaria a Messianic movement, a rudimentary attempt at a Jewish crusade, aimed at the conquest of Palestine by force of arms. The initiator of the movement was a Khazar Jew, one Solomon ben Duji (or Ruhi or Roy), aided by his son Menahem and a Palestinian scribe. They wrote letters to all the Jews, near and far, in all the lands around them.... They said that the time had come in which God would gather His people from all lands to Jerusalem, the holy city, and that Solomon Ben Duji was Elijah, and his son the Messiah." Duji's movement later became known as Zionism.

British journalist Douglas Reed, author of the 1938 influential book *Insanity Fair*, wrote in his 1978 volume *The Controversy of Zion:* "From [the time of Napoleon] on the ruling sect of Jewry bent all its efforts on reducing the authority of the original Sephardic Jews and increasing that of their compact Ashkenazi in the East, from this moment on the Ashkenazi began to move into Europe (and later into America), to assume the leadership of the world revolution and to carry with them everywhere the assault on all legitimate government, religion and nationhood."

To complicate matters, in 1666, a Cabalist rabbi named Sabbatai Zevi proclaimed himself the long-anticipated Jewish Messiah. Zevi was born in 1626 to affluent Jews living in Anatolia, which encompassed Asia Minor and most of Turkey. A charismatic leader, by the mid-seventeenth century his followers included about half of the world's Jewish population. His popularity also stemmed from Zevi's use of the *Lurianic Kabbalah*, named after Rabbi Isaac Luria, a sixteenth-century mystic who proclaimed a new version of the Cabala, which used

Cabalist rabbi Sabbatai Zevi declared himself the Messiah in 1666. His many followers were dismayed when Zevi later converted to Islam.

numerology and codes to predict the coming of a Messiah. Zevi and his followers came to be called Sabbateans.

German-born Israeli historian Gershom Scholem, an authority on the Cabala, described the Shabbatean movement as "the largest and most momentous messianic movement in Jewish History."

Due to his unorthodox views, Zevi was expelled from Jerusalem by rabbinical leaders but found support from the Sultan of the Ottoman Empire and his sect flourished until the Sultan grew uneasy over its growing power. Zevi reportedly was offered the choice of "Your head or the turban," meaning death or conversion to Islam. It was an easy choice. Much to the dismay of many of his followers, Zevi became a Muslim and took the name of Aziz Mehmed Effendi (the Power of Muhammed). Some supporters excused this conversion by believing that as the new Messiah, Zevi represented an opportunity to merge the two religions.

The new interpretations taught in the Lurian Cabala are thought by some scholars to provide the spiritual justification for proactive Zionism that eventually led to the creation of Israel.

Zevi and his Sabbateans practiced a contrary form of religious practice. They believed that by violating the old Jewish laws, the new Messiah could more easily lift them up to redemption. They feasted during fast days, ate food forbidden by Jewish dietary law, and believed in the transmigration of souls, or reincarnation. Another aspect of the Sabbateans' theology involved secrecy.

Anthropologist and author Robert Sepehr in his 2015 book *1666: Redemption through Sin* explained the Sabbatean view of secrecy: "This theme of a secret, hidden, or occult identity became part of this evolving religious philosophy. In essence, a true act cannot be committed publicly, before the eyes of the world. Like the true faith, the true act was concealed, for only through concealment could it negate the falsehood of what is explicit. Through a revolution of values, what was formerly sacred became profane and what was formerly profane had become sacred."

Following Zevi's death in 1676, the movement's leadership fell to Polish-born Jacob Frank, who claimed to be the reincarnation of Zevi as well as the biblical patriarch Jacob. Adopting the Sabbatean practice of posing as something he or she was not, Frank preached to his followers that the only way to preserve themselves was to pose as Christians. He taught that the overthrow and destruction of society was the only way to save mankind. The Sabbateans, who came to include many members of the Jewish middle class, soon became known for practicing Frankism—also Illuminated or Sabbatean Franks. It was a belief system that disregarded the strict Judaic rules, including those on modesty, and it even approved of wife swapping, sex orgies, and incest.

Practicing an early form of "Do as thy wilt," Frank preached the Gnostic view that the Old Testament God was evil and that the most appropriate

Jacob Frank believed that the God of the Old Testament was evil and that people should disregard Judaic rules, even indulging in orgies and incest.

way to imitate the true God was to transgress every old taboo. Stating "No man can climb a mountain until he first descended to the foot," he explained that to become free, one must throw off all conventions. He practiced this philosophy by converting to both Catholicism and Islam and he slept with certain members of his flock, including his daughter, Eva Frank. Perhaps reflecting the Frankish ideology of intermarriage, history professor Howard M. Sachar noted, "As they set about protecting their vast estates, moreover, these Jewish dynasts [Rothschild associates and relatives] often found it useful in the United States as in western Europe to marry among each other. Solomon Loeb and Abraham Kuhn, it is recalled, married each other's sisters, and Jacob Schiff became an instant partner by marrying Loeb's daughter. In turn, Felix Warburg, scion of a distinguished Hamburg banking family, assured himself a senior partnership in Kuhn, Loeb [& Co.] by marrying Schiff's daughter Frieda. Felix's brother Paul married Solomon Loeb's daughter Nina—from Loeb's second wife—and thus became his own brother's uncle. Another partner, Otto Kahn, married Adelaide Wolff, daughter of one of the firm's original investors. At Goldman, Sachs & Co., two Sachs boys married two Goldman daughters."

The Polish ecclesiastical authorities tried to ban Frankism, the "Sabbatean heresy," at an assembly at Lwów in 1722 but with marginal effect. In 1786, Frank moved near Frankfurt, Germany, and it was here that his contacts become important to our story. His previous financial troubles suddenly ended. According to Rabbi Marvin S. Antelman, an internationally recognized biochemist and chief justice of the Supreme Rabbinic Court of America, Frank became suddenly wealthy because he was supported by the German Jew Meyer Amschel Bauer, who later took the name Mayer Amschel Rothschild (Red Shield) and who had established a banking house in Frankfurt about 1764. An early Rothschild red shield featured the six-pointed Star of David.

The Rothschilds are Ashkenazi Jews, described as those Jews who come from Eastern Europe. Many researchers claim they are in fact descendants of the Khazars. By the time of World War II, Ashkenazi Jews represented 92 percent of the world's Jewry. According to the Hebrew University of Jerusalem, today there are more than 10 million Ashkenazi Jews around the world, including 2.8 million in Israel.

Author Koestler in his 1976 book pointed out, "This was written before the full extent of the holocaust was known, but that does not alter the fact that the large majority of surviving Jews in the world are of Eastern European—and thus perhaps mainly of Khazar origin. If so, this would mean that their ancestors came not from the Jordan but from the Volga, not from Canaan but from the Caucasus, once believed to be the cradle of the Aryan race; and that genetically they are more closely related to the Hun, Uigur and Magyar tribes than to the seed of Abraham, Isaac and Jacob. Should this turn out to be the case, then the term 'anti-Semitism' would become void of meaning, based on a misapprehension shared by both the killers and their victims. The story of the Khazar Empire, as it slowly emerges from the past, begins to look like the most cruel hoax which history has ever perpetrated."

A 2014 DNA study, funded by the National Institutes of Health and the National Science Foundation along with several private foundations, found that Ashkenazi Jews came from the Mesopotamia area of the Middle East more than 20,000 years ago. This bolsters the idea that they may be descendants of the ancient Sumerians who fled north after the devastation of Sumer in early biblical times. In support of this notion, it should be noted that during the twentieth century, the Rothschilds were the largest financial supporters of archaeological digs in Mesopotamia and Palestine. The famous Masada dig of the 1950s was actually called the "Edmond de Rothschild Masada Dig." Several sources report that the Rothschilds believe themselves descended from the Sumerian god King Nimrod, the great-grandson of Noah. According to the prestigious genealogical publication *Burke's Peerage*, one Rothschild child born in 1922 was named Albert Anselm Salomon Nimrod Rothschild. According to legend, Nimrod was the first person to seek power for his or her own sake and this desire for power spawned cruelty and decadence.

Others of the wealthy elite have long associated themselves with past royalty and the ancient gods. It does not matter if one believes in such connections. The point is that they do. "There are major families, which call themselves the Sons of Marduk, the Bush's, and Banksters, which might shed a little light on why the Earth is in its predicament. They are the war and disease profiteers," wrote James Gilliland, author of the 2016 book *Anunnaki Return, Star Nations and the Days to Come*.

Mayer Rothschild, perhaps with the knowledge of skillful money handling from the Khazarian bankers who lived along the "Silk Road" trade route, developed the concept of fractional banking, the practice of lending more money than held by the bank. He had five sons who exported his financial acumen and eventually controlled the central banks of England, France, Germany, Austria, and Italy. Antelman went on to explain, "Frankfurt at the time was the

Marduk was a Mesopotamian god. Some wealthy, influential families of today have reportedly called themselves the "Sons of Marduk."

headquarters of the Jesuits, Adam Weishaupt, founder of the Illuminati, as well as Rothschild Brothers' financial empire. This is worth repeating: Frankfurt was the birthplace of both the Illuminati and the Rothschild Empire. When Jacob Frank entered the city, the alliance between the two had already begun. Weishaupt provided the conspiratorial resources of the Jesuit Order, while the Rothschilds contributed the money. What was missing was a means to spread the agenda of the Illuminati...."

That missing piece proved to be Jacob Frank, who added Jewish Cabala mysticism to the Illuminati structure of Weishaupt backed by the financial support of Rothschild. The Frankists also increased the reach of the Order with their network of agents throughout the Christian and Islamic worlds.

Antelman wrote that Rothschild persuaded Weishaupt to accept Frankish doctrine, which included subverting the world's religions and creating a one-world government headquartered in Jerusalem. This was an early attempt at creating a Jewish state in Palestine.

Canadian journalist Barry Chamish, a graduate of the Hebrew University of Jerusalem and who fought with the Israeli Defense Force (IDF) in the 1982 Lebanon War, wrote, "We all owe a huge debt to Rabbi Marvin Antelman, the first Jew to try to decipher the real conspiracy to destroy Jews and Judaism, which, as we all know, is in full swing today. Way back in 1974, before any of us had heard of the illuminati or the Council on Foreign Relations (CFR), Rabbi Antelman published his book *To Eliminate the Opiate* and exposed their covert war against religion, focusing on their battle plan to extinguish Judaism, but with great implications for Christianity as well.

"This book ... has drawn praise for its deep scholarship even from researchers who clearly have no great love for Jews. Its crowning achievement was to prove that Jews are the chief victims of the New World Order, not its chief promulgators."

Rabbi Antelman wrote that even as the Illuminati was being exposed and outlawed in Germany, Weishaupt had already set in motion the dissemination of

Illuminati goals in other nations. By infiltrating Illuminati agents into the Freemasonic lodges of England and Scotland, the Illuminati soon had centers of activity in both Germany and Britain. According to Chamish, "It was from Germany to London that the apostate Jews Karl Marx and Frederick Engels were sent to devise the rot of communism. Shortly after that task was done, the Rothschilds sent their agents John Jacob Astor and Jacob Schiff from Germany to America. They financed the robber barons like Rockefeller and Morgan, who in 1922, founded the Council on Foreign Relations (CFR), to overthrow the American constitution and switch the nation's diplomacy to Illuminism."

Chamish said it was Shabbateans that started Zionism—named after the hill Zion outside Jerusalem—with its ultimate goal of creating a Shabbatean state in Palestine, the historical homeland of the Semitic Hebrews. But Zionist progress was slow. Conferences of rabbis held in 1845, 1869, and 1885—all rejected the call to return to Palestine. Frustrated Zionists felt some impetus was needed to force Jews back to their homeland, so the Sabbateans in Russia took the initiative, formed socialist organizations, and encouraged the Czarist government to increase pogroms against the Jewish people. "The deal was simple: The Jesuits provided the Cossacks, the Frankists, the communists. And naturally, the Rothschilds would provide the moolah," explained Chamish.

"The Frankists were bent not only on the eradication and humiliation of the majority of the Jewish community, who refused to accept their deviations ... but of all religions, and they exploited the Zionist ideals to disguise their quest for world domination. The Frankists believed that ... all that had been prohibited [by the Torah] was now permitted, or even mandatory. This included prohibited sexual unions, orgies and incest....," wrote David Livingstone, author of *Terrorism and the Illuminati: A Three-Thousand-Year History*.

A Viennese reporter named Theodore Herzl soon became the front man for Zionism with the publication of his book *Der Judenstaadt (The Jewish State)* in 1896. It has been pointed out that Herzl claimed to have written the book one summer in Paris. Yet, it has also been claimed that the book was written for him by the Sabbateans. "Herzl wasn't in Paris when he said he wrote the most influential book of Zionism," noted Chamish. "It had to have been written for him. Anyone who reads Herzl's dreadful plays, has to doubt his sudden departure from literary mediocrity."

Herzl became the face of Zionism, particularly his brand of "Political Zionism," that advocated that any area could be considered Jewish territory. Herzl went to Britain in 1901, where he sought a Jewish sanctuary in British-controlled East Africa. "If the idea caught on, it would neutralize the Shabbateans' game plan [for a state in Palestine]," said Chamish, adding, "Herzl died not long after and not one biography of him tells us how. He entered a Paris sanatorium for an unknown condition and never emerged."

An Austro-Hungarian journalist, Theodore Herzl was the author of *Der Judenstaadt,* one of the most influential books on Zionism.

British Freemasons, influenced by Shabbatean and Illuminati theology, selected a German-educated Jew named Chaim Weizmann to succeed Herzl. It was near the end of World War I that the goal of Sabbatean/Frankist Zionism was realized. Britain was at war with the Ottoman Empire that controlled Palestine. Weizmann met with David Lloyd George, who in 1916 became British prime minister, and Arthur Balfour, who became foreign secretary. Weizmann gained the support of these key politicians. The final push for Zionism came in 1917 when, after serving as a member of the British Parliament, Zionist Second Lord Lionel Walter Rothschild—the eldest son of Nathan Rothschild, who by 1815 controlled the Bank of England—received a reply letter from British foreign secretary Balfour expressing approval for Rothschild's plan for the establishment of a home for Jews in Palestine. This letter later became known as the Balfour Declaration. In 1922, the League of Nations approved the Balfour mandate in Palestine, thus paving the way for the later creation of Israel. Baron Edmond de Rothschild, who built the first pipeline from the Red Sea to the Mediterranean to bring Iranian oil to Israel and founded the Israel General Bank, was called "the father of modern Israel." Today, some conspiracy writers believe that the Rothschild plan to create the Israeli state in Palestine was more about gaining a foothold in the oil-rich Middle East than in a genuine desire for a Jewish homeland. "The Balfour Declaration may have been delivered by patrician British diplomats in the imperial splendor of Whitehall, but in many ways it had been conceived 200 miles further north, amongst the second-generation Jewish immigrants of industrial Manchester [where] Chaim Weizmann and a band of ambitious young Jewish intellectuals and businessmen launched an upstart campaign which culminated in the declaration of 1917," wrote Josh Glancy in a 2012 edition of *The Jewish Chronicle Online.*

Zionists pushed their agenda farther along in World War I with an audacious scheme, one that has largely and diligently been kept from the public. Benjamin Harrison Freedman, the Jewish American part owner of Woodbury Soap Company, who as a young man had converted to Roman Catholicism, revealed this alternative history in a 1961 speech at the Willard Hotel in Washington, D.C.:

> Nineteen-hundred and fourteen was the year in which World War One broke out. There are few people here my age who remember that. Now that war was waged on one side by Great Britain, France, and Russia; and on the other side by Germany, Austria-Hungary, and Turkey [the Ottoman Empire]. What happened?
>
> Within two years Germany had won that war: not alone won it nominally, but won it actually. The German submarines, which were a surprise to the world, had swept all the convoys from the Atlantic Ocean, and Great Britain stood there without ammunition for her soldiers, stood there with one week's food supply facing her—and after that, starvation.
>
> At that time, the French army had mutinied. They lost 600,000 of the flower of French youth in the defense of Verdun on the Somme. The Russian army was defecting. They were picking up their toys and going home, they didn't want to play war anymore, they didn't like the Czar. And the Italian army had collapsed.
>
> Now Germany—not a shot had been fired on the German soil. Not an enemy soldier had crossed the border into Germany. And yet, here was Germany offering England peace terms. They offered England a negotiated peace on what the lawyers call a *status quo ante* basis. That means: "Let's call the war off, and let everything be as it was before the war started."
>
> Well, England, in the summer of 1916 was considering that. Seriously! They had no choice. It was either accepting this negotiated peace that Germany was magnanimously offering them, or going on with the war and being totally defeated.
>
> While that was going on, the Zionists in Germany, who represented the Zionists from Eastern Europe, went to the British War Cabinet and—I am going to be brief because this is a long story, but I have all the documents to prove any statement that I make if anyone here is curious, or doesn't believe what I'm saying is at all possible—the Zionists in London went to the British war cabinet and they said: "Look here. You can yet win this war. You don't have to give up. You don't have to accept the negotiated peace offered to you now by Germany. You can win this war if the United States will come in as your ally."
>
> The United States was not in the war at that time. We were fresh; we were young; we were rich; we were powerful. They [the

Zionists] told England: "We will guarantee to bring the United States into the war as your ally, to fight with you on your side, if you will promise us Palestine after you win the war."

In other words, they made this deal: "We will get the United States into this war as your ally. The price you must pay us is Palestine after you have won the war and defeated Germany, Austria-Hungary, and Turkey."

Zionists in all areas of the United States circulated mass-media, anti-German propaganda to whip up Congress and the public. But, as throughout history, a provocation was needed to push a recalcitrant public into war. This provocation was the sinking of the ocean liner *Lusitania*.

Britain's Winston Churchill, who was appointed First Lord of the Admiralty in 1911, wanted America to join England as an ally. In a later book, *The World Crisis*, Churchill wrote, "The maneuver which brings an ally into the field is as serviceable as that which wins a great battle."

Under the existing rules of war, both British and German warships were to give the crew of enemy vessels a chance to escape before sinking them. For submarines this meant surfacing and challenging the enemy. In 1914, Churchill ordered British merchant ships to disregard any challenge, even counterattack if they were armed. This order forced German U-boat commanders to launch torpedoes while submerged for protection. Churchill also ordered British ships to remove their hull names and to fly the flags of neutral nations when in port. Churchill freely admitted his orders were a ploy to cause the Germans to attack neutral ships that would involve other nations in the war. His ploy worked. On May 7, 1915, a German U-boat commander torpe-

The RMS *Lusitania* (shown here in 1906 in New York) was sunk by a German U-boat in 1915, sparking international outrage. It was later revealed the ship was carrying ammunition for the British.

doed the British liner RMS *Lusitania* en route from New York to Liverpool. Nearly 2,000 persons went down with the ship, including 128 Americans. This act set off a firestorm of anti-German feeling throughout the United States, fanned by the Rockefeller-Morgan dominated press.

Only in later years did the facts of the *Lusitania's* demise become public. Contrary to claims regarding U.S. neutrality, the ship carried 600 tons of gun cotton explosive, six million rounds of ammunition, 1,248 cases of shrapnel shells, plus other war materials. The Imperial German Embassy in Washington, fully aware that tons of war materials were being carried into the war zone around England, aside from vainly protesting to the U.S. government, made an effort to prevent tragedy. Embassy officials attempted to place ads in fifty East Coast newspapers.

The ad read: "NOTICE! TRAVELERS intending to embark on the Atlantic voyage are reminded that a state of war exists between Germany and her allies and Great Britain and her allies; that the zone of war includes the waters adjacent to the British Isles; that, in accordance with formal notice given by the Imperial German Government, vessels flying the flag of Great Britain, or of any of her allies, are liable to destruction in those waters and that travelers sailing in the war zone on ships of Great Britain or her allies do so at their own risk."

Of the fifty newspapers slated to carry this notice, only the *Des Moines Register* ran it on the date requested because of intervention by the U.S. State Department. Government officials cowed editors into pulling the ads by claiming that due to the possibility of libel suits, they should first obtain approval by State Department lawyers.

President Woodrow Wilson was alerted to the situation yet did nothing to stop the shipment or alert the crew of the danger. Adding support to those who believed the *Lusitania* was consciously sent to her fate, British commander Joseph Kenworthy, on duty when the ship was sunk, later revealed that her military escort was withdrawn at the last minute and her captain ordered to enter at reduced speed an area where a German U-boat was known to be operating. Survivors and later investigations revealed that the German torpedo did not sink the *Lusitania*. Its destruction was caused instead by a secondary internal explosion, most probably the tons of stored explosives and ammunition on the ship. The German High Command, in a studious effort to avoid antagonizing the United States following the sinking of several merchant ships, including the *Lusitania*, in September 1915, suspended unrestricted submarine warfare.

Whether the sinking of the *Lusitania* was contrived or not, the incident was not enough to propel the war-wary American public to action. Despite all the maneuvering on the part of Wilson and Churchill, it was the Germans themselves that finally pushed America into the war. This event involved Mexico and, more specifically, the one man who more than any other launched World War I. This was Arthur Zimmermann, who by January 1917, had been appointed German foreign secretary. On January 16, he sent a coded telegram to the German minister in Mexico by way of the German ambassador in Washington D.C., authorizing the proposal of a German alliance with Mexico and Japan. Both of these nations had strained relations with the United States. At the time, Brigadier General John "Black Jack" Pershing, who would become the commander of the American Expeditionary Force in France, was in the process of chasing Mexican revolutionary Pancho Villa. Zimmermann advised Mexican president Venustiano Carranza that Germany was about to resume unrestricted submarine warfare. In the event that war with the United States ensued, Germany promised to assist Mexico "to regain by conquest her lost territory in Texas, Arizona and New Mexico."

I n the event that war with the United States ensued, Germany promised to assist Mexico "to regain by conquest her lost territory in Texas, Arizona and New Mexico."

While this promise was, in all likelihood, merely the usual wartime diplomatic maneuvering, it was just the catalyst needed to put America into the war. The sensational telegram was intercepted by British cryptographers who spent days deciphering the document before it was given to the American ambassador on February 25. It was made public on March 1 and initially was greeted with great skepticism. It was thought the text was a ruse perpetrated by the French and English to get America into the war.

But any question regarding the authenticity of the telegram ended on March 3 at a Berlin news conference. Here a Hearst news correspondent, who later turned out to be a German agent, gave Zimmermann every chance to deny the telegram. "Of course, Your Excellency will deny this story," urged the correspondent. Zimmermann then inexplicably announced, "I cannot deny it. It is true." This simple confession produced the desired effect in America. Newspaper editorials railed against the "Hun" and public pressure for war against the German Kaiser [emperor] grew irresistible. Wilson, who had been reelected to office in 1916 on the motto "He kept us out of war," declared war on Germany on April 6, 1917. Eight days later, money began to flow when passage of the War Loan Act authorized $1 billion in credit to the empty banks of the Allies.

In 1936, Congress's Special Committee on Investigation of the Munitions Industry, better known as the Nye Committee, after its chairman, Senator Gerald Nye, reported that while the United States had loaned Germany some $27 million between 1915 and 1917, during that same period, loans to the United Kingdom and her allies amounted to $2.3 billion. According to the committee, the United States did not enter the war because of the Zimmermann telegram but because it could not afford for Britain to lose the war.

With the arrival of the fresh American Expeditionary Forces later that year, the war truly stalemated, resulting in the Armistice of 1918 and the Versailles Treaty, which was so odious to the Germans that it set the stage for the rise of Hitler and his Nazis. The only real winner of that war were the Zionists, as they were awarded Palestine by the British after the defeat of the Ottoman Turks. But one huge problem remained for them. Many Orthodox Jews did not subscribe to Zionism, arguing that when their Messiah arrived he would designate their new homeland and that they should not take land away from indigenous residents. Also, most Jews living in Europe were not anxious to move to the Middle East. To solve this problem, Balfour recruited Russian-born rabbi Abraham Isaac Kook as first Chief Rabbi in Palestine while Weizmann was made the first head of the Jewish Agency. Kook, while initiating the idea of "the purity of land redemption," proceeded to take both land and political rights away from both the Palestinians and the Orthodox Jews.

Meanwhile, back in Europe, plans were laid within the Sabbatean/Frankist Zionists to force Jews to Palestine. In Germany, Adolf Hitler came to power thanks to the help of foreign banks and corporations, including the Bank of England, City National Bank (now Citigroup), Union Banking Corp. (represented by Prescott Bush, the father of President George H. W. Bush), Ford Motor Co., the Rockefellers' Standard Oil, and IBM.

When Hitler became chancellor in 1933, fewer than one percent of German Jews supported Zionism. But life for German Jews grew increasingly worse as the Nazis stepped up their anti-Semitic agenda. According to Barry Chamish, many tried to escape from Nazism by boat to Latin and North American ports but the Western nations turned them back. "Any German Jew who rejected Palestine as his shelter would be shipped back to his death," noted Chamish. "By 1934, the majority of German Jews got the message and turned to the only Jewish organization allowed by the Nazis, the Labor Zionists."

Early in his career, Hitler supported the views of German economist Gottfried Feder, who advocated monetary control through a nationalized central bank rather than private banks and proposed that financial interests had enslaved the population by controlling the money supply. One of the platforms of the Nazi Party was the breaking of "debt-slavery," that is, interest payments.

German economist Gottfried Feder gave Adolf Hitler the idea that having a nationalized central bank was the best way to stabilize and control the economy.

"When listening to Gottfried Feder's first lecture about the 'Breaking of the Tyranny of Interest,' I knew immediately that the question involved was a theoretical truth which would reach enormous importance for the German people's future," wrote Hitler in *Mein Kampf*. "… Germany's development already stood before my eyes too clearly for me not to know that the hardest battle had to be fought, not against hostile nations, but rather against international capital…. The fight against international finance and loan capital has become the most important point in the program of the German nation's fight for its independence and freedom." Hitler's viewpoint eventually narrowed to only Jewish finance.

In his effort to break free from the international bankers, Hitler failed to follow the wishes of the moneyed elite to borrow money. He instead issued his own debt-free money, "Reichmarks," and put the Germans back to work on public projects such as the autobahn highway system, other public works, and the production of war materials.

By the 1936 Berlin Olympics, Germany had become an economic powerhouse, with nearly full employment and a stable monetary system. The wealthy elite could not afford to have the rest of the world see the benefits of interest-free money, as sought by Benjamin Franklin, Thomas Jefferson, and many others throughout history. Winston Churchill, a member of the aristocratic and wealthy elite, summed up the issue when he said, "Germany's unforgivable crime before the second world war was her attempt to extricate her economic power from the world's trading system and to create her own exchange mechanism which would deny world finance its opportunity to profit."

Compounding the problems for Germany's Jews was the Transfer Agreement (*heskem haavara* in Yiddish) signed on August 25, 1933, between the new Nazi government and German Zionist Jews that facilitated the immigration of Jews to Palestine, but only after they were forced to give up their possessions in exchange for exported German goods once settled in Palestine.

As detailed in Edwin Black's 1983 award-winning book *The Transfer Agreement: The Dramatic Story of the Pact between the Third Reich and Jewish Palestine*, the Transfer Agreement, which allowed the movement of some 60,000 Jews and $100 million of their assets to Palestine, was in exchange for halting a worldwide boycott of German goods initiated by the Zionists in response to Hitler's election. "The deal cut worked like this," explained Chamish. "The German Jews would first be indoctrinated into Bolshevism in Labor Zionism camps and then, with British approval, transferred to Palestine. Most were there by the time the British issued the White Paper banning further Jewish immigration. The Labor Zionists got the Jews they wanted, and let the millions of religious Jews and other non-Frankists perish in Europe without any struggle for their survival."

He added, "Into this plot against the Jews we add the Jesuits, who wished with all their hearts, to wreck the land that produced Luther [Germany] … [and] to America where the Jewish leadership used all their contacts and resources to make good and certain that the unwanted non-Shabbataian Jews of Europe never again saw the light of day."

According to Ralph Schoenman, a former personal secretary to British philosopher and socialist Bertrand Russell, it was indeed Zionists who broke the back of the Jewish boycott of German goods following the 1933 election of Hitler. He wrote, "[T]he World Zionist Organization [WZO] Congress in 1933 defeated a resolution calling for action against Hitler by a vote of 240 to 43. During this very Congress, Hitler announced a trade agreement with the WZO's Anglo-Palestine Bank, breaking, thereby, the Jewish boycott of the Nazi regime at a time when the German economy was extremely vulnerable. It was the height

Author Livingston also saw the Sabbatean/Frankist Zionists as the force behind the Illuminati, the Nazis, and more modern movements.

of the Depression and people were wheeling barrels full of worthless German Marks. The World Zionist Organization broke the Jewish boycott and became the principal distributor of Nazi goods throughout the Middle East and Northern Europe. They established the *Ha'avara*, which was a bank in Palestine designed to receive monies from the German-Jewish bourgeoisie, with which sums of Nazi goods were purchased in very substantial quantity."

Henry Makow, himself Jewish, was even more pointed when he wrote in "The Half-Jewish Conspiracy" in 2015:

> The satanic plague devouring humanity originated with the Sabbatean-Frankist cult, a Satanic Jewish movement based on the Cabala that absorbed half the Jews of Europe in the 17th/18th Century. They were chameleons. Pretending to convert, these Satanist Jews infiltrated and subverted all important religions, organizations and governments. They are the progenitors of the Illuminati, Zionism, Communism, Fascism and they control Freemasonry. The NWO [New World Order] is their goal. In 1988, Rabbi Gunther Plaut described Illuminati founder Jacob Frank in these terms, and implied that the Nazis were a Sabbatean-Frankist creation.

Author Livingston also saw the Sabbatean/Frankist Zionists as the force behind the Illuminati, the Nazis, and more modern movements. He claims to have traced the genealogies of the Khazarian bloodlines to include the Rothschilds, the Hapsburgs, the Sinclairs, the Stuarts, the Merovingians, the Lusignans, and the Windsors. "The great secret of history is this story of the ascent of heretical Cabalists to world power," wrote Livingstone. "Ordinary Jews and people in general have no idea how they are being manipulated."

He added, "It is easy to recognize the origin of communism and anarchism in this demented philosophy. It is easy to recognize the terror of the French and Bolshevik revolutions, the Soviet Gulags and Nazis' concentration

Hillary Clinton is shown here getting an award at Chatham House in London. The Royal Institute of International Affairs there is connected to the Illuminati, some say.

camps, the killing fields of Cambodia and China, the 'Shock and Awe' of Iraq, and the dust of the World Trade Center. It is easy to recognize that this degenerate Jewish sect is the reason why all Jews have been tainted with suspicion of immorality and subversion. Many Jews were tricked by the (Frankish) communist promise of economic justice and public ownership. (This is what the Cabalist means by 'magic'—deception and lies.) Yet ordinary Jews have been slow to distance themselves from this pernicious movement, and its Zionist, Neo-conservative and Masonic manifestations (which are not what they pretend)."

One Jewish dissenter of Zionism is Josef Antebi, an Orthodox Jewish rabbi born in Palestine but relocated to Amsterdam. He told the Jewish Telegraphic Agency (JTA) he had been tortured and exiled from his home in Israel because he, like many Orthodox Jews, rejects Zionism. In the summer of 2013 the then-fifty-year-old was assaulted on the streets of Amsterdam. He told a German news reporter, "The one to blame is the Zionist state, which is doing a lot of bad things to people."

Antebi is one of the *Neturei Karta* ("Guardians of the City") who consider themselves "true Jews" and oppose Zionism and believe a promised land was to be provided by the Jewish Messiah when he arrives. Ignored by the mainstream media and viewed as a cult by the Anti-Defamation League (ADL), an activist branch of Zionism, Rabbi Antebi and his group believe Israel is creating problems throughout the world, and should be dismantled peacefully. Such thoughts were echoed by author Henry Makow, who wrote:

> Most Jews are unaware of the Illuminati agenda.… The Illuminati hides behind the skirts of ordinary Jews. The cult that hijacked the world is the tiny nucleus of Cabalistic bankers and Masons based in London and directed by the House of Rothschild.
>
> They govern through their subtle control of large corporations (cartels—especially finance, oil, defense, pharmaceuticals, media); government, mass media, secret societies, intelligence agencies, the military, law, churches, foundations, think tanks,

NGO's and education. Chatham House in London (The Royal Institute of Internal Affairs) and Pratt House in New York (Council on Foreign Relations) are two main control mechanisms. Illuminati power is omnipresent yet the masses don't even know it exists.

This thesis was further expounded on a website called *The Judeo-Masonic Conspiracy:*

> The case is that it is true that the plot had its origins in the usury practiced by some European Jews, and that some individuals from Jewish origin and secret societies like Freemasonry were fundamental for the conspiracy to succeed. But it is also true that not all the Jews practiced usury, that not every Jew that practiced usury had anything to do with the conspiracy, nor with the international bankers, and it is also quite likely that even the Jewish individuals and the secret societies that were directly involved in the plot did not know they were doing so, nor that there was even a worldwide conspiracy going on. In other words: they were simply used by the international bankers, and for the bankers' benefit. The case is that none of these Jewish individuals or secret societies knowingly worked to fulfil the bankers' agenda. Instead, it was the bankers who chose, funded and supported those causes, societies, groups or individuals that would ultimately help them achieve their goals while pursuing their own agenda; like in the case of Weishaupt's Illuminati against church and state, or the Bolsheviks against the Czar. This tactic is still used to this day by some governments, which support revolutionaries and terrorist groups against their enemies; even though their ultimate goals differ. For example: the US funding and supporting the Mujahidin against the Soviets—even though they did not share the same ideology—and once they got rid of the Soviet, the Mujahidin would be dealt with by the US.

While it may be true that secret organizations in the past were built along both racial and religious grounds, attempting to bring race or religion into a discussion of modern secret societies and conspiracies only serves to confuse the issue and repel conscientious researchers. Although many international financiers are of Jewish descent, it is no more fair to accuse all Jews of an international conspiracy than it would be to blame all Christians for the acts of Hitler's Nazis.

One commentator summed it up as follows: "By blaming 'the Jews' for the NWO, patriots are falling into an Illuminati trap. Patriots and Jews alike need a new paradigm. The Jewish people, and indeed all religions and nations, are led by Frankist (Illuminati) Satanists, their lackeys and dupes."

Summary

Zionism is a political movement that involves predominately Jews but also many fundamentalist Christians who believe in the inerrancy of the Bible. This movement is concerned with the establishment of a predominately Jewish nation in the Middle East. Ironically, it began in Russia in the 1800s by peoples far removed from Palestine. It is a separate issue from Judaism, the religion, or Hebrews, a term now used to identify the Semitic race that inhabited the Holy Land in the past.

While most feel it is improper to discriminate against anyone because of their race or religion, any political undertaking should be open to examination and criticism. Yet, proponents of Zionism have quite effectively smeared anyone critical of Israel as anti-Semites. A fitting response to the charge of anti-Semitism might be "Oh, no, I like the Palestinian Arabs!" After all, both the Semitic Palestinians and the Semitic Israelis ironically both trace their lineage back to the biblical patriarch Abraham, who, as has been shown, was neither a Jew nor an Arab but rather a Sumerian nobleman. The real scriptural basis for Zionism may have begun with the early writings of the tribe of Judah, which had fought not only with the other Hebrew tribes but suffered defeat at the hands of the Assyrians, Babylonians, and Egyptians. About 621 B.C.E. the Levi priests produced a text entitled *Deuteronomy*. This work became the basis for both the *Torah* (the Law) and the later Pentateuch, an earlier version of the Talmud. Reportedly the direct word handed down from Moses—though this idea is controversial—*Deuteronomy* laid the groundwork for alteration of previous Jewish law and even advocated racial and religious intolerance and the complete destruction of enemies.

> **T**he real scriptural basis for Zionism may have begun with the early writings of the tribe of Judah....

The concept of destruction as an article of faith must have derived from *Deuteronomy*, argued British journalist Douglas Reed in his 1985 book *The Controversy of Zion*, "...for there is no other discoverable sources," he wrote, adding, "Deuteronomy is to formal Judaism and Zionism what *The Communist Manifesto* was to the destructive revolution of our [twentieth] century. It is the basis of the *Torah* ... the *Pentateuch* ... the *Talmud* ... which together constitute the Judaic 'law.'" Reed noted that from the time the Judah tribe was rejected by the Israelites, they were ruled by a priesthood that taught that destruction was the chief command of Jehovah and they were the chosen ones to carry this out. A prolific author, Reed, who had been praised for his incisive writings later, was shunned by publishers following his exposé of Zionism.

The majority of Jews living in Israel today did not originate in the Middle East but are Ashkenazi Jews from Eastern Europe who migrated westward from the Khazarian Empire, which existed between the years 652 and 1016 C.E.

in the area between the Black and Caspian Seas in what is today mostly Georgia. The Khasarian leadership had a problem. Sitting astride the famous Silk Road, the major trade route between the East and the West, they had built their empire by raiding the passing caravans. But this was dangerous work as caravan drivers often fought back. It was decided that a much safer and profitable way to increase their wealth was to enter the business of exchanging and lending money. But there was a new problem—one third of the Khazar population was Christian and another third Muslim, both of which declared that lending money at interest was a sin and unacceptable. Only the last third of the population, the Jews, thought it appropriate to charge interest on a loan, especially if it was to non-Jews. So, in 740 C.E., the king of Khazaria proclaimed he had converted to Judaism and, like the Romans under Emperor Constantine, his subjects followed. In 969 C.E. Khazaria was overrun by Scandinavian migrants called the Rus and dissolved. The area now came to be called Russia. The now-Jewish Khazars fled west into Europe, called themselves Ashkenazi Jews, and prospered as they spread across Europe and then to America. They later became the originators of Zionism despite the fact that these people had no connection whatsoever to the Hebrews of Palestine. According to author Reed, "When the Khazars became converted the Talmud was complete, and after the collapse

> The now-Jewish Khazars fled west into Europe, called themselves Ashkenazi Jews, and prospered as they spread across Europe and then to America.

of their kingdom (in about 1000 C.E.) they remained the political subjects of the Talmudic government, all their resistance to Russia being governed by the Talmudic, anti-Christian law … though they had no Judahite blood…. The area where they congregated, under Talmudic direction, because the centers of the anti-Russian revolution which was to become 'the world revolution' in these parts, and through these people, new instruments of destruction were forged, specifically for the destruction of Christianity and the West."

It may well have been the Talmudic exhortation to destroy of all things not of themselves that led to the masses submitting to the hysteria of revolutionary France, communism in Russia, and National Socialism in Germany.

Adding to this conflict and confusion was the rise in 1666 of a Cabalist Rabbi named Sabbatai Zevi, who proclaimed himself the long-anticipated Jewish Messiah. Although expelled from Jerusalem by rabbinical leaders, Zevi and his followers, termed Sabbateans, created conflict within Judiasm by their belief that by rejecting all Jewish laws, they might prompt the arrival of their messiah. Under great secrecy, they feasted during fast days, ate food forbidden by Jewish dietary law, and believed in the transmigration of souls, or reincarnation. After Zevi's death in 1676, the movement's leadership fell to Polish-born Jacob Frank, who claimed to be the reincarnation of Zevi as well as the biblical patriarch Jacob. Frank adopted the Sabbatean practice of posing as something they were not. He preached that the only way to preserve themselves was to pose as Christians and that the overthrow and destruction of society was the only way to save mankind. The Sabbateans soon became known as practicing Frankism, also known as the Illuminated or Sabbatean Franks. Frank preached the Gnostic view that the Old Testament God was evil and that the most appropriate way to imitate the true God was to transgress every old taboo.

By posing as something they were not and by intermarrying with both Jews and Gentiles, the subversive Franks became difficult to locate and define. But some of the knowledge of the old sky gods remained within the Sabbatean and Frankish movement. The Rothschilds believe themselves descended from the Sumerian god King Nimrod, the great-grandson of Noah. According to the prestigious genealogical publication *Burke's Peerage*, one Rothschild child born in 1922 was named Albert Anselm Salomon Nimrod Rothschild. It is said that Nimrod was the first person to seek power for his or her own sake and from this desire for power came cruelty and decadence. It does not matter if one believes in such things. What matters is that some of those in high and powerful positions do believe in such occult matters. It is also imperative to realize that even before the turn of the nineteenth century, anti-Jewish sentiment had become connected with Illuminism ideals, despite the fact that many Jews were being enrolled into Freemasonry and its Illuminized lodges. From the Illuminized Freemason lodges from Germany to London, the Jewish socialists Karl Marx and Frederick Engels devised the plan for communism. It was the Shabbatean Jews who started Zionism, the name coming from the hill Zion outside Jerusalem. Its ultimate goal was to create a Shabbatean state in Palestine, the historical homeland of the Semitic Hebrews. However, rabbinical conferences conducted in 1845, 1869, and 1885 all rejected the call to return to Palestine. Frustrated Zionists decided to force Jews back to Palestine, so Sabbateans in Russia pressured the Czarist government to increase pogroms against the Jewish people. The Jesuits encouraged the Cossacks while the Frankist/Sabbateans egged on the communists. The result was continual turmoil in Russia, causing many Jews to flee. A Viennese reporter named Theodore Herzl became the front man for Zionism with the publication of his book *Der Judenstaadt (The Jewish State)* in 1896. In 1901, Herzl moved to England and called for a Jewish homeland in British-controlled East Africa. This was not to the liking of Zionist leaders, who had their eye on Palestine, and Herzl soon disappeared. British Freemasons, influenced by Shabbatean and Illuminati theology, selected a German-educated Jew named Chaim Weizmann to succeed Herzl.

In World War I, Britain was also at war with the Ottoman Empire that controlled Palestine. Weizmann gained the support of David Lloyd George, who in 1916 became British prime minister, and Arthur Balfour, who became foreign secretary. The final push for Zionism came in 1917 when, after serving as a member of the British Parliament, Zionist Second Lord Lionel Walter Rothschild—the eldest son of Nathan Rothschild, who, by 1815, controlled the Bank of England—received a reply letter from British foreign secretary Balfour expressing approval for Rothschild's plan for the establishment of a home for Jews in Palestine. This letter later became known as the Balfour Declaration.

> It was the Shabbatean Jews who started Zionism, the name coming from the hill Zion outside Jerusalem. Its ultimate goal was to create a Shabbatean state in Palestine....

In 1922, the League of Nations approved the Balfour mandate in Palestine, thus paving the way for the later creation of Israel. Baron Edmond de Rothschild, who built the first pipeline from the Red Sea to the Mediterranean to bring Iranian oil to Israel and founded the Israel General Bank, was called "the father of modern Israel." Some researchers today believe that the Rothschild plan to create the Israeli state in Palestine was more about gaining a foothold in the oil-rich Middle East than in a sincere desire for a Jewish homeland. Furthermore, some historical researchers believe that it was the Zionists who convinced the British leaders not to sign an armistice with Germany in 1916 by pledging that their influence in the United States could bring that neutral nation into World War I and tilt the balance in favor of the Allies. It is true that Germany, while suffering tremendous losses, had not been invaded nor lost any significant territory. It was in a much better bargaining position than either France or Britain. Sure enough, back in the United States, along with provocations such as the sinking of the *Lusitania* and the scandal of the Zimmerman note advocating a German invasion from Mexico, Zionists in all areas of the counry circulated mass-media, anti-German propaganda to stir up the public. And in April 1917, President Woodrow Wilson, a Democrat who had pledged to keep the nation out of the war, declared war on Germany with the approval of Congress.

With the arrival of the American Expeditionary Forces in 1917, the war stagnated and lasted until the Armistice of November 11, 1918. The subsequent heavy-handed and unfair Treaty of Versailles resulted in the rise of Hitler and his Third Reich, leading to World War II.

In 1930s Germany, Adolf Hitler was consolidating his power thanks to help from foreign banks and corporations, including the Bank of England, City National Bank (now Citigroup), Union Banking Corp. (represented by Prescott Bush, the father of President George H. W. Bush), Ford Motor Co., the Rockefellers' Standard Oil, and IBM. Ardent Zionists continued to be thwarted in their efforts to get European Jews to move to Palestine.

The orthodox Jewish leadership proved the biggest opponents to the idea of Zionism. They argued it was not proper to take land away from its existing occupants and that when their Messiah finally arrived, he would show them their new homeland. Furthermore, most Jews, even in Germany, were not eager to pack up and leave their homes for the deserts of the Middle East. A forcible exit was accomplished through the Transfer Agreement reached in 1933 between the Zionist leadership and the Nazis. With the election of Hitler, a worldwide boycott of German goods was proclaimed by Jewish leaders. This threatened the German export business when it was struggling through an economic downturn, just as America was dealing with the Great Depression. As the Nazis began to persecute Jews, the socialist Labor Zionists concluded a transfer agreement with Hitler's National Socialist regime that allowed some 60,000 German Jews to immigrate. However, the western nations of the United States, England, and France declined to take them in and they were forced to go to Palestine. But first, they had to leave any valuable assets behind and, once in Palestine, they were moved onto communal farms (the Kibbutz), indoctrinated in socialism, and forced to buy only German-made goods. It was a win-win situation for both the Nazis, who made huge profits, and for the Zionists, who gained Jewish settlers in the Middle East. So it would seem the real Holocaust was more about destroying the Orthodox Jewry, and particularly its leadership, to further the aims of the Zionism. Some researchers today blame the Sabbatean/Frankist Zionists for discrimination against Jews, who are sometimes characterized as being immoral and subversive. These researchers believe that Jews were manipulated by Zionists (both Jewish and Gentile) with glowing promises of socialism, economic justice, and public ownership. It is certainly true that Jews, far from being the chief instigators, have largely been the chief victims of Illuminati-initiated movements like communism, Nazism, and today's New World Order. And Illuminati doctrines made their way into Zionism just as in Freemasonry, the largest secret society in the world.

Freemasons

In just eleven short years of existence, the Illuminati not only infiltrated nearly all courts of the Holy Roman Empire but also managed to penetrate the Freemasons, one of the oldest and most secretive societies in the world.

Weishaupt decided the Illuminati would infiltrate Freemasonry because as a secret society its members were bound by oath not to divulge anything they might hear or learn. It was a perfect cover for Illuminati subversion. Weishaupt blended his brand of Illuminism with Freemasonry after joining the Masonic Order's Lodge Theodore of Good Counsel in 1777.

The French Revolutionary leader and Illuminati member Mirabeau noted in his memoirs, "The *Lodge Theodore de Bon Conseil* at Munich, where there were a few men with brains and hearts … resolved to graft on to their branch another secret association to which they gave the name of the Order of the *Illumines*. They modeled it on the Society of Jesus [the Jesuits], while proposing to themselves views diametrically opposed." It was in this Freemason Lodge where Mirabeau and the Illuminati formulated the anti-clerical and anti-government agenda proposed at France's Constituent Assembly twelve years later.

They also recruited many of the most prominent men of the Enlightenment. For example, the German Mason Karl Gotthelf, Baron von Hund und Altengrotkau, already a member of the Frankfurt Masonic Lodge, who in 1751 formed an extension of its Scottish Rite called the Order of the Strict Observance. Strict Observance members even proclaimed themselves "Knights of the Temple," whose lineage traced back to the Knights Templar. Hund had learned that this Order was based on an earlier Rosicrucian rite called the Order of the Gold and Rosy Cross while visiting in Paris in 1743. It was this order that was joined by Weishaupt and his Illuminati.

The Rite of Strict Observance was meant to attract more non-nobility members into Freemasonry by appealing to German national pride. It also meant to reform Masonry through strict discipline and the regulation of rites, particularly the elimination of occultism then rampant in many lodges. Oddly enough, despite this goal, the Rite of Strict Observance carried with it an oath of unquestioning obedience to mysterious and unseen "superiors."

Hund claimed to be carrying out the orders of "unknown superiors" who were never identified or located. Most researchers believe they probably were Jacobite supporters of the Stuart royal line who died or lost faith following the defeat of English King James II, the "Young Pretender," but others claimed these "superiors" were not human. Who, or whatever, they were, these superiors provided Hund with a list of names reported to have been ongoing grand masters of the Knights Templar, thought to have become extinct in the mid-1300s. A nearly identical list discovered recently was connected to the mysterious Priory of Sion headquartered in Rennes-le-Château in southern France through an Austrian historian named Leo Schidlof and his *Dossiers secrets*, or secret files. This list, except for the spelling of a single surname, matched precisely the list Hund produced, providing strong support for the belief that both the Priory may have been real and, as stated by Freemason Hund, directly tied to the Knights Templar and their claim of holding knowledge of ancient gods.

Karl Gotthelf, Baron von Hund und Altengrotkau, the Freemason who founded the Rite of Strict Observance.

Even more troubling aspects of the Strict Observance Rite began to be noticed. Critics claimed Masonic members of the Rite were attempting to take over orphanages for profit, founding military academies for control and infiltrating governments. Such accusations, along with the mystery concerning unseen superiors and the claims of Templar heritage, prompted dissatisfaction among the Masons and finally led to the Congress of Wilhelmsbad in 1782.

The Wilhelmsbad Congress was held in the summer home of William I of Hanau on July 16, 1782. It was about this same time that Jews were first allowed to enter Freemasonry. William later became William IX, Landgrave of Hesse-Kassel. William eventually named Mayer Rothschild to handle his financial affairs. According to several authors, the Rothschild family fortune was built upon money embezzled from William IX, who was paid an enormous sum by the British government to provide 17,000 Hessian soldiers to fight American colonists during the Revolutionary War. William handed over this money to Mayer for investment but instead it reportedly was used to establish his son Nathan as head of the London branch of the Rothschild banking house. Mayer eventually repaid the money but as Rothschild biographer Derek Wilson acknowledged, "… it was the temporary diversion of the immense sums of money originating in Hesse-Kassel which enabled N. M. (as Nathan liked to be called) to launch his banking operation, providing him with both liquidity and prestige."

According to Albert Mackey, one time secretary general of the Supreme Council of the Ancient and Accepted Scottish Rite for the Southern Jurisdiction of the United States, the Congress of Wilhelmsbad was "the most important Masonic Congress of the eighteenth century." Chief of the Illuminati contingent at the Congress was Baron Franz Dietrich von Ditfurth, an assistant judge in the court council of Brunswick and to the Imperial Court. One of the first issues at the congress was to determine the real objectives of the Strict Observance. Led by Ditfurth, the Illuminists carried the day by claiming the Strict Observance Lodges were not descended from the Knights Templar. They also maintained that the Observance Lodges were controlled by the "unknown superiors," whom they claimed were actually Jesuits in disguise.

The Illuminati contingent to the Congress revealed the power of their fledgling Order as they voted down the Strict Observance supporters. The Strict Observance Rite was abolished, at least temporarily, and the notion of "unknown superiors" was declared a fraud. Masonic author Mackey wrote, "Vanquished by the powerful rival, the Strict Observance ceased temporarily to exist and Illuminism was left in possession of the field."

Another organizer of the Wilhelmsbad Congress was a French silk manufacturer named Jean-Baptiste Willermoz, who traveled in the same circles as Mayer Rothschild. A Christian mystic, Willermoz is considered by many as the founder of modern spiritualism. He joined the Freemasons in 1750, quickly rising to the position of venerable master at the age of twenty-three. His French lodge accepted the Rite of Strict Observance and Willermoz came into contact with Hund. Together they established various systems of higher Masonic degrees and reforms in both France and Germany.

At the Congress, Willermoz helped create the Rectified Scottish Rite to replace the disbanded Strict Observance and persuaded many Masons there to accept his reforms, despite opposition from the Illuminati.

After hiding out during the French Revolution, Willermoz later became active again in Masonry, to which he dedicated himself until his death at age ninety-four in 1824. Although Ditfurth was in charge at the Masonic Congress of Wilhelmsbad, Knigge was active in Weishaupt's absence, enticing

Jean-Baptiste Willermoz devised the Rectified Scottish Rite to replace the Rite of Strict Observance created by Karl Gotthelf von Hund.

attending Masons to join the Illuminati with promises to reveal the Order's secrets. He persuaded many of the German and French delegates to join the Illuminati, the means through which Illuminism would spread into their lodges. Top leaders of German Freemasonry were recruited by Knigge, bringing all of German Freemasonry under Illuminati control.

With the loss of the Strict Observance Rite, many former members joined the Illuminati, inflating its ranks. Author Melanson also noted, "Both Landgrave Karl von Hessen-Kassel and the Duke Ferdinand of Brunswick, the two heads of the Strict Observance and indeed German Freemasonry as a whole, were recruited into the Illuminati soon after; and it was because of the contacts (and good impression) made at the Congress of Wilhelmsbad that the Illuminati truly became a formidable power throughout Europe."

Although Weishaupt was absent, Knigge and Ditfurth were most effective representing the Illuminati. Knigge, under his code name "Philo," had been traveling across Germany preaching the reformation of Freemasonry. At Wilhelmsbad, with the authority of Weishaupt backing him, Knigge was able to enroll into the Illuminati a number of officials, including magistrates, scientists, clergy, academics, and ministers of state.

Although Knigge and Weishaupt later quarreled and parted ways, the baron proved instrumental in merging the Illuminati with the higher degrees of Freemasonry.

According to author William T. Still, the same year as the Wilhelmsbad Congress, "the headquarters of Illuminized Freemasonry was moved to Frankfurt, the stronghold of German finance under the control of the Rothschilds." He added, "For the first time, Jews were admitted into the Order. Previously, Jews had only been admitted to a division of the Order called 'the small and constant Sanhedrin of Europe.'"

In his book *Jews and Freemasonry in Europe*, Jacob Katz wrote that the founders of the Frankfurt Lodge of Freemasonry included Frankfurt Rabbi Zvi Hirsch Kalischer, Rothschild chief clerk Sigismund Geisenheimer, and in fact all of the city's leading bankers. It was the Rothschild banking dynasty that would later fund the Rockefellers, Morgans, and Britain's Cecil Rhodes, who founded the Round Table groups, a precursor of the Council on Foreign Relations and its offshoot, The Trilateral Commission.

Although the Order of Strict Observance officially disappeared after the Wilhelmsbad Congress, authors Lynn Picknett and Clive Prince argued that the Rectified Scottish Rite accepted there was merely the Strict Observance under a different name. Mason Waite confirmed that, following the Wilhelmsbad Congress, Strict Observance was "transformed" into other rites and "Hidden Grades."

With divisive issues seemingly settled and the Illuminati safely hidden away within Freemasonry, the Congress of Wilhelmsbad proved a turning point for the Order. Anti-Illuminati author Nesta Webster in 1921 wrote: "What passed at this terrible Congress will never be known to the outside world, for even those men who have been drawn unwittingly into the movement, and now heard for the first time the real designs of the leaders, were under oath to reveal nothing."

But, in fact, one participant, the Comte de Virieu, a member of an occult masonic lodge at Lyons, may have revealed more than he should. Upon his return to Paris, Virieu was asked for details of the Wilhelmsbad Congress. Apparently a shaken man, he responded, "I do not entrust them to you.... I can only tell you is that all this is far more serious than you think. The conspiracy happening is so contrived, that it will be virtually impossible for the Monarchy and the Church to escape it."

Enlarging on Virieu's comments, journalist William T. Still wrote, "From the Frankfurt Lodge, the gigantic plan of world revolution was carried forward. The facts show that the Illuminati, and its lower house, Masonry, was a secret society within a secret society."

Exuberant with the Order's success at the Congress, Weishaupt wrote of his plans: "That we shall have a Masonic lodge of our own. That we shall regard this as our nursery garden. That to some of these Masons we shall not at once reveal that we have something more than the Masons have. That at every opportunity we shall cover ourselves with this (Masonry). All those who are not suited to the work shall remain in the Masonic Lodge and advance in that without knowing anything of the further system."

Others have voiced similar opinions. "While the Illuminati have attempted to subvert Freemasonry, it should be noted that Freemasonry per se is suspect despite the fine people who join its ranks," cautioned Rabbi Marvin S. Antelman. "Lower degree Masons have been duped into thinking that the Masonry building symbols were connected with Solomon's Temple. Many Jewish Freemasons erroneously think that there is some sort of Jewish element or tradition in Freemasonry because of this. If they knew the truth their hair would stand on end. In effect, Freemasonry supports the Islamic concepts of conquest of Judaism and its destruction as taught in the Koran, and today the Dome of the Rock is a perpetual symbol of the destruction of the Temple."

Antelman added, "While we are focusing on apostate Jewish Illuminati, it must be reiterated that the Bundist-Illuminati were predominantly of Christian birth, both among the membership and the leadership. However, they found it most suited to their ends, as the Communists or the CFR [Council on Foreign Relations] elitists of today do, to utilize the intellectual talents of these Jewish-born apostates. They were especially placed in conspicuous positions so as to insure a victory of sorts if they would not succeed—thus polarizing among the masses those who would be stupid enough to blame the Jews for Illuminism, Revolution, Bundism [a secular Jewish Socialist movement], Socialism or Communism."

Master Mason Albert Pike, in his 1871 book *Morals and Dogma of the Ancient and Accepted Scottish Rite of Freemasonry*, explained the procession from ancient knowledge to the secret societies of the modern era:

The Occult Science of the Ancient Magi was concealed under the shadows of the Ancient Mysteries: it was imperfectly

While many think that the symbolism behind Masonry refers to Solomon's Temple, others such as Rabbi Marvin S. Antelman assert that it references the Dome of the Rock (pictured) and, therefore, symbolizes the destruction of the Temple and Judaism.

revealed or rather disfigured by the Gnostics: it is guessed at under the obscurities that cover the pretended crimes of the Templars; and it is found enveloped in enigmas that seem impenetrable, in the Rites of the Highest Masonry. Magism was the Science of Abraham and Orpheus, of Confucius and Zoroaster. It was the dogmas of this Science that were engraven on the tables of stone by Enoch and Trismegistus. Moses purified and re-veiled them, for that is the meaning of the word reveal. He covered them with a new veil, when he made of the Holy Kabbalah the exclusive heritage of the people of Israel, and the inviolable Secret of its priests. The Mysteries of Thebes and Eleusis preserved among the nations some symbols of it, already altered, and the mysterious key whereof was lost among the instruments of an ever-growing superstition. Jerusalem, the murderess of her prophets, and so often prostituted to the false gods of the Syrians and Babylonians, had at length in its turn lost the Holy Word, when a Prophet announced by the Magi by the consecrated Star of Initiation [Sirius], came to rend asunder the worn veil of the old Temple, in order to give the Church a new tissue of legends and symbols, that still and ever conceal from the Profane, and ever preserves to the Elect the same truths.

However, another Masonic historian, Arthur Edward Waite, attempted to distance Freemasonry from the Illuminati by writing, "The connection of the Illuminati with the older Institution is simply that they adopted some of its Degrees and pressed them into their own service."

Likewise, Laurence Gardner, a ranking Master Mason, disparaged any connection between the Illuminati and the Masons. While acknowledging that Illuminati members "influenced the thinking of a great many people, and possibly assisted the mind-set for the French Revolution," he argued, "they never once influenced any government except against themselves."

"As for their attachment to Freemasonry," he added. "it too was non-existent. Weishaupt founded the group specifically because he was unimpressed with German Freemasonry. It is impossible to presume that, in the context of all this, the Illuminati managed to contrive a powerful New World Order, and have since been running a conspiratorial global network for the past 200 years. The Illuminati simply do not exist, neither in the top echelons of Freemasonry, nor anywhere else."

While it may be true that Freemasonry was not fully illuminized, this secretive organization certainly provided a made-to-order mechanism to promote the Illuminati agendas to the more sinister elements of European society—unrepentant Knights Templars, early-day Zionists, calculating bankers, and would be revolutionaries. Do all Masons know this sordid history? Not according to Joseph "Doc" Marquis, a former U.S. Army medic and Christian writer who claims to have once been a member of the Illuminati. Marquis wrote, "About 95 percent of all Masons haven't a clue as to what is really going on in their own lodges. Only 30th degree Masons and above may be allowed to know these secrets. Of those Masons who are 30th and above, only 5 percent of them know the full truth, because they have already been initiated into the Illuminati. Most of the time, an Illuminist will enter into the ranks of Masonry simply to continue the infiltration process. Eventually, this Illuminist will become one of the high ranking Masons and will, therefore, be able to better control the Masonic world because of his degree and power.... Truly, Freemasonry is a series of long hallways of smoke and mirrors, designed to lead all but a handful of Masons astray, and to deceive 100 percent of all Non-Masons. No organization that engages in deliberate lying can call itself Christian."

> **W**hile it may be true that Freemasonry was not fully illu-minized, this secretive organization certainly provided a made-to-order mechanism to promote the Illuminati agendas....

Venerable Masonic author Albert Pike has support-ed Marquis's claim of Masons' ignorance of their own order by writing in *Morals and Dogma*, "The Blue Degrees are but the outer court or portico of the Temple. Part of the symbols are displayed there to the Initiate, but he is intentionally misled by false interpretations. It is not intended that he shall understand them; but it is intended that he shall imagine he understands them. Their true explication is reserved for the Adepts, the Princes of Masonry.... It is well enough for the mass of those called Masons, to imagine that all is contained in the Blue Degrees; and who so attempts to undeceive them will labor in vain.... Masonry is a veritable Sphinx, buried up to the head in sands heaped round it by the ages."

Summary

Becoming disenchanted with his experience with the Freemason lodge in Munich and perhaps encouraged by his companions, such as Knigge, Zwack, and others, Weishaupt began to not only infiltrate the lodge with his philosophies but to actually change some of its rituals and traditions. While many Masons remained true to their upbringing to trust and revere both church and state, others were susceptible to the revolutionary ideals of their Illuminati brethren. They even felt allegiance to the proclaimed "invisible superiors," even though no one knew if these were hidden Jesuits, secret Illu-minati leaders, or perhaps even supernatural or non-human entities.

Controversies within the Freemasons, not the least of which were ques-tions over the order's connection to the outlawed Knights Templars or the rites being initiated by Illuminized members, resulted in the 1782 Congress of

Wilhelmsbad, a convocation of some of the most Illustrious Masons in Europe. Although Weishaupt was absent, apparently fearing arrest following the edict issued by Regent Theodore, it was here that the powerful Order of Strict Observance was discarded, as were the official references to the Templars. Illuminati members were quick to recruit into their ranks the disillusioned members of the Strict Observance rite, swelling their numbers considerably.

Knigge and other Illuminati were especially effective at the congress, recruiting many French and other delegates, including important government officials, magistrates, scientists, clergy, academics, and even ministers of state. During this time, the headquarters of Illuminized Freemasonry moved to Frankfurt, Germany, that center of finance controlled by the Rothschilds, and at last Jews were permitted to join the Freemasons within a group known as the "Small and Constant Sanhedrin of Europe." Not everyone was pleased with this secretive infusion of Illuminism within Freemasonry. One concerned French delegate, the Comte de Virieu, returned home and warned, "The conspiracy happening is so contrived, that it will be virtually impossible for the Monarchy and the Church to escape it." Weishaupt, following the congress, wrote that the Illuminati plan for world revolution was now covered by the guise of Freemasonry and that those within the lodges not privy to the plan would know nothing about it. Master Mason Albert Pike in the late 1800s outlined the plan thusly: "The Occult Science of the Ancient Magi was concealed under the shadows of the Ancient Mysteries: it was imperfectly revealed or rather disfigured by the Gnostics: it is guessed at under the obscurities that cover the pretended crimes of the Templars; and it is found enveloped in enigmas that seem impenetrable, in the Rites of the Highest Masonry." He did not mention the infusion of Illuminism, either by mistake or design, although it is clear he was referring to the ancient mysteries. Despite attempts by some Masonic writers to disassociate Freemasonry from the Illuminati, it appears quite clear that that Illuminati theology spread widely through the European lodges of the eighteenth and nineteenth centuries. Even Pike, the author of the masonic bible *Morals and Dogma*, acknowledged, "The Blue Degrees are but the outer court or portico of the Temple. Part of the symbols are displayed there to the Initiate, but he is intentionally misled by false interpretations. It is not intended that he shall understand them; but it is intended that he shall imagine he understands them. Their true explication is reserved for the Adepts, the Princes of Masonry."

Having effectively gained control over Freemasonry in Europe, the miscreants of the Illuminati turned their attention to the Church, which had become an easy target

While many Masons remained true to their upbringing to trust and revere both church and state, others were susceptible to the revolutionary ideals of their Illuminati brethren.

due to its past transgressions, tyranny, and growing spiritual discontent, thanks to the knowledge being spread by the Age of Enlightenment and the proliferation of Bibles in print since 1454. With more and more of the population reading the word of God for themselves, the priesthood was increasingly being viewed as irrelevant.

The Church

First Freemasonry, both before and after the infusion of Illuimnati theology, provided a major connection for the covert teachings of the Ancient Mysteries to the modern era. This provoked both anger and offense within the Catholic Church, which was still grappling with the Protestant Reformation begun on October 31, 1517, when Martin Luther by legend nailed his Ninety-five Theses to a cathedral door in Wittenberg, Germany.

Manly P. Hall confirmed this connection by stating, "Freemasonry is therefore more than a mere social organization a few centuries old, and can be regarded as a perpetuation of the philosophical mysteries and initiations of the ancients."

Masonic historian W. L. Wilmshurst also confirmed this link to older mysteries. He wrote, "When Christianity became a state religion and the Church a world power, the materialization of its doctrine proceeded apace and has only increased with the centuries. Instead of becoming the unifying force its leaders meant it to be, its association with 'worldly possessions' has resulted in making it a disintegrative one. Abuses led to schisms and sectarianism … whilst the Protestant communities and so-called 'free' churches have unhappily become self-severed altogether from the original tradition and their imagined liberty and independence are in fact but a captivity to ideas of their own, having no relation to the primitive gnosis and no understanding of those Mysteries which must always lie deeper than the exoteric popular religion of a given period.… Since the suppression of the Mysteries in the sixth century, their tradition and teaching have been continued in secret and under various concealments and to that continuation our present Masonic system is due."

Another secret of the Freemasons and the later Illuminati is that both groups have passed along knowledge inimical and dangerous to organized religion with its rigid structure of beliefs and traditions, all of which evolved from the Roman Catholic Church. While espousing the Christian ideals of brotherly love, charity, and truth, even Masonic authors make it clear that Freemasonry is not an adjunct to the formal Christian religions. The innermost secrets of the Order, some of which appear to be the antithesis of Christianity, have raised considerable suspicion and concern over the years, including an early church prohibition. On April 28, 1738, just one year after the Mason Andrew Michael Ramsay, called the Chevalier, publicly connected Freemasonry to the outlawed Knights Templar, Pope Clement XII issued his famous "bull," *In Eminenti*. He condemned Freemasonry as pagan and unlawful and threatened with excommunication any Catholic who joined. Some conspiracy writers still view the Masons as subversive to organized religion.

> **Author Laurence Gardner explained that to control a population, a climate of fear and trepidation must be instilled and a common enemy must be created.**

However, journalist William T. Still, after lengthy study, saw an ambivalent public view on religion at best in both Freemasonry and the Illuminati. He wrote, "Every aspect of Masonry seems to have both a good and a bad side to it—an evil interpretation and a benign interpretation. Those who wish to find a Christian interpretation in its symbols can find ample published Masonic justifications. Those who wish to show that Masonry is really a form of Deism—built for all religions and faiths—can easily do so."

Author Laurence Gardner explained that to control a population, a climate of fear and trepidation must be instilled and a common enemy must be created. "The Church has Satan or the strangely defined Antichrist but, to be effective in their mission, scaremongers must ignore the Church because it promised salvation and this would defeat their objective," he noted. "There has to be an adversary that is beyond clerical confrontation—someone or something that is so powerful at a secular level as to be insurmountable. In this regard, the name of a long defunct eighteenth century organization from Bavaria called the Illuminati has been resurrected … these emissaries of global damnation.…"

Nesta Webster, a Freemason author and critic, noted in 1924: "The truth is that Freemasonry in a generic sense is simply a system of binding men together for any given purpose, since it is obvious that allegories and symbols, like the *x* and *y* of Algebra, can be interpreted in a hundred different manners."

But Masonic authors themselves reveal that the Order is not without metaphysical thought, rather it is very much devoted to divine understanding. "Freed of limitations of creed and sect, (the Mason) stands master of all faiths," wrote Manly P. Hall. "Freemasonry … is not a creed or doctrine but a universal expression of Divine Wisdom … revealing itself through a secret hierarchy of illumined minds."

Wilmshurst, though writing in the 1920s, echoed the ideas of present-day New Agers. He wrote of "positive energy," reincarnation or regeneration of the spirit, as well as a person's "aura [the energy field surrounding the human body]," which he explained as the biblical Joseph's "coat of many colors." He even went so far as to state that "Just as our Craft organization has its higher assemblies and councils … so in the mighty system of the universal structure there are grades of higher life, hierarchies of celestial beings working and ministering … beyond our ken."

Wilmshurst stated that the "secrets" of Freemasonry deal with introspection of the human soul but that "beyond this brief reference to the subject it is inexpedient here to say more." Obviously, all Masonic secrets are not publicly available despite a wealth of published material.

One can readily see why Christian authors such as Still, Epperson, and Webster saw in both Freemasonry and the Illuminati an insidious attempt to subvert Christianity. Still claimed Masonic initiation rites "provide a system to gradually and gently realign a man's religious beliefs. Thus, a Christian is slowly encouraged to become a Deist (one who believes in no supernatural aspects of God); a Deist becomes an Atheist; an Atheist to a Satanist."

At another point, journalist Still backed away from the claim that Masons are Satanists. He stated the god of masonry is actually Lucifer, defined as "the Shining One" or the "Light Bringer." He explained the difference is that "Luciferians think they are doing good [while] Satanists know they are evil."

Anti-communist author Carr determined that those whom he saw directing the Luciferian conspiracy showed in their writings that their purpose was to enslave "all lesser human beings absolutely, physically, mentally, and spiritually, and force them to accept the Luciferian ideology by application of Satanic despotism." He added, "This being a fact, those who claim that the W. R. M. [World Revolutionary Movement] is a Jewish, Roman Catholic, Communist, Nazi, Masonic, or any other kind of conspiracy, talk utter nonsense, because evidence in [my] book will prove how the conspirators intend to destroy all forms of government and religion.

"This TRUTH [emphasis in the original] is made abundantly clear in the writings of both Adam Weishaupt and Albert Pike. They say that when the Luciferian conspiracy is finally imposed on what remains of the Human Race, the King-Despot will be served by a FEW millionaires, economists, and scientists, who have been proven to be devoted to the Luciferian Cause, assisted by sufficient soldiers and police (the United Nation's International Police?) to enforce the will of the dictator upon the masses (Goyim)," Carr explained. "All the Goyim, without exception, are to be reduced to the state of human cattle by a process of integration on an international scale. After the human race has been turned into a vast conglomeration of humanity, breeding will be limited to types and numbers considered sufficient to fill the requirements of the State (God). Artificial insemination will be used to accomplish this purpose. Less than five percent of the males, and 30 percent of the females, will be selected and used for breeding purposes."

It should be noted that while the Hebrew word *goyim* has been used as a pejorative name for non-Jews, its original meaning was simply a "nation of people." Tracey Rich, who described herself as "just a traditional, observant Jew," hosts a website called jewfaq.com. She explained, "The most commonly used word for a non-Jew is goy.... There is nothing inherently insulting about the word 'goy.' In fact, the *Torah* occasionally refers to the Jewish people using the term 'goy.'"

Masonic author and thirty-third degree master Albert Pike explained both the duplicity and fundamental belief of the Freemasons when he wrote of the Luciferian Doctrine to Masonic officials in July 1889:

> That which we must say to a crowd is—We worship a God, but it is the God that one adores without superstition. To you, Sovereign Grand Inspectors General, we say this, that you may repeat it to the Brethren of the 32nd, 31st, and 30th degrees—The Masonic Religion should be, by all of us initiates of the high degrees, maintained in the purity of the Luciferian Doctrine. If Lucifer were not God, would Adonay whose deeds prove his cruelty, perfidy and hatred of man, barbarism and repulsion for science, would Adonay and his priests, calumniate him? Yes, Lucifer is God, and unfortunately Adonay is also god. For the eternal law is that there is no light without shade, no beauty without ugliness, no white without black, for the absolute can only exist as two gods: darkness being necessary to the statue, and the brake to the locomotive. Thus, the doctrine of Satanism is a heresy; and the true and pure philosophical religion is the belief in Lucifer, the equal of Adonay; but Lucifer, God of Light and God of Good, is struggling for humanity against Adonay, the God of Darkness and Evil."

Luciferians believe God has a duel nature—the loving side Lucifer and the bad side Adonai, both equal in power but opposite in intent. This concept is symbolized by the circular yin-yang symbol of the Buddhists or the black-and-white checkerboard pattern on the floor of Masonic lodges. This belief in two separate but equal gods provides significant support to those connecting Freemasonry and Illuminism directly to the ancient Cathars of France and the earlier Gnostics, both of whom were mercilessly exterminated by the Catholic Church. Both of these sects were known dualists, those who believe in the equal power of good and evil, light and dark.

It would appear that the philosophies found within the Illuminati, like those of the Freemasons, were not just a simple God versus Satan. Even the anti-Mason author Epperson noted that Pike's book *Magnum Opus*, stated, "All have admitted two gods with different occupations, one making the good and the other the evil found in nature. The former has been styled 'God,' and the latter 'Demon.' The Persians or Zoroaster named the former Ormuzd and the latter Ahriman; of whom they said one was of the nature of Light, and the other that of Darkness. The Egyptians called the former Osiris, and the latter Typhon, his eternal enemy."

Some anti-Masonic writers saw in the Masonic symbols of ancient Egypt a return to the worship of the pagan Sun God. However, Pike, in his book *Morals and Dogma of the Ancient and Accepted Scottish Rite of Freemasonry*, intended only for the inner core of Masonry, made it clear that

Confederate general, journalist, and Sovereign Grand Commander Albert Pike declared that there can only be two gods: one black and one white, which is the Luciferian doctrine.

worship of the sun was an adulteration of an earlier belief. "[T]housands of years ago, men worshipped the sun.... Originally they looked beyond the orb [our solar system's sun] to the invisible God.... The worship of the Sun [the invisible God] became the basis of all of the religions of antiquity," he wrote.

Egyptian mythology, which was centered on sun worship, has obvious connections between the Masonic myth of Hiram Abiff (known as the Widow's son), the chief architect of King Solomon's Temple, and of the Egyptian god Osiris. Like the story of Osiris, Abiff is killed and his body hidden away. According to Pike, the ancients "personified the Sun, and worshipped him under the name Osiris.... The moon became Isis, the wife of Osiris, and Winter, as well as the desert or ocean into which the Sun descended, became Typhon, the Spirit or Principle of Evil, warring against and destroying Osiris." Osiris has been connected to the Sumerian Anunnaki god Enki.

The Illuminati also appropriated the Masonic view of a supreme creative being, referred to as the Great Architect of the Universe (G.A.O.T.U.) Master Mason Pike described humankind's place in all this: "Satan created and governs the visible world. But the soul of man emanated from God, and is the same substance with God. Seduced by the evil spirits, it passes through various bodies, until, purified and reformed, it rises to God and is strengthened by His light. The powers of evil hold mankind in pledge; and to redeem this

A stained glass window at St. John's Church in Chester, England, depicts the figure of Hiram Abiff, the architect of Solomon's Temple.

pledge, the Savior, Christ the Redeemer, came and died upon the cross of expiation, thus discharging the written obligation."

Many authors draw a distinction between the celestial "sun" and the "Sun" God which, they say, is the bringer of light. The gift of light—light usually being interpreted as knowledge—is greatly venerated in Masonic rituals under the name Lucifer. Interestingly enough, the appellation "Morning Star" and "Bringer of Light" were at times applied to Jesus.

According to lecturer and psychic David Wilcock, "The secret beliefs of the Illuminati included the idea that there is a 'Great Architect' of the Universe, divided into two polarities—the Christian God, which they called Adonay, and Lucifer. In this system, Lucifer is not seen as "the bad guy"—merely one of the two Divine aspects of the Great Architect. The idea of Lucifer falling and becoming "Satan" is rejected within the inner teachings of this philosophy. In the Bible, Lucifer originally appears as the highest and brightest angel of all. Illuminists believe Lucifer was kicked out because the Christian God was actually the bad guy. Their arguments were founded on the Church's suppression of freedom, sexuality and scientific inquiry—wisdom. The Church was the government back then, and they demanded obedience."

The cabalists, on the other hand, believed the name of Satan was simply the name Yahveh reversed and that the Devil is not a dark god but only the personification of atheism, the absence of God. Others believe that God represents a force of liberty or free will, which while created for good, can be used for evil.

So we find that one inner Masonic secret echoes the belief of the ancient Gnostics, Cathars, and Cabalists, namely that there is only one great creative cosmic God referred to in Masonic literature as the Great Architect of the Universe, but that there may be two opposing aspects to this deity. A hidden aspect of this conviction is that of belief in ancient "gods," powerful non-human beings found in the Hebrew Bible and even earlier Babylonian and Sumerian legends who brought humans civilization and science. Researchers of the ancient astronaut theory see the conflict between Adonay and Lucifer as possibly representing the enmity between the Anunnaki commanders and step-brothers Enlil and Enki.

Inner-core Illuminati understood scientific principles as well as metaphysical ones as exemplified by their veneration of the collection of Greek writings called *Hermes Trismegistus* by Plato's disciples. These writings were named after the Greek god Hermes, who established alchemy and geometry, and to the Greek philosopher Pythagoras. Both Pythagoras, who stated the earth moved around the sun, and the Hermetic writings were said to have utilized secret "science" that survived Noah's Flood. Hermes, deified as Thoth by the Egyptians and Ninurta by the Sumerians and thought to have intimate knowledge of the gods and the stars, voiced the principle "As above, so below." This indicated a knowledge of universal unity, comparing favorably with Albert Einstein's "Unified Field Theory." "From the smallest cell to the widest expanse of the galaxies, a repetitive geometric law prevails and this was understood from the very earliest of times," explained author Laurence Gardner.

Alchemy, known as the "Hermetic science," along with Freemasonry and the Illuminati, contains both Hermetic branches and Hermetic rites. The mythical and magical practice of alchemy was passed down from the Egyptians. From philosophy and hermeticism to sacred geometry and cosmology, these philosophies permeated the secret societies.

"There can be no doubt that in some of what are called the High Degrees [in Illuminism and Freemasonry] there is a very palpable infusion of a Hermetic element. This cannot be denied," wrote Masonic historian Mackey. Such philosophy also may be found in the competitive society of the Rosicrucians.

A careful study will find that all religions are a collection of truths, legends, parables teaching morality, both real and imagined history, philosophies, and admonitions for living a happy and productive life. But the preponderance of these cautionary tales can be traced back to the mythologies of the Romans, Greeks, Egyptians, and Sumerians, all of whom are connected to the original accounts of the Anunnaki who came from the heavens to the Earth.

After they withdrew from sight of humans, their memory founded the basis for the earliest religions, the basic beliefs of which—gather to worship, tithe to the church, care for the Earth, proselytize, and primarily obey church dogma—are still with us today.

Summary

During the time of the Bavarian Illuminati, the Roman Catholic Church was still powerful, exerting its influence by lending money and spiritual largess to European royalty as well as keeping a close eye on the daily lives of the peasants through the confessional system of the priests, which proved to be sort of an early-day National Security Agency.

Deep within the Church were hidden many of the secrets of the ancients handed down through the centuries, first by word of mouth, then by clay tablets, and finally by passages written down on scrolls and papyrus. Much of the information contained in these writings had been kept secret from the public, thought to be too ignorant to understand, much less to understand and accept, their messages.

After becoming a world religion following the edict of the Roman Emperor Constantine, the priesthood and clerical hierarchy grew jealously possessive of both their knowledge and exalted position within society. Long before the arrival of the Illuminati, Pope Clement XII in 1738 issued a papal decree condemning Freemasonry as an unlawful pagan cult and forbade Catholics from joining the order. This edict remained in effect until the early 1983 when Pope John Paul II issued a Code of Canon Law that, while still voicing opposition to members joining the Masons, failed to mention the Freemasons specifically but only called for the excommunication of apostates and heretics. While all Masons admit to recognizing a Great Architect of the Universe, the interpretations of Masonic symbols and lore can be used to support the idea that Masons support the Christian God or they pay homage to Lucifer, the Bringer of Light. A Masonic historian, Manly P. Hall, described Freemasonry simply as "not a creed or doctrine but a universal expression of Divine Wisdom … revealing itself through a secret hierarchy of illumined minds."

However, Mason leader Pike clearly stated a dualist belief within Freemasonry when he wrote, "Yes, Lucifer is God, and unfortunately Adonay is also god. For the eternal law is that there is no light without shade, no beauty without ugliness, no white without black, for the absolute can only exist as two gods: darkness being necessary to the statue, and the brake to the locomotive."

Critics have claimed the order is designed to gradually turn religious belief in God into Deism, then into atheism and ultimately into becoming a Satanist. Still others contend that many Masons are followers of Lucifer, meaning "the Light Bringer" or in the King James version a "Shining One." After all, one cannot experience light without dark, or good without evil as a comparison. Many disavow the oft-stated belief that Lucifer is the same as the Devil or Satan. Journalist William T. Still explained the difference in that Luciferians think they are doing good whereas Satanists know they are practicing evil. Secret societies then are either expressing a belief in a dual god or they surreptitiously understand that the deity of the Old Testament actually referred to separate beings—the vengeful and jealous god (the Anunnaki Enlil?) and the loving merciful god (Enki?). Such a concept fits well with the known references and imagery found within Freemasonry. And none of this misinterpretation precludes the existence of one omnipotent all-knowing universal creative force that fits the perception of God within a growing number of people today.

METHODOLOY

The methods employed by the Illuminati to keep members in line and silent were varied but most effective.

One strategy was to publicly present an image of the Illuminati as a charitable and philanthropic organization. Such an image drew many academics and clergy to the Order, as many were convinced that the objective of the Order was a Christian effort to unify all society into one big happy family. Such a goal has been advocated by many movements, from National Socialism (Nazis) to communist socialism.

Weishaupt explained, "These [government] powers are despots when they do not conduct themselves by [the Order's] principles; and it is therefore our duty to surround them with its members, so that the profane [non-illuminated persons] may have no access to them. Thus we are able most powerfully to promote [the Order's] interests. If any person is more disposed to listen to Princes than to the Order, he is not fit for it, and must rise no higher. We must do our utmost to procure the advancement of Illuminati into all important civil offices."

Author McIlhany noted, "Many of these [important offices] were ministers, lawyers, doctors, and even a few princes. None were members of the lower classes, the agricultural working masses, or the serfs. The influence of the Order on German education and the German clergy was devastating. By 1800 many German ministers no longer believed the most basic tenets of Christian doctrine. They had been converted to the worship of 'reason.'"

Illuminati critic Nesta Webster saw an insidious scheme in the recruitment of new members for the Order. "Weishaupt's followers were enlisted by the most subtle methods of deception and led on towards a goal entirely unknown to them," noted Webster. "It is this that … constitutes the whole difference between honest and dishonest secret societies."

"The art of illuminism lay in enlisting dupes as well as adepts and by encouraging dreams of honest visionaries or the schemes of fanatics; By flattering the vanity of ambitious egotists; By working on unbalanced brains or by playing such passions as greed and power to make men of totally divergent aims serve the secret purpose of the sect. People with money were welcomed but kept oblivious of actual secrets. The purpose is to win power and riches. To undermine secular or religious government and attain the masters of the world," she wrote.

E. Michael Jones is a Catholic-reared professor at St. Mary's College of Notre Dame, who was dismissed because of his adverse views of the school's support of pro-choice, secularism, and feminism. Today the editor of *Culture Wars* magazine, Jones made this comment regarding what he sees as the result of Illuminati practices:

> [M]uch as the Illuminatist papers called for the toppling of the throne and altar, the significance of Illuminism did not lie in exhortation. Rather … Illuminism seemed to propose an especially effective system which would bring about these ends. Weishaupt had not just issued a manifesto calling for revolution, he had created a system of control that would create disciplined cells which would do the bidding of their revolutionary masters often, it seemed, without the slightest inkling that they were being ordered to do so. Weishaupt's intentions were clearly revolutionary, but the shocking thing about the Illuminati was the mechanism whereby he put those intentions into effect by controlling the secret society members' minds. Weishaupt had created an instrument of psychic control which was effective precisely because it did not derive from the mechanistic philosophy of the Enlightenment.

In his book, Jones claimed the development of communication technologies, reproduction, and psychic control, including psychotherapy, behaviorism, advertising, sensitivity training, pornography, and plain old blackmail, has "allowed the Enlightenment and its heirs to turn [Saint] Augustine's insight on its head and create masters out of men's vices." St. Augustine was an early Christian theologian who separated the act of love (from God) from lust (materialism).

So it is worthwhile to consider the structure of the Bavarian Illuminati, as it may still be in use today.

Structure

Weishaupt created an organizational structure that guaranteed him total control over the Order. It was pyramidal organization with himself at the top. Under him were two immediate subordinates, who in turn had two men under them. And on it went. At any given time, all Illuminati members could know—and identify if questioned—only two others. Weishaupt described his system in a letter to Zwack. He said, "Immediately under me, I have two [subordinates] into whom I infuse my whole spirit; these two in turn correspond with two others, and so on. In this manner, and with the simplest means possible, I will inflame a

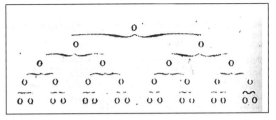

Weishaupt's drawing in a letter to Zwack, showing how the Bavarian Illuminati could be organized. Members would only know the names of those near them in the chart.

thousand men into action. Similarly, this is the same method by which secret societies necessarily operate within the political sphere." He included the diagram shown on this page to illustrate the organization.

No member, except for a handful of the Areopagites immediately below Weishaupt, knew the names of others. These cells were kept separate with leaders knowing only the names of their immediate superior and their subordinates. This tactic has been seen in modern times within the structure of the communist cells operating outside the old Soviet Union and today's terrorists. To add to the secrecy, code names were used in all correspondence. To his fellow Illuminati, Weishaupt was known by his code name "Spartacus," in honor of the slave who led a bloody revolt against the Romans in 73 B.C.E. Other code names all came from classical literature or mythology, such as Alexander, Cato, Brutus, Pythagoras, Socrates, Hannibal, Hercules, Adonis, Sulla, Odin, Confucius, and Osiris. Undoubtedly, the names of the Sumerian Anunnaki gods would have been also used had they had been known in Weishaupt's time. The Sumerian tablets and friezes were not discovered and translated until the mid-nineteenth century. Even cities and locations had code names. For example, Vienna's code name was "Rome," Austria's was "Egypt," Frankfurt am Main's was "Thebes," Munichs was "Athens," and France's was "Illyria."

Illuminati recruiters especially sought educated young men between the ages of eighteen and thirty, from wealthy and well-connected families.

The few members who proved especially dedicated to the Order were awarded all the material and sensual benefits available, for as Weishaupt once wrote, "the power of the Order must be turned to the advantage of its members. All must be assisted. They must be preferred to all persons otherwise of equal merit. Money, services, honor, goods, and blood must be expended for the fully proved Brethren."

Despite his enmity toward the Jesuits, Weishaupt's pyramidal structure for the Order was largely based on the Jesuit organizational configuration. Weishaupt then added the structures of the Freemasons to this Jesuit system to include a similar system of degrees, esoteric instruction, and secret methods of recognition. In Freemasonry, initiates find three basic Lodges—the Blue Lodge, which is divided into three stages or degrees; the York Rite, composed of ten more degrees; and the Scottish Rite with a total of thirty-two degrees. The thirty-third degree represents the human head atop the thirty-three vertebrae of the back. This is the highest publicly known degree. Masonic literature, however, makes clear that only those initiates who progress beyond thirty-three-degree status are educated in the group's true goals and secrets.

In 1827, it was disclosed in Captain Morgan's book *Illustrations of Masonry, by One of the Fraternity Who Has Devoted Thirty Years to the Subject* that the initiate into the First Degree of the Blue Lodge pledged to "binding myself under no less penalty than to have my throat cut across, my tongue torn out by the roots, and my body buried in the rough sands of the sea at low-water mark, where the tide ebbs and flows twice in 24 hours...." The penalties in higher degrees grew progressively more gruesome.

Likewise, the structure of the Illuminati was broken into three primary classes—the Nursery, the Masonry, and the Mysteries. Any candidate deemed unsuitable for higher degrees were termed *Sta Bene* (Stand Well) and were given dead-end assignments that precluded any further advancement.

> The candidate knew only the name of his recruiter, called an Insinuator, and was totally unaware of Order spies, called Scrutators, whose job was to constantly surveil new members.

The demeaning-sounding Nursery class was divided into four degrees—Preparation, Novice, Minerval, and Illuminatus Minor. The first three degrees were awarded with no particular regard for any specific order. Preparation was simply the initial stage of recruiting a new member, with particular emphasis on determining the initiate's views on the church and state. The candidate knew only the name of his recruiter, called an Insinuator, and was totally unaware of Order spies, called Scrutators, whose job was to constantly surveil new members. As he moved into the Novice stage, the initiate was required to sign a non-disclosure agreement called "Silentio" and given a notebook in which he was expected to write down his observations of all he saw and felt during his daily experiences. According to the anti-Illuminati author Abbé Augustin Barruel, the Novice, whose probationary period could last from one to three years, depending on his age, was instructed to record the weaknesses, prejudices, actions, financial status, interests, and passions of everyone he met, including his own family, friends, and even strangers. As any true spy, he was told to write down his impressions of any local or national event or activity. He also was required to pen a history of his immediate superior, usually his recruiter, called a "Brother Insinuator," in hopes he would see him as a role model to aid in understanding what was expected of him as a member of the Order. He further was to delve into the lives and writings of historical authors, philosophers, and mythological heroes to better understand the references in Illuminati documents.

Professor Vernon L. Stauffer acknowledged: "An important part of the responsibility of the Novice consisted in the drawing-up of a detailed report (for the archives of the Order), containing complete information concerning his family and his personal career, covering such remote items as the titles of the books he possessed, the names of his personal enemies and the occasion of their enmity, his own strong and weak points of character, the dominant passions of his parents, the names of their parents and intimates. Monthly reports were also required, covering the benefits the recruit had received from and the services he had rendered to the Order." Such sharing of intimate knowledge was later adopted by the Skull & Bones Society.

Novices were also conditioned to obedience. They were to take orders from their superiors without question. They were also instructed to keep all Order activities from the "profane," members of the secular population unknowing and uncaring of religious and spiritual matters. Novices who met the approval of their Brother Insinuator moved on to become a Minerval. According to the Masonic Dictionary, within the Illuminati, "Anyone otherwise qualified could be received into the Degree of Novice at the age of eighteen; and after a probation of not less than a year he was admitted to the Second and Third Degrees, and so on to the advanced Degrees; though but few reached the Ninth and Tenth Degrees, in which the inmost secret designs of the Order were contained, and, in fact, it is said that these last Degrees were never thoroughly worked up."

"The ceremony of initiation through which the Novice passed into the grade Minerval was expected to disabuse the mind of the candidate of any lingering suspicion that the order had as its supreme object the subjugation of the rich and powerful, or the overthrow of civil and ecclesi-

A 1788 pamphlet published by the Bavarian Illuminati includes the owl of Minerva symbol, which was named after the Roman goddess of wisdom.

astical government," wrote Stauffer. "It also pledged the candidate to be useful to humanity; to maintain a silence eternal, a fidelity inviolable, and an obedience implicit with respect to all the superiors and rules of the order; and to sacrifice all personal interests to those of the society."

Minervals were named after Minerva, the Roman goddess of wisdom, symbolized by the Minerval Owl. According to author Melanson, "The class of Minerval was a relatively low rank in the scheme of things. However, it was the soul of the Order, and functioned as a sort of assembly line for recruits. Candidates advanced from Novice to the Minerval degree, where they were properly vetted, scrutinized, and indoctrinated.... The Minerval Superior—a Minor or Major Illuminatus—was given the code: *Nosce te ipsum; Nosce alios* [Know thyself; Know others]."

Minervals who proved themselves prepared for a deeper commitment to the Order advanced to the rank of Illuminatus Minor. Here they were instructed that the only obstruction to the Order's goal of universal happiness was the power being held by the Church along with governments of the world. This meant, of course, that leaders of these institutions had to be either brought under the control of the Order or destroyed. Should this prospect frighten or horrify the fledgling Illuminatus Minor, he was kept from advancing until his ethics could be modified. As Weishaupt wrote in a letter to Zwack in 1778, "We cannot use people as they are, but begin by making them over."

Barruel wrote that during the meetings of Minerval initiates, they were required to read a wide variety of classic works by men such as Seneca, Marcus Aurelius, and Confucius. The fact that this schooling included the Bible infuriated Barruel, who argued this would "make the pupils view the Bible in a similar light with the works of the pagan philosophers." According to Barruel, the Minervals were encouraged to donate books to their assemblies, purchase books from store and courts and even "secretly stealing such books or manuscripts, and putting them into possession of the sect."

"They are called the Brethren of Minerva, and are under the direction of the Major or Minor Illuminatees," wrote Barruel, who described a Minerval gathering. "The academy, properly so called, is composed of ten, twelve, and sometimes fifteen Minervals, under the direction and tuition of a Major Illuminatus. In the calendar of the sect, the days on which the academy meets are called *Holy*, and its sittings are generally held twice a month, always on the full moon. The place where they meet is called, in their language, *a Church* [emphasis in the original]. It must always be preceded by an antechamber, with a strong door armed with bolts, which is to be shut during the time of the meeting; and the whole apartment is to be so disposed, that it shall be impossible for intruders either to see or hear anything that is going forward."

The Minerval initiation was always conducted at night when the candidate was placed by himself in a dark room to meditate on his fate. Within the light from three lanterns, representing the three major Illuminati grades, the candidate pledged complete loyalty to the Order, blind obedience to his superiors, and complete silence as to his knowledge of the Illuminati, agreeing to whatever punishment the Order might impose upon his breaking this silence. Only then would the candidate, now called a "Disciple of Minerva," be given the phrase needed to join in the Minerval assemblies and academies—"Away, away, you profane." In the final stage of the Nursery grade, the Illuminatus Minor, the candidate was gradually introduced to the structure and objectives of the Order. It was in this degree, also called Illuminatus Master, that the Nursery member received the degree's password, hand grip, and sign of recognition along with a medallion. The initiate was urged to closely watch and report on his fellow members becoming snitches called Scrutators. Those who did well in this capacity could be moved up to the degree of Illuminatus Major.

> **The Minerval initiation was always conducted at night when the candidate was placed by himself in a dark room to meditate on his fate.**

The Masonry class was divided into two parts with a total of five degrees—Symbolic, comprising Apprentice, Fellow Craft, Master Mason, and Illuminatus Major; and Scots, made up of the Illuminatus *Dirigens*, or Scottish Knights.

Moving into the Symbolic degrees, the candidate was initiated in a darkened room all covered in black material with participants dressed in black. It was here he was introduced to the equivalent of Masonic degrees. Here he was told the Illuminati secretly controlled all Masonic lodges. He also was introduced to an activity that extended their role as Scrutators. Called "Know others," this required the member to describe in detail his fellow members, right down to their physical characteristics, facial features, expressions, education, use of language, emotions, and even sleeping habits.

In the Illuminatus Major degree, the member was required to write down a complete biographical sketch of himself, called a *Pensum*, which was compared with the views of both his Brother Insinuator as well as his fellow initiates. If his autobiographical notes matched well with the other data, the initiate moved to a higher degree where he began to learn the deeper secrets of the Order. If it did not match, this was another step in weeding out undesirable candidates. Oddly, the Illuminatus Major was required to learn how to write with both hands.

The Illuminatus Major's password was *Nosce te ipsum* (Know thyself). After the Symbolic degrees came the Scottish Knight degree, encompassing Illuminatus *Dirigens* or Scottish Knights, where administrators for the Order were developed. These carefully vetted men were put in charge of the Illuminized Masonic lodges, thus creating a secret society with a secret society.

Initiated in rooms decorated in green, the Illuminati *Dirigens* initiation was sometimes followed by a reception of the *Dirigens* known as Agape.

The final grade of Mysteries was also divided into two parts with four degrees—Lesser Mysteries with Prince and Priest degrees and Greater Mysteries composed of the Magus and King degrees. The Lesser Mysteries degree of Prince was reserved for top administrators of the Order. During initiation, their hands were tied, signifying the bondage of state and church tyranny. After professing that he wanted to be a free man, the candidate was led into the main initiation room where he received the trappings of his degree—a uniform, a red cap representing liberty, an olive branch, a shepherd's crook, and a crown.

> **D**uring their initiation their hands were tied, signifying the bondage of state and church tyranny.

The password for a Prince was *Redemptio* (Redemption). The Priests, who met once a year in what was known as a Synod, were driven about blindfolded in a carriage to keep the location of their initiation secret. The ritual was presided over by a chief priest called a Decanus. Illuminati Priests were given the choice of directing one of these sciences—physics, medicine, mathematics, natural history, politics, the arts, or the occult sciences. Priests also were taught to spurn material possessions and that owning property led to inequality and the loss of freedom. They were taught that great wealth could only be obtained at the expense of others. Candidates for the priesthood were presented with a choice of riches, including gold, jewelry, a sword, a crown, or a coarse woolen robe. If he chose the robe, he would advance. The Priest's code word was "I-N-R-I," which represented *Iesus Nazarenus Rex Iudaeorum* ("Jesus King of the Jews").

The Mysteries Grade was divided in the Lesser Mysteries and the Greater Mysteries. These degrees were secret even from other Order members and officiated by Weishaupt personally. Only a very few members ever reached these degrees, which were derived from the knowledge of the Greek and Egyptian Mystery Schools as well as the Eleusinian Mysteries. It was here the Magus member finally learned some of the most intimate Illuminati secrets, undoubtedly those passed down from the ancient gods.

A candidate with his absolute devotion to the Order proven was allowed to enter the top-level circle of initiates as a Magus, ranked only below the position of King held by Weishaupt. "By now, all conventional idealism had been purged from the candidate and he was told about the real objectives of the Order: rule of the world, to be accomplished after the destruction of all existing governments and religions. He was now required to take an oath which bound his every thought and action, and his fate, to the administration of his superiors in the Order," explained author McIlhany.

The role of Illuminati Rex, or King, was reserved only for Weishaupt, whose first law and watchword for his Illuminati was secrecy. In one 1794 letter to a fellow Illuminatus, Weishaupt stated, "The great strength of our Order lies in its concealment. Let it never appear in any place in its own name, but always covered by another name, and another occupation. None is fitter than the three lower degrees of Freemasonry; the public is accustom[ed] to it, expect little from it, and therefore takes little notice of it. Next to this, the form of a learned or literary society [the Thule Society] is best suited to our purpose.... By establishing reading societies and subscription libraries … we may turn the public mind which way we will. In like manner we must try to obtain an influence in … all offices which have any effect, either in forming, or in managing, or even in directing the mind of man."

> **W**eishaupt not only set out to deceive the public, but he reminded his top leaders they should hide their true intentions from their own initiates....

Weishaupt not only set out to deceive the public, but he reminded his top leaders they should hide their true intentions from their own initiates by "speaking sometimes in one way, sometimes in another, so that one's real purpose should remain impenetrable to one's inferiors."

Even correspondence between Order members was to be coded. Weishaupt stated, "… he [the member] must make himself master of that cypher, which is to serve him until initiated into the higher degrees, when he will be entrusted with the hieroglyphics of the Order."

In September 1785, the defecting academics, Utzschneider, Grünberger, and Cosandey, in a joint deposition for Duke Theodore, described the inner working of the Illuminati thusly:

> The object of the first degrees of Illuminism is at once to train their young men, and to be informed of everything that is going forward by a system of espionage. The Superiors aim at procuring from their inferiors diplomatic acts, documents, and original writings. With pleasure they see them commit any treasons or treacherous acts, because they not only turn the secrets betrayed to their own advantage, but thereby have it in their power to keep the traitors in a perpetual dread, lest, if they ever showed any signs of stubbornness, their malefactions should be made known.—*Oderint dum metuant* [Detest fate], let them hate, provided they fear, is the principle of their government.
>
> The Illuminees from these first degrees are educated in the following principles:

I. The Illuminee who wishes to rise to the highest degree must be free from all religion; for a *religionist* (as they call every man who has any religion) will never be admitted to the highest degrees."

II. The *Patet Exitus*, or the doctrine on Suicide, is expressed in the same terms as in the preceding deposition.

III. *The end sanctifies the means* [emphasis added]. The welfare of the Order will be a justification for calumnies, poisonings, assassinations, perjuries, treasons, rebellions; in short, for all that the prejudices of men lead them to call crimes.

IV. One must be more submissive to the Superiors of Illuminism, than to the sovereigns or magistrates who govern the people; and he that gives the preference to sovereigns or governors of the people is useless to us. Honor, life, and fortune, all are to be sacrificed to the Superiors. The governors of nations are despots when they are not directed by us. They can have no authority over us, who are free men.

V. The love of one's prince and of one's country are incompatible with views of an immense extent, with the ultimate ends of the

Working behind the scenes to stir up trouble in the world, the Illuminati have taken credit for causing or helping to cause wars and revolts such as the French Revolution (*Run on the Tuileries* by Jean Duplessis-Bertaux, 1793).

Order, and one must glow with ardor for the attainment of that end.

The Superiors of Illuminism are to be looked upon as the most perfect and the most enlightened of men; no doubts are to be entertained even of their infallibility.

It is in these moral and political principles that the Illuminees are educated in the lower degrees; and ... later admitted to the higher degrees.

They use every possible artifice to get the different post-offices in all countries entrusted to the care of their adepts only. They also boast that they are in possession of the secret of opening and reclosing letters without the circumstance being perceived.

"Deception and blackmail were the Order's ways to reach its aims, Weishaupt had advised his closest Illuminati brothers," noted the *Biblioteca Pleyades* ("Library of Pleyades"), a website devoted to the "many scientists, scholars, philosophers and seekers of truth who confirm it again and again ... that we are not alone in the universe, that beings from other planets and galaxies as well as from other dimensions are and always have been in contact with Humanity, sharing our True Story, as well as making our present-day reality."

In notes confiscated from Sandersdorf Castle (owned by an Illuminati leader named Baron Dominikus de Bassus in Germany), Weishaupt wrote, "Devote yourselves to the art of deception, the art of disguising yourselves, of masking yourselves, spying on others and perceiving their innermost thoughts." To make sure that the secrets of the Order were not leaked, Weishaupt created a secret police corps within the Order that he called the "insinuating brothers." These worked in the same manner as the Bolshevik's Cheka and its successors: denunciation, provocation, blackmail and terrorism. "The 'insinuating brothers' acted with full force during the reign of terror which is called the Great French Revolution, which was largely the work of Illuminati agents," according to one website.

Much like the Jesuits, whose structure Weishaupt tried to emulate, the Illuminati Order was operated along strict and military lines. Members were expected to surrender their individual will and thoughts upon the promise of ancient wisdom if they attained higher grades and ranks. The higher they rose in the initiations, the more secrets would be imparted to them.

Knowledge within the Illuminati was strictly on a "need-to-know" basis and members were exhorted to spy on one another, as well as report their experiences outside the Order. They were required to make sealed reports on a regular basis to their immediate superior. These reports flowed upward to Weishaupt and his closest confidants.

Symbology

Symbols are material things—whether drawings, icons, objects, or nonfigurative marks—that represent something else, often an abstract idea. Symbols, such as the American eagle, the Nazi swastika, the dollar sign, and the various icons that characterize commercial products have been utilized for centuries to convey messages to the public. Symbols can be extremely effective in communicating ideas.

The Illuminati early on learned to use symbols to convey information secretly to its members. Many of the symbols used by the Order and other secret societies can be traced back through the Knights Templar, Assassins, and the Mystery Schools of Greece and Egypt to the Babylon Mystery School, which reportedly held secrets remembered from the ancient Anunnaki. Examples of this symbolism include the Maltese Cross, once used to represent the god Baal, then used by the Christian Templars; the double-headed eagle, used by the ancient Egyptians, Knights Templars, and Romans, on into Freemasonry and the Illuminati; and the Caduceus, a serpent-entwined staff used by the Sumerians and still used as the symbol of physicians. It should be noted that the eagle is also prominently found on the crest of the Rothschild family as well as being the national bird of the United States.

One key symbol of the Illuminati is the All-Seeing Eye of Horus, also known as the Eye of the sun god Ra, a symbol seen repeatedly since the days of the Pharaohs. It is an ancient Egyptian symbol of royal power, good health, sacrifice, healing, restoration, and protection and refers to both Horus, god of the sky and kingship, and Osiris, god of life, death, and resurrection.

According to Isaac Weishaupt ("which obviously isn't my real name. I use the moniker because this is my hobby; not my full time job. I'm a working professional and need to keep the anonymity"), who operates the website Illuminatiwatcher.com, "… one of the most ancient interpretations of the eye and the concept of a deity watching over us [is] the idea of an omnipresent

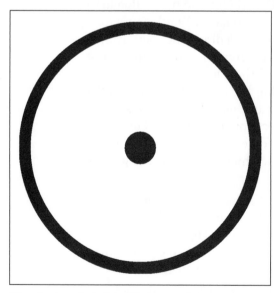

The chief symbol of the Illuminati, the secret cypher used in all communications between members, was a dot within a circle. This apparently was meant to signify the sun radiating knowledge, or illumination, to outer circles.

being watching over us as referenced in the Bible several times (1 Peter 3:12 and Proverbs 22:12) and this also includes the Biblical reference to The Watchers, aka the Nephilim. These were the hybrid offspring of extraterrestrials who were called the 'sons of God' in Genesis and the daughters of men at the time on Earth…. The Nephilim were said to be giants, approximately 300 cubits, or 450 feet tall, based on the translation of the Hebrew Bible and the Book of Enoch."

According to Masonic author Albert Mackey, "[The] all-seeing eye [is] an important symbol of the Supreme Being, borrowed by the Freemasons from the nations of antiquity. Both the Hebrews and the Egyptians appear to have derived its use from the natural inclination of figurative minds to select an organ as the symbol of the function which it is intended…. On the same principle, the open eye was selected as the symbol of watchfulness, and the eye of God as the symbol of Divine watchfulness and care of the universe."

Many students of the occult believe the Eye of Horus actually refers to the pineal gland or the Third Eye, located in the center of the forehead. The third eye, a conceptual symbol used by the ancient Egyptians and Hindus in reference to the pineal gland, is believed to be the gateway to higher consciousness and enlightenment. The third eye has often been associated with religious visions, clairvoyance (remote viewing), the ability to observe chakras (thought by some to be the seven centers of spiritual power within the human body) and auras, precognition, and out-of-body experiences. In fact, the one regulator of consciousness in the brain, the thalamus, looks amazingly like the ancient symbol of the Eye of Horus.

One self-proclaimed modern Illuminati defector known only as Svali claims, "The pyramid and the 'eye of Horus' on the back of the dollar bill are Illuminati symbology. The pyramid is an ancient form based on the holiness of the number three to the ancient mystery religions (it, not six, is considered the most spiritual number), and a pyramid was a structure used specifically to call up the demonic, or occult, a point of psychic activity.

"The eye is the all seeing eye of Horus (remember the emphasis on Egyptian magical religious practices? The book of the undead, etc.?) and the fact that no one can escape his magical reach. This eye is considered a demonic eye in the group, or the eye of the deity, and in Illuminati mythology is either open or closed, depending upon the spiritual time of year and the state of the person psychically. Young children are given

The Eye of Horus was an Egyptian symbol of power, protection, and good health.

'psychic surgery' where the eye is placed inside, and they are told that Horus will snatch their soul if they ever try to leave, or if they tell, or that the eye will explode. The symbol on the dollar is reinforcement for every Illuminati child who sees one, and the reminder that they are being watched."

Another major Illuminati symbol is the Owl of Minerva (see the chapter on "The Church"). An original insignia of the Bavarian Illuminati, the Owl of Minerva symbolized wisdom and was perched on top of an opened book. The Minerval owl is found on an Illuminati pamphlet printed around 1776, the year of the Order's formation. The owl was prominent in the lower degrees of the Order and represented the Roman goddess Minerva, the Greek goddess Athena, known to the Egyptians as Isis and to the Sumerians as Ninhursag. Illuminati initiates were called Brethren of Minerval and met in Minerval Assemblies.

Some ardent conspiracy researchers even claim that the Minerval owl can be found hidden in the details of a dollar bill. They see this as proof that some form of the Illuminati is still active and powerful enough to place its symbols on U.S. currency.

Some even detect the outline of the Minerval owl in overhead views of the nation's Capitol.

Researchers wonder if it is sheer coincidence that the Minerval owl, symbol of the Illuminati, is also the symbol of the mysterious and secretive Bohemian Club of San Francisco, which sponsors the yearly gatherings at Bohemian Grove, a nearby 2,700-acre campground. Here some of the most powerful and prominent men (no permanent women members since its inception in 1872) in the world gather every July to engage in rituals involving pageantry, pyrotechnics, and exotic costumes. Besides the owl, another club motto is "Weaving spiders come not here," which can be interpreted as a prohibition against conducting conspiracies or simply that the daily concerns of commerce and politics are to be left outside.

The all-seeing eye symbol appears on many buildings throughout Europe. Here's one example that can be found on Aachen Cathedral in Germany.

A thirty-foot-tall concrete owl, reportedly symbolizing knowledge, overlooks the Grove's lake and is the backdrop for the yearly Cremation of Care ceremony, conducted as "an exorcising of the Demon to ensure the success of the ensuing two weeks." Critics claim it is a reenactment of a human sacrifice ritual.

The secrecy, trappings, and level of prominence of its members, not to mention the Minerval owl, has resulted in accusations that the Bohemian Club and the Bohemian Grove festivities are offshoots of the old Illuminati.

The symbols that have drawn the most attention are found on the reverse side of the dollar bill, which is rife with Masonic, and hence some Illuminati, symbols. The number thirteen appears frequently in occult literature. In numerology, the number thirteen is considered a karmic number of great power reflecting upheaval and breaking ground for new beginnings. According to the website Biblestudy.org, "The number 13 is symbol of rebellion and lawlessness. Nimrod, the mighty hunter who was 'before the Lord' (meaning he tried to take the place of God—Genesis 10:9), was the 13th in Ham's line (Ham was one of Noah's three sons who survived the flood). Thirteen represents all the governments created by men, and inspired by Satan, in outright rebellion against the Eternal."

Thirty-three-degree Mason and occult author Manly P. Hall has written, "European mysticism was not dead at the time the United States of America was founded. The hand of the Mysteries controlled in the establishment of the new government, for the signature of the Mysteries may still be seen on the Great Seal of the United States of America."

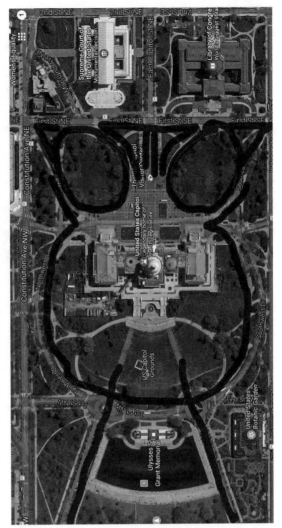

Some even detect the outline of the Minerval owl in the overhead view of the U.S. Capitol. (Imagery copyright ©2017 Google. Map data copyright ©2017 Google.)

The all-seeing eye and the pyramid on the reverse side of the seal were proposed by Congress in 1782. After six years and three separate committees, which included Founding Fathers Thomas Jefferson, John Adams, and Benjamin Franklin, the seal was finally approved by Congress in 1789. As will be seen, Jefferson and Franklin had more than passing knowledge of the Illuminati.

The official explanation for the pyramid is that it merely signifies strength and duration. The unfinished top denotes that work was still needed to complete the destiny of the United States. The all-seeing eye and the motto "Annuit coeptis" pertain to the idea that God, Providence or the Great Archi-

ANNUIT COEPTIS — 'announcing conception'

Illumined eye — Great architect 'Lucifer'

NOVUS ORDO SECLORUM — 'Secular New Order'

13 letters in motto E PLURIBUS UNUM — 'One of Many'

13 illuminated Stars - 13 enlightened Colonnies

13 Layers of Brick - 13 Original collonies 72 Bricks - 72 Powers of the name of God in Qabbalah

MDCCLXXVI - 1776 Date 'illuminati' formed mDCcLXxVI = 666

13 Arrows, 13 leaves 13 Berries - Different powers possessed by the 13 colonies

Pheonix not an eagle rising from the ashes, or ignorant world

9 Tail feathers - 9 spheres risen through to return to heavenly state

One possible interpretation of the symbols on the back of the U.S. dollar bill.

tect of the Universe, blesses the American cause. The Latin numerals at the base of the pyramid are said to denote the date of the signing of the Declaration of Independence.

Illuminati influence on the Great Seal was hinted at by Masonic occultist Manly P. Hall, who wrote, "Not only were many of the founders of the United States government Masons, but they received aid from *a secret and august body existing in Europe* [emphasis added] which helped them to establish this country for a peculiar and particular purpose known only to the initiated few. "The Great Seal is the signature of this exalted body—unseen and for the most part unknown—and the unfinished pyramid upon its reverse side is a trestle board [a board for symbols or designs] which is setting forth symbolically the task to the accomplishment of which the United States Government was dedicated from the day of its inception."

Even more to the point was Emanuel Josephson, an ardent anti-communist, who in 1955 published an attack on the late president Franklin D. Roosevelt entitled *Roosevelt's Communist Manifesto*. In this work, Josephson argued that Roosevelt's New Deal to combat the Great Depression was based on Adam Weishaupt's plans for the Illuminati.

Speaking of the Great Seal, Josephson wrote, "The above insignia of the Order of Illuminati was adopted by Weishaupt at the time he founded the

Order, on May 1, 1776. It is that event that is memorialized by the MDC-CLXXVI [Roman numerals for 1776] at the base of the pyramid, and not the date of the signing of the Declaration of Independence, as the uninformed have supposed."

Although the year was correct, the date is missing. We all know the document was signed on July 4, Independence Day. But that's not correct, either.

According to History.com, "The Declaration of Independence wasn't signed on July 4, 1776. On July 1, 1776, the Second Continental Congress met in Philadelphia, and on the following day twelve of the thirteen colonies voted in favor of Richard Henry Lee's motion for independence. The delegates then spent the next two days debating and revising the language of a statement drafted by Thomas Jefferson. On July 4, Congress officially adopted the Declaration of Independence, and as a result the date is celebrated as Independence Day. Nearly a month would go by, however, before the actual signing of the document took place. First, New York's delegates didn't officially give their support until July 9 because their home assembly hadn't yet authorized them to vote in favor of independence. Next, it took two weeks for the Declaration to be "engrossed"—written on parchment in a clear hand. Most of the delegates signed on August 2, but several—Elbridge Gerry, Oliver Wolcott, Lewis Morris, Thomas McKean and Matthew Thornton—signed at a later date. Two others, John Dickinson and Robert R. Livingston, never signed at all...."

Josephson explained the significance of the design on the Great Seal as follows: "[T]he pyramid represents the conspiracy for destruction of the Catholic (Universal Christian) Church, and establishment of a One World, or UN dictatorship, the 'secret' of the Order; the eye radiating in all directions, is the 'all-spying eye' that symbolizes the terroristic, Gestapo-like, espionage agency that Weishaupt set up under the name of 'Insinuating Brethren,' to guard the 'secrets' of the Order and to terrorize the populace into acceptance of its rule. This 'Ogpu' [early secret police of the Soviet Union] had its first workout in the Reign of Terror of the French Revolution, which it was instrumental in organizing. It is a source of amazement that the electorate tolerates the continuance of use of this insignia as part of the Great Seal of the U.S."

"ANNUIT COEPTIS means 'our enterprise (conspiracy) has been crowned with success,'" explained Josephson. "Below, NOVUS ORDO SECLORUM explains the nature of the enterprise: and it means 'a New Social Order,' or 'New Deal'.... Benjamin Franklin, John Adams (a Roosevelt kinsman) and Thomas Jefferson, ardent Illuminist, proposed the above as the reverse of the seal, on the face of which was the eagle symbol.... It can only mean that with the advent of the New Deal the Illuminist-Socialist-Communist conspirators, followers of Professor Weishaupt, regarded their efforts as beginning to be crowned with success."

The shape of a pyramid is triangular, a geometric figure used in Freemasonry to represent the Great Architect of the Universe. Henry A. Wallace, who served as secretary of agriculture, vice president, and secretary of commerce under Roosevelt, acknowledged in the 1950s how Roosevelt, a thirty-second-degree Mason and member of Holland Lodge No. 8 in New York City, helped alter the Great Seal's symbols:

> I noted the colored reproduction of the reverse side of the Seal. The Latin phrase *Novus Ordo Seclorum* impressed me as meaning the New Deal of the Ages.

> I was struck by the fact that the reverse side of the Seal had never been used. Therefore I took the publication to President Roosevelt and suggested a coin be put out with the obverse and reverse sides of the Seal.

> Roosevelt, as he looked at the colored reproduction of the Seal, was first struck with the representation of the "All Seeing Eye," a Masonic representation of The Great Architect of the Universe. Next, he was impressed with the idea that the foundation for the new order of the ages had been laid in 1776, but that it would be completed only under the eye of the Great Architect. Roosevelt like myself was a 32nd degree Mason.

> He suggested that the Seal be put on the dollar bill rather than a coin and took the matter up with the Secretary of the Treasury. He brought it up in a Cabinet meeting and asked James Farley [postmaster general and a Roman Catholic] if he thought the Catholics would have any objection to the "All Seeing Eye" which he as a Mason looked on as a Masonic symbol of Deity. Farley said "no, there would be no objection." The new bills, which were silver certificates, were released in the summer of 1935.

The pyramid was a most prominent symbol of the Bavarian Illuminati and the fact that it is included in the Great Seal has caused many researchers to suspect the influence of the Order on the design of the seal.

Officially, the thirteen-step pyramid signifies strength and duration as well as the thirteen original colonies. The pyramid is uncapped and unfinished, signifying that America is still an incomplete nation. However, the pyramid also represented the Order of the Bavarian Illuminati itself with the stones lying before it representing the idea that the Order's work was not yet

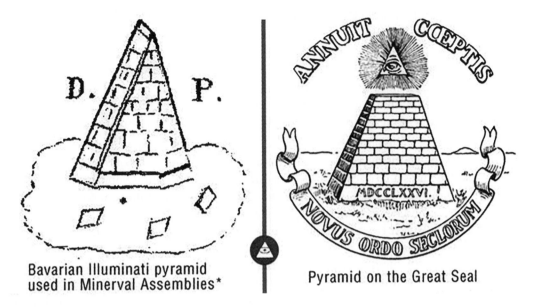

D. P.

Bavarian Illuminati pyramid
used in Minerval Assemblies*

Pyramid on the Great Seal

A comparison of the Illuminati pyramid and the pyramid of the great seal used on the U.S. dollar.

finished. The pyramid was a prominent feature of all Minerval assemblies of the Order.

The thirteen-letter motto *Annuit cúptis* means "God has favored our undertakings," a reference to God's pleasure with the American cause. Interestingly enough, the letters D and P seen on the Illuminati's pyramid meant *Deo Proximo*, or "close to God," a close comparison to *Annuit cúptis*. And the year in Latin MDCCLXXVI [1776] might represent the year the Illuminati was first formed more than the founding of the United States. After all, the American Revolution was well underway when the Declaration of Independence was adopted by the Second Continental Congress, and grievances against British rule dated back to at least 1763 when King George's prohibition of westward expansion was seen as interference with the affairs of the colonies. The famous Boston Massacre occurred in 1770, the First Continental Congress in 1774, and the battles of Lexington and Concord in 1775.

According to Illuminati researcher and evangelist Texe Marrs, some aspects of the Great Seal were instigated by a representative of the Rothschilds. "... in 1772, Haym Salomon, a European Rothschild agent and the man honored in the classic textbook, *A History of Jews in America*, as the 'Financier of the American Revolution,' came to the American colonies and used Rothschild money to further influence American colonial leaders," noted Marrs. "... Later, Salomon caused the All-Seeing eye symbol of the Illuminati to be made the reverse of the Great Seal of the United States. Today, this occultic and mysterious eye is found on our one-dollar bill, just above the Illuminati's pyramid."

According to Johnny Silver Bear, "American and British Intelligence have documented evidence that the House of Rothschild has financed both sides of every war, since the American Revolution. Financier Haym Salomon, an Illuminati agent, supported the patriots during the American Revolution, then later made loans to James Madison, Thomas Jefferson, and James Monroe."

The Great Seal's motto *Novus ordo seclorum* also has been the topic of much controversy. Officially translated as "A new order of the ages," many still see it as a rendition of "New World Order." The phrase apparently was taken from the Roman poet Virgil's *Eclogues* in which a child comes from the heavens and begins a new order of the ages. Although the identity of the child is unclear, it has commonly been thought to refer to Christ, which may explain why the early Christians did not destroy this work as they did with so much other Roman literature. There is even controversy over the American eagle, the preeminent symbol of the United States. Researchers have noticed that the bird represented on the first version of the Great Seal has a much longer neck and a noticeable tuft of feathers on the back of its head. The body is much thinner with shorter wings. It is believed the bird originally was to represent the Phoenix, the Greek mythological bird that rises from the ashes of its predecessor. The idea being that the states comprising the United States arose from the ashes of Old World colonization.

The Phoenix has long been an occult symbol. Apparently, someone thought the Phoenix was too closely associated with secret societies such as the Illuminati, which were attempting to tear down old religious and state systems and replace them with something new. So the mythical bird was replaced by the eagle in later versions. It is of interest that for some time former first lady and Secretary of State Hillary Clinton was pictured wearing a lapel pin that, upon close inspection, appeared to be a Phoenix bird atop a globe. No explanation was offered as to why she would wear an emblem of the Illuminati.

Founding Father Benjamin Franklin, a member of the Hell Fire Club, wanted the national bird to be the turkey, not the bald eagle, a symbol of the Illuminati.

Founding Father Benjamin Franklin, a member of the pagan Hell Fire Club of London and undoubtedly friendly with Illuminati members or sympathizers, in a letter to his daughter disparaged the eagle by writing, "For my own part I wish the Bald Eagle had not been chosen the representative of our Country. He is a bird of bad moral character. He does not get his living honestly. You may have seen him perched on some dead tree near the river, where, too lazy to fish for himself, he watches the labor of the Fishing Hawk; and when that diligent bird has at length taken a fish, and is bearing it to his nest for the support of his mate and young ones, the Bald Eagle pursues him and takes it from him.

"I am on this account not displeased that the figure is not known as a Bald Eagle, but looks more like a turkey. For the truth the turkey is in comparison a much more respectable bird, and withal a true original Native of America.… He is besides, though a little vain and silly, a bird of courage, and would not hesitate to attack a grenadier of the British Guards who should presume to invade his farm yard with a red coat on."

Several Masonic authors have linked the eagle to the ancient Egyptian sun god Amun Ra, as it can fly closer to the sun than any other creature.

"Some Masons created the Great Seal in 1782, and other Masons put it on the back of the American dollar in 1935," noted A. Ralph Epperson. "And it appears that all involved knew the meaning of the concealed symbols portrayed therein. There is an abundance of evidence that the Masons were heavily involved in the founding of the United States and the design of the Great Seal." As we have seen, the Masons were liberally infiltrated with Illuminati doctrine.

The Protocols

*T*he *Protocols of the Learned Elders of Zion*, sometimes called *The Protocols of the Wise Men of Zion*, is a list of procedures for usurping national governments and gaining world domination. This document may have wreaked more havoc than almost any other piece of literature in recent history.

A version of the *Protocols* first appeared in 1864 in France in a book entitled *Dialogue in Hell Between Machiavelli and Montesquieu.* It was written anonymously by a French lawyer named Maurice Joly and viewed as a political satire against the Machiavelli-inspired machinations of Napoleon III. Joly was a member of the Rosicrucians, which influenced his writing. A 1921 exposé by Lucien Wolf, an English Jewish journalist, revealed Joly's work as the crude plagiarism of two previous books. One of these books was written in 1859 by Jacques Crétineau-Joly, a French Catholic journalist, who reportedly had received documents from Pope Gregory XVI. The documents were taken from

> This document may have wreaked more havoc than almost any other piece of literature in recent history.

an Italian secret society called the *Haute Vente Romaine*, headed by an Italian prince who had been initiated by Weishaupt intimate Knigge. This society was believed to be nothing more than a reincarnation of the Illuminati, which strengthens the argument that the *Protocols* originated within the Order.

When Maurice Joly's identity was discovered, he received a fifteen-month prison sentence for his impertinence and his work was almost forgotten.

In the mid-1890s, Joly's obscure book was rewritten and reissued with anti-Semitic material on orders of the Russian Ochrana, the czar's secret police. It was added to the work of a religious writer named Sergei Nilus and published to coincide with the founding of the first official Zionist assembly at the 1897 World Congress of Jewry in Basel, Switzerland. The *Protocols* were included as an appendix to Nilus's book, partially titled *The Anti-Christ Is Near at Hand*. The objective was to relieve public pressure on the czar by portraying Russian revolutionaries as pawns of an international Jewish conspiracy. Without naming the Illuminati, Nilus's book charged that a clique of Jews and Freemasons had joined forces to create a one-world government based on liberalism and socialism, a conspiracy theory still alive today. For example, on June 13, 2013, during a speech at Moscow's Jewish Museum and Tolerance Center, Russian president Vladimir Putin, speaking of the old communist government, said, "The decision to nationalize this library was made by the first Soviet government, whose composition was 80–85 percent Jewish." Putin added that the politicians in the predominantly Jewish Soviet government "were guided by false ideological considerations and supported the arrest and repression of Jews, Russian Orthodox Christians, Muslims and members of other faiths. They grouped everyone into the same category. Thankfully, those ideological goggles and faulty ideological perceptions collapsed."

Putin may have known of which he was speaking. The first Soviet government, the Council of People's Commissars, was formed in 1917 and comprised sixteen leaders, including Vladimir Lenin and Leon Trotsky, both Jewish, and Joseph Stalin. According to the anti-Zionist website *Jew Watch*, Stalin's real name was Joseph David Djugashvili, a typical Jewish name indicating a Jewish heritage. Additionally, Stalin had three wives—Ekaterina Svanidze, Kadya Allevijah, and Rosa Kaganovich—who were all Jewish. The site also stated that Stalin's daughter, Svetlana, who defected to the United States in 1967, had four husbands, three of them Jewish.

It is such claims of Jewish conspiracy that have kept the *Protocols* in circulation since its inception. Today, many modern conspiracy writers see "historical truth" in the *Protocols*, believing they represent a real program that predates Nazism or communism. Some conspiracy researchers have claimed the

Frenchman Joly simply incorporated in his book concepts he picked up as a member of the Illuminati. Just as likely is the idea that the *Protocols* originated with the Italian secret society headed by a prince initiated into the Illuminati. Some saw a remarkable resemblance between the *Protocols* and confiscated Illuminati documents containing numerous Masonic references. Michael Baigent, Richard Leigh, and Henry Lincoln, the authors of *Holy Blood, Holy Grail*, had this take on the *Protocols*. They noted that the original Nilus edition contained references to a King as well as a "Masonic kingdom," concepts clearly not of Jewish origin. Furthermore, it concluded with the statement "Signed by the representatives of Sion of the 33rd degree." These authors argued that Nilus produced a "radically altered text" based on a legitimate original created by "some Masonic organization or Masonically oriented secret society that incorporated the word 'Sion'" and that it may indeed have been a serious blueprint for infiltrating Freemasonry and gaining global domination.

The cover of the 1905 Russian edition of *The Protocols of the Learned Elders of Zion,* an anti-Semitic text outlining how the Jewish people planned to take over the world.

The *Protocols* may indeed reflect a deeper conspiracy beyond its intended use to encourage anti-Semitism, one hidden within the secret upper ranks of the Illuminati and Freemasonry. They still chill readers with their prophetic description of the methodology for tyranny by a few. The *Protocols'* message fits quite well with the theology of the Illuminati as well as the outlook of the wealthy global elite of today:

> We are the chosen, we are the only true men. Our minds give off the true power of the spirit; the intelligence of the rest of the world is merely instinctive and animal. They can see, but they cannot foresee; their inventions are merely corporeal. Does it not follow that nature herself has predestined us to dominate the whole world? Outwardly, however, in our 'official' utterances, we shall adopt an opposite procedure, and always do our best to appear honorable and cooperative. A statesman's words do not have to agree with his acts [a premonition of today's politicians?]. If we pursue these principles, the governments and peoples which

U.S. General Maxwell Davenport Taylor, a former chair of the Joint Chiefs of Staff, once said that the world's population should be reduced on purpose through the deliberate use of war, disease, and starvation.

we have thus prepared will take our I. O. U.'s for cash. One day they will accept us as benefactors and saviors of the human race. If any State dared to resist us, if its neighbors make common cause with it against us, we will unleash a world war.

The *Protocols* explain that the goal of world domination will be accomplished by controlling how the public thinks by controlling what they see and hear; by creating new conflicts or restoring old orders; by spreading hunger, destitution, and plague; and by seducing and distracting the youth. "By all these methods we shall so wear down the nations that they will be forced to offer us world domination," they proclaim.

These same sentiments were echoed in the 1980s by a four-star general, former chairman of the Joint Chiefs of Staff, and ambassador to Vietnam during the conflict there: General Maxwell Davenport Taylor. Taylor said it would be necessary to reduce the world's population, mostly in third-world countries, using methods such as disease, starvation, and regional wars. He concluded, "I have already written off more than a billion people…. The population crisis and the food-supply question dictate that we should not even try. It's a waste of time."

Some of the twenty-four Protocols bear a brief summary. If any part of them is to be believed, they provide a clear connection to the Illuminati, Freemasonry, and the Ancient Mysteries as well as an amazing road map for world conquest. Because the *Protocols* were rewritten and attributed to Jews before World War I in Russia with the intent of inciting anti-Jewish sentiment, their use of the term *goyim*, a Jewish word for non-Jews, has been substituted with the term "masses." The remainder is true to the document. Pertinent points include:

- The Protocol plan "will remain invisible until the moment when it has gained such strength that no cunning can any longer undermine it." [Protocol 1]
- "[W]ars, so far as possible, should not result in territorial gains." [Protocol 2]
- "[The] minds [of the masses] must be diverted towards industry and trade. Thus, all the nations will be swallowed up in the pursuit of gain

and ... will not take note of their common foe." [Protocol 4]—"We shall create an intensified centralization of government," [Protocol 5] "... we must develop [a] Super-Government by representing it as the Protector and Benefactor of all those who voluntarily submit.... We shall soon begin to establish huge monopolies [this was written before the rise of the giant multinational corporations]...." [Protocol 6]— "The intensification of armaments, the increase of police forces ... [so that] in all the States of the world, besides ourselves, [there will be] only the masses of the proletariat, a few millionaires devoted to our interests, police and soldiers." [Protocol 7]

- "[W]e shall put [government power] in the hands of persons whose past and reputations are such that between them and the people lies an abyss, persons who, in case of disobedience to our instructions, must face criminal charges...." [Protocol 8]

- "We have fooled, bemused and corrupted the youth of the [masses] by rearing them in principles and theories which are known to us to be false...." [Protocol 9] "[W]e shall destroy among the [masses] the importance of the family and its educational value." [Protocol 10]

- "[W]e have invented this whole policy and insinuated it into the minds of the [masses] ... to obtain in a roundabout way what is ... unattainable by the direct road.... It is this which has served as the basis for our organization of secret Masonry which is not known to, and aims which are not even so much as suspected by, these ... cattle, attracted by us into the 'Show' army of Masonic Lodges in order to throw dust in the eyes of their fellows." [Protocol 11]

- "What is the part played by the press [media] today?... it serves selfish ends ... it is often vapid, unjust, mendacious and the majority of the public have not the slightest idea what ends the press really serves. We shall saddle and bridle it with a tight curb.... Not a single announcement will reach the public without our control.... [Protocol 12]

- "The need for daily bread forces the [masses] to keep silent and be our humble servants.... In order that the masses themselves may not guess what they are about we further distract them with amusements, games, pastimes, passions, people's palace [no TV or movies at that time]. Soon we shall begin through the press to propose competitions in art, in sport of all kinds...." [Protocol 13]

- "[I]t will be undesirable for us that there should exist any other religion than ours.... We must therefore sweep away all other forms of belief." [Protocol 14] "Freedom of conscience has been declared everywhere, so that now only years divide us from the moment of the complete wrecking of that Christian religion, as to other religions we shall have still less difficulty in dealing with them." [Protocol 17]

- "When we at last definitely come into our kingdom by the aid of *coups d'etat* prepared everywhere for one and the same day ... we shall make it our task to see that against us such things as plots shall no longer exist. With this purpose we shall slay without mercy all who take arms in hand to oppose our coming ... anything like a secret society will also be punishable with death...." [Protocol 15]

- "In our program one-third of [the masses] will keep the rest under observation from a sense of duty, on the principle of volunteer service to the State. It will be no disgrace to be a spy and informer, but a merit ... how else [are] we to ... increase ... disorders?" [Protocol 17] "Sedition-mongering is nothing more than the yapping of a lap-dog at an elephant.... In order to destroy the prestige of heroism, for political crime we shall send it for trial in the category of thieving, murder and every kind of abominable and filthy crime. Public opinion will then ... brand it with the same contempt." [Protocol 19] "[U]ntil [dissenters] commit some overt act we shall not lay a finger on them but only introduce into their midst observation elements...." [Protocol 18]

Later Protocols deal with finances. Protocol 20 called for general taxation—"the lawful confiscation of all sums of every kind for the regulation of their circulation in the State." This would be followed by "a progressive tax on property" and then finally a graduated income tax, a "tax increasing in a percentage ratio to capital," as well as taxes on sales, "receipt of money," inheritance, and property transfers. There was a discussion of "the substitution of interest-bearing paper" money since "Economic crises have been produced by us ... by no other means than the withdrawal of money from circulation." The *Protocols* discuss at great length loans, which "hang like a sword of Damocles over the heads of rulers, who, instead of taking from their subjects by a temporary tax, come begging with outstretched palm to our bankers."

Whoever produced the *Protocols* clearly understood the secrets of banking. In a passage that could have been entitled "The National Debt of the United States," Protocol 20 stated, "A loan is an issue of government bills of exchange containing a percentage obligation (interest) commensurate to the sum of the loaned capital." It proceeded to explain, "If the loan bears a charge of five percent [hefty interest in those more knowledgeable times] then in 20 years the State vainly pays away in interest a sum equal to the loan borrowed, in 40 years it is paying a double sum, in 60—treble, and all the while the debt remains an unpaid debt...."

The writer also determined that no one would figure out what was happening. "We shall so hedge about our system of accounting that neither ruler nor the most insignificant public servant will be in a position to divert even the smallest sum from its destination without detection or to direct it in another direction...."

The *Protocols* also demonstrate a linkage to the Ancient Mysteries, referring to bloodlines such as "the seed of David," "secret mysteries," and even the "Symbolic Snake," an icon of the earliest cults.

Despite their dubious origin, the *Protocols* were taken seriously by many powerful people. Adolf Hitler already has been mentioned. Others included Germany's Kaiser Wilhelm II, Russia's Czar Nicholas II, and American industrialist Henry Ford, who used them to help persuade U.S. senators not to join President Woodrow Wilson's League of Nations.

However, in Russia the Ochrana's plan may have backfired. Incensed by the

A photo taken after the 1906 Bialystok pogrom in which over eighty Jews were killed. Now part of Poland, the city was then under Russian rule and subjected to anti-Semitic sentiments inflamed, in part, by the *Protocols*.

Czarist propaganda, a counter-revolution took place and pogroms against Russian Jews were instituted by vigilantes called "The Black Guard." Continuing instability and violence finally resulted in a Russian Revolution in 1905, during which the *Protocols* again were trotted out by pro-Czarist elements to inflame the public.

Author Konrad Heiden, an anti-Nazi contemporary of Hitler, while denying the authenticity of the *Protocols*, also saw a certain reality there. "Today the forgery is incontrovertibly proved, yet something infinitely significant has remained: a textbook of world domination ... the great principle of inequality fights to preserve its rule; the ruling class philosophy of a natural hierarchy, of innate differences between men. Once this principle is expressed in the form of historical events, it also soon assumes the aspect of conspiracy.... The spirit of the *Protocols*, therefore, contains historical truth, though all the facts put forward in them are forgeries."

In the summer of 1917, a young Estonian Jew named Alfred Rosenberg was a student in Moscow, where a stranger gave him a copy of the *Protocols*. Later that year, following the Russian Revolution, the anti-Bolshevik Rosenberg fled to Germany, where he used the book to gain entry to the secret society in Munich, a move that was to have far-reaching effects for the world.

In late 1918, Rosenberg presented the *Protocols* to an aging Munich newspaper publisher named Dietrich Eckart. A boozing bon vivant and one of Germany's better known poets at the time, Eckart was enthralled by this plan for world domination. He introduced Rosenberg to fellow members of the *Thule Gesellschaft*, or Thule Society, a "literary discussion" group founded by Baron Rudolf Freiherr von Sebottendorff. The society proved to be merely a front for a more secret society, the *Germanenorden*, or German Order. Both were anti-Semitic nationalist organizations laced with beliefs in the supernatural and more than a few Illuminati. Sebottendorff, Eckart, and others within the Thule Society were directly linked to the rise of Hitler and his Nazis, which were far more than simply a political movement. They saw themselves leading a quasi-religious movement born out of secret organizations whose goals were the same as those found in the Illuminati and Freemasonry, as will be detailed later. Sounding like Adam Weishaupt, Hitler acknowledged this by stating, "Anyone who interprets National Socialism merely as a political movement knows almost nothing about it. It is more than religion; it is the determination to create a new man."

> This idea of creating a new kind of human was nothing new. The concept had stirred around in several occult and esoteric societies for centuries.

This idea of creating a new kind of human was nothing new. The concept had stirred around in several occult and esoteric societies for centuries. But, since the time of the Roman Empire, such ideas of freedom and self-determination had continually been suppressed by the Catholic Church.

"The Illuminati simply means 'Holders of the Light' just as the word 'Protocols' means 'Original written draft of a plan designed to achieve a definite stated purpose," noted author Carr. "The Illuminati has existed since Cain defected from God. The Protocols were written just as soon as man mastered the art of expressing his thoughts, and recording his future plans by writing on material which could be preserved. The Protocols were written long before Zion was ever heard of.... My studies have convince me that Illuminism, under the name 'Perfectionism,' was practiced within the Jesuit Order long before Weishaupt defected from God and became a Luciferian. Both movements, Illuminism and Perfectionism, were started to encourage human beings to become as near perfect as possible. There is an old saying 'The road to hell is paved with the good intentions of those who failed to put them into practice.'"

Many of those who have studied the *Protocols* at length believe they were originally written in the 1700s as an Illuminati document and only later appropriated by the Frenchman Joly. Their relevance can be demonstrated simply by comparing the schemes advanced in the *Protocols* to the headlines of today.

Author Douglas Reed, while admitting the *Protocols* did not originate as minutes of a secret meeting of Jewish elders, nevertheless stated, "In every other respect it is of inestimable importance, for it is shown by the conclusive test (that of subsequent events) to be an authentic document of the world-conspiracy first disclosed by Weishaupt's papers."

If the *Protocols* were indeed an Illuminati game plan for world conquest, what was the theology used to support it?

Theology

Imbued with Illuminati theology, members were happy to be indoctrinated with ancient esoteric knowledge and felt they were superior to what they saw as the tyranny of the Catholic Church and the national governments it supported. "Man is not bad," Weishaupt wrote, "except as he is made so by arbitrary morality. He is bad because religion, the state, and bad examples pervert him. When at last reason becomes the religion of men, then will the problem be solved." Weishaupt also evoked a philosophy that has been used with terrible results down through the years by Hitler and many other tyrants. "Behold our secret. Remember that the end justifies the means," he wrote, "and that the wise ought to take all the means to do good which the wicked take to do evil." So, for the enlightened or illuminated, any means to gain their ends is acceptable—even the use of lies, deceit, theft, murder, or war.

Furthermore, according to Illuminati documents found in Baron Bassus's castle, Order members were bound by this oath: "I shall perform an action, if asked by the Order, which I may not consent to, inasmuch as it (when seen as a whole) would truly be wrong. Furthermore, even if it might seem so from a certain point of view, it would cease to be improper and wrong if it served as a means to thereby achieve blessedness or the final aim of the whole."

Such an oath left wide open the possibilities for immoral or illegal activities on the part of the Illuminati. Despite his rhetoric against church and state, many people, including Thomas Jefferson, believed Weishaupt was far from an atheist but instead a deeply religious man in his own manner. But as has been seen so many times in history, initial good intentions within supposedly benevolent organizations have been infiltrated and taken over by people with evil designs. Such diversion from original purposes can be seen in the rise of the Bolsheviks in Russia and the National Socialists in pre-war Germany.

But regardless of Weishaupt's true motives or the best intentions of the Illuminati, original documents of the Order included detailed instructions for fomenting hatred and bloodshed between different racial, religious, and ethnic groups, and even between the sexes. "The idea of promoting hatred between children and their parents was introduced. There were even instructions about the kinds of buildings to be burned in urban insurrections. In short, virtually every tactic employed by 20th-century subversives

> **S**o, for the enlightened or illuminated, any means to gain their ends is acceptable—even the use of lies, deceit, theft, murder, or war.

was planned and written down by Adam Weishaupt over 200 years ago," wrote William H. McIlhany.

Weishaupt openly voiced his intention of concealing the Illuminati within Freemasonry when he wrote: "We must consider how we can begin to work under another form. If only the aim is achieved, it does not matter under what cover it takes place, and a cover is always necessary. For in concealment lies a great part of our strength. For this reason, we must always cover ourselves with the name of another society. The lodges that are under Freemasonry are in the meantime the most suitable cloak for our high purpose, because the world is already accustomed to expect nothing great from them which merits attention.... As in the spiritual Orders of the Roman Church, religion was, alas! only a presence, so must our Order also in a nobler way try to conceal itself behind a learned society or something of the kind.... A society concealed in this manner cannot be worked against. In case of a prosecution or of treason the superiors cannot be discovered.... We shall be shrouded in impenetrable darkness from spies and emissaries of other societies."

The idea of a hostile takeover of the Illuminati was strongly supported by Masonic historian Albert G. Mackey, who wrote, "Illuminism, it is true, had its abundant errors, and no one will regret its dissolution. But its founder had hope by it to effect much good; that it was diverted from its original aim was the fault, not of him, but of some of his disciples; and their faults he was not reluctant to condemn in his writings." And in his own defense, Weishaupt once wrote:

> Whoever does not close his ear to the lamentations of the miserable, nor his heart to gentle pity; whoever is the friend and brother of the unfortunate; whoever has a heart capable of love and friendship; whoever is steadfast in adversity, unwearied in the carrying out of whatever has been once engaged in, undaunted in the overcoming of difficulties; whoever does not mock and despise the weak; whose soul is susceptible of conceiving great designs, desirous of rising superior to all base motives, and of distinguishing himself by deeds of benevolence; whoever shuns idleness; whoever considers no knowledge as unessential which he may have the opportunity of acquiring, regarding the knowledge of mankind as his chief study; whoever, when truth and virtue are in question, despising the approbation of the multitude, is sufficiently courageous to follow the dictates of his own heart,—such a one is a proper candidate.

Mackey went so far as to write, "The truth is, I think, that Weishaupt has been misunderstood by Masonic and slandered by un-Masonic writers. His success in the beginning as a reformer was due to his own honest desire to do good. His failure in the end was attributable to ecclesiastical persecution, and to the faults and follies of his disciples. The master works to elevate human nature; the scholars, to degrade. Weishaupt's place in history should be among the unsuccessful reformers and not among the profligate adventurers."

But what some might see in Weishaupt's words as fledgling humanism was seen by others as Satanism, for in the Bible, Adam and Eve were told by the serpent that if they utilized the apple from the Tree of Knowledge, they could be like gods, but in Exodus 20:3, the Lord decreed, "Thou shalt have no other gods before me." After being assured in the Bible that there is only one true God, Genesis 1:26 quoted the singular God as saying, "Let us make man in our image, after our likeness...."

Those who have studied the accounts of the ancient Anunnaki find it highly interesting that the monotheistic God of the Old Testament should speak in the plural and of other gods. Such verses may carry two explanations: first, that the plural *Elohim* of the Old Testament, interpreted as "God" by the monotheists who

One view about Adam is that he was the genetic creation of the Anunnaki Assembly, which created him out of an existing species.

wrote Genesis, indeed may have referred to the Anunnaki Assembly, which approved the creation of man, and, second, the idea of creating man "in our image" meant simply genetic manipulation of an existing species, not the creation of a new race. As mentioned previously, such alteration of DNA produced the *Adama*, or Adam, the first hybrid born on Earth. This was not an incidence of creation but one of merely improving the breed, just as humans have done with animals for centuries. The real key to Illuminati control was its secrecy. In one 1794 document, *Die neuesten Arbeiten des Spartacus und Philo in dem Illuminaten-Orden*, Weishaupt declared:

> The great strength of our Order lies in its concealment. Let it never appear in any place in its own name, but always covered by another name, and another occupation. None is fitter than the three lower degrees of Freemasonry; the public is accustom[ed] to it, expect little from it, and therefore takes little notice of it. Next to this, the form of a learned or literary society [the Thule Society?] is best suited to our purpose.... By establishing reading societies and subscription libraries ... we may turn the public

mind which way we will. In like manner we must try to obtain an influence in … all offices which have any effect, either in forming, or in managing, or even in directing the mind of man.

Anti-Illuminist John Robison wrote of the Illuminati's public relations efforts, stating:

Like them they hired an Army of Writers; they industriously pushed their writings into every house and every cottage. Those writings were equally calculated for inflaming the sensual appetites of men, and for perverting their judgments. They endeavored to get the command of the Schools, particularly those for the lower classes; and they erected and managed a prodigious number of Circulating Libraries and Reading Societies.… They took the name of OECONOMISTS, and affected to be continually occupied with plans for improving Commerce, Manufactures, Agriculture, Finance, &c. and published from time to time respectable performances on those subjects. But their daring project was to destroy Christianity and all Religion, and to bring about a total change of Government. They employed writers to compose corrupting and impious books— these were revised by the Society, and corrected till they suited their purpose. A number were printed in a handsome manner, to defray the expense; and then a much greater number were printed in the cheapest form possible, and given for nothing, or at very low prices, to hawkers and peddlers, with injunctions to distribute them secretly through the cities and villages. They even hired persons to read them to conventicles of those who had not learned to read.

Weishaupt, in his zeal to bring change, not only set out to deceive the public, but he reminded his top leaders they should hide their true intentions from their own initiates by "speaking sometimes in one way, sometimes in another, so that one's real purpose should remain impenetrable to one's inferiors."

Nesta Webster wrote, "Weishaupt's followers were enlisted by the most subtle methods of deception and led on towards a goal entirely unknown to them. It is this that … constitutes the whole difference between honest and dishonest secret societies."

Unlike anarchists who seek an end to all government, Weishaupt and his Illuminati sought a world government based on their philosophy of human-centered rationalism. This world government, naturally, would be administered by themselves. Weishaupt proclaimed, "The pupils (of the Illuminati) are convinced that the Order will rule the world. Every member therefore becomes a ruler."

Weishaupt also blamed nationalism for much of the world's troubles. "With the origin of nations and peoples the world ceased to be a great family.... Nationalism took the place of human love," he wrote.

To Order members, Weishaupt confided, "Do you realize sufficiently what it means to rule—to rule in a secret society?" he wrote. "Not only over the lesser or more important of the populace, but over the best men, over men of all ranks, nations, and religions, to rule without external force, to unite them indissolubly, to breathe one spirit and soul into them, men distributed over all parts of the world?"

In articulating this goal, Weishaupt may have revealed a basic agenda found in some secret societies right up to today—the desire for ultimate and absolute power.

> Unlike anarchists who seek an end to all government, Weishaupt and his Illuminati sought a world government based on their philosophy of human-centered rationalism.

It is critical at this point to understand that Illuminism is an "ism"—not unlike National Socialism (Nazis), communism, capitalism, and socialism. It is a belief system that is not relegated to any one individual or group in any given period of time.

The beneficial goals of the Illuminati, such as freedom from church dogma and government tyranny, lived on to modern times in France, America, and Russia. But the more sinister aspects of the Order, such as inherent secrecy, duplicity, violence (recall the poison formulas), and the drive for absolute power lived on too in unscrupulous men. Robert Anton Wilson opined, "The one safe generalization one can make is that Weishaupt's intent to maintain secrecy has worked; no two students of Illuminology have ever agreed totally about what the 'inner secret' or purpose of the order actually was (or is ...)."

As Wilson once fancifully told a radio audience, "Maybe the secret of the Illuminati is that you don't know you're a member until it's too late to get out."

Summary

A variety of methods were used by the Illuminati leadership to ensure both silence and compliance within the Order. Ironically, while Weishaupt had grown to despise the Jesuit order, he nevertheless generally modeled his Illuminati after its organizational structure. He also copied many of the Freemason's system of degrees for his Order. For example, the Masonic Blue Lodge is divided into three stages or degrees—the York Rite, composed of ten more degrees or the Scottish Rite with a total of thirty-two degrees. The thirty-third degree represents the human head atop the thirty-three vertebrae of the back. Similar degrees were initiated for the fledgling Illuminati Order with others added as the organization grew larger and stronger. No recruit was aware of any degrees higher than his own and he was required to accept orders from "unknown superiors" above him.

All members were carefully conditioned to blind obedience, whether orders came from their immediate Insinuator or the invisible ones.

Initially, the Order was broken into three classes—the Nursery for newcomers, the Masonry for general members, and the Mysteries for the more adept. Each class contained degrees:

- The Nursery—Preparatory Literary Essay, Novice, Minerval, Illuminatus Minor.
- The Masonic—Apprentice, Fellow Craft, Master (Scots Major Illuminatus and Scots Illuminatus Dirigens).
- The Mysteries—Lesser (Presbyter, Priest, or Epopt and Prince or Regent) and Greater (Magus and Rex or King).

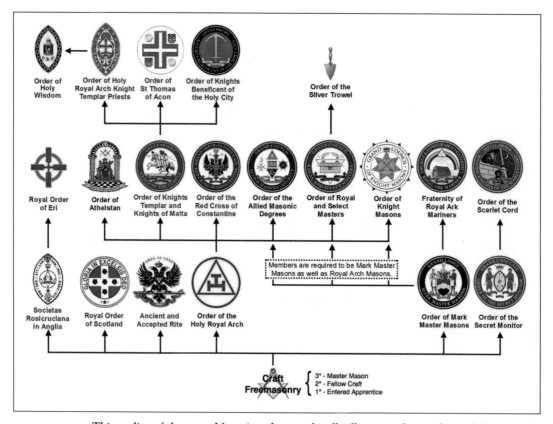

This outline of the many Masonic orders graphically illustrates the number and diversity of branches within Freemasonry. It also makes it easy to understand how members of one order may not know the inner agenda of the others. Secrecy has always been the key to the advancement of secret society programs down through the ages.

The Illuminati Rex or King was, of course, reserved for Weishaupt. All classes were kept in line through the use of their recruiter, called Insinuators, and a network of spies and snitches called Scrutators. To add to this intimidating system of spying, each member was constantly called upon to produce a written report covering his own daily activities but also those of his fellow members, friends, and acquaintances. This type of snooping was quite effective and would have been most welcome in the Nazi Gestapo.

The sheer knowledge that the Order held such intimate information provided strong impetus to keep members quiet and compliant. Added incentives, such as expensive gifts, higher advancement, and even women, were provided to those who proved loyal and effective to the Order. Those who failed to live up to expectations were held back or drummed out.

Absolute secrecy was the order of the day. As Weishaupt once wrote to a fellow Illuminatus, "The great strength of our Order lies in its concealment. Let it never appear in any place in its own name, but always covered by another name, and another occupation." The most outward means of preserving secrecy was to present a public image at odds with the true inner working of the Illuminati. Posing as a Christian-based charitable organization, members were instructed to infiltrate professional and government offices to include the military using any explanation that would work. In its later years, facing persecution by the authorities, members would meet posing as a literary society, a political discussion group, or even as a social gathering.

Illuminati recruiters were careful to target younger men, preferably between the ages of eighteen and thirty. They especially sought candidates from wealthy families well connected to royalty, government, or the professional class. One such potential member would lead them to others of a similar caliber.

Prospective members were flattered and extolled as valuable recruits. Their most base instincts or most fanciful dreams were addressed as obtainable goals by the Illuminati adepts. New members were never told the true agenda of the Order. Many served for years without an inkling of the purposes envisioned by Weishaupt and his top commanders.

Such mental control over his subjects proved most effective as most members, educated and professional men, were already conditioned to the process of reason encouraged by the Age of Enlightenment. Rational thought was the order of the day and beneficial-sounding rationales could always be presented for every activity requested by the Order.

The pyramidal structure of the Illuminati reinforced the flow of both information and command within the Order. Sitting at the top of this structure, Weishaupt was in complete control of the organization. Such structure insured that authority rested at the pinnacle of the organization with orders flowing downward, a configuration later copied by authoritarians such as the Soviet communists and Hitler's Nazis.

As a forerunner to the terrorist cells of today, Weishaupt saw to it that one Illuminatus could know the identity and control only two others. These two could control two between them and so on. Thus, if one cell was discovered by the authorities, only three persons would be compromised. The remainder of the Order would be safe. No one with the exception of Weishaupt and a few of his top officers, known as Areopagites, knew the names of the cell leaders.

Adding to the overall secrecy of the Illuminati was the use of code words, not only false names for cities and states but for personal identities as well. Members used aliases known as "Order Names," usually taken from classical Greek or Roman literature, such as Pericles, Theseus, Cassiodorus, Zeno, Anacharsis, and Tamerlane. Only the top echelon of Areopagites knew the true identities of the members. The false names, as well as code words for locations, were always used in written reports and letters, along with cyphers and codes, which caused considerable consternation among the authorities who struggled to understand the correspondence acquired in Illuminati raids.

Another method utilized to confound the authorities was the use of the Persian calendar in their correspondence. Weishaupt's use of the Persian calendar commemorated the death of the Persian King Yazdegerd III, which represented the end of the millennium of Zoroaster. This calendar of 360 days was configured around religious observances and festivals, assuring that the names of major deities were in constant use. Each Illuminati novice was tutored in the used of both the Persian calendar and the codes used by the Order.

The followers of Zoroaster, called Parsis, fled to India from Iran around the tenth century to escape persecution by the Muslims. They continue to use the same dating system today. The Illuminati novice was taught to date his correspondence with this calendar, which begins with the year 630 C.E. Author Terry Melanson quoted Abbé Augustin Barruel as explaining, "The year begins with the Illuminees on the first of *Pharavardin*, which answer to the 21st of March. Their first month has no less than forty-one days; the following months, instead of being called May, June, July, August, September, and October, are *Adarpahascht, Chardad, Thirmeh, Merdedmeh, Shaharimeh, Meharmeh*: November and December are *Abenmeh, Adameh*: January and February, *Dimeh*, and *Benmeh*: The month of March only has twenty days, and is called *Asphandar*."

Over and above the secret codes, calendars, and cyphers, compartmentalization played a huge roll in keeping Illuminati secrets, both from the unknowing public and each other. All information was strictly on a need-to-know basis. Most often the left hand did not know what the right hand was about. Furthermore, severe penalties were imposed on errant members. Deception was practiced on the public while blackmail, using information gleaned through the regular readings of reports and diaries, kept the membership in line. Illuminati members had to surrender their individual will. They were promised initiation into the higher mysteries and ancient knowledge if they dutifully fulfilled their assigned tasks and performed to their superior's expectations. In this cult-like atmosphere, very little information about the Order found its way into the public until the authorities began raiding the homes of the membership once the Illuminati agenda became known.

The use of symbols was another effective way to convey messages and ideas to the Illuminati while leaving the authorities and the public in the dark about the meaning of symbols, such as the Maltese cross, the double-headed eagle, and the Caduceus that are still in use today. These and many other such cyphers can be traced back through the Knights Templar, Assassins, and the Mystery Schools of Greece and Egypt to the Babylon Mystery School, which held bits of knowledge passed down from the Anunnaki. A dot within a circle, apparently representing the sun radiating light (or knowledge) to the surrounding figure, was a major symbol to the Illuminati and was found on all communications. Another key symbol was the All-Seeing Eye of Horus, which dates back to at least the time of the pharaohs and represented power and health. The eye is also thought to represent the eye of the Supreme Being who is watching over the entire Earth. A more mundane explanation is that the eye, sometimes called the Third Eye, represents the human pineal gland located in the center of the forehead and believed by some to be the center of higher consciousness and enlightenment. It is interesting to note that the symbolic eye bears a remarkable resemblance to the human thalamus, a walnut-shaped mass in the forebrain thought to control both sensory and motor signals as well as regulate consciousness, sleep, and alertness. The all-seeing eye within a pyramid was a prominent symbol within the Illuminati and is still found on the reverse side of the U.S. dollar bill along with the date 1776 in Roman numerals. While some suspect this refers to the founding year of the Illuminati, most argue it represents the year the Declaration of Independence was written and approved. Some researchers even claim to have found a tiny Minerval owl, an Illuminati symbol, within the scrollwork on the face of a dollar bill, but this is far from conclusive.

What is certain is that the Minerval owl plays a prominent role in the secretive Bohemian Club of San Francisco, sponsor of the yearly gatherings at Bohemian Grove, which has been the subject of conspiracy theories after the names of notable attendees such as George H. W. Bush, Warren Christopher, Joseph Coors, David Gergen, Bobby Ray Inman, Henry Kissinger, George Shultz, Caspar Weinberger, and many others surfaced. Activities at Bohemian Grove include ceremonies in torchlight conducted under a thirty-foot statue

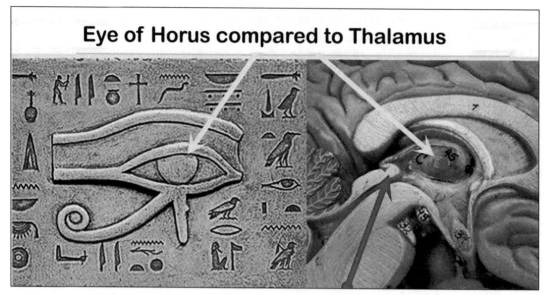

Eye of Horus compared to Thalamus

The thalamus in the human brain bears a remarkable resemblance to the symbol of the Eye of Horus.

of an owl, the depiction of which is a logo for the group. The secrecy, trappings, and level of prominence of its members, not to mention the Minerval owl, have resulted in accusations that the Bohemian Club and the Bohemian Grove festivities are but reincarnations of the old Illuminati.

Such speculation is invigorated by other signs and symbols on the dollar bill, particularly the abundance of the number thirteen found in the stars, layers of bricks, leaves, arrows, and, of course, the thirteen original colonies. Some claim the number thirteen represents rebellion and lawlessness. It should be noted that the thirteen-step unfinished pyramid topped by an all-seeing eye on the dollar bill was another prominent symbol used by the Illuminati. The motto *Annuit cúptis,* interpreted as "God has favored our undertakings," contains thirteen letters. Occult symbolism connected to the Illuminati is also ascribed to the Great Seal of the United States. The all-seeing Eye and the Motto *Annuit coeptis* pertains to the idea that God, Providence, or the Great Architect of the Universe blesses the American cause. The Latin numerals at the base of the pyramid are said to denote the year of the signing of the Declaration of Independence although it is also the year the Illuminati was founded.

Mason and occultist Manly P. Hall may have connected the Freemasons who founded the United States to the outlawed Illuminati when he wrote, "... they received aid from a secret and august body existing in Europe which helped them to establish this country for a peculiar and particular purpose known only to the initiated few." Even the Great Seal's motto *Novus ordo seclorum,* usually translated as "A New Order of the Ages," has been the topic of controversy, with some viewing it as a rendition of the term "New World Order."

There has even been controversy over the American eagle as a symbol of the nation. It seems originally that this distinction was going to the mythical Phoenix bird that rose afresh from the ashes of its old self. But apparently too many drew the connection with the revolutionaries of Europe, especially the Illuminati. So the honor went to the eagle, although Benjamin Franklin argued that a turkey would be more relevant as it was a native American bird and not a scavenger like the eagle.

All of Washington, D.C., is rife with Masonic symbols, right down to the layout of the streets, statuary, and numerous zodiacs located around the city, indicating an interest in astrology. No discussion of the Illuminati and its theology would be complete without considering the much-maligned *The Protocols of the Learned Elders of Zion*, sometimes called *The Protocols of the Wise Men of Zion*.

> **All of Washington, D.C., is rife with Masonic symbols, right down to the layout of the streets, statuary, and numerous zodiacs located around the city....**

Although usually brushed off as a crude forgery used to incite hatred and violence toward Jews, a close examination reveals deeper aspects of this extraordinary document that may have had its origins in the Illuminati. Popularly thought to have grown from the satirical mind of Frenchman Maurice Joly, a 1921 exposé determined Joly's work was based on earlier books, one of which was based on papers from an Italian secret society linked to the Illuminati. It is true that Joly's book was rewritten and filled with anti-Semitic material in the 1890s by the Russian Czar's secret police, the Ochrana. The purpose was to relieve public pressure on the Czar by portraying Russian revolutionaries as pawns of an international Jewish conspiracy.

The *Protocols*, with additions by a religious writer named Sergei Nilus, were published to coincide with the founding of the first official Zionist assembly at the 1897 World Congress of Jewry in Basel, Switzerland. The document lists a number of practices that could be used to take control over whole governments and societies. They reveal how to accomplish world domination by guiding how the public thinks by directing what they see and hear (media control); by creating new conflicts or restoring old orders (terrorism); by spreading hunger, destitution, and plague; how to enslave a population through a debt-based society; and by seducing and distracting the youth (dumbed down education and entertainment). "By all these methods we shall so wear down the nations that they will be forced to offer us world domination," proclaim the *Prtotocols*.

Many people, including Adolf Hitler and Henry Ford, believed the *Protocols* to reflect a genuine agenda for world domination simply because so many of them have come to pass in so many countries. The audacity of the

Protocols has been kept alive over decades due to the fact that many of the protocols deal with money as a control mechanism and that so many of the Russian communist revolutionaries were Jews. But it is no more fair to blame all Jews for communism than to blame all Catholics for Nazism. The original *Protocols* share ideology more with the Illuminati than with Jewish leadership, although the connections between the two beginning with the spread of Illuminism in Frankfurt, home of the Rothschilds, should not be forgotten. Following World War I, the *Protocols* surfaced in Germany where Munich newspaper publisher Dietrich Eckart introduced them to the secret societies of the *Thule Gesellschaft*, or Thule Society, and its predecessor the *Germanenorden*, or German Order. Both these societies were instrumental in the rise of Hitler and his Nazis. The *Protocols* may have encouraged Hitler's anti-Semitism.

> **W**eishaupt wrote that humans are not born bad or evil but gain such attributes through the arbitrary morality imposed by religion and the state.

The *Protocols* did indeed reflect the theology of the Illuminati. Weishaupt wrote that humans are not born bad or evil but gain such attributes through the arbitrary morality imposed by religion and the state. He felt that freed from such conventional morality, human beings could achieve enlightenment through reason.

One's view of Weishaupt depends on how one views the world. Those comfortable with the strictures of church, state, and society would see him as a radical or dissenter at best and a revolutionary or anarchist at worst. Free-thinkers might see Weishaupt as an earlier Henry David Thoreau seeking a peaceful, balanced life on Walden Pond. It's all in one's perception. Weishaupt, though he realized the serious responsibility of the changes he sought, nevertheless was probably conflicted within himself. It was the men around him who turned his Illuminati into a force for change, whether for better or worse. It was yet another example of the quest for power becoming a force for evil. In the words of the English historian Lord Acton, "Power tends to corrupt and absolute power corrupts absolutely. Great men are almost always bad men, even when they exercise influence and not authority; still more when you superadd the tendency of the certainty of corruption by authority."

A basic tenet of the Illuminati as voiced by Weishaupt has wreaked untold havoc down through the years—"Behold our secret. Remember that the end justifies the means."After all, if one can justify the end of his or her desires, then under this principle anything can be applied to achieve it, whether this be lying, cheating, stealing, even murder. And, in line with Illuminati doctrine, such action can be masked behind any excuse or reason. Aldous Huxley, the futurist author of *Brave New World*, was correct in noting, "The nature of the universe is such that ends can never justify the means. On the contrary, the means always determine the end."

One clear-cut example of this Illuminati principle carried to extreme is the deaths of so many people in the Holocaust of the Nazis, who cold-bloodedly decided that the most expedient method to eliminate undesirables in their society was to kill them. Although the number killed in the Holocaust is debatable, any large-scale murder condoned by an established government should be considered a holocaust. It is this belief, that the end justifies the means, that has been twisted by men into dark actions and it might not all be laid at the feet of Weishaupt. Many people, including Thomas Jefferson, thought Weishaupt a truly religious man with the best of intentions. But when men and women begin to accept this principle, there can be dire consequences. Sheer intellectual reason must not always prevail. For example, the Nazis moved from an intellectual belief that some segments of society were undesirable to downright persecution and finally killing. The Bolsheviks in Russia and Pol Pot in Cambodia murdered millions in the hopes of producing a Utopian future. It must be understood that Illuminism is an "ism"—not unlike National Socialism (Nazis), communism, capitalism, and socialism. It is a belief system that is not relegated to any one individual or group in any given period of time. It was Illuminism that guided rebellions from the French, American, and Russian Revolutions through the rise of communism and National Socialism. It is the Illuminati dream of power and control that still lives on in unscrupulous persons. And it was the Illuminati's penchant for secrecy and abrupt change that inevitably led to its downfall.

SUPPRESSION

Friday, October 13, 1307, was the day that French authorities began a campaign to exterminate the Knights Templar. From that time onward, there has been a sinister connotation to any Friday the thirteenth. The number thirteen also proved unlucky for Weishaupt and his Illuminati, for thirteen years after its founding, the Order found itself in deep trouble.

It all began on June 22, 1784. Bavarian Duke Karl Theodor, acting on various damaging rumors being spread about Illuminati and Masonic anti-clerical and anti-government teachings, issued an edict banning all secret societies not officially authorized.

In part, the edict stated, "Whereas all communities, societies and associations without approval from a public authority and the confirmation of the Monarch are illegal, prohibited by law, suspect and dangerous things in of themselves, His Electoral Highness has decided not to tolerate them in his State...."

This total ban of all secret societies in Bavaria also included severe penalties for failure to obey the order. Weishaupt suddenly found that the power he had achieved over Freemasonry did not include real political power. Although the Illuminati was forced to go underground in Bavaria, it simply moved its revolutionary efforts elsewhere. Furthermore, the edict did little to deter the Order. Many members, especially prominent and professional men, thought the edict so general in nature as not to specifically include themselves. Membership continued to grow, spreading into France, as Order members waited for things to calm down and normal activities to resume.

Some members tried to approach Karl Theodor to offer explanations and excuses for the criticisms against the Illuminati but were rebuffed. Word must have reached Karl Theodor's ear as to the intransigence of the Illuminati in obeying his earlier edict, for On March 2, 1785, he issued a second edict, this time specifying both the Illuminati and certain Masonic lodges. Karl Theodor wrote that he was "deeply affected and displeased to learn that various Lodges of so-called Freemasons and Illuminati who are still in our States, have taken so little heed of our General Prohibition issued on June 22nd of last year against all fraternal societies clandestine and unapproved, as to not only continue to hold meetings in secret, but even to raise funds and recruit new members, seeking to further increase the already large number of adepts. We had deemed this Society, very much degenerated and of primitive institution, too suspect, both in regards to religious concerns and from a social and political point of view, so that we could no longer tolerate it in our States...."

> In this harsh edict, leaving no room for evasion, Karl Theodor also ordered "all money and any funds collected illegally" by the groups to be confiscated....

In this harsh edict, leaving no room for evasion, Karl Theodor also ordered "all money and any funds collected illegally" by the groups to be confiscated and shared between the poor and whoever came forward to denounce the society, even if he were a member.

This edict, more forceful and specific than the first, drove the Illuminati even deeper underground. Some members began feverishly burning or otherwise destroying many incriminating Illuminati documents.

Meanwhile, Weishaupt was probably tipped off to the second edit by Karl Theodor as he suddenly left Bavaria in February, two weeks prior to its issuance. He later gave the feeble excuse that he left because of an argument with the University of Ingolstadt librarian over some books he needed for his classes. Another version stated he was in trouble for attempting to place revolutionary books in the Ingolstadt library.

Author Melanson gave this interesting account of Weishaupt's departure: "As he tried to leave Ingolstadt, he realized that guards were posted throughout the city with orders for his arrest. Weishaupt hid in the house of a master locksmith, fellow Illuminatus Joseph Martin, and managed to escape a few days later by disguising himself in the clothes of a working craftsman."

After a short stop in Nuremburg, by April, Weishaupt had moved on to Regensburg, where he was greeted by Illuminati member Duke Ernest II of Saxe-Gotha-Altenburg and given work in civil service with a pension. It was here that he began a prolific writing career, churning out many letters and pamphlets defending Illuminism and attacking its enemies.

Also, in April, a leading Illuminatus sent out a circular to members stating "you are released from all duties, excepting only secrecy, which you have accepted upon entering our Order." However, this in no way dissolved the Order.

In fact, many branches of the Order were still functioning as late as 1788, although communications, specifically the delivery of reports and new protocols, apparently had ceased. On September 9, 1785, the three professors who had defected from the Order in 1783 and sent the defaming letter to the sister-in-law of Karl Theodor—Joseph von Utzschneider, Georg Grünberger, and Johann Sulpitius Marquis de Cosandey—signed a revealing deposition. This was one of the first accounts of Illuminati's secrets and its intent made public. Their deposition stated:

> In consequence of our acquaintance with this doctrine of the Illuminees, with their conduct, their manners, and their incitements to treason, and being fully convinced of the dangers of the Sect, we … left the Order … though the Illuminees sought to impose upon us shamefully, by assuring us that his Electoral Highness was a member of their Order. We clearly saw that a Prince knowing his own interests, and wholly attending to the paternal care of his subjects, would never countenance a Sect, spreading through almost every province under the cloak of Free-Masonry; because it sows division and discord between parents and their children, between Princes and their subjects, and among the most sincere friends…. Experience had convinced us, that they would soon succeed in perverting all the Bavarian youth. The leading feature in the generality of their adepts were irreligion, depravity of morals, disobedience to their Prince and to their parents, and the neglect of all useful studies. We saw that the fatal consequence of Illuminism would be, to create a general distrust between the prince and his subjects, the father and his children, the minister and his secretaries, and between the different tribunals and councils. We were not to be deterred by that threat so often repeated, *That no Prince can save him that betrays us.* We abandoned, one after the other, this Sect, which *under different names,* as we have been informed by several of our former Brethren, has already spread itself *in Italy, and particularly at Venice, in Austria, in Holland, in Saxony, on the Rhine, particularly at Frankfort, and even as far as America* [emphasis in the original]. The Illuminees meddle as much as possible in state affairs, and excite troubles wherever their Order can be benefited by them.

The defectors claimed they were never aware of the invisible superiors mentioned in Illuminati rites, but they suspected they were men of higher degrees. They also claimed to have been threatened and harassed by members following their desertion of the Order.

The Marquis de Cosandey went so far as to reveal that one disquieting Illuminati doctrine—*Patet Exitus* (a clean exit)—dictated that a member should commit suicide rather than betray the Order.

Utzschneider admitted that the goal of Illuminism was "to introduce a worldwide moral regime which would be under their control in every country."

Pope Pius VI believed that those who were members of the Order posed a danger to the Church.

Adding to the problems for the Illuminati, in June 1785, Pope Pius VI sent a letter to the Bishop of Freising in Bavaria advising that membership in the Order was dangerous and incompatible with church traditions.

Then in July, Weishaupt and a fellow Illuminatus, Friar Johann Jakob Lanz (code name Socrates) were riding near the gates of Regensburg when Lanz was struck dead by lightning. Some saw this as divine retribution as Father Lanz undoubtedly knew the anti-church position of Illuminism. Weishaupt miraculously was uninjured. By one account, Lanz had stopped at Regensburg while on a scouting mission for the Illuminati to Silesia.

There was a dispute over the disposition of Lanz's body, which was eventually returned to his diocese in Freising, where he had co-founded the Illuminati/Masonic Lodge *Augusta zu den drei Kronen* (Augusta at the Three Crowns) in 1781. Found sewn into his clothing were secret Illuminati documents, including a membership list and a tract written by Weishaupt expounding on the Order's plan to create a New World Order through world revolution. Another account said Lanz was an Illuminati courier, and that both he and his horse were killed and that Order messages were found in the undamaged saddlebags. Two years later, the unrepentant Weishaupt wrote, "When my late friend Lanz was struck by lightning at my side in the year 1785 in Regensburg, what an opportunity this could have provided me to play the penitent and remorseful hypocrite, and thus gain the confidence of my persecutors." But instead of acting contrite for his assaults against the church and state, Weishaupt stayed on his course. Attempts were made to arrest Weishaupt in connection with Lanz's death but he remained at large as Regensburg was a free imperial city and the officials lacked jurisdiction, especially as Weishaupt was under the protection of Duke Ernest II.

The impounded material found on Lanz indicating the Order was still active infuriated Karl Theodor, who issued yet another edict requiring all Illuminati to repent and register with the government or face even more severe punishments.

In Ingolstadt, the judicial authorities of a special commission to investigate the Illuminati stepped up their probe of the Order. Those members unlucky enough to fall into the hands of the inquisitors made formal confessions. The investigations revealed that many members of the military were involved with the Illuminati or its doctrine, as well as state officials, professors, teachers, and students. Many lost their positions or were exiled. Some saw this as an effort by Jesuits and Rosicrucians to finally exterminate the Illuminati.

Despite the protection of Duke Ernest in Regensburg, who sent letters to Karl Theodor advising that as Weishaupt was a member of his Privy Council and thus immune from any warrants, Weishaupt was under constant surveillance by agents from Munich.

The Duke, fearing that Weishaupt might be kidnapped and returned to Munich, arranged for him to relocate to Gotha. Even here, Weishaupt was forced to hide in a chimney for three days when posters with orders for his arrest were circulated throughout the city.

Further troubles came in October 1786, when police raided the home of Franz Zwack in Landshut. The authorities had been slowly, but meticulously, seeking out Illuminati members. The documents found on Lanz eventually led them to Zwack. The raid on Zwack's house produced a treasure trove. Zwack's home was a repository of important Illuminati documents.

In addition to secret communications between the Illuminati Adepts, police found descriptions of the Order's symbols and the Persian calendar they used. Also, according to Melanson, "… membership rosters, statutes, instructions for recruiters, ceremonies of initiation and imprints of the Order's insignia; a eulogy of atheism and a copy of a manuscript entitled *Better Than Horus*; a proposal for a branch of Illuminism for women; several hundred impressions of Government seals (with a list of their owners, princes, nobles, clergymen, merchants, etc.) for the purposes of counterfeiting; instructions for the making of the poison *Aqua Toffana*, poisonous gas and secret ink; 'an infernal machine' for the safeguarding of secret papers—apparently a strong box that would blow up, destroying its contents; and receipts for procuring abortion and a formula for making a tea to induce the [abortion] procedure."

More than two hundred letters between Weishaupt and the Illuminati Areopagites were recovered, many dealing with the most sensitive matters. There were also tables containing the Order's secret symbols and geographical terms belonging to the Order, along with instructions for the primary initiation ceremonies. Illuminati leaders or adepts, whose names were found in the Zwack documents, were rounded up and interrogated. "Out of the mouths of its friends, the accusations which its enemies made against the order were to be substantiated," noted author Stauffer. "By the admissions of its leaders, the system of the Illuminati had the appearance of an organization devoted to the overthrow of religion and the state, a band of poisoners and forgers, an association of men of disgusting morals and depraved tastes. The publication of these documents amounted to nothing less than a sensation."

Even before the end of the year, Weishaupt quickly produced at least nine pamphlets defending the Illuminati. Among these were *Apologie der Illuminaten* and *Vollständige Geschichte der Verfolgung der Illuminaten in Bayern* (*Complete History of the Persecution of the Illuminati in Bavaria*). His pro-Illuminati works were spread widely but to little effect. Weishaupt tried to resurrect the Illuminati but there is no record of success.

A year later, even more Illuminati materials became available after a search of the Sandersdorf castle, which belonged to one of the Order's leaders, Thomas Maria Baron de Bassus, who ranked as a Superior with the code name Hannibal.

The Baron had become close friends with Weishaupt while studying in Ingolstadt. He joined the Illuminati in 1778 and was made an Areopagite the next year. As part of his work for the Illuminati, de Bassus procured a Bavarian printing press, which was shipped to his hometown of Poschiavo, a small municipality in Switzerland, where he went to live. Aided by printer Giuseppe Ambrosini, another Illuminatus, de Bassus also opened a book shop where the pair sold their printed books criticizing the Church and the pope. They also published the first edition of the Italian version of the autobiographical novel *The Sorrows of Young Werther,* by Johann Wolfgang von Goethe, reportedly also an Illuminati member. The printing operation also was one of the first to disseminate revolutionary ideals on the eve of the French Revolution, according to Italian historian Franco Venturi.

Thomas Maria Baron de Bassus became a leader among the Illuminati, even allowing them to make use of his residence at Sandersdorf Castle.

De Bassus's castle was confiscated and, due to the escalating animosity against the Illuminati, he and his family moved back to Bavaria, where he died peacefully in 1815.

Following the raid, the Bavarian authorities published the documents found in de Bassus's castle in two volumes, entitled *Einige Originalschriften des Illuminaten Ordens* ("Some Original Writings of Illuminati Order"). But there was some editing. "While reproducing letters and official reports, the editors usually censored the real identity of any noble or other high-ranking individual listed, making it difficult from the beginning to gain a complete picture of the Order," explained Melanson.

One picture did clearly emerge—that of an organization dedicated to worldwide revolution, or as described by Weishaupt in the documents, "By this plan, we shall direct all mankind in this manner. And, by the simplest means, we shall set all in motion and in flames. The occupations must be so allotted and contrived that we may, in secret, influence all political transactions."

These volumes were sent to the governments of England, France, and Russia, but with little effect. Foreign noblemen, having been exposed to Illuminati propaganda, still thought of the Illuminati as honest and noble-minded Freemasons.

But now the true objectives of the Illumnati began to be perceived by the public. In the seized documents were plans for a global revolution and it was clear this was to be accomplished by clandestine groups using secrecy and deceit. It was also clear that this was to be the work of only the most illuminated (educated) and well-placed individuals. Ordinary working stiffs need not apply. It was due to the many professional and highly placed Illuminati members that the Bavarian police work was slow and careful, even tedious. But scurrilous information on the Order began to pile up, accusations ranging from simple sedition to Satan worship and human sacrifice.

The final nail in the Order's coffin came when it was found that the Illuminati had considered opening its doors to women, a preposterous proposition in the eighteenth century. Letters and notes were found in the raids on Zwack and de Bassus that outlined these plans. Arkon Daraul reported:

> The famous memorandum detailing the plan to win over women … states that women are the best means of influencing men. They should be enrolled, and into their minds put a hope that they might themselves in time be released from the "tyranny of public opinion." Another letter asked how young women can be influenced, since their mothers would not consent to their being placed under the Illuminati for instruction. Five women were suggested by one member, as a start. They were four step-daughters of one of the Illuminati, who were to be placed in the care of the wife of yet another Illuminated One. They, in their turn would, enlarge the society through their friends. It was further mentioned that women are not considered to be really suitable for such an undertaking, because they are "fickle and impatient."

With the extent of the Order's shocking activities becoming more documented, Duke Karl Theodor on August 16, 1787, issued a third and final edict against the Illuminati. It was literally a death knell for the Order as it prescribed the death penalty for anyone recruiting for the Illumnati. In part, this edict stated:

> As more time passes it is further realized how harmful and dangerous the Order of the Illuminati will be for the State and reli-

In the seized documents were plans for a global revolution and it was clear this was to be accomplished by clandestine groups using secrecy and deceit.

gion, if allowed to flourish here and beyond…. Accordingly, his Electoral Highness not only reiterates by the present text the defense contained in the previous Edicts, but give them more strength; His orders are to proceed with criminal indictments and carry them out irrespective of person, dignity, standing or status, against anyone who has allowed recruiting in his States or beyond: for the recruiter he is to be deprived of life by the sword, and for the recruited he will be sentenced to have his property confiscated and be banished for life from all States of his Electoral Highness, with a promise of never being allowed to return. Under the same penalties of forfeiture and expulsion, the prohibited Lodges of the Illuminati, under whatever name they may hide and carefully present themselves, in all places, must be subject to rigorous surveillance. Those in Lodge attire will be held and treated as if they had attended meetings in secret, in suspect places, such as hotels or particular houses, and we will not allow the futile excuse usually given—an honest society of good friends—especially when those present have already been suspected of impiety and Illuminism.

The Illuminati was destroyed as an organization but not silenced. Its membership and teachings lived on. Much like the "flame wars" of today's Internet, Weishaupt and his detractors exchanged volley after volley of claims and counter claims in pamphlets and letters, attacking each other vehemently.

In separate writings in 1787, Weishaupt defended the Illuminati with this description of an ideal member:

> Whoever does not close his ear to the lamentations of the miserable, nor his heart to gentle pity; whoever is the friend and brother of the unfortunate; whoever has a heart capable of love and friendship; whoever is steadfast in adversity, unwearied in the carrying out of whatever has been once engaged in, undaunted in the overcoming of difficulties; whoever does not mock and despise the weak; whose soul is susceptible of conceiving great designs, desirous of rising superior to all base motives, and of distinguishing himself by deeds of benevolence; whoever shuns idleness; whoever considers no knowledge as unessential which he may have the opportunity of acquiring, regarding the knowledge of mankind as his chief study; whoever, when truth and virtue are in question, despising the approbation of the multitude, is sufficiently courageous to follow the dictates of his own heart—such a one is a proper candidate.

Despite the laws against this Order, Illuminati members merely continued to hide themselves away within the ranks of the Freemasons. Having successfully merged with continental Freemasonry earlier in that decade, they simply went further underground.

Their ideals were advanced right on through the secret Round Tables of Cecil Rhodes in the twentieth century, backed by the might of the Frankfurt Lodge, which was under the control of Hessian royalty, the Rothschilds, and their associates.

By 1790, the Illuminati appeared to have disbanded, but many members, those who had not hid themselves within the Freemasons, simply fled to other countries while retaining their loyalty to the Order's ideals. It would appear that the Illuminati philosophy was unwittingly spread by the Bavarian government's crackdown. When the authorities saw the Illuminati as a direct threat to the established order and outlawed the organization, it prompted many members to flee Germany, which only sowed their philosophies farther afield. Secret and shadowy Illuminati Orders sprang up in France, Italy, England, and even the new lands of America.

Some former members turned against the Order. Leopold Alois Hoffmann, a Freemason who briefly joined the Illuminati, was swayed by Rosicrucian material opposing the Order. The Rosicrucians had gone to the extent of infiltrating the Order and creating an espionage system within it. Hoffmann later wrote, "A group of us pledged ourselves to work for the overthrow of Illuminism, and I was selected as spokesman for the group. My new acquaintances handed me secret papers whose content stimulated my zeal and indignation."

Ludwig Adolph Christian von Grolman, a friend of Knigge and member of the Masonic Order of Strict Observance, was recruited into the Illuminati in 1782. But after reaching the position of Perfect, he made friends with a man named Johann August von Starck, a virulent anti-Illuminati, and began to have second thoughts about his membership. Grolman was eventually thrown out of the Order, perhaps for learning from Knigge the plans for world conquest. Grolman and Starck in 1795 began publishing a journal entitled *Eudaimonia* (a state of contentment), which postulated that the Illuminati had not only spawned the French Revolution but had dastardly designs on both world politics and religion. Other members suspected that the Order had been appropriated by sinister

An author of political and theological works, Johann August von Starck was against the Illuminati, asserting that they started the French Revolution.

forces. Duke Ferdinand of Brunswick, a Grand Master of German Freemasonry who was inducted into the Illuminati in 1783 and rose to the position of Regent, actually recommended the dissolution of all Freemasonry in a 1794 letter to his fellow Masons, warning:

> I have been convinced that we, as an Order, have come under the power of some very evil occult Order, profoundly versed in science, both occult and otherwise, though not infallible, their methods being black magic, that is to say, electromagnetic power, hypnotism, and powerful suggestion. We are convinced that the Order is being controlled by some Sun Order, after the nature of the Illuminati, if not by that Order itself. We see our edifice … crumbling and covering the ground with ruins, we see the destruction that our hands no longer arrest … a great sect arose, which taking for its motto the good and the happiness of man, worked in the darkness of the conspiracy to make the happiness of humanity a prey for itself. This sect is known to everyone, its brothers are known no less than its name. It is they who have undermined the foundations of the Order to the point of complete overthrow; it is by them that all humanity has been poisoned and led astray for several generations…. They began by casting odium on religion…. Their masters had nothing less in view than the thrones of the earth, and the governments of the nations was to be directed by their nocturnal clubs … the misuse of our order … has produced all the political and moral troubles with which the world is filled today … we must from this moment dissolve the whole Order.

Weishaupt, in an effort to show that his own agenda for the Order remained undeterred, defiantly wrote, "I have foreseen everything, and I have prepared everything. Let my whole Order go to rack and ruin; in three years I will answer to restore it, and that to a more powerful state than it is in at present.… I [shall] rise stronger than ever.… I can sacrifice whole provinces, the desertion of a few individuals, therefore, will not alarm me."

The Jesuit abbot Augustin Barruel taught grammar in France until sentiment against the Jesuits forced him to move east to the Austro-Hungarian Empire. He returned to France in 1773 when the Jesuits were banned by the pope. In the waning days of the French Revolution, Barruel published a book entitled *Mémoires pour Servir à l'Histoire du Jacobinisme* (*Memoirs Illustrating the History of Jacobinism*). Jacobins were members of the Jacobin Club, whose members were dedicated to protect the revolution from aristocratic reaction. They soon gained a reputation for radical political activity and revolutionary zeal.

Between 1797 and 1799, only ten years after the banning of the Illuminati, Barruel published four volumes of this book, which immediately became quite popular, were translated into several languages, and laid the groundwork for many modern conspiracy writers. This was one of the first major works to demonize the Illuminati.

In his third book, Barruel connected the Illuminati and Freemasons together and claimed they collectively comprised more than 300,000 members, "all zealous for the Revolution, and all ready to rise at the first signal and to impart the shock to all other classes of the people."

He attributed the French Revolution to an Illuminati/Freemason conspiracy. He also claimed the Illuminati, by appropriating the secret structures of the Freemasons, had to radicalize the movement against the church and state and had predisposed the population to their hidden principles. He said after studying Masonic mysteries, he concluded the order had long held atheistic and anti-government beliefs.

Barruel also confirmed that even after the Illuminati were outlawed in Bavaria, many members survived and continued the Order's mission with little opposition. He wrote:

Augustin Barruel, a Jesuit priest, was the first critic to publicly name members of the Illuminati and show the link between them and the Freemasons.

> If we except Weishaupt, no adept in Bavaria had been condemned to a severer punishment than exile or short imprisonment. In other parts … not a single inquiry had been made concerning their lodges. Many of those adepts who had been convicted of the deepest guilt had met with protection instead of indignation in the different courts. Notwithstanding that the deepest proofs of his guilt had been adduced, we see Zwack, a very few days after, producing certificates of his probity and fidelity to his prince.… Spartacus [Weishaupt] himself tranquilly enjoyed his asylum and a pension at a court, though he had conspired to annihilate every Prince. Never has so monstrous a conspiracy been discovered or so publicly been denounced; yet never were conspirators so amply supplied with the means of continuing their plots by those even against whom they were conspiring.

In his writings, Barruel was one of the first critics to actually name known members of the Order. Of sixty-seven names published by Barruel, ten were professors, thirteen were nobles, seven were in the church, three were lawyers, and the rest came from the emergent middle class, of which most were government officials and men of commerce along with a few military officers. He also linked the Illuminati to the Assassins, Knights Templar, and a worldwide Zionist plot and believed that the Order merely regrouped under different front names after 1785 and that their theology still continued. Barruel's work continues to be influential though controversial. But some still support his work. Author Jones pointed out:

> Freemasonry's attack on Christ was inspired by the Talmudic literature in the Cabala. Barruel's book powerfully brought together previously unknown material in three important areas—the writings of the philosophes, the Freemasons, and the Illuminati. Its lack of a coherent explanation of how those parts fit together should not blind us to its genius: no one had published anywhere near this volume of material before Barruel. No one had gotten to the theological roots of the revolution in Talmudic Judaism either, because no one had studied the Masonic texts in such detail. Barruel witnessed the attack on Christ that began in the Lodge first hand....

Author Douglas Reed agreed, writing that Talmudic philosophy was embraced by some Russian Jews "though they had no Judahite blood" and that the "areas where they congregated, under Talmudic direction, became the centers of that anti-Russian revolution which was to become 'the world revolution.'"

Finally, fearing the violence of the French Revolution, Barruel sought sanctuary in England. Interestingly, in his subsequent works, he appeared to absolve English Freemasonry of the crimes he ascribed to the Illuminati, including inciting the French Revolution. This may have been due to the fact that it was Englishmen, particularly the Irish-born English philosopher Edmund Burke, who granted him asylum and supported him financially while he wrote his volumes.

Another important critic of the Illuminati was John Robison, a Scottish physicist and mathematician and a professor of philosophy at the University of Edinburgh in the late 1700s. He gained prominence after inventing the siren and working with inventor James Watt, who developed the steam engine. Watt once described Robison as "a man of the clearest head and the most science of anybody I have ever known."

Robison became disenchanted with what he considered an excess of the Enlightenment and, as a Freemason, was asked to join the Illuminati. Upon investigation, he declined and instead authored a book in 1797 with the protracted title *Proofs of a Conspiracy against all the Religions and Governments of Europe, Carried on in the Secret Meetings of Freemasons, Illuminati and Reading*

Societies. This ponderous work essentially accused Weishaupt and his Illuminati of maliciously infiltrating Freemasonry and fomenting the French Revolution.

Robison had read a German periodical, *Religions Begebenheiten* ("Religion Events"), which came to his notice in 1795. He became so entranced with the Masonic rituals and degrees contained therein, he decided he must share his discoveries with the public. Robison wrote:

> I have found that the covert of a Mason Lodge had been employed in every country for venting and propagating sentiments in religion and politics, that could not have circulated in public without exposing the author to great danger. I found, that this impunity had gradually encouraged men of licentious principles to become more bold, and to teach doctrines subversive of all our notions of morality—of all our confidence in the moral government of the universe—of all our hopes of improvement in a future state of existence—and of all satisfaction and contentment with our present life, so long as we live in a state of civil subordination. I have been able to trace these attempts, made, through a course of fifty years, under the specious pretext of enlightening the world by the torch of philosophy, and of dispelling the clouds of civil and religious superstition which keep the nations of Europe in darkness and slavery. I have observed these doctrines gradually diffusing and mixing with all the different systems of Free Masonry; till, at last, an association has been formed for the express purpose of rooting out all the religious establishments, and overturning all the existing governments of Europe. I have seen this Association exerting itself zealously and systematically, till it has become almost irresistible: And I have seen that the most active leaders in the French Revolution were members of this Association, and conducted their first movements according to its principles, and by means of its instructions and assistance, formally requested and obtained: And, lastly, I have seen that this Association still exists, still works in secret, and that not only several appearances among ourselves show that its emissaries are endeavoring to propagate their detestable doctrines, but that the Association has Lodges in Britain corresponding with the mother Lodge at Munich ever since 1784.... The Association of which I have been speaking is the Order of Illuminati, founded, in 1775 [*sic*], by Dr. Adam Weishaupt, professor of Canon-law in the University of Ingolstadt, and abolished in 1786 by the Elector of Bavaria, but revived immediately after, under another name, and in a different form, all over Germany. It was again detected, and seemingly

broken up; but it had by this time taken so deep root that it still subsists without being detected, and has spread into all the countries of Europe.

The "proofs" alluded to by Robison have been assailed right to this day. Author Stauffer commented, "Bringing out into bold relief the most malignant and brutal of the anticlerical and anti-Christian utterances of Voltaire and his friend,. as well as all available evidence of a crafty strategy on the part of the conspirators to avoid detection of their plan, Barruel was emboldened to affirm a desperate plan to overturn every altar where Christ was adored, whether in London, Geneva, Stockholm, Petersburg, Paris, Madrid, Vienna, or Rome, whether Protestant or Catholic."

Masonic Author Mackey in his *Masonic Dictionary* was also critical of Barruel but admitted, "But it cannot be denied, that in process of time, abuses had crept into the Institution [Freemasonry] and that by the influence of unworthy men the system became corrupted; yet the coarse accusations of such writers as Barruel and Robison are known to be exaggerated, and some of them altogether false."

"Neither Robison nor Barruel deny that the professed goal of the Order was to teach people to be happy by making them good—to do this by enlightening the mind and freeing it from the dominion of superstition and prejudice," noted Trevor W. McKeown on a Masonic website. "But they refused to accept this at face value. Where Weishaupt and Knigge promoted a freedom from church domination over philosophy and science, Robison and Barruel saw a call for the destruction of the church. Where Weishaupt and Knigge wanted a release from the excesses of state oppression, Robison and Barruel saw the destruction of the state. Where Weishaupt and Knigge wanted to educate women and treat them as intellectual equals, Robison and Barruel saw the destruction of the natural and proper order of society."

A mathematician, physicist, and University of Edinburgh professor, John Robison was another intellectual who, after the French Revolution, accused the Freemasons of being under the Illuminati's influence.

Author Steven Luckert explained the spread of anti-Illuminati literature thusly:

By 1798, the Illuminati complot thesis truly had become international. Robison and Barruel had taken this German-born conspiracy theory, systematized it, and circulated it to large audiences throughout the Western world.... Though neither Barruel [nor] Robison were the originators of the Illuminati complot theory, their names ... have been indelibly linked to this conspiracy theory. In the end, this grandiose conspiratorial vision outlived all those who promoted it, and survived with some changes well into the 20th century.

It is indeed ironic that the anti-Illuminati books of Barruel and Robison spread the doctrines of the Order far more than Weishaupt could have ever dreamed. Both books were translated into dozens of languages and gained a worldwide readership. It should be noted that neither Barruel nor Robison had complete access to Illuminati documents. Many original papers of the Bavarian Illuminati have been translated into English only in recent years. Both Barruel and Robison said they were not aware of the other until their writings were published. They argued the fact that they both investigated the Order independently of each other but came to many of the same conclusions and confirmed the legitimacy of their claims against the Illuminati. Barruel later explained, "It will be perceived that we are not to be put in competition with each other; Mr. Robison taking a general view while I have attempted to descend into particulars: as to the substance we agree."

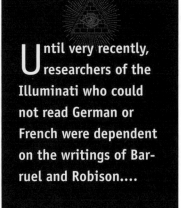

Until very recently, researchers of the Illuminati who could not read German or French were dependent on the writings of Barruel and Robison....

The writings of both Barruel and Robison were well known to America's Founders, such as George Washington, James Madison, Thomas Jefferson, among others. More on their thoughts later.

Until very recently, researchers of the Illuminati who could not read German or French were dependent on the writings of Barruel and Robison, both of whom had access to primary source material. However, both Barruel and Robison were Christian critics of the Order and wrote from that perspective, as did another vocal critic, Nesta Webster.

The daughter of a partner in Britain's Barclays Bank, Nesta Helen Webster was born in 1876, educated at Westfield College, and had traveled extensively before marrying Captain Arthur Templer Webster, a superintendent of the British Police in India.

In 1920, she and others penned a series of articles for the London *Morning Post* entitled "The Jewish Peril," largely based on the controversial *Protocols of the Learned Elders of Zion*, the authenticity of which she said was an "open question."

Webster is best known for her book *World Revolution: The Plot against Civilization*, which postulated that Illuminati ideals, under many different guises, continued to plague humankind well into the twentieth century. She saw Order members as occultists plotting world domination.

"Weishaupt … knew how to take from every association, past and present, the portions he required and to wield them all into a working system of terrible efficiency," wrote Webster, "… the disintegrating doctrines of the Gnostics and Manicheans, of the modern philosophers and Encyclopeadists, the methods of the Ismailis and the Assassins, the discipline of the Jesuits and Templars, the organization and secrecy of the Freemasons, the philosophy of Machiavelli, the mystery of the Rosicrucians—he knew moreover, how to enlist the right elements in all existing associations as well as isolated individuals and turn them to his purpose."

Webster also noted, "The extravagance of the [Illuminati] scheme … rendered it unbelievable, and the rulers of Europe, refusing to take Illuminism seriously, put it aside as a chimera." Many researchers claim this same incredulous attitude has helped protect the descendants of the Illuminati even today.

Writers Pauli Poisuo and M. Asher Cantrell, on a website entitled *Cracked*, typify some antagonistic views of Webster, writing,

> Nesta Webster was a 1920s British historian, writer, propagandist and Nazi sympathizer who had a less-than-secret vendetta against Jews.… If you've read *The Sun Also Rises*, or a biography of Henry Ford, you know that anti-Semitism was up there with stupid-looking pants and the Charleston in terms of things rich white people lost their goddamned minds over.

> Webster was married to a superintendent of the British police, which rendered her pretty much untouchable, and she was even tight with Winston Churchill a few decades before he came to his goddamn senses.… Webster struck gold when she proposed an elaborate historical bad-guy cult that worked in alliance with the Jews and was responsible for everything bad that had ever happened. She was studying a fringe conspiracy theory that the French Revolution was secretly orchestrated by a tiny, long extinct secret society called the Bavarian Illuminati, when she decided "What if *that*, but like the Jews are in on it, too!?"

However, others thought Webster may have been onto something. One such was none other than Winston Churchill, castigated by the writers above because of his support of Webster. In a 1920 article Churchill wrote, "This [revolutionary] movement among the Jews is not new.… It played, as a modern writer, Mrs. Webster, has so ably shown, a definitely recognizable part in the tragedy of the French Revolution. It has been the mainspring of every subversive movement during the Nineteenth Century.…"

More recently, author Ralph Epperson echoed Churchill's concern when he wrote in *The Unseen Hand*, "The fact that the rulers of Europe wouldn't believe the goals of the Illuminati is a problem that is recurring all over the world today. It is difficult for the observer to believe that such a giant, well-organized conspiracy does exist, and that the goals they envision for the world are real. This disbelief by the public is what fuels their success and it behooves the conspiracy to plan their moves in such a way that the truth becomes so incredible and so preposterous that no one would believe that they were intentionally created."

Another more modern writer also saw validity in the early critics. Evangelist Texe Marrs has stated that after extensive research, he can now state unequivocally that "there is a secret organization of illuminized men that exists. It is the Money Power of America, Europe, and Asia. I call the men who lead it the *Secret Brotherhood*. The members of this clandestine group believe themselves to be men of a superior race and bloodline. They are convinced that their destiny is to be served. *We are to become their economic slaves* [emphasis in the original]. Over the centuries, these diabolical men, agents of a magical underworld known only to a few, have banded together in secret societies, amassing untold wealth and material treasures. But because greed is never satiated, their hungry appetite for more and more money—and for more and more absolute, unchallenged power—grows daily."

British Prime Minister Winston Churchill agreed with the ideas of Nesta Webster that the Illuminati were behind the French Revolution and "every subversive movement during the Nineteenth Century."

He went on to proclaim, "It put Woodrow Wilson and FDR in office, and protected Bill Clinton during impeachment proceedings. This clique hated Richard Nixon and drove him from office.... The Illuminati leaders of Mystery Babylon have put their stooges in the highest offices. Alan Greenspan, [former] chairman of the Federal Reserve, is one of them. So is Russian President Vladimir Putin, France's President ... and Britain's Prime Minister.... Secret agents of this calculating and cruel cabal have funded revolutions around the globe. They were financial backers of Karl Marx, and they used the Zionist Movement to found the nation of Israel. They have long used communism and Zionism as twin hammers to destroy their enemies, depose political leaders, and topple governments.... The awful, staggering truth must get out. We are no longer a free people. *Illuminati Mystery Babylon* is reaching the zenith of its power, and our very lives are now at risk."

"History is unfolding according to the Illuminati's long-term plan. Wars are plotted decades in advance and orchestrated to achieve the destruction of nations and natural elites, depopulation, demoralization, and of course power and profit," wrote commentator Henry Makow. "The super rich have organized themselves into a Satanic cult to prey on mankind and to establish their permanent hegemony. Put yourself in the central bankers' shoes. The nations of the world owe you trillions based on money you printed for the cost of paper and ink. The only way to protect this 'investment' is to establish a thinly disguised dictatorship, using sophisticated methods of social and mind control. This is the true meaning of the 'War on Terror.' It's not directed at 'Muslim terrorists.' It's directed at you and me."

> **N**umerous websites and anonymous tracts can be found that identify some nebulous world elite as the latest reincarnation of the Bavarian Illuminati.

This negative view of the Order has persisted down to today. Numerous websites and anonymous tracts can be found that identify some nebulous world elite as the latest reincarnation of the Bavarian Illuminati. They view the Illuminati as a secret society within secret societies, supported by a banking elite led by the Rothschild Dynasty, advancing a plan of abolishing religion and overturning civil governments to centralize everything under their control—in essence, the New World Order.

Other writers, such as Masonic historian Trevor W. McKeown, view the Illuminati as hardly worth mentioning in the long view of history. "Evidence would suggest that the Bavarian Illuminati was nothing more than a curious historical footnote. Certainly, this is the opinion of Masonic writers. Conspiracy theorists though, are not noted for applying Occam's razor and have decided that there are connections between the Illuminati, Freemasonry, the Trilateral Commission, British Imperialism, International Zionism and communism … that all lead back to the Vatican (or if David Icke is to be believed, the British house of Windsor and extra-terrestrial lizard people) in a bid for world domination. Believe what you will but there is no evidence that any Illuminati survived its founders."

In fact, it seems the Masons have attempted to absolve Freemasonry of any liability in the Illuminati story. The *Masonic Dictionary* stated that following the edicts of Elector Karl Theodor, "[T]he Order began to decline, so that by the end of the eighteenth century it had ceased to exist. Adopting Freemasonry only as a means for its own more successful propagation, and using it only as incidental to its own organization, it exercised while in prosperity no favorable influence on the Masonic Institution, nor any unfavorable effect on it by its dissolution."

Many saw Weishaupt's Illuminism as the public manifestation of a centuries-old struggle between organized religious dogma and a humanism based on ancient esoteric knowledge both theological and secular. Such knowledge required great secrecy because of the unrelenting attacks by both the church and the monarchies.

In 1785, with his Illuminati in disarray, Weishaupt was fired by the University of Ingolstadt and sent away with a small pension. However, he refused the pension, blaming his dismissal on the machinations of the Jesuits. He moved to Regensburg, where he sought asylum with Ernest II, Duke of Saxe-Gotha-Altenburg. Weishaupt was later appointed a professor at the University of Gottingen, where he remained until his death on November 18, 1830, reportedly a somewhat bitter and largely forgotten man. That's what conventional history records. Many today believe his Illuminati ideals live on and some theorists even conjecture he traveled incognito to America and took the place of George Washington. More on that later.

Summary

A mere thirteen years after its founding, in 1784 the Illuminati was the object of a broad edict by Bavarian Duke Karl Theodor, banning any secret society not officially authorized. This was the result of rumors being spread about the anti-clerical and anti-state writings and speeches of some members of both Freemasonry and the Illuminati.

This edict was largely ineffective as many Illuminati believed the decree was not aimed at them specifically nor would be vigorously prosecuted. In fact, the ban prompted many Illuminati members to move to other principalities and countries, further spreading Illuminati theology and increasing membership.

Incensed by the lack of effect by his decree, Karl Theodor issued a second edict nine months later, this time specifying both certain Masonic lodges and the Illuminati. Stating he was "deeply affected and displeased to learn that various Lodges of so-called Freemasons and Illuminati who are still in our States, have taken so little heed of our General Prohibition…," Karl Theodor ordered a halt to all society activities and even ordered the confiscation of "all money and any funds collected illegally" by such groups.

This new decree left no loop holes and signaled the end of any public demonstration of Illuminati activity. Possibly warned of this action ahead of time, Weishaupt was conveniently absent when the decree was issued, having slipped out of Ingolstadt disguised as a workman.

Weishaupt ended up in Regensburg where he was given a civil service job by Duke Ernest II of Saxe-Gotha-Altenburg, a member of his Illuminati. In addition to his work, Weishaupt took this opportunity to write many letters and pamphlets defending Illuminism and attacking its enemies.

Although Order members were now divided from each other and forced to operate in secrecy, the Illuminati did not dissolve. It was merely forced further underground. Although all outward manifestations of the Order ceased, some branches continued to operate as late as 1788.

Yet as members were arrested and compelled to talk and Illuminati papers began to become public, the Order came under further disrepute. Disgruntled whistleblowers accused the Illuminati leadership of being irreligious, depraved, immoral, disobedient to authorities, and neglectful of work and duties. Some defectors claimed to have been threatened and harassed for leaving the Order and even described the Illuminati doctrine of *Patet Exitus*, which advocated committing suicide rather than betraying the Order.

Adding to all these troubles, in 1785 Pope Pius VI sent a letter to the Bishop of Freising in Bavaria warning that membership in the Illuminati was dangerous and incompatible with church traditions.

> **Although Order members were now divided from each other and forced to operate in secrecy, the Illuminati did not dissolve.**

In July of that same year, the Illuminatus Friar Johann Jakob Lanz was struck and killed by lightning while riding with Weishaupt near the gates of Regensburg. On Lanz's body were Illuminati documents including a membership list containing the names of prominent men throughout Europe. The papers also indicated that the Illuminati were still quite active in spite of the Bavarian law.

An angered Prince-Elector Karl Theodor was moved to issue yet another edict, this one specifically requiring all Illuminati to register with the government and repent of their transgressions or face severe punishment. In Ingolstadt, a special commission convened to investigate the Illuminati stepped up their efforts. Known members were arrested and interrogated while their homes and workplaces were thoroughly searched. Karl Theodor sought to have Weishaupt arrested and returned to Bavaria to face trial but was stymied by Duke Ernest, who claimed Weishaupt as a member of his privy council and thus immune to arrest.

In a raid on the home of Franz Zwack, the authorities found a treasure trove of Illuminati documents, including membership rosters, statutes, instructions for recruiters, initiation ceremonies, various insignia, a proposal for the enlistment of women, official government seals used for counterfeiting, instructions for making a tea to induce abortions, poisons, deadly gases and secret ink, and even a strong box that would explode destroying its contents if tampered with. Also recovered were hundreds of letters dealing with sensitive Illuminati matters as well as tables containing the Order's secret symbols, geographical code words, and the procedures for initiation ceremonies. The ongoing revelations concerning the Illuminati caused a major sensation at the time as the contents of its own documents gave the appearance of an organization composed of poisoners and forgers, men of disgusting morals and depraved tastes dedicated to the overthrow of religion and government.

From his home in exile, Weishaupt produced a number of pamphlets attempting to defend the Order but with little effect. The damage had been done. Following additional raids that garnered even more evidence against the Order, the Bavarian authorities published two volumes of Illuminati documentation entitled *Einige Originalschriften des Illuminaten Ordens* (or "Some Original Writings of Illuminati Order"). These volumes were sent to the governments of England, France, and Russia but with no great effect, as foreigners, who had been exposed to Illuminati propaganda, still thought of the Order as honest and noble-minded Freemasons. They could not believe the true objectives of the Illuminati included plans for global revolution accomplished by clandestine groups using secrecy and deceit. Foreign noblemen also disdained the idea of any woman participating in manly efforts at rebellion and sedition.

In 1787, Karl Theodor issued a final edict ordering the death penalty for anyone recruiting for the Illuminati, which he called "harmful and dangerous."

While the Order was destroyed as a formal organization, its doctrines and religion were not eradicated. Weishaupt and others continued to publish Illuminism ideals in newspapers and pamphlets while many Illuminati simply hid themselves within the ranks of the Freemasons. After all, Illuminism is a view of life. It is not readily apparent such as in the form of a uniform, armband, or badge.

The crackdown by the Bavarian authorities may have had the opposite effect from that intended as many Illuminati fled to other countries, spreading their doctrine of world revolution. Secret and shadowy Illuminati Orders sprang up in France, Italy, England, Russia, and even the new lands of America. And no one had any control over the persons who were promoting Illuminism. "I have been convinced that we, as an Order, have come under the power of some very evil occult Order, profoundly versed in science, both occult and otherwise...." warned Duke Ferdinand of Brunswick, a Grand Master of German Freemasonry who had been inducted into the Illuminati in 1783.

Such sentiments were voiced by anti-Illuminati writers years after Karl Theodor's final decree by such men as Jesuit abbot Augustin Barruel and physicist John Robison. Both these men, operating from a background of religion, could only see the anti-clerical aspects of the Order and attacked it accordingly. It is quite ironic that the popularity of the anti-Illuminati works of Barruel and Robison may have spread the doctrines of the Order far beyond anything Weishaupt could have dreamed.

A more modern critic of the Illuminati also had a strict religious heritage and wrote extensively about the dangers of Illuminism. Nesta Helen Webster, beginning

> They could not believe the true objectives of the Illuminati included plans for global revolution accomplished by clandestine groups using secrecy and deceit.

with a series of newspaper articles in 1920, preached against what she perceived as Illuminati occultists plotting world domination. This theme was continued in her persuasive 1921 book entitled *World Revolution: The Plot Against Civilization*. Webster has been criticized as an anti-Semite and pro-Nazi by her detractors, although Winston Churchill supported her.

Webster argued that the sheer audacity and extravagance of the Illuminati scheme for global control rendered it unbelievable to world leaders, who refused to take it seriously. "Weishaupt ... knew how to take from every association, past and present, the portions he required and to wield them all into a working system of terrible efficiency," she wrote.

Some writers today, such as evangelist Texe Marrs and conspiracy researchers Ralph Epperson, still view the Illuminati and their descendants as belonging to a secret organization, based on wealth, race, and bloodline, who continue to try and make economic slaves of the human race. Marrs wrote, "Secret agents of this calculating and cruel cabal have funded revolutions around the globe. They were financial backers of Karl Marx, and they used the Zionist Movement to found the nation of Israel."

Other commentators see history unfolding according to the Illuminati's long-term plan. They see wars being plotted decades in advance and designed to destroy whole nations and their natural elites, along with depopulation, demoralization, and the quest for power and profit.

What is undeniable is that the doctrines of the Illuminati played a role in the revolutions of the future.

REVOLUTION

While the Illuminati may have emerged from the shadows in the late 1700s to foment revolution in the British colonies of America, such involvement has not been clearly established. It was in France that the Order's revolutionary spirit emerged most clearly, accompanied by uncontrollable violence.

France

Contrary to some conventional accounts, the French Revolution was not a spontaneous uprising of the downtrodden public. Prior to the bloodletting between 1787 and 1799, the French monarchy had allowed considerable political and social reform. The lives of the commoners had actually improved. The violent revolution that followed the storming of the Bastille was not by chance but rather an orchestrated effort to create a new political order. And behind this was the shadow of the Illuminati. Once popularly believed to have begun due to a public uprising over lack of food and government representation, the record is quite clear that the revolution was instigated by cells of French Masonry and the German Illuminati, often intermingled. It was plainly a major world event inspired by secret society machinations. *The New Encyclopedia Britannica* reported that in France "there arose a political system and a philosophical outlook that no longer took Christianity for granted, that in fact explicitly opposed it.... The brotherhood taught by such groups as the Freemasons, members of secret fraternal societies, and the Illuminati, a rationalist secret society, provided a rival to the Catholic sense of community."

In a speech shortly before the French revolution broke out, Weishaupt proclaimed, "Salvation does not lie where strong thrones are defended by swords, where the smoke of censers ascend to heaven or where thousands of strong men pace the rich fields of harvest. The revolution which is about to break will be sterile if it is not complete."

Italian adventurer Giuseppe Balsamo, a student of the Jewish Cabala, a Freemason, and a Rosicrucian, became known as Louis XIV's court magician Count Alessandro di Cagliostro. He wrote how the German Illuminati had infiltrated the French Freemason lodges for years and added, "By March, 1789, the 266 lodges controlled by the Grand Orient were all 'illuminized' without knowing it, for the Freemasons in general, were not told the name of the sect that brought them these mysteries, and only a very small number were really initiated into the secret.

Nesta H. Webster was even more pointed, writing in 1924, that the Masonic book *A Ritual and Illustrations of Freemasonry* contains the following passage, "The Masons ... originated the Revolution with the infamous Duke of Orléans at their head."

Key instigators of the French Revolution were Louis Philippe II, the Duke of Orléans, once the Grand Master of French Masonry's Grand Orient of France, and Marie-Joseph Paul Yves Roch Gilbert du Motier, the Marquis de Lafayette, who was initiated into Freemasonry by no less than George Washington and who played an important role in both the American and French revolutions. It has also been noted that the Jacobin Club, the radical nucleus of the French revolutionary movement, was founded by prominent Freemasons.

The Judeo-Masonic Conspiracy website gave this explanation for the involvement of both the Illuminati and Freemasonry in the French Revolution: "The Illuminati order vanished; though it's not clear what happened with the more than 2000 adepts recruited over a period of 10 years throughout Europe. What is a fact is that not all the members were arrested; not even in Germany (i.e. Ernest II and Weishaupt himself). The truth is that, for the purpose of the

A self-styled magician who performed for King Louis XIV, Giuseppe Balsamo was also an occultist who claimed French Freemasonry had been compromised by the Illuminati.

French Revolution, it makes no difference whether or not they were still opera-tive, since all the key figures from the French Revolution (either Freemasons or founders of the Jacobin Club) were already well into Weishaupt's revolutionary philosophy, and would eventually go on with Weishaupt's plans (i.e. Lafayette, Robespierre, Voltaire, Louis Philippe II Duke of Orléans, etc.)." Further expla-nation came from Professor Stauffer, who noted:

> By the beginning of 1789 the lodges of the Grand Orient had received the secrets of the Illuminati. The Duke of Orléans, who had been "illuminated" by Mirabeau, and whose personal politi-cal ambitions were strongly stressed by Robison, gave hearty sup-port to the enterprise; and thus in a very short time the Masonic lodges of France were converted into a set of secret affiliated societies, all corresponding with the mother lodges of Paris, and ready to rise instantly and overturn the government as soon as the signal should be given.

With Weishaupt hiding within the Saxe-Gothe court, the leadership of the Illuminati was passed to Johann Joachim Christoph Bode in 1786. The next year Bode founded the Illuminati Lodge *Philalèthes* in Paris. A 1789 docu-ment found later stated the *Philalèthe* was largely responsible for the revolution started that year. According to Dr. Dennis L. Cuddy, a university teacher and former senior associate with the U.S. Department of Education, "It is entirely logical that the Illuminati would be a prime instigator of the French Revolu-tion as the theories of French philosopher Jean Jacques Rousseau, who greatly influenced Weishaupt, inspired the Revolution."

Another prominent leader of the revolution was Honoré Gabriel Riqueti, comte de Mirabeau, hailed as a hero of the people but later found to be an agent of foreign enemies of France. He reportedly made a speech at the Wilhelmsbad Congress in which he stated he was a member of an organiza-tion linked to the Knights Templar, whose aim was the destruction of both the church and state. Stauffer elaborated: "Mirabeau, during his residence at Berlin, in the years 1786 and 1787, came into contact with the Illuminati of that city and was received as an adept into the Order. Upon his return to Paris he made the attempt to introduce Illuminism into that particular branch of Masonry of which he was also a member, the *Philalèthes* or *Amis Réunis*. To give force to his purpose, he called upon the Illuminati in Berlin to send to his assistance two talented and influential representatives of the Order. The men chosen by the Illuminati circle in Berlin, Bode and von dem Busche, arrived in Paris in the early summer of 1787…. Meantime, the lodges of the *Philalèthes*, and through them the French Masonic lodges in general, were inoculated with the principles of Illuminism. French Freema-sonry thus became committed to the project of forcing the overthrow of thrones and altars."

Honoré Gabriel Riqueti, comte de Mirabeau, was a complicated figure in French history, first as a nobleman on the side of the king, and later an apparent champion of the people and then a traitor. He once admitted being part of a secret organization.

However, Staufffer, whose work is posted on the website of the Grand Lodge of British Columbia and Yukon, also attempted to play down the idea of Illuminati involvement in the revolution by writing, "The much more important contention that the Illuminati were instrumental in starting the French Revolution, shows a lack of historical perspective that either leaves out of account or obscures the importance of the economic, social, political, and religious causes, tangible and overt, though complex, that rendered the Revolution inevitable."

Author E. Michael Jones also attempted to shift blame for the revolution away from the Illuminati. He wrote:

By making German Illuminism the "smoking gun," Barruel let Freemasonry off the hook. He also diverted attention from England, which everyone then saw as the historical and geographical source of the Lodge. Even if we eliminate the shadowy Rosicrucian brotherhood of the 1620s, Scottish Freemasonry had agents on the continent by the 1650s. Whig-controlled lodges were founded during the first three decades of the eighteenth century, and their numbers increased dramatically in France up to the outbreak of the French Revolution. It is perverse to discount that activity by shifting responsibility to an organization that came into existence in 1776 and that for the first few years of its existence—until the initiation of the Prussian Baron von Knigge—was little more than a college fraternity. Barruel argued the Illuminati took over existing lodges, but this explanation is not persuasive, given the number of lodges that needed to be subverted, and the time that would take. If German Illuminism is responsible for the French Revolution, Weishaupt and von Knigge had to complete the takeover in the six years following the 1781 Masonic convention in Wilhelmsbaden.

While famine and hunger among the common people did provoke the French uprising, research reveals it was the Duke of Orléans who reportedly bought all the grain in 1789 and either sold it abroad or hid it away, thus creating near starvation among the commoners. Galart de Montjoie, a contemporary, blamed the Revolution almost solely on the Duke of Orléans and hinted that the Illuminati was behind him, claiming the Duke "was moved by that invisible hand which seems to have created all the events of our revolution in order to lead us towards a goal that we do not see at present...."

The economic woes that contributed to the uprising were also caused by the key role France played in the American Revolution. King Louis XVI's support was largely encouraged by the colonies' ambassador, Benjamin Franklin. A primary instigator of the French Revolution was the infamous Jacobin Club, which became the radical nucleus of the revolutionary movement, and was founded by prominent Freemasons.

Pro-revolutionary members of France's National Constituent Assembly had formed a group that became known as the Society of the Friends of the Constitution. After the assembly moved to Paris, this group met in a hall leased from the Jacobins Convent of Catholic Dominican friars. These revolutionaries, sworn to protect the revolution from the aristocrats, soon were known as the Jacobin Club. Since that time, revolutionaries have been called Jacobins. The anti-Illuminati writer John Robison wrote of the Jacobins, stating, "The intelligent saw in the open system of the Jacobins the hidden system of the Illluminati."

French Masons were heavily involved in the political events of that day. All revolutionaries of the Constituent Assembly were initiated into the third degree of Illuminized Masonry. These included revolutionary leaders with familiar names such as the Duke of Orléans, Valance, Lafayette, Mirabeau, Garat, Rabaud, Marat, Robespierre, Danton, and Desmoulins.

Revolutionary leader Mirabeau indeed espoused ideals that were identical to those of Adam Weishaupt. In personal papers, Mirabeau called for the overthrow of all order, all laws and all power to "leave the people in anarchy." He said the public must be promised "power to the people" and lower taxes but never given real power "for the people as legislators are very dangerous [as] they only establish laws which coincide with their passions." He said the clergy should be destroyed by "ridiculing religion."

Mirabeau ended his tirade by proclaiming, "What matter the means as long as one arrives at the end?"—the same end-justifies-the-means philosophy preached from Weishaupt to Lenin to Hitler.

In February 1787, French noblemen were summoned to an assembly by the controller general of finances, who proposed increasing taxes on the wealthy to reduce the national debt. Needless to say, the wealthy noblemen rejected this idea and instead called for a meeting of the Estates-General, the three estates composed of the nobles, the clergy, and the commoners. The Estates-General, France's parliament, had not met in nearly 200 years. The

A primary instigator of the French Revolution was the infamous Jacobin Club, which became the radical nucleus of the revolutionary movement, and was founded by prominent Freemasons.

three Estates met at Versailles on May 5, 1789, and were immediately divided over how voting should be tabulated. Popular votes would favor the majority, primarily the commoners, while a vote by the Estates would favor the nobles and clergy. The Third Estate commoners, gaining support from some of the priests, won out and King Louis XVI grudgingly called for a National Constituent Assembly to devise a new French constitution while secretly gathering troops to suppress the gathering.

Word of these troop movements spread and in the ensuing Great Fear of July 1789, a crowd in Paris stormed the king's chief prison, the Bastille, where they released only seven prisoners—most were mental patients—but acquired much-needed guns and powder. It was an event that has long been misrepresented and romanticized. Only one out of every thousand people in Paris participated in this event. Bastille guards were lackluster in their defense, and only one of the fifteen available cannons was fired at the crowd.

This attack was not the spontaneous action of a downtrodden mob, according to some. "That brigands from the South were deliberately enticed to Paris in 1789, employed and paid by the revolutionary leaders, is a fact confirmed by authorities too numerous to quote at length.... In other words,

The storming of the Bastille in Paris in 1789, which ignited the French Revolution, is a highly romanticized event in history. Actually, only seven prisoners were released and the prison was not staunchly defended, and the attack may have been orchestrated and exaggerated by secret societies.

the importation of the contingent of hired brigands conclusively refutes the theory that the Revolution was an irrepressible rising of the people," wrote Webster.

Meanwhile mounted couriers dispatched by the secret societies rode from town to town warning the fearful peasants that conspirators against the nation were hiding in the aristocrats' castles and chateaux. They were told the king planned to attack them. Chaos and violence were soon widespread and seen as a revolution.

"We see in the French Revolution the first time where grievances were systematically created in order to exploit them," wrote author Still.

Such exploitation began with the Freemasons as early as 1772 when the Grand Orient Lodge was firmly established in France, counting 104 lodges. This number grew to 2,000 lodges by the time of the Revolution, with 447 lodge members participating in the 605-member Estates General. According to several researchers, the Grand Orient Lodges were the core of the Illuminati penetration of Freemasonry.

French Masonry soon split into two factions—the Grand Lodge of France with its Templar tradition infused with Illuminism and the expelled Grand Lodge Lacorne, which in 1772 became the Grand Orient Lodge with the future duke of Orleans at its head. In 1786, the lodges combined under the leadership of the "illuminized" duke and the base of the revolution was formed. The combined Lodge officers acted as a central committee whom, as early as 1776, began instructing their deputies in the lodges throughout France to prepare the brethren for insurrection.

Alarmed over the spreading havoc, the national assembly in 1789 hastily introduced a Declaration of the Rights of Man and of the Citizen, proclaiming liberty, equality, the inviolability of property and the right to resist oppression—all basic longtime tenants of Masonry.

When the king refused to approve the declaration, a Parisian mob marched to Versailles and took him to Paris, where the assembly continued to hammer out new laws and policies. One was to nationalize property of the Roman Catholic Church to pay off the national debt. This action drove a wedge between the commoners and their supporters within the clergy, increasing hostility on both sides. The assembly then attempted to create a constitutional monarchy similar to England but the weak and fearful Louis tried to flee the country in June 1791. He was captured at Varennes and returned to Paris under guard. Meanwhile, encouraged by the turmoil in France, Masonic-based Revolutionary Clubs sprang up in other countries, including England, Ireland, the German states, Austria, Belgium, Italy, and Switzerland. Tensions between outside nations and France rose until 1792 when France declared war on Austria and Prussia.

Confronted with both a war and a revolution, France degenerated into the Reign of Terror, during which time King Louis XVI, Marie Antoinette, and many thousands, chiefly aristocrats, were executed. In a move similar to Hitler 150 years later, the Jacobins closed down all Masonic lodges in 1791, ironically fearful that Freemasonry's organizing power might turn against them.

Author Epperson, after an exhaustive study of the subject, wrote, "The invisible hand that guided the entire French Revolution was the Illuminati, only 13 years in existence, yet powerful enough to cause a revolution in one of the major countries of the world."

It may be significant to note that the French revolutionaries wore the Phrygian red cap, symbol of the Illuminati and the Greek Phrygian mysteries, comparable to the Eleusinian Mysteries, and that the Illuminati symbol of the eye in the triangle was found on many revolutionary documents.

Wars, riots, and coups continued in France until young General Napoleon Bonaparte finally seized complete control in 1799. Although he carried on his own brand of terror in Europe for years, Napoleon proclaimed an end to the revolution. France was in shambles. Hundreds of thousands had died of starvation, war, violence, and the guillotine. The dream of the Illuminati was realized—the power of both the monarchy and the monolithic church had been largely destroyed. Following the French Revolution, the Illuminati faced more troubles due to the panicked reactions of the royalty of Europe. Aghast at the violence against the throne of France, other royal houses joined Karl Theodor in banning all secret societies and attacks against them were increased. In 1792, an officer of the Illuminati was lynched in Versailles by an angry mob as persecutions of Freemasons and Rosicrucians began. Misgivings about such societies increased greatly with the 1798 publication of John Robison's *Proofs of Conspiracy.*

> **I**n a move similar to Hitler 150 years later, the Jacobins closed down all Masonic lodges....

Freemason lodges and other secret societies were infiltrated by Napoleon's, who was determined to eliminate all subversive organizations to protect his authority and power. "Rather than profiting from the Revolution, the Freemasons suffered greatly from its excesses under the Terror which the Revolution unleashed," noted Christian historian and Vietnam War veteran S. R. Shearer. "The Freemasons were hunted down mercilessly and guillotined by the hundreds by the Jacobins."

The Illuminati appeared to be finally crushed for good.

America

The confidence to start a major revolt such as the French Revolution may have been gained in the new lands of America. While the American Revolution, which ended six years prior to the uprising in France, was not the sole basis for the creation of secret societies as it was in France, there was nevertheless a definite undercurrent of secret society agitation based on religious and philosophical ideas brought from Europe.

The Illuminati had several chapters already in America and they, then and now, were accused of conspiring to bring about the American Revolution of 1776. It is certainly true that many of the leading colonists were Freemasons and supporters of the Enlightenment. As noted by author David Livingston, "The American constitution itself was inspired by the French Revolution, and the ideals of Freemasonry. It enshrined 'Liberty,' meaning freedom from the yoke of Christian morality, rules which it attempted to replace with 'unalienable rights,' a concept originally discussed among the secret meetings of the Illuminati."

Almost every war and revolution seems to be founded on finances. One little known factor precipitating the American Revolution was that in 1764 King George III of England, pressured by the Nathan Rothschild-controlled Bank of England, outlawed the creation of colonial script, the money used by the colonies based on available goods and services. This forced the colonists to sell bonds of indebtedness to the Bank of England and use its bank notes. "The colonies would gladly have borne the little tax on tea and other matters had not it been that England took away from the colonies their money, which created unemployment and dissatisfaction," wrote Benjamin Franklin.

England's King George III's policies toward the American colonies led to the Revolution, but it was his ban on colonial script that ignited the rebellion more than the tea tax.

The Illuminati and men following their doctrine of fighting political and religious tyranny may have used the outrage at the taxes to further incite rebellion. After all, most of America's Founding Fathers could be called Illuminati, for they supported, as exemplified by the Constitution, guarantees on personal, political, and religious freedom. And it is certainly true that in the times preceding the American Revolution, it was the secrecy of the Masonic Lodges that provided the colonial patriots the opportunity to meet and plan their strategy. The Boston Tea Party was entirely Masonic, carried out by members of St. John's Lodge after an adjourned meeting. Others have identified the Lodge as St. Andrew's, but the point is made. There is no documentation to establish if these lodges had been "illuminized." Of the fifty-six signers of the Declaration of Independence, only one was not a Freemason. Masonic writer Manly P. Hall, in his book *The Secret Teachings of All Ages*, told of a most mysterious incident at the time of the signing of this historic document. As the debate over the future of the new country reached a crescendo and many hesitated to sign the declaration, realizing they would be putting their life on the line, a tall stranger with a pale face suddenly spoke out. No one knew who he was or where he came from, but the force of his oration was transfixing. His stirring words ended with the cry, "God has given America to be free!" Amid emotional cheers, every man rushed forward to sign the declaration, except the stranger. "He had disappeared," wrote Hall, "nor was he ever seen again or his identity established." Hall said this episode paralleled similar incidents in world history, when strange unknown men suddenly appeared just in time for the creation of some new nation. "Are they coincidences," he asked, "or do they demonstrate that the divine wisdom of the Ancient Mysteries still is present in the world, serving mankind as it did of old?"

In John Robison's *Proofs of Conspiracy*, he noted that the banning of the Illuminati in Bavaria was largely a formality, with many members reappearing in reading societies known as the German Union. He quoted Weishaupt as proclaiming, "I have considered everything, and so prepared it, that if the Order should this day go to ruin, I shall in a year re-establish it more brilliant than ever." He clearly suspected machinations by the Order in America.

Following the suppression of Illuminism in 1788, Karl Bahrdt and Baron von Knigge sought to revive it under the name of a reading society called the German Union. This hybrid Illuminati soon controlled the publishing and book-selling business in Germany. Such control assured that only those books on religion, philosophy, and politics acceptable to the Order would be available to the public. Although this control of reading matter kept Illuminism alive, it was not until 1808 that there was an overt attempt to revive the Order in the now established

> Such control assured that only those books on religion, philosophy, and politics acceptable to the Order would be available to the public.

nation of Germany. It was called the *Tugendbund,* or League of Virtue, and was founded in Prussia by what has been described as a "quasi-Masonic secret society" in an effort to revive Prussian pride following Prussia's defeat by Napoleon. Apparently the *Tugendbund* was too identifiable with the Illuminati as it was banned after only a year by Napoleonic decree and by Frederick William III. A similar effort was made via the establishment of the League of the Just, with branches in London, Brussels, Paris, and Switzerland. More on that later.

The public was inflamed against such efforts as it was a reading group meeting that attracted attention from the authorities and led them to Illuminatus Zwack's home where secret papers of the Order were discovered. One of these documents was a list of Illuminati lodges existing prior to 1786, a year before the start of the French Revolution. This list identified five lodges in Strasburg; four in Bonn; fourteen in Austria; "many" in Livonia, Courland, Alsace, Hesse, Poland, Switzerland, and Holland; two in Warsaw; eight in England; two in Scotland; and even "several" in North America.

"But, although I cannot consider the German Union as a formal revival of the Order under another name, I must hold those *United,* and the members of those Reading Societies, as *Illuminati* and *Minervals* [emphasis in the original]. I must even consider the [German] Union as a part of Spartacus's work," concluded Robison.

It also may well have been the transfer of Illuminati ideals of freedom and liberty, initiated in Europe, that were brought back by the officers and men of the French and Hessian soldiers who fought in the American Revolution. Robison reported that "their officers and soldiers who returned from America, imported the American principles, and in every company found hearers who listened with delight and regret to their fascinating tale of American independence."

It may even be that Illuminati ideals were imported to the American colonies long before the revolution. Texe Marrs explained:

> In the year 1760, Masonic Illuminati agent Stephen Morin came over from France to the New World. By funneling bribes to U.S. and West Indies politicians, Morin was able to open up dozens of illuminized Masonic chapters throughout the Americas. In these clandestine lodges, thousands were initiated into the Secret Order. Then, in 1772, Haym Salomon … used Rothschild money to further influence American colonial leaders. The result was the American Revolutionary War against King George's Great Britain.

Warnings against the Illuminati came from many quarters. Professor Robison, utilizing the Order's own internal papers, saw clearly in his mind that the organization was created for the "express purpose of rooting out all the religious establishments and overturning all the existing governments of Europe."

Reverend Jedidiah Morse, who was a geographer and father of Samuel Morse of Morse code fame, feared that the anti-Federalists were controlled by the French Illuminati.

The Reverend Jedidiah Morse, an ardent Federalist, in his sermons cited from Robison's book and warned of an Illuminati conspiracy in America. On May 9, 1798, Morse, in a sermon at the New North Church in Boston, addressed the Illuminati by proclaiming, "Practically all of the civil and ecclesiastical establishments of Europe have already been shaken to their foundations by this terrible organization; the French Revolution itself is doubtless to be traced to its machinations; the successes of the French armies are to be explained on the same ground. The Jacobins are nothing more nor less than the open manifestation of the hidden system of the Illuminati. The Order has its branches established and its emissaries at work in America. The affiliated Jacobin Societies in America have doubtless had as the object of their establishment the propagation of the principles of the illuminated mother club in France...."

In his last sermon on the Illuminati, Morse sounded much like Senator Joe McCarthy 150 years later by claiming to have "... an official, authenticated list of the names, ages, places of nativity, professions, &c. of the officers and members of a Society of *Illuminati* (or as they are now more generally and properly styled *Illuminees*) [emphasis in the original] consisting of *one hundred* members, instituted in Virginia, by the *Grand Orient* of France." It turned out his proof of Illuminati infiltration was merely a congratulatory letter from Wisdom Lodge No. 2660 in Portsmouth, Virginia, warranted by the Grand Orient of France, to the newly constituted Union Lodge No. 14 in New York, warranted by the Grand Orient of New York. The letter had been provided by a Federalist Party official intending to discredit Republicans.

Morse's claims were controversial even at the time and, when he could not substantiate his assertions, he was ridiculed and nothing was heard from him until the rise of the Anti-Masonic Party. Yet fear of the Illuminati continued unabated in the new nation.

According to author Rev. Duane L. Wildie, even after the founding of the United States, the Illuminati attempted to export Jacobin-style revolution to the infant United States. "The U.S. was established as a constitutional republic in 1789, the same year the Illuminati's devastation of France began.

Shortly thereafter, agents of the Illuminati, such as French agitator Edmond-Charles Genêt [the French ambassador to America], began organizing insurrectionary and secessionist movements to destroy the American Republic. Their efforts were delayed by widespread public exposure, thanks in no small measure to George Washington, who condemned 'the nefarious, and dangerous plan, and doctrines of the Illuminati....'" According to some researchers, Genêt's real purpose was to gain political favor for France while spreading Illuminism through the establishment of "Democratic Clubs."

John Quincy Adams, who later became a U.S. president, reportedly organized the New England Masonic lodges.

John Quincy Adams, who later became a U.S. president, reportedly organized the New England Masonic lodges. About 1807, Adams wrote three letters to Colonel William C. Stone, a ranking Mason, charging that Thomas Jefferson was using the Masonic lodges for subversive Illuminati purposes. David Allen Rivera, author of *Final Warning: A History of the New World Order*, claimed, "These letters were allegedly kept at the Rittenburg Square Library in Philadelphia, but have since mysteriously vanished. Adams [had written earlier] to Washington, saying that Jefferson and Alexander Hamilton were misusing Masonic lodges for Illuminati purposes and the worship of Lucifer [which is recorded in the Adams Chronicles]."

In 1798, the Reverend G. W. Snyder sent Robison's book to former president George Washington requesting his thoughts on the matter of the Order's activities. In a reply letter, Washington wrote:

> It was not my intention to doubt that, the Doctrines of the Illuminati, and principles of Jacobinism had not spread in the United States. On the contrary, no one is more truly satisfied of this fact than I am. The idea that I meant to convey, was, that I did not believe that the Lodges of Free Masons in this Country had, as Societies, endeavored to propagate the diabolical tenets of the first, or pernicious principles of the latter (if they are susceptible of separation). That Individuals of them may have done it, or that the founder, or instrument employed to found, the Democratic Societies in the United States, may have had these objects; and actually had a separation of the People from their Government in view, is too evident to be questioned. I have heard much of the nefarious, and dangerous plan, and doctrines of the Illuminati, but never saw the Book until you were pleased to send it to me.... The fact is, I preside over none, nor have I been in one more than once or twice, within the last thirty years. I believe notwithstanding, that none of the Lodges in this Country are contaminated with the principles ascribed to the Society of the Illuminati.

Shortly after he became the third president of the United States, Thomas Jefferson wrote that he found some aspects of Weishaupt's credo to be not without merit.

Washington, while not denying that the doctrines of the Illuminati had spread to the new nation, apparently believed it was only the work of certain individuals and not the official agenda of clubs or parties, to include his fellow Freemasons. But if it seemed that Washington was trying to distance himself from the Illuminati, such was not the case with Founding Father and author of the Declaration of Independence, Thomas Jefferson. In an 1800 letter Jefferson wrote a defense of Weishaupt, stating, "As Weishaupt lived under the tyranny of a despot and priests, he knew that caution was necessary even in spreading information, and the principles of pure morality. This has given an air of mystery to his views, was the foundation of his banishment.... If Weishaupt had written here, where no secrecy is necessary in our endeavors to render men wise and virtuous, he would not have thought of any secret machinery for that purpose."

Jefferson, a Freemason and Founding Father, who would become president the next year, wrote in 1800 to Bishop James Madison in Philadelphia about his thoughts on Barruel's anti-Illuminati book. He almost appeared to exhibit admiration for Weishaupt as he wrote:

> I have lately by accident got a sight of a single volume (the 3d.) of the Abbe Barruel's "Antisocial conspiracy," which gives me the first idea I have ever had of what is meant by the Illuminatism against which "illuminate Morse" as he is now called, & his ecclesiastical & monarchical associates have been making such a hue and cry.

> Barruel's own parts of the book are perfectly the ravings of a Bedlamite [inmates of the infamous London insane asylum]. But he quotes largely from Wishaupt [sic] whom he considers as the founder of what he calls the Order. As you may not have had an opportunity of forming a judgment of this cry of "mad dog" which has been raised against his doctrines, I will give you the idea I have formed from only an hour's reading of Barruel's quotations from him, which you may be sure are not the most favorable. Wishaupt [sic] seems to be an enthusiastic Philanthropist.

He is among those … who believe in the indefinite perfectibility of man. He thinks he may in time be rendered so perfect that he will be able to govern himself in every circumstance so as to injure none, to do all the good he can, to leave government no occasion to exercise their powers over him, & of course to render political government useless. This you know is … what Robinson [sic], Barruel & Morse had called a conspiracy against all government. Wishaupt [sic] believes that to promote this perfection of the human character was the object of Jesus Christ. That his intention was simply to reinstate natural religion, & by diffusing the light of his morality, to teach us to govern ourselves. His precepts are the love of god & love of our neighbor. And by teaching innocence of conduct, he expected to place men in their natural state of liberty & equality. He says, no one ever laid a surer foundation for liberty than our grand master, Jesus of Nazareth. He believes the Free Masons were originally possessed of the true principles & objects of Christianity, & have still preserved some of them by tradition, but much disfigured.

The means he proposes to effect this improvement of human nature are "to enlighten men, to correct their morals & inspire them with benevolence. Secure of our success, said he, we abstain from violent commotions. To have foreseen the happiness of posterity & to have prepared it by irreproachable means, suffices for our felicity. The tranquility of our consciences is not troubled by the reproach of aiming at the ruin or overthrow of states or thrones."

As Wishaupt [sic] lived under the tyranny of a despot & priests, he knew that caution was necessary even in spreading information, & the principles of pure morality. He proposed therefore to lead the Freemasons to adopt this object & to make the objects of their institution the diffusion of science & virtue. He proposed to initiate new members into his body by gradations proportioned to his fears of the thunderbolts of tyranny.

This has given an air of mystery to his views, was the foundation of his banishment, the subversion of the Masonic order, & is the color for the ravings against him of Robinson [sic], Barruel & Morse, whose real fears are that the craft would be endangered by the spreading of information, reason, & natural morality among men.

The Federalists under Alexander Hamilton had spread the rumor that Thomas Jefferson and his Democratic-Republican Party were puppets of the European Illuminati and, judging from Jefferson's letter, either Jefferson lacked knowledge of the inner Illuminati teachings, which is hard to believe, or the Federalists were correct in charging him with being a secret member of the Order. Although no concrete evidence has been made public that Jefferson was an Illuminatus, from the writings of both he and Franklin, it is apparent that they both were most familiar with the ideals of the Rosicrucians and, hence, the Illuminati.

At George Washington's inauguration in 1789, the oath of office was administered by Robert Livingston, Grand Master of the New York Grand Lodge. On September 18, 1793, Washington dedicated the U.S. Capitol. Author David Livingstone described this Masonic ceremony, writing, "Dressed in Masonic apron, the president placed a silver plate on the cornerstone and covered it with the Masonic symbols of corn, oil and wine. The plan of the city of Washington, D.C., itself was designed by Freemason and architect Pierre Charles L'Enfante [sic] in the form of a pentagram, or five-pointed star. In 1848, in a Masonic ceremony, the cornerstone was laid of the Washington Monument, an obelisk or pillar, like those formerly dedicated to the dying gods of ancient Middle East. And, every president of the United States since Independence has purportedly been a 33rd degree Freemason." The question left unanswered was "How many of the Masonic lodges involved in the revolution and its successful aftermath had been illuminized?"

Some wags have even proposed that Washington's identity was surreptitiously taken by none other than Adam Weishaupt. It is true that Weishaupt's activities after 1790 are disputed, with various versions offered of his life following the outlawing of his Order. Robert Shea and Robert Anton Wilson in their trilogy *Illuminatus!* suggested that Weishaupt traveled to America, murdered George Washington, and assumed his personae.... In Part I, they quoted from "a small left-wing newspaper in Chicago," stating, "No historian knows what happened to Adam Weishaupt after he was exiled from Bavaria in 1785.... The possibility that Adam Weishaupt killed George Washington and took his place, serving as our first President for two terms, is now confirmed.... The two main colors of the American flag are, excluding a small patch of blue in one corner, red and white: these are also the official colors of the Hashishism [the Assassins]. The flag and the Illuminati pyramid both have thirteen horizontal divisions: thirteen is, of course, the traditional code for marijuana ... and is still used in that sense by Hell's Angels among others. Now, 'Washington' formed the Federalist party. The other major party in those days, The Democratic Republicans, was formed by Thomas Jefferson [and] there are grounds for accepting the testimony of the Reverend Jedediah [sic] Morse of Charleston, who accused Jefferson of being an Illuminati agent. Thus, even at the dawn of our government, both parties were Illuminati fronts.... In spite of the fact that his face appears on billions of stamps and dollar bills, and his portrait hangs in every public building in the country, no one is quite sure what Washington looks like ... contemporary portraits of the first President ... do not even seem to be the same man.... Some of the portraits can be found in *Encyclopedia Britannica* and the resemblance to portraits of Weishaupt is undeniable."

One critic of this Washington-substitution theory astutely observed, "Washington took command [of the Continental Army] on July 3, 1775, and the war lasted five years. The Bavarian Illuminati was founded allegedly in 1776. Either George grew wings and quickly flew to Germany during a break from tactical maneuvers, or Weishaupt, newly arrived from Germany, was for some reason given command of the Continental army. George would have been the first general up to that era to travel across the ocean and back (takes a while each way) while managing a revolutionary army facing a relatively superior enemy."

Shea and Wilson ultimately put the kibosh on their own theory of Weishaupt substituting for the Father of our Country. They correctly pointed out that while Washington was cultivating his hemp crop, "Adam Weishaupt was very definitely still in Bavaria, teaching canon law at the University of Ingolstadt."

In tune with the psychedelic 1960s, Shea and Wilson did connect Washington with the Illuminati in that both reportedly smoked marijuana for

The portrait on the U.S. dollar bears a strong resemblance to Adam Weishaupt, founder of the Illuminati.

THE ILLUMINATI: THE SECRET SOCIETY THAT HIJACKED THE WORLD

the medicinal and hallucinatory benefits. They noted that separating male from female hemp plants is "not required for the production of hemp rope but is absolutely necessary if one wants to use the flowering tips of the female for marijuana." Indeed, Washington's diary entry for August 7, 1765, read, "Began to seperate [sic] the Male from the Female hemp at Do—rather too late." This indicated he wanted to separate the male from the female to increase potency before fertilization.

Some researchers have suggested the British looted and burned Washington, D.C., in the War of 1812 to destroy incriminating documents exposing treason against the United States by Illuminati operatives within the government.

The followers of Thomas Jefferson, known as Jeffersonian Republicans, were anti-monarchy and anti-federalist. They divided in 1796 when members, those advocating states' rights, farming interests, and more democratic procedures, became Democratic-Republicans. In 1826, they became known simply as Democrats and, in 1854, the National Republicans shortened their name to just Republicans. This two-major party system has remained until today.

By the time of the War between the States, much of the secret society machinations had been forgotten by the American public thanks to the Anti-Masonic Movement of the early 1800s.

> It is historical fact that for some years the Rothschilds ... had financed major projects in the United States on both sides of the Mason-Dixon Line.

It is historical fact that for some years the Rothschilds, financial supporters of the Illuminati, had financed major projects in the United States on both sides of the Mason-Dixon Line. Nathan Rothschild, who owned a large Manchester textile plant, bought his cotton from Southern interests and financed the importation of Southern cotton prior to the war. At the same time, wrote Rothschild biographer Wilson, "He had made loans to various states of the Union, had been, for a time, the official European banker for the U.S. government and was a pledged supporter of the Bank of the United States."

Rothschild interest in North America reached back at least as far as 1837, when a German-born representative of the Rothschild banking empire arrived in the United States and changed his name from August Schoenberg to August Belmont. He was rumored to be an illegitimate Rothschild himself. Whatever the truth, Belmont was in daily correspondence with the Rothschilds and became their acknowledged representative in the United States.

With no apparent capital of his own, Belmont soon was buying up government bonds and within a few short years had created one of the largest banking firms in the nation, August Belmont & Company. Thanks to Belmont's aggressive business tactics, the Rothschilds soon had American investments in industry, banks, railroads, federal and state bonds, tobacco, cotton, and, of course, gold. Belmont was instrumental in later financing both North and South during the Rebellion. He strongly influenced bankers in both England and France to support the Union war effort by the purchase of government bonds. At the same time, he quietly bought up the increasingly worthless bank bonds of the South at great discounts, with the idea that the South would be forced to honor them in full after the war.

Salomon Rothschild, one of the younger family members, visited America at the onset of the war and was as openly pro-Confederate as their agent Belmont was pro-Union. Rothschild disparaged President Lincoln, stating, "He rejects all forms of compromise and thinks only of repression by force of arms. He has the appearance of a peasant and can only tell barroom stories."

The idea that the machinations behind America's sectional war were instigated by the European financial elite was confirmed by German chancellor Otto von Bismarck. "The division of the United States into federations of equal force was decided long before the Civil War by the high financial powers of Europe. These bankers were afraid that the United States, if they remained in one block and as one nation, would attain economic and financial independence, which would upset their financial domination over the world. The voice of the Rothschilds prevailed…. Therefore they sent their emissaries into the field to exploit the question of slavery and to open an abyss between the two sections of the Union," proclaimed Bismarck.

If the gambit indeed was to split the republic in two and regain North America for the European bankers, presidential aspirant Abraham Lincoln saw it clearly. He often tried to explain that his goal was to save the American union, not emancipate the slaves. During his famous debates with Stephen Douglas in 1858, Lincoln made his personal position on race quite clear: "I will say, then, that I am not, nor ever have been, in favor of bringing about in any way, the social and political equality of the white and black races…. I, as much as any other man, am in favor of having the superior position assigned to the white race."

Anti-slavery advocates in both North and South realized that technological advances meant the demise of slavery was only a matter of time. But extremists on both sides, encouraged by agents of the European financiers, continually fanned the fires of discontent.

One leader of this agitation came from yet another secret society—the Knights of the Golden Circle (KGC), a secret society founded by surgeon and author George W. L. Bickley, who in 1854 built his first knightly "castle" in Cincinnati, Ohio. Bickley drew liberally from the rites and rituals of Freemasonry. The Knights have similar passwords, handshakes, and temples to serve as meeting halls for their lesser, grand, and supreme councils. According to author G. Edward Griffin, the KGC "had close ties with a secret society in France called The Seasons, which itself was a branch of the Illuminati."

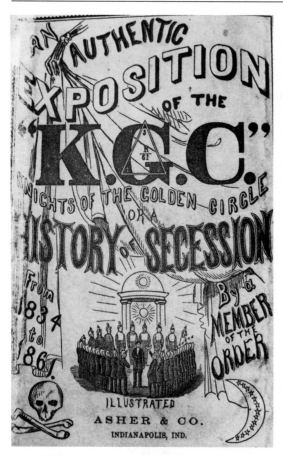

An 1854 book published by the Knights of the Golden Circle and advocating secession for southern slave states.

The name Knights of the Golden Circle was derived from a grandiose plan to create a huge slave-holding empire 2,400 miles (3,862 kilometers) in circumference with Cuba as the center point. This new nation was to include the southern United States, Mexico, part of Central America, and the West Indies in Order to gain a monopoly over the world's supply of tobacco, sugar, rice, and coffee. Historian Shelby Foote used the term "Jacobins" to describe the secessionists of the era—disrupters of the established social, religious, and political Order—who had been operating in America since the late 1700s. The Jacobins, and their form of "illuminized" Freemasonry, were the connective tissue that tied the secret societies of the Old World to hidden manipulation in the New World.

They had crossed the Atlantic after successfully destroying the "Old World Order" in France and were looking for new worlds to conquer. These fugitives were former members and the offspring of members of elder secret societies, including the outlawed Bavarian Illuminati, which traced its origins back to the dawn of humankind.

Even the assassin of President Lincoln, Southern sympathizer John Wilkes Booth, was a known member of the Knights of the Golden Circle (along with the famous outlaw Jesse James and Sam Houston). Various conspiracy researchers have connected Booth to the Illuminati, the Italian Carbonari, and through fellow Knights member Judah Benjamin, who was the secretary of state for the Confederacy, to the House of Rothschild. After the war, Benjamin, often called the "sinister power behind the throne" of Confederate president Jefferson Davis, fled to England where he became a successful attorney, reportedly representing the Rothschilds. Benjamin's mentor was U.S. senator John Slidell of Louisiana, whose niece married Rothschild agent August Belmont. Benjamin's connection to Slidell further connected Benjamin to European banking, which funded the Confederacy. As previously mentioned, the Rothschilds had established a central bank system in the major European nations since the late eighteenth century. The idea of a central bank, providing cheap credit and expandable money to commercial interests, was pushed through the Continental Congress in 1781 by Congressman Robert Morris, a Philadelphia financier born in England who initially voted against the Declaration of Independence, yet whose firm, Willing and Morris, profited handsomely by trading in arms and loans to the fledgling American government.

Along with Federalist Alexander Hamilton, who was called "Morris' youthful disciple," the pair was instrumental in scraping the old Articles of Confederation in favor of a new Constitution, which essentially established an American system of mercantilism and Big Government copied after that of England, under which the colonists had just rebelled. Morris was able to create the first central bank in America, the Bank of North America. When this enterprise failed after only three years, it was Hamilton, by then secretary of the treasury, who created a second central bank, the First Bank of the United States, which Jefferson and his followers strongly opposed.

Hamilton's bank, like that of Morris, was closely modeled after the Rothschild-controlled Bank of England and created a partnership between the government and banking interests. Twenty percent of the bank's capital was obtained through the federal government, with the remaining 80 percent pledged by private investors, including foreigners such as the Rothschilds. "Under the surface, the Rothschilds long had a powerful influence in dictating American financial laws. The law records show that they were the power in the old Bank of the United States," wrote author Gustavus Myers.

Although no direct evidence can be found that Hamilton was a Rothschild agent, the fact that he acted to establish a private bank in America certainly indicates his fealty to the European banking system. As a supporter of a federal bank and his founding of the Federalist Party in 1791, it is evident he was working for the banking elite. Hamilton worked against the ideals of the Founding Fathers. Both today and at the time, many felt Hamilton's monetary policy was unconstitutional and based on fraudulent statements. Franklin, Jefferson, Madison, and other supporters of Republican government fought Hamilton's banking system and his federalism. As it seems evident that Illuminati-connected European bankers and their New World associates were trying to gain control over America's money supply, it is especially fascinating to note that the first assassination attempt on a U.S. president was against Andrew Jackson, who in 1836 ended the effort to establish a central bank, claiming it was unconstitutional and "a curse to a republic; inasmuch as it is calculated to raise around the administration a moneyed aristocracy dangerous to the liberties of the country."

America's first assassination attempt of a president was made on Jackson in 1835 by a man named Richard Lawrence, whose pistols misfired. Lawrence claimed to be "in touch with the powers in Europe." Two U.S. presidents who issued debt-free currency—Lincoln in 1862 and John F. Kennedy in 1963—also were assassinated under controversial circumstances. It should be

In 1835 an attempt was made on President Andrew Jackson's life. It was the first such attack on a U.S. president, and some feel it might have been because Jackson was opposed to the idea of a central bank.

noted that Jackson was a Freemason, which indicates that his Masonry, unlike that of the Illuminized European Masons, was not under the thrall of the international banking elite who had used Freemasonry as a cover for their Illuminati ideals.

If indeed the War Between the States was a plot to split the United States by the secret societies, as claimed by a Knights of the Golden Circle tract published in 1861, and backed by the European Rothschilds, it very nearly succeeded. In the fall of 1863, France and Britain, both badly needing Southern cotton for their textile mills, came dangerously close to both recognizing and militarily aiding the South; it was Russia's pro-North Czar Alexander II who tipped the balance. After receiving information that England and France, pending an end to the rebellion in North America, were plotting war to divide up the Russian Empire, Alexander ordered two Russian fleets to the United States. One anchored off the coast of Virginia, while the other rested at San Francisco. Both were in perfect position to attack British and French commercial shipping lines. No threats or ultimatums were made public, but it was clear that should war come, the Russian Navy was in a position to wreak havoc.

Faced with the possibility of World War I a half century before they were ready, the leaders of France and Britain hesitated, and the South, running out of money, manpower, and materials, was devastated. Adding insult to this loss were the harsh Reconstruction policies of the Republican government, which caused the South to suffer under punitive economic policies well into the 1960s. Reconstruction generated enduring hatred and bitterness into the twentieth century as well as the growth of other secret societies in the South, such as the Ku Klux Klan. It should be recalled that well into the 1960s there were no Republicans, only Democrats, in the Solid South. The men who created societies such as the Klan, Knights of the Golden Circle, the Thule Society, and Cecil Rhodes's Round Table Groups drew from a long history of clandestine European organizations. Eric Dubay, an American yoga teacher living in Thailand, is author of *The Atlantean Conspiracy*. After researching the "New World Order," he concluded:

> Before the Revolutionary War, the "New World" of the Americas lacked unity and autonomous identity. For almost 300 years there was no military, constitution, or federal government. Then within two short years, the snap of a historical finger, America had Continental Marines, Continental Congress, and the Arti-

cles of the Confederation. With the Declaration of Independence, the British colonialists (or "Americans") officially separated from the British nationalists. Freemason and bloodline General George Washington became first President of the now United States of America, and royal rule of America switched from overt to covert. Royal and secret society rule had not changed, only the perception of governance changed while the same DNA stayed in office. Instead of peasants well-aware of their plight, knowing the Monarchs/Emperors oppressing them, we became peasants who actually believed we were born into a free and open system.

Russia

The Russian Revolution—indeed the very creation of communism—sprang from Western conspiracies involving Illuminati theology long before World War I. "One of the greatest myths of contemporary history is that the Bolshevik Revolution in Russia was a popular uprising of the downtrodden masses against the hated ruling class of the Czars," wrote author Griffin. The planning and funding for the revolution came from outsiders, especially financiers in Germany, Britain, and the United States operating under Illuminati theology.

However, according to author Douglas Reed, a former London *Times* correspondent, communism sprang directly from the Illuminati. "When Weishaupt died in 1830," he wrote, "his order was probably stronger than it had ever been, but was about to change its name; the same organization with the same aims, was in the late 1840's to emerge as communism." Reed concluded that a "permanent organization of secret conspirators in all lands" brought about the "emergence of world revolution as a permanent idea and ambition."

Reed also said communism and the Russian Revolution also were the "greatest Judaic triumph and vengeance on record" as they were "organized, directed and controlled by Jews who had grown up in the Talmud-controlled areas" of Russia. He said that by following the Talmud law "Thou shall reign over every nation ...." and "the Lord thy God shall set thee on high above all nations of the earth," the Jewish leaders of the revolution organized as a permanent destructive force with a permanent center of governance and a permanent armed force ready to conquer other nations.

However, some Bolsheviks and their communist descendants traced their origins to revolutionaries in nineteenth-century Italy called the Car-

> **R**eed concluded that a "permanent organization of secret conspirators in all lands" brought about the "emergence of world revolution as a permanent idea and ambition."

bonari, or charcoal-burners. Being a secret society, their true origin is undocumented. However, the Sufi author Idries Shah of India, writing under the pen name Arkon Daraul, claimed the Carbonari originated in Scotland, later the refuge of the outlawed Knights Templar. Spreading to the continent, they lived a communal life in the forests burning wood to make charcoal. Under the pretense of carrying their charcoal for sale, they traveled freely, communicated with members, and recruited followers.

By the early 1800s, the Carbonari were established in France, Germany, Poland, and Italy. They practiced a primitive form of Freemasonry, complete with secret signs, symbols, and lodges ruled by a High Lodge commanded by a grand master.

The anti-authoritarian socialism of the Carbonari, Illuminized Freemasonry, and other rationalist and humanist groups that flourished during the Age of Enlightenment added to the aggravation of the Roman Catholic Church.

"In our day, if Masonry does not found Jacobite or other clubs, it originates and cherishes movements fully as Satanic and as dangerous. Communism, just like Carbonism, is but a form of the illuminated Masonry of (Illuminati founder) Weishaupt," warned Monsignor George Dillon in 1885.

One such movement was the International Working Men's Association—better known as the First International—the direct forerunner of communism, convened in London in 1864 and soon under the leadership of Karl Marx.

Marx was born Moses Levy Mordecai in 1818 in Trier, Germany, to Heinrich and Henrietta Marx, both descended from a long line of Jewish rabbis and hence undoubtedly familiar with the mystical traditions of the Torah and Cabala. To deter anti-Semitism, both Karl and his father were baptized in the Evangelical Established Church. Both were greatly influenced by the humanism of the Age of Enlightenment.

Following his graduation from the University of Bonn, Marx enrolled in the University of Berlin in 1836 where he joined a secret society called the Doctor Club filled with devotees of German philosopher and professor Georg Hegel and his philosophy. Although earlier expressing devout Christian ideals, Marx joined these Hegelians in moving from a belief that the Christian Gospels were "human fantasies arising from emotional needs" to outright atheism. Some modern conspiracy writers even claim that Marx eventually became a Satanist. They point to his eventual criticism of Hegel as not material enough in his thinking, to the anti-social societies in which he moved and a work written by Marx as a student that stated, "If there is a something which devours, I'll leap within it, though I bring the world to ruins ... that would be really living." Such metaphysical views of Marx indicate his acquaintance with Illuminati lore. Richard Wurmbrand, a Christian minister of Hebrew descent who spent fourteen years in a communist prison in his homeland of Romania, in his 1986 book *Marx and Satan* stated, "Marx's chief aim was the destruction of religion. The good of the workers was only a pretense."

The goals of Russian communists and Karl Marx were largely the same goals of the Illuminati and continental Freemasonry. They were also almost identical to the major platform goals of Hitler's National Socialists (Nazis), indicating they all stemmed from a common source.

First consider the basic goals of the Illuminati:

The author of *The Communist Manifesto*, Karl Marx was born a Jew, but he was baptized and his name was changed to protect him from anti-Semites in Germany.

1. Establish a New World Order.
2. Abolition of all ordered national governments.
3. Abolition of inheritance.
4. Abolition of private property.
5. Abolition of national sovereignty and patriotism.
6. Abolition of the individual home and family life.
7. Abolition of all established religions.

Now consider the ten steps to create an "ideal state" as offered by Karl Marx in his *Communist Manifesto*:

1. Abolition of private property.
2. A progressive or graduated income tax.
3. Abolition of all inheritance.
4. Confiscation of property of dissidents and immigrants.
5. Creation of a monopolistic central bank.
6. Centralize all communication and transport.
7. Control over all factories and farm production.
8. Central ownership of capital with deployable work force.
9. Blur the distinction between rural country and cities.
10. Free public education to indoctrinate all children.

Finally, we see these same goals reflected in the Nazi Party's major platform points, aside from their racial segregation:

1. A strong central government with unquestioned authority.
2. Creation of a New World Order.
3. Demand colonization of others' property.
4. Control of allocation of work force.
5, Halt further immigration into Germany.
6. Abolition of inheritance.
7. Confiscation of war profits.
8. Nationalization of all corporations.
9. Creation of National retirement plans.
10. The expropriation without compensation of land for public purposes.
11. Free public education.
12. Elevate national health through compulsory physical training.
13. The creation of a national army.
14. Laws against art and literature which have a destructive effect on our national life.
15. Allow only religions that do not endanger the State or its morality concepts.

It seems clear that the original goals of Illuminism while remaining substantially the same, nevertheless have been somewhat tailored through the years to match the desires of any current movement.

These goals are all a real-world model of the theory of Hegel's dialectic, which proposes one side of a conflict (thesis) be pitted against the other (antithesis) to create a compromise (synthesis). This formula—with the added element of actually creating the conflict—has been used successfully by the students of Hegel, which include the Illuminati, Cecil Rhodes's Round Tables, Hitler's Nazis, and members of the modern secret societies. Hegel himself also was connected to the Illuminati by his immersion in the Hermetic tradition.

> In fact, many researchers claim communism was created by illuminized men as the perfect antithesis to the Western thesis of capitalism....

In fact, many researchers claim communism was created by illuminized men as the perfect antithesis to the Western thesis of capitalism so that the resulting synthesis (the Cold War) would eventually lead to their New World Order.

The term communism itself can be traced back to French author Nicolas-Edme Restif, who in 1785, four years before the French Revolution, used the word in a published book review. Like Weishaupt, Restif was greatly influenced by French philosopher Rousseau. He also was a collaborator on publications by Nicolas de Bonneville, honored by Marx as having begun the modern revolutionary movement. Christian author and former Satanist/Illuminist Joseph "Doc" Marquis states emphatically that he was taught that communism was created by the Illuminati. In fact, he said the very name "communism" is simply another way of expressing Illuminism.

At the height of the McCarthy communist scare, a California State Senate report from the Committee on Education, stated:

> Communism and Russia are by no means synonymous. Russia merely occupies the unfortunate position of being communism's first victim. Communism is synonymous with world revolution and seeks the destruction of all nations, the abolition of patriotism, religion, marriage, family, private property, and all political and civil liberties.... So-called modern communism is apparently the same hypocritical and deadly world conspiracy to destroy civilization that was founded by the secret order of Illuminati in Bavaria in May 1, 1776, and that reared its hoary head here in our colonies at critical periods before the adoption of our federal Constitution.

This view was echoed by Gary Allen in his 1971 book *None Dare Call It Conspiracy*. He wrote, "'communism' is not a movement of the down-trodden masses but a movement created, manipulated and used by power-seeking billionaires in order to gain control over the world ... first by establishing socialist governments in the various nations and then consolidating them all through a 'Great Merger,' into an all-powerful world Socialist Super-State probably under the auspices of the United Nations."

Throughout the twentieth century, many people saw the telltale signs of conspiracy, the reach for world domination, within both Europe and America, but blamed it first on international Jewry and then on communism. They failed to see the hidden hand of Illuminism that was pulling the strings of the leaders advocating a one-world government. One such leader was Karl Marx, who in 1843 married and moved to Paris, a hotbed of socialism and extremist groups already known as communists. It was in Paris that Marx befriended German philosopher Friedrich Engels. Marx and Engels both became confirmed communists

Friedrich Engels became a friend and cohort to Karl Marx after the two met in Paris. Together they collaborated on *Das Kapital.*

and collaborated in writing a number of revolutionary pamphlets and books, the most famous being three volumes discussing capital, *Das Kapital.* Ironically, it was Engels, the son of a wealthy capitalist, who would financially subsidize Marx, champion of the working class, most of his life.

Long a devoted Hegelian, Engels had been converted to socialist humanism by Moritz Moses Hess, known as the "communist rabbi," and by Robert Owen, a utopian socialist and spiritualist openly hostile to traditional religion.

Owen, greatly influenced by Illuminatus Johann Heinrich Pestalozzi, organized the first socialist movement in Britain and then came to America. At New Harmony, Indiana, in 1825, Owen established the first commune in the United States. There, in words ringing with Illuminati theology, Owen proclaimed, "I am come to this country to introduce an entire new order of society; to change it from an ignorant selfish system, to an enlightened social system, which shall gradually unite all interests into one and remove all cause for contest between individuals."

Some claim it was Rabbi Hess who introduced both Marx and Engels to the Illuminati. It was in London in 1847 that Marx and Engels entered another secret society called the League of the Just, composed primarily of German emigrants, many of whom were thought to be escaped members of the outlawed Illuminati. It was Hess who advocated changing the name of The League of the Just into the Communist Party. At the same time both Marx and Engels were Thirty-First Degree Masons. William Josiah Sutton, in his 1983 book *The Illuminati 666*, explained:

> Napoleon, when he came into power, would not tolerate the activities of the Jacobin Clubs with their independent opposition, so he completely suppressed it. However, the Illuminati just operated under other names. It was under the name of "The League of the Just" that Karl Marx became a member. He was hired to update the writings of Adam Weishaupt, written seventy years earlier. Weishaupt died in 1830, but his revolutionary plans were carried on by a list of his successors. In 1842, Karl Marx began to write revolutionary propaganda for the League of the Just, hoping to cause a spirit of unrest. In 1844, in collaboration with Friedrich Engels, and under the supervision of The League of the Just, Marx began to write the infamous "*Manifest der Kommunistichen Partei,*" commonly known today as the "The Communist Manifesto," which appeared at the beginning of 1848. Later, the Illuminati operating under the name of The League of the Just, changed their name to "The League of Communists."

Further confirmation of the connection between the communists and the Illuminati came in the days following the Russian Revolution when socialist revolutionaries in Germany organized and called themselves Spartacists, after Adam

Weishaupt's Illuminati pseudonym. They were led by Rosa Luxemburg, the founder of the *Spartakusbund* or Spartacist League and led to a worker's rebellion in early 1919 called the Spartacist uprising. Later, in Russia they became known as Bolsheviks and then communists. Some say they celebrate May 1 as the birth of their revolutionary movement because it was the birthday of the Illuminati.

It is interesting to note that in 1851 Marx was a correspondent for Horace Greeley's *New York Herald Tribune*. The paper praised the German Marx as "one of the clearest and most vigorous writers that country has produced—no matter what may be the judgment of the critical upon his public opinions in the sphere of political and social philosophy." Greeley along with Clinton Roosevelt was financially assisting the Communist League in London with its publication of the *Communist Manifesto*. Apparently Marx also was receiving support from the Rothschilds, as reportedly two checks made payable to Marx by Nathan Rothschild were found on display at the British Museum in London.

> Apparently Marx also was receiving support from the Rothschilds, as reportedly two checks made payable to Marx by Nathan Rothschild....

In a 1961 speech, President John F. Kennedy remarked on Marx's newspaper career, stating, "We are told that foreign correspondent Marx, stone broke, and with a family ill and undernourished, constantly appealed to Greeley and managing editor Charles Dana for an increase in his munificent salary of $5 per installment, a salary which he and Engels ungratefully labeled as the 'lousiest petty bourgeois cheating.' But when all his financial appeals were refused, Marx looked around for other means of livelihood and fame, eventually terminating his relationship with the *Tribune* and devoting his talents full time to the cause that would bequeath the world the seeds of Leninism, Stalinism, revolution and the Cold War. If only this capitalistic New York newspaper had treated him more kindly; if only Marx had remained a foreign correspondent, history might have been different. And I hope all publishers will bear this lesson in mind the next time they receive a poverty-stricken appeal for a small increase in the expense account from an obscure newspaper man."

"[W]hile Karl Marx was writing the *Communist Manifesto* under direction of one group of Illuminists, Professor Karl Ritter of Frankfurt University was writing the antithesis under direction of another group, so that those who direct the conspiracy at the top could use the differences in these two ideologies to start dividing larger and larger numbers of the human race into opposing camps so they could be armed and then made to fight and destroy each other, together with their political and religious institutions," wrote author Carr. "The work Ritter started was continued by the German so-called philosopher Friedrich Wilhelm Nietzsche (1844–1900) who founded Nietzscheism. Nietzscheism was developed into Fascism and later into Nazism and used to enable the agentur of the Illuminati to foment World Wars One and Two."

Estonian author Juri Lina, who called Soviet communism "a social catastrophe," reported that on "17 November 1845, Karl Marx became a member of the lodge *Le Socialiste*. In February 1848, Marx published his 'Communist Manifesto' on the orders of the Masonic leadership."

Author William H. McIlhany also argued that by 1815 the Illuminati had begun to extend its influence into many parts of the world beyond Bavaria and France. He noted:

> Among the personages and organizations responsible for extending the Illuminati's infiltration and power throughout Europe were Filippo Michele Buonarroti and his *Sublimes Maîtres Parfaits* [Sublime Perfect Masters], and Louis Auguste Blanqui and the *Société des Saisons* [Society of the Seasons]. Those two branches of the Illuminati formed the source of the League of the Just.... The Illuminists provided the unseen hand behind the staged communist revolts of 1848, which convulsed France, Austria-Hungary, and Russia. This inaugurated the era of communist subversion, infiltration, and control of governments across the globe—an era which has not ended, contrary to "polite" opinion.

Marx's manifesto set forth the immediate steps to create an ideal communist state. As previously demonstrated, they bear a striking resemblance to the *Protocols of the Learned Elders of Zion* and the goals of the Illuminati. The proposals of Marx were so remarkably similar to the steps for creating the ideal society proposed by the Bavarian Illuminati that it suggests a common origin. "In fact, the [communist] Internationale can hardly be viewed as anything but Illuminated Masonry in a new disguise," commented author Still.

In 1848, Marx failed to incite a socialist revolution in Prussia and, after evading prison, returned to London. Personality clashes, petty bickering, and fractious fights over ideology prevented the Communist League from becoming an effective force. Militant factions chided Marx for being more concerned with speeches than revolutions and he gradually withdrew into isolation, which only ended with his attendance at the 1864 First International. He died of apparent lung abscesses on March 14, 1883, depressed over the suicides of his two daughters and just two months after the death of his wife.

Following an abortive revolution in 1905, thousands of Russian activists had been exiled, including Leon Trotsky, whose Hebrew name was Lev Davidovich Bronstein, and Vladimir Ilyich Lenin, a revolutionary intellectual who adapted the theories of Hegel, Fichte, Ruskin, and Marx to Russia's political and economic predicament. After years of attempts at reform, the czar was forced to abdicate on March 15, 1917, following riots in St. Petersburg (then Petrograd) believed by many to have been instigated by British agents. The czar and his entire family were murdered by the Bolsheviks a year later in July 1918 at Yekaterinburg in central Russia. When the Bolsheviks were forced to hastily flee from Yekaterinburg, they had no time to destroy all the telegraph tape strips in the telegraph building. Nikolai Sokolov, who participated in an investigation in 1919 by "White Russians," reported that the anti-communist leader Alexander Kolchak found and kept the telegraph tapes, which later were deciphered by experts in Paris in 1922. The tapes revealed that orders to the communists originated outside of Russia.

"The order to murder the Czar and his family came from New York. Lenin had hardly any say in the matter," noted Jewish Canadian writer Henry Makow. "The chairman of the [communist] Central Executive Committee, Yakov Sverdlov, sent a message to Yakov Yurovsky where he relayed that after he had told Jacob Schiff in New York about the approach of the White army, he had received orders from

Vladimir Lenin, leader of the Russian Revolution, was a believer in the ideals of Marx, Engel, Hegel, and others who advocated overturning the social order.

Schiff to liquidate the Czar and his entire family at once. This order was delivered to Sverdlov by the American Representation, which then lay in the town of Vologda."

So it is clear that communism did not spring spontaneously from poor, downtrodden masses of workers, but was the result of long-range schemes and intrigues by Illuminati refugees and adherents of Illuminism. Author Douglas Reed contended that the labor uprisings in various European countries following the publication of the Manifesto indicated that the secret societies were colluding together in promoting the Illuminati's world revolution. He proclaimed the cause of all this: "Karl Marx and his Communist Manifesto were the outward and visible signs of a significant historic event: Talmudic Judaism had taken over the world revolution."

Citing author Lina's charge that about 150 million people died as a result of the Bolshevik Revolution, some researchers viewed the resulting communism as being subsidized by the Illuminati and the banking cartel behind it. It is ironic, and largely unknown to the public, that Western leaders, guided by the banking elite, pledged to oppose the Bolsheviks but in fact defended and financed them. They betrayed the White Russians who were our allies in World War I and ensured a Bolshevik victory through their intervention.

It is true that in January 1917, Leon Trotsky was living in New York City working as a reporter for *The New World*, a communist newspaper. Trotsky had escaped an earlier failed attempt at revolution in Russia and fled to France, where he was expelled for his revolutionary behavior. "He soon discovered that there were wealthy Wall Street bankers who were willing to finance a revolution in Russia," wrote journalist Still.

One of these bankers was the previously mentioned Jacob Schiff, whose family had lived with the Rothschilds in Frankfurt. Another was Elihu Root, attorney for Paul Warburg's Kuhn, Loeb & Company. According to the *New York Journal-American*, "[I]t is estimated by Jacob's grandson, John Schiff, that the old man sank about $20 million for the final triumph of Bolshevism in Russia." Root, a member of the Council on Foreign Relations, contributed yet another $20 million, according to the *Congressional Record* of September 2, 1919.

According to *The Reformation Online* website, "In Wall Street and the Bolshevik Revolution, we noted that revolution related financiers were concentrated at a single address in New York City, the same Equitable Office Building. In 1917 the headquarters of the No. 2 District of the Federal Reserve System, the most important of the Federal Reserve districts, was located at 120 Broadway; of nine directors of the Federal Reserve Bank of New York, four were physically located at 120 Broadway, and two of these directors were simultaneously on the board of American International Corporation. The American International Corporation [A.I.C.] had been founded in 1915 by the Morgan interests with enthusiastic participation by the Rockefeller and Stillman groups. The general offices of A.I C. were at 120 Broadway. Its directors were heavily interlocked with other major Wall Street financial and industrial interests, and it was determined that American International Corporation had a significant role in the success and consolidation of the 1917 Bolshevik Revolution."

A.I.C. directors included names like Rockefeller (representing Rothschild interests), Lovett and Stillman, and Frank Vanderlip, one of the Jekyll Island conspirators who created the Federal Reserve, and George Herbert Walker, whose daughter married Prescott Bush, the father and grandfather of the two Bush presidents. Gary Allen, author of *None Dare Call It Conspiracy*, concluded, "In the Bolshevik Revolution we have some of the world's richest and most powerful men financing a movement which claims its very existence is based on the concept of stripping of their wealth men like the Rothschilds, Rockefellers, Schiffs, Warburgs, Morgans, Harrimans and Milners. But obviously, these men have no fear of international communism. It is only logical to assume that if they financed it and do not fear it, it must be because they control it. Can there be any other explanation that makes sense?"

It is also factual to note that nearly all of the leading communists who took control of Russia from 1917 to 1920 were Jewish or had Jewish family members in the past. It is not hard to suspect that some, if not most, were "illuminized" with esoteric and Cabalistic theology. Even Vladimir Ilyich Ulyanov, known simply as Lenin, had a Jewish grandfather on his mother's side. According to Ruth Wisse, writing on the myjewishlearning.com website, "The declassification of documents since the collapse of the Soviet Communist tyranny in 1991 has brought irrefutable proof that Lenin's maternal great-grandfather was a *shtetl* Jew named Moshko Blank. Whether or not Lenin himself was aware of this piece of information is uncertain, but by the time of his death in 1924 his sister had possession of the facts—and, by order of the Central Committee of the Communist party, was forced to keep them secret. The order held firm until the dissolution of the Soviet Union in the early 1990s."

Another leader of the Russian Revolution was Leon Trotsky, who was the son of David Bronstein, a wealthy Jewish farmer from what is now the Ukraine.

David R. Francis, the last U.S. ambassador to pre-communist Russia, warned about the international aspect of the revolutionaries in a January 1918 dispatch to Washington: "The Bolshevik leaders here, most of whom are Jews and 90 percent of whom are returned exiles, care little for Russia or any other country but are internationalists and they are trying to start a worldwide social revolution."

This conspiratorial view was echoed by none other than Winston Churchill, who in a February 8, 1920, article in the *Illustrated Sunday Herald* entitled "Zionism versus Bolshevism," he wrote, "This movement among the Jews is not new. From the days of Spartacus-Weishaupt to those of Karl Marx, and down to Trotsky (Russia), Bela Kun (Hungary), Rosa Luxembourg (Germany), and Emma Goldman (United States), this worldwide conspiracy for the overthrow of civilization and for the reconstitution of society on the basis of arrested development, of envious malevolence, and impossible equality, has been steadily growing. It played, as a modern writer, Mrs. Webster, has so ably shown, a definitely recognizable part in the tragedy of the French Revolution. It has been the mainspring of every subversive movement during the Nineteenth Century; and now at last this band of extraordinary personalities from the underworld of the great cities of Europe and America have gripped the Russian people by the hair of their heads and have become practically the undisputed masters of that enormous empire."

It must clearly be understood that these world revolutions cannot be blamed on all persons of the Jewish faith. In fact, whether in revolutionary France or Russia, and certainly in Germany, the majority of victims were Jewish. The trouble seems to have come only from those deeply involved in the Zionist movement, which originated in Russia. In fact, both in the French and Russian revolutions, atheism was declared the national religion.

If there is one, single motivating factor behind the horror and tragedy experienced in the twentieth century, it is surely anti-communism. The animosity between the so-called democracies of the West and the communism of the East produced continuous turmoil from 1918 through the end of the century.

The flight of the privileged elite from communism in Russia during 1918 and from China in 1949 sent shock waves through the capitals of Europe and America, which prompted a backlash that lasted for decades. Anti-communism became the basis for much of the horror and tragedy in the twentieth century. The cry of "Workers of the world unite!" struck fear in the capitalists of Western industry, banking, and commerce who were not in the know. This fear trickled through their political representatives, employees, and on into virtually every home. Thoughtful people were mystified as to how such high-level capitalists as the Morgans, Du Ponts, Warburgs, Schiffs, and Rockefellers could condone, much less support, an ideology that overtly threatened their position and wealth.

To understand this seeming dichotomy, one must understand that the Illuminati operated largely on the Hegelian Dialectic, utilized so well by Weishaupt, Marx, and Hitler. The application of the Hegelian Dialectic could explain how Western capitalists created communism on one side (thesis) as a perceived enemy to the democratic nations (antithesis) on the other side. The ensuing conflict produced huge markets for finance and armaments and eventually a leveling of both sides (synthesis). Often during the past fifty years, it was said, the United States was getting more like Russia and Russia was getting more like the United States.

Social activists and bureaucrats alike have learned this both-ends-against-the-middle stratagem well, whether by experience, intuition, or study. Demand more than you really need (thesis) from your opposition (antithesis) and, after compromises, you'll usually end up with what you wanted in the first place (synthesis).

"This revolutionary method—the systematic working of thesis vs. antithesis = synthesis—is the key to understanding world history," declared conspiracy author Texe Marrs. Others have described this Hegelian dialectic as problem, reaction, solution.

Trotsky, carrying a passport authorized by President Woodrow Wilson and accompanied by nearly 300 revolutionaries along with funds provided by Wall Street, was sent to Russia by ship on March 27, 1917, just days before

America entered World War I. Trotsky openly revealed the plan in a speech before leaving New York. "I am going back to Russia to overthrow the provisional government and stop the war with Germany," he proclaimed.

As Trotsky traveled to Russia with an American passport and Wall Street funding, Lenin also left exile. Aided by the Germans and accompanied by about 150 trained revolutionaries, Lenin was put on a "sealed train" in Switzerland along with at least $5 million. The train passed through wartime Germany unhindered as arranged by Max Warburg and the German High Command. Warburg was the brother of Paul Warburg, one of the creators of the Federal Reserve and who handled World War I finances for the United States. Here was a classic example of internationalists/globalists—in this incidence, two brothers—managing opposing sides of the same war.

Both Lenin and Trotsky were labeled German agents by the government of Alexander Kerensky, the second of provisional governments created following the czar's abdication. By November 1917, Lenin and Trotsky, backed by Western funds, had instigated a successful revolt and seized the Russian government for the Bolsheviks.

Because of the 1917 revolution, the Russians pulled out of World War I, which had the effect of allowing German forces to divert their forces back to the Western Front.

But the communist grip on Russia was not secure. Internal strife between the "Reds" and the "Whites" lasted until 1922 and cost some twenty-eight million Russian lives, many times the war loss. Lenin died in 1924 from a series of strokes after helping form the Third International or Comintern, an organization to export communism worldwide. Trotsky fled Russia when Stalin took dictatorial control and in 1940 was murdered in Mexico by a Stalinist agent.

The Russian Revolution not only took Russia out of the war, freeing millions of German soldiers on the Eastern Front for transfer to the Western Front in France, but at the Illuminati globalist level, communism become entrenched and ready to stimulate worldwide fear and mistrust in communism vs. capitalism vs. fascism.

Even Lenin apparently came to understand that he was being manipulated by more powerful forces. "The state does not function as we desired," he once wrote. "A man is at the wheel and seems to lead it, but the car does not drive in the desired direction. It moves as another force wishes."

This other "force" may well have been members of the secret societies operating in the shadow of the Illuminati, who were behind the birth of communism itself. Lenin described them as "monopoly finance capitalists."

William Guy Carr, a former intelligence officer in the Royal Canadian Navy who was introduced to Bolshevik theories while onboard a ship to Asia in 1909, in his book *Pawns in the Game*, wrote, "Once these revolutionaries [who put Lenin in power] had served their purpose most of them were condemned to exile or death. It was only a comparatively short time before all original members of the First International were either dead, in prison, or in exile. The history of the Lenin and Stalin Dictatorships should convince any unbiased person that the masses of the world's population, regardless of color, or creed have been used as pawns in the game of international chess played by the 'Red' international bankers and the 'Black' Aryan Nazi War Lords as directed by the Illuminati."

With the subjugation of Russia by the communists, Carr said the leaders of the World Revolutionary Movement went into action. He wrote:

> The Central Committee [of the communists] was ordered to prepare the Temples and Lodges of the Grand Orient for action. The members were to be made active, proselytizing their revolutionary and atheistic ideology. The Party Line was to unite all revolutionary bodies for the purpose of bringing all the big capitalistic countries into war with each other so that the terrific losses suffered, the high taxation imposed, and the hardships endured by the masses of the population, would make the majority of the working classes react favorably to the suggestion of a revolution to end wars. When all countries had been Sovietized then the Secret Powers would form a Totalitarian Dictatorship and their identity need remain secret no longer. It is possible

that only Lenin knew the secret aims and ambitions of the Illuminati who molded revolutionary action to suit their purposes.

One such secret aim was to prepare for a Great War, which within Illuminati-inspired groups was being planned even before the Russian Revolution had been completed.

Summary

Although, as will be seen, there were the fingerprints of Illuminism, if not actual Order members, involved in the American Revolution, it was later in France that a definite connection between rebellion and the Illuminati may be found.

It is popularly believed, and sometimes taught, that the French Revolution was caused by a public uprising due to lack of food and unequal government representation. However, close examination reveals that the upheaval was the result of agitation by cells of French Freemasonry and the German Illuminati, which oftentimes were intermingled. Even the stodgy *New Encyclopedia Britannica* noted that the revolutionary spirit was encouraged by a "brotherhood taught by such groups as the Freemasons, members of secret fraternal societies, and the Illuminati, a rationalist secret society...."

One observer of the scene, an Italian who took the name Cagliostro and served as court magician to King Louis XVI, wrote that by 1789, the year revolution broke out, some 266 lodges of the Masonic Grand Orient of France had become imbued with Illuminati philosophy, many without knowing it. Only a small number of French Masons were initiated into the secrets and rituals of the Illuminati.

Not only were prominent leaders of the revolution, such as the Duke of Orléans and the Marquis de Lafayette, ranking Freemasons but the infamous Jacobin Club, which provided the bulk of the radicals at the heart of the rebellion, was itself a creation of Illuminzed Freemasons. Another notable revolutionary leader, Count Mirabeau, achieved the status of an Illuminati Adept while living in Berlin. Note also that it was the theories of French philosopher Rousseau that had so inspired Weishaupt. The illuminated lodges were in close communication with the Grand Orient Lodge in Paris and were prepared to rise up when the signal was given.

Contrary to popular accounts, the French monarchy in the decade prior to the revolution had permitted considerable political and social reforms improving the lives of the commoners. One theory at the time was that the Duke of Orléans, influenced by the Illuminati, bought up all the grain in 1789, thus causing starvation among the commoners.

As the three Estates squabbled over voting rights at Versailles in May 1789, King Louis XVI called for a National Assembly while secretly summon-

Louis Philippe II, Duke of Orléans, supported the French Revolution but was still killed during the Reign of Terror. One theory was that he incited the rebellion by depriving commoners of grain.

ing troops to suppress the gathering. Word of the troop movements created fear among the population and in July a Paris crowd assailed the King's prison, the Bastille, where they released a paltry seven prisoners, most of them mental patients, but did seize much-needed weapons and gunpowder. The storming of the Bastille has been greatly romanticized, considering only one in every thousand Parisians participated and the defense was lackluster with only one of the fifteen available cannons being fired at the crowd. Even this event was blamed on agitation and encouragement by *agents provocateur* sent from the south.

Meanwhile couriers sent from the secret societies rode from town to town warning fearful peasants that the king intended to attack them. They were told their enemies were hiding in the homes of the aristocrats and soon violence became widespread.

The insurrection was inspired by the fusion of two Masonic Grand Lodges into one grand assembly in 1786 headed by the Duke of Orléans, who began to prepare it for revolution.

As chaos grew in 1789, the national assembly at Versailles introduced the Declaration of the Rights of Man and of the Citizen, which proclaimed liberty, equality, and the rights to property and to resist oppression. When King Louis XVI refused to sign the declaration, a mob seized him and took him to Paris. Encouraged by the success of the Illuminati-inspired French rebellion, Revolutionary Clubs sprang up in England, Ireland, Austria, Belgium, Italy, Switzerland, and the German states. Tensions between the nations grew until 1792 when France declared war on Austria and Prussia. The resulting war and violence degenerated into the Reign of Terror in which King Louis XVI, Marie Antoinette, and many thousands of aristocrats were led to the guillotine. The chaos continued until 1799 when a young Napoleon Bonaparte took control and proclaimed an end to the revolution. It is interesting to note that following their success at igniting a revolution, the Jacobins shut down all the French Masonic lodges, apparently fearful that the organizing power of Freemasonry might be turned against them. Likewise, the remnants of the Bavarian Illuminati did not fare well after the revolution.

Aristocrats who fled to neighboring countries raised the alarm over Illuminati machinations and soon other nations joined German Elector Karl Theodor in banning all secret societies. Both Freemasons and anyone identified as an Illuminatus were hunted down and executed, particularly by the Jacobins in France. It appeared to be the end of the Illuminati until one considers its influence in another revolution, this one in the new lands of America. Although the American Revolution had ended six years before violence broke out in France, many of the same secret society influences were accused of fomenting insurrection within the thirteen colonies. Illuminati documents discovered in the raid on the home of Zwack noted there were "several" Illuminati chapters or lodges in North America before the revolution and even at the time they were accused of fostering insurrection. These chapters often included leading Freemasons and avid supporters of the Enlightenment. The slogans of the American Revolution—Liberty and Equality—inspired those of the French Revolution. The concept of "unalienable rights" for the individual was first discussed within the Illuminati. Most of America's Founding Fathers supported the concept of individual freedom from political and religious tyranny, thereby supporting Illuminati goals. And above all, a majority of the patriots were practicing Freemasons, within which flowed the currents of Illuminati doctrines.

> **M**ost of America's Founding Fathers supported the concept of individual freedom from political and religious tyranny, thereby supporting Illuminati goals.

While some Masons had been "Illuminized" in European lodges before immigrating to America, others received training as members of newly formed lodges in the colonies. It was the secrecy inherent in America's Masonic lodges that provided cover for the planning necessary for the revolution. It was also thought that the Illuminati ideals of individual freedom from church and state may have been absorbed by the officers and men of the French and Hessian soldiers sent across the Atlantic during the revolution. It was said that these troops were delighted and intrigued by the tales of American independence and carried discontent back to Europe.

Even the Founding Fathers were not immune to the divisiveness over the Illuminati. Recall that John Quincy Adams accused Thomas Jefferson of subverting Masonic lodges with Illuminism. George Washington, responding to a friend who had sent him John Robison's anti-Illuminati book in 1798 wrote, "It was not my intention to doubt that, the Doctrines of the Illuminati, and principles of Jacobinism had not spread in the United States. On the contrary, no one is more truly satisfied of this fact than I am."

Jefferson, always the free thinker and champion of individual liberty, as late as 1800, wrote in defense of Weishaupt, noting that it was "the tyranny of a despot and priests" that caused the great secrecy within the Illuminati and was the principal cause of its crusade against church and state. He also charac-terized Barruel's anti-Illuminati screed as the "the ravings of a Bedlamite." Jef-ferson's defense of Weishaupt prompted his political enemies, particularly Fed-eralist Alexander Hamilton, to accuse the author of the Declaration of Independence of being a puppet of the European Illuminati. Although no con-crete evidence has been made public that Jefferson was an Illuminatus, from the writings of both he and Benjamin Franklin it appears obvious that both men were familiar with the ideals of the Rosicrucians and, hence, the Illumi-nati. And it is well known that the Freemasons, whether illuminized or not, played a major role in the founding of the United States. When dedicating the U.S. Capitol, Washington wore his Masonic apron. Researchers have claimed that every president since Washington has been at least a Thirty-three-Degree Mason. One disproven conspiracy theory even claimed that Weishaupt secret-ly came to America where he murdered Washington and took his place as president.

One theory that has been proven true based on the letters of the Found-ing Fathers is that many of them, including Washington and Jefferson, grew cannabis hemp (marijuana) and smoked it for its medicinal and hallucinatory properties, just as within the Illuminati. It is known that the Boston Tea Party was entirely a Freemason operation performed by members of a Boston lodge, identified by some as St. John's and by others as St. Andrew's. Every signatory to the Declaration of Independence, except one, was known to be a Freema-son. After the revolution, the French ambassador to America, Edmond-Charles Genet, made attempts to organize insurrection against the new Amer-ican Republic and establish Illuminism but was stymied by patriots, including George Washington, who condemned "the nefarious, and dangerous plan, and doctrines of the Illuminati...." Meanwhile, attempts to revive the Illuminati in Germany by reorganizing as reading societies proved a failure, and some, such as the *Tugendbund* or League of Virtue, were banned by Napoleonic decree. Attempts in other European nations met similar fates. Except for the Freemasons, secret societies had a difficult time becoming established in the new nation of the United States, where men prided themselves on individual freedom from both government and religion. Individualism had a strong hold on the men and women who tamed the wilderness areas. Public attention was again turned to secret societies in the early 1800s with a scandal involving the Freemasons, whether Illumininized or not. Following the disappearance and presumed murder of Captain William Morgan in 1826, who had threatened to reveal Masonic secrets, coupled with the lack of investigation by Masonic offi-cials, public outrage prompted an anti-Masonic backlash that caused the clo-sure of more than 2,000 lodges with more than 45,000 Masons resigning. For the first time a third political party was formed in the United States—the Anti-Masonic Party. It was a serious blow to Freemasonry. The party was formed by opponents of President Andrew Jackson, himself a Freemason but who opposed the international bankers and their attempts at creating a central bank. Many of the Founding Fathers had argued that a central bank would be injurious to the new nation. John Adams in 1811 wrote, "[E]very bank of discount, every bank by which interest is to be paid or profit of any kind made by the [lender], is downright corruption. It is taxation for the public for the benefit and profit of individuals...."

The First Bank of the United States created by the efforts of Alexander Hamilton's mentor Robert Morris was closely modeled after the Bank of England. It created a partnership between the government and banking interests. The new federal government provided 20 percent of the bank's capital with the remaining 80 percent pledged by private investors, including foreigners such as the Rothschilds. It appeared conspiring European bankers and their New World associates were trying to gain control over America's money supply. This bank

Captain William Morgan, a veteran of the War of 1812, threatened in 1826 to publish the secrets of the Freemasons. Shortly afterwards, he was kidnapped and presumably killed by Masons as depicted in this engraving.

also caused inflation by the creation of fractional-reserve notes. Money merchants prospered but the average citizen suffered. In 1811, when the bank's twenty-year charter came up for renewal, it was defeated by one vote in both the Senate and the House.

The Second Bank of the United States was created by Alexander Hamilton in 1816 to combat chaotic banking conditions following the War of 1812. This central bank ended in 1836, after President Jackson vetoed a congressional bill to extend its charter, precipitating what became known as the "Bank War." Jackson, the first president from west of the Appalachian Mountains, denounced the central bank as unconstitutional as well as "a curse to a republic; inasmuch as it is calculated to raise around the administration a moneyed aristocracy dangerous to the liberties of the country."

It is interesting to note that America's first presidential assassination attempt was made on Jackson in 1835 by a man named Richard Lawrence, whose pistols misfired. Lawrence claimed to be "in touch with the powers in Europe." The unharmed, but infuriated, Jackson withdrew government funds from the "den of vipers" and Second Bank resident Nicholas Biddle retaliated by curtailing credit nationally, causing widespread economic panic. According to some researchers, Biddle was an agent of Jacob Rothschild in Paris. Jackson was censured by Biddle's friends in the Senate for failure to obtain Congressional authorization to withdraw the funds, but the censure was annulled in 1837. Biddle disappeared from the scene and "Old Hickory," the hero of the Battle of New Orleans, by the end of his two terms had managed to eliminate the national debt. There were other attempts to resurrect a central bank but none succeeded until the creation of the Federal Reserve System in 1913.

With the anti-Masonic scandal and the decimation of its membership, a very distinct rift was opened between the lodges of North America, which in the confusion lost understanding of the arcane knowledge and became more like social clubs, and their European brothers, who managed to hold on to some of the prehistoric lore and traditions. A similar loss of ancient knowledge had occurred in England when King James II in 1688 went into exile in France, taking with him traditional Masonic knowledge gained from the Scots, beneficiaries of the Knights Templar teachings. His followers were known as Jacobites, James being derived from Jacob.

> Those left behind attempted to restore the Masonic traditions but knew that much of the original information passed down through the centuries was lost.

Those left behind attempted to restore the Masonic traditions but knew that much of the original information passed down through the centuries was lost. In 1714, following Georg, the Elector of Hanover, Germany, being placed on the throne of England and installed as King George I, the Grand Lodge of London was formed and from there came most of the traditions of modern Masonry. British author and Masonic scholar Laurence Gardner wrote that Masonic texts prepared about 1717 most likely were produced by Sir Francis Bacon, believed by some to be the real author of the Shakespeare material as well as the person who masterminded the forty-six scholars who produced the King James Bible. A coded clue as to Bacon's contributions can be found in in the King James Version of Psalms 46—count forty-six letters from the beginning to get the word "Shake" and forty-six words from the end to get the word "Spear." The number forty-six was Bacon's cypher.

Following the anti-Masonic Movement of the early 1800s, much of the secret society machinations during the revolution had been forgotten by the American public. But the European bankers had not forgotten about America. By 1860 the Rothschilds, financial supporters of the Illuminati, had financed major projects on both sides of the Mason-Dixon Line. Nathan Rothschild, who owned a large Manchester textile plant, bought his cotton from Southern interests and financed the importation of Southern cotton prior to the war. Concurrently, he had made loans to various states of the Union, serving as the official European banker for the U.S. government and a pledged supporter of the Bank of the United States. Nathan also was represented in the United States by Rothschild agent August Schoenberg, who arrived in America in 1837, changed his name to August Belmont, and was instrumental in financing both the South and the North prior to the Confederate rebellion. Salomon Rothschild, one of the younger family members, visited America at the onset of the war and was as openly pro-Confederate as Belmont was pro-Union. Again, this was an example of the non-partisan machinations of the internationalists.

The idea that European bankers, led by the Rothschilds, were behind America's sectional war was confirmed by German chancellor Otto von Bismarck, who said the bankers feared economic independence in the United States would "upset and their financial domination over the world." "The voice of the Rothschilds prevailed," said Bismarck. "Therefore they sent their emissaries into the field to exploit the question of slavery and to open an abyss between the two sections of the Union." Apparently the one man who clearly saw this attempt to divide the American Republic and thereby regain mastery over it for the French and British was Abraham Lincoln, who often explained his goal was to save the American union, not emancipate the slaves.

One secret society that worked to divide the nation prior to the War Between the States was the Knights of the Golden Circle (KGC), a secret society founded by surgeon and author Dr. George W. L. Bickley, who in 1854 founded his first knightly "castle" in Cincinnati, Ohio. Bickley liberally copied the rites and rituals of the Freemasons and reportedly had close ties to a French branch of the Illuminati called "The Seasons." Respected historian Shelby Foote described the southern secessionists as "Jacobins," who had crossed the Atlantic after successfully destroying the "Old World Order" in France. John Wilkes Booth, the assassin of Lincoln, was a member of the KGC, as was Confederate secretary of state Judah Benjamin, himself connected to the Rothschilds. The plot by the secret societies to split the United States, as claimed by a Knights of the Golden Circle tract published in 1861, very nearly succeeded. In the fall of 1863, France and Britain, both badly needing Southern cotton for their textile mills, came dangerously close to both recognizing and militarily aiding the South.

John Wilkes Booth, the famous actor who killed President Lincoln, was a member of the Knights of the Golden Circle.

It was Russia's pro-North Czar Alexander II, after learning that England and

France were plotting to divide up the Russian Empire at the conclusion of the war in America, who changed the course of history. He ordered two Russian fleets to the United States, one to Virginia and the other to San Francisco, where they were in position to attack British and French commerce shipping lines. No threats or ultimatums were made public, but it was clear that should war come, the Russian Navy was in a position to wreak havoc. Faced with the possibility of World War I a half century before they were ready, the leaders of France and Britain hesitated and the South, out of money, manpower, and materials, was crushed. The harsh Reconstruction policies of the Republican government, which caused the South to suffer under punitive economic policies well into the 1960s, generated enduring hatred and bitterness well into the twentieth century and prompted the growth of other secret societies, such as the Ku Klux Klan. But if the plan by secret societies to divide the United States was thwarted, their goal of world revolution continued. The planning and funding for the revolution in Russia came from financiers in Germany, Britain, and the United States operating under Illuminati theology.

It has been stated that the Illuminati merely changed names in the late 1840s. Tracing their anti-authoritarian socialism back to the charcoal-burners, or *Carbonari*, radicals carried on the world revolution ideals of the Illuminati under the name communism. One group leading the way to socialism was the International Working Men's Association, called the First International. This direct forerunner of communism was convened in London in 1864 and soon under the leadership of Karl Marx, the German-born son of a long line of Jewish rabbis. Marx undoubtedly was familiar with the mystical traditions of the Torah and Cabala and Illuminati theology. The basic goals of the Russian communists under Marx were largely the same as those of the Illuminati and continental Freemasonry, indicating a common origin. These goals included the establishment of a New World Order and the abolition of all ordered national governments, inheritance, private property, national sovereignty and patriotism, the individual home and family life, and all established religions. These same Illuminati goals, which bear a striking resemblance to the *Protocols of the Learned Elders of Zion*, can be found within the platform of the later Nazi Party. These goals are all a real-world model of the theory by German philosopher Georg Hegel, whose dialectic theory proposes one side of a conflict (thesis) be pitted against the other (antithesis) to create a compromise (synthesis). This formula—with the added element of actually creating the conflict—has been used successfully by the Illuminati, Hitler, and members of the modern secret societies.

Hegel was connected to the Illuminati by his immersion in the Hermetic tradition. One devoted follower of Hegel, Friedrich Engels, who with Marx composed the theories of Marxist communism, had been converted to socialist humanism by Moritz Moses Hess, the "communist rabbi," and by Robert

Owen, a utopian socialist and spiritualist. Owen, greatly influenced by Illuminatus Johann Heinrich Pestalozzi, organized the first socialist movement in Britain and then brought his socialism to America.

In 1847, Marx and Engels, both Freemasons, joined a secret society in London called the League of the Just, composed primarily of German emigrants many thought to be escaped members of the outlawed Illuminati. On the suggestion of Rabbi Hess, the name of the League was changed to the Communist Party. One researcher claimed Marx wrote his "Communist Manifesto" on the orders of the Masonic leadership.

On the suggestion of Rabbi Hess, the name of the League was changed to the Communist Party.

In 1917, as World War I was reaching a crescendo, rebellion in Russia forced the abdication of the czar, who later, along with his entire family, was murdered by the Bolsheviks, who took control of Russia and withdrew from the war, freeing millions of German soldiers for action on the Western Front. It was the Bolsheviks, the forerunners of communism, who were funded by bankers in London and New York.

In fact, when the Russian Revolution broke out, the future leaders of the communist movement—Leon Trotsky and Vladimir Lenin—were not even in Russia. Lenin, who had been in exile in Switzerland, passed through wartime Germany aided by the German intelligence service, which included Max Warburg, brother of Paul Warburg, who had immigrated to the United States in 1902, had helped create the Federal Reserve System and the Council on Foreign Relations, and was instrumental in securing U.S. financing for the war effort. The two brothers ran the war from opposite sides.

Trotsky was living in New York and, armed with an American passport and Wall Street funding, he left with a ship full of revolutionaries for Russia. One of his backers was Jacob Schiff, whose family had lived with the Rothschilds in Frankfurt. His grandson, John Schiff, estimated Schiff spent about $20 million ensuring the final triumph of Bolshevism in Russia.

A like amount was provided by Elihu Root, attorney for Paul Warburg's Kuhn, Loeb & Company, and a Council on Foreign Relations member.

As noted by *None Dare Call It Conspiracy* author Gary Allen, the fact that some of the world's wealthiest and most powerful men financed a movement calling for the stripping of wealth from such persons as themselves displayed a lack of fear of communism. Since they did not fear it, they must have controlled it.

Furthermore, the Communist Party in Russia was largely composed of Jewish Zionists, who saw themselves as internationalists and supporters of a worldwide social revolution. The connection between Zionism, Illuminism, and communism was pointed out in a 1920 article by Winston Churchill.

But it is clear that past world revolutions cannot be blamed on persons of the Jewish faith. In fact, whether in revolutionary France or Russia, and certainly in Germany, the majority of victims were Jewish. In fact, both in the French and Russian revolutions, atheism was declared the national religion. The Russian Revolution not only took Russia out of the war, but at the Illuminati globalist level, communism became entrenched, creating fear among the peoples of the West. Anti-communism can today be identified as a prime motivation behind the subsequent wars of the twentieth century. It was the application of the Hegelian Dialectic by Western capitalists that created communism on one side (thesis) as a perceived enemy to the democratic nations (antithesis) on the other side. The ensuing synthesis, known as the Cold War, produced huge markets for finance and armaments and eventually a leveling of both sides. Often during the past fifty years, it was said, the United States was getting more like Russia and Russia was getting more like the United States.

In World War II, we saw the same stratagem working as socialist Russia was pitted against socialist Germany, their populations mere pawns in a rigged game being played by Illuminized globalists. The doctrines, first synthesized from older traditions and groups by the Illuminati, continued to spread into our modern time.

Modern Illuminati

The shadow of Illuminism continued to stretch across the globe long after the demise of the original Order of the Bavarian Illuminati. After the revolutions in America and France ended, as had the life of Adam Weishaupt, the principles of Illuminism continued to thrive within Freemasonry and other offshoot secret societies.

Weishaupt exhibited a clear understanding of Illuminism whether applied for good or evil. Addressing new *dirigens* of the Order, he once proclaimed, "Do you realize sufficiently what it means to rule—to rule in a secret society? Not only over the lesser or more important of the populace, but over the best of men, over men of all ranks, nations, and religions, to rule without external force, to unite them indissolubly, to breathe one spirit and soul into them, men distributed over all parts of the world?"

As far back as 1829 a secret meeting was conducted in New York, at which a British Illuminist named Frances "Fanny" Wright addressed the assembly. An associate of socialist Robert Dale Owen, son of the aforementioned utopian socialist Robert Owen, this Scottish woman had moved to New York and, along with Owen, started a publication called the *Free Enquirer*.

According to author David Allen Rivera, "At the meeting, she spoke of equal rights, atheism, and free love, as she promoted a Women's Auxiliary of the Illuminati. Those present were told that an international movement of subversives was being developed along the lines of Illuminati principles, which would be used to foment future wars. They were to be known as 'communists.' This movement was to be used to make the idea of a one-world government more appealing by bringing chaos to the world through war and revolution, so the Illuminati could step in to create order."

According to Canadian naval commander Carr, the leaders of the Illuminati-inspired World Revolutionary Movement (WRM), along with high officers of Europe's Illuminized Freemasonry, met in Switzerland in 1912 and ordered the assassination of Austrian archduke Franz Ferdinand to bring about World War I.

Just as today, the Balkan states were locked in a cycle of war, revolution, and ethnic conflict. Since political tensions in Europe had been rising for several years, accompanied by an arms race, the assassination of Franz Ferdinand was not the cause of the war but the trigger.

According to author William T. Still, a 1952 Masonic publication stated that Bosnian Serb Gavrilo Princip, who on June 28, 1914, shot Franz Ferdinand and his wife Sophie in Sarajevo, Bosnia, was a Freemason. In fact, another Serb named Milan Ciganovic was a leader of a secret society

Feminist and abolitionist Frances "Fanny" Wright advocated for a utopian society that included sexual freedom. Was she part of a new Illuminati-inspired movement?

known as the "Black Hand," which carried out the assassination. During the trials of society members, it was learned that Ciganovic also was a Mason and had told one of the assassins the Freemasons had turned to the Black Hand because they could not find any Masons willing to carry out the archduke's murder.

The Austro-Hungarian government demanded the assassins be sent to Vienna for trial but the prime minister of Serbia refused, claiming it would be a violation of Serbia's Constitution. Three days later Austro-Hungary declared war on Serbia, which set off a chain reaction of ultimatums and mobilizations that ultimately spread war from the Balkans to the whole of Europe.

In an interesting sidelight, Albert Pike, a Master Mason, author of the Masonic *Morals and Dogma,* and former Confederate general, has been widely reported as being not only connected to the Illuminati but in a letter reportedly predicted three world wars. "Documentary evidence proves that Pike was not only a false Christ; he was, before he died, the High Priest of the Luciferian ideology on this earth, and as such, controlled the Synagogue of Satan," accused Commander Carr. "His military blueprint called for three world wars, and three major revolutions, to bring Weishaupt's revised version of the age-old Luciferian conspiracy to its final stage. In the 1860's he is recorded as saying his military program might take one hundred years or a little longer to reach the day when those who direct the conspiracy AT THE TOP [emphasis in the original] will crown their leader King-despot of the entire world, and impose a Luciferian totalitarian dictatorship upon what is left of the human race."

Giuseppe Mazzini, a nineteenth-century revolutionary in Italy and a thirty-third-degree Mason, has been named as a post-Weishaupt leader of the Illuminati. When Mazzini's revolutionaries required money, they robbed banks, extorted business for protection money, and kidnapped for ransom, which led to the phrase *Mazzini Autorizza Furti, Incendi e Attentati*, (Mazzini authorizes theft, arson, and kidnapping), or the acronym MAFIA. Working for Italian unity, Mazzini saw the spread of Freemasonry as a means to destroy the Roman Catholic Church.

In January 1870, Mazzini communicated with Pike, instructing him on how to insinuate Illuminati theology into Freemasonry. Mazzini wrote, "We must allow all the [Masonic] federations to continue just as they are, with their systems, their central authorities and their diverse modes of correspondence between high grades of the same rite, organized as they are at the present, but we must create a super rite, which will remain unknown, to which we will call those Masons of high degree whom we shall select. With regard to our brothers in Masonry, these men must be pledges to the strictest secrecy. Through this supreme rite, we will govern all Freemasonry which will become the one international center, the more powerful because its direction will be unknown."

The next year, Pike published *Morals and Dogma of the Ancient and Accepted Scottish Rite of Freemasonry*, a Masonic handbook detailing the lower degrees of that order. According to Michael Haupt, who in 2003 started the website threeworldwars.com, "After Mazzini's death on March 11, 1872, Pike appointed Adriano Lemmi (1822–1896, 33rd degree Mason), a banker from Florence, Italy, to run their subversive activities in Europe. Lemmi was a supporter of patriot and revolutionary Giuseppe Garibaldi, and may have been active in the Luciferian Society founded by Pike. Lemmi, in turn, was succeeded by Lenin and Trotsky, then by Stalin. The revolutionary activities of all these men were financed by British, French, German, and American international bankers; all of them dominated by the House of Rothschild."

Italian journalist and politician Giuseppe Mazzini is credited for helping unify Italy. He was also a Mason and supposedly believed that the Illuminati should destroy the Catholic Church.

The site also propagates the story that Albert Pike prophetically predicted three world wars, stating, "Between 1859 and 1871, Pike worked out a military blueprint for three world wars and various revolutions throughout the world which he considered would forward the conspiracy to its final stage in the 20th Century." According to accounts posted by Haupt, Pike predicted:

A First World War would be brought about in order to permit the Illuminati to overthrow the power of the Czars in Russia and of making that country a fortress of atheistic Communism. The divergences caused by the "agentur" (agents) of the Illuminati between the British and Germanic Empires will be used to foment this war. At the end of the war, Communism will be built and used in order to destroy the other governments and in order to weaken the religions.

A Second World War would be fomented by taking advantage of the differences between the Fascists and the political Zionists. This war would be fought so that Nazism is destroyed and that the political Zionism become strong enough to create a sovereign state of Israel in Palestine. During the Second World War, International Communism must become strong enough in order to balance Christendom, which would be then restrained and held in check until the time when we would need it for the final social cataclysm.

A Third World War must be fomented by taking advantage of the differences caused by agents of the Illuminati between the political Zionists and the leaders of Islamic World. The war must be conducted in such a way that Islam (the Muslim Arabic World) and political Zionism (the State of Israel) mutually destroy each other. Meanwhile the other nations, divided on this issue, will be constrained to fight to the point of complete physical, moral, spiritual and economical exhaustion.

Author Carr even quoted Pike as predicting the results of World War III, writing, "We shall unleash the Nihilists and the atheists, and we shall provoke a formidable social cataclysm which in all its horror will show clearly to the nations the effect of absolute atheism, origin of savagery and of the most bloody turmoil. Then everywhere, the citizens, obliged to defend themselves against the world minority of revolutionaries, will exterminate those destroyers of civilization, and the multitude, disillusioned with Christianity, whose deistic spirits will from that moment be without compass or direction, anxious for an ideal, but without knowing where to render its adoration, will receive the true light through the universal manifestation of the pure doctrine of Lucifer, brought finally out in the public view. This manifestation will result from the general reactionary movement which will follow the destruction of Christianity and atheism, both conquered and exterminated at the same time."

Like so many other revelations found on the Internet, the attributions for Pike's word, eerily prescient as they may seem, lead in circles, with one writer quoting another and that one going back to the first. Despite being often quoted on the Internet, no one has found conclusive proof that such a letter ever existed. Diligent researcher Terry Melanson finally traced the Pike quotes though several publications, including those of Canadian author Carr, back to an 1892 French book entitled *The Devil in the 19th-century* by a Dr. Bataille, who subsequently turned out to be Gabriel Jogand-Pagès. This book alleged that Pike and Mazzini belonged to a secret Satanist society called the Palladian Society, headquartered in Charleston, South Carolina. In this work there was no mentioned of world wars. Bataille/Jogand-Pagès in 1897 finally admitted his story was a hoax.

"Exactly what William Guy Carr was trying to pull, I'll never know," said Melanson. "... perhaps you're disappointed to have found nothing about a prediction of three world wars, Communism, Nazism and Zionist Illuminati—or anything of the sort.... What it truly represents is the scurrilous fantasies, and militant anti-Catholicism of its author...."

But other claims of revolutionary actions attributable to Illuminati influence cannot be so easily dismissed. Evidence available today indicates World War II was brought on by agents and members of secret societies connected to the Illuminati and Freemasonry in both Germany and Britain. It was in this "good war" that the older mystic societies seeking freedom from both church and state merged with the modern secret societies, concerned primarily with wealth, power, and control. "Sir Winston Churchill himself ... was insistent that the occultism of the Nazi Party should not under any circumstances be revealed to the general public," wrote author Trevor Ravenscroft, who claimed to have worked closely with Dr. Walter Johannes Stein, a confidential adviser to Churchill. "The failure of the Nuremberg Trials to identify the nature of the evil at work behind the outer facade of National Socialism convinced him that another three decades must pass before a large enough readership would be

Dr. Walter Johannes Stein was a philosopher who knew Hitler personally before the war, including the Nazi leader's obsession with the occult. In exile after 1933, Stein was an advisor to the British government.

present to comprehend the initiation rites and black magic practices of the inner core of Nazi leadership."

This remarkable statement was corroborated by Airey Neave, one of the post-war Nuremberg prosecutors, who said the occult aspect of the Nazis was ruled inadmissible because the tribunal feared both the psychological and spiritual implications in the western nations. They also thought that such beliefs, so contrary to public rationalism, might be used to mount an insanity defense for Nazi leaders.

Further confirmation of the mysticism behind Hitler and his Nazis came from Nazi researchers and author Ethel K. "Dusty" Sklar, who wrote, "These cults, from those connected with [occultists] George Ivanovitch Gurdjieff, Madame Helena Petrovna Blavatsky, and Rudolf Steiner to their present reincarnations, shared certain features: an authoritarian obedience to a charismatic and messianic leader; secrecy; loyalty to the group above all other ties, a belief in supernatural possibilities open to members only, a belief in reincarnation; initiation into superhuman sources of power; literal acceptance of the myth of ancient 'giants' or supermen who handed down an oral tradition to a chosen people and who were guiding us now; and, in uncommon cases, Satanic practices."

Many books, articles, and even TV specials have been produced documenting the ties between Hitler's Nazis and occult societies, but few have made it plain that Hitler was their creation. Adolf Hitler's Nazis were far more than simply a political movement. They saw themselves leading a quasi-religious movement born out of secret organizations whose goals were the same as those found in the Illuminati and Illuminized Freemasonry. "[T]hey were a cult ... [and] as with any typical cult, its chief enemies were other cults," noted author Peter Levenda in a well-researched book dealing with Nazis and the occult.

This Nazi cult grew from a variety of organizations, theologies, and beliefs present in Germany at the end of World War I—all stemming from the mysteries of older groups such as Weishaupt's Bavarian Illuminati, the *Germanenorden*, Freemasonry, and the Teutonic Knights.

"The rationale behind many later Nazi projects can be traced back ... to ideas first popularized by Blavatsky," wrote Levenda, who detailed connections with other European secret organizations. "[W]e have the Theosophical Society, the OTO (*Ordo Templi Orientis* or Oriental Templars), [Dr. Rudolf Steiner's] Anthroposophical Society and the [Order of] the Golden Dawn all intertwined in incestuous embrace."

Post-World War I Munich was flooded with anti-communist Russian refugees, and the occult societies began to merge with political activism, particularly in southern Germany.

Dietrich Eckart, the journalist and politician who founded the German Workers Party, which later evolved into the National Socialist German Workers Party, or NAZI, found in the *Protocols* what he saw as the final proof of the long-theorized Jewish-Masonic-Bolshevik world conspiracy. He saw to its immediate publication and the book swiftly spread throughout Germany and Europe and even to America. "The story of the circulation of *The Protocols of the Wise Men of Zion* would seem to indicate the existence of an international network of secret connections and cooperating forces ... described clearly enough in the *Protocols* themselves," commented author Konrad Heiden, who wrote a wartime book on Hitler.

> **Dietrich Eckart ... founded the German Workers Party, which later evolved into the National Socialist German Workers Party....**

As previously mentioned, one of the most important secret societies supporting Hitler's rise to power was the Thule Society. "The inner core within the Thule Group was all Satanists who practiced Black Magic," wrote Trevor Ravenscroft, author of *The Spear of Destiny*. "That is to say, they were solely concerned with raising their consciousness by means of rituals to an awareness of evil and non-human Intelligences in the Universe and with achieving a means of communication with the Intelligences. And the Master-Adept of this circle was Dietrich Eckart."

It has been documented that in post-World War I Munich there were several hundred unsolved "political" murders and kidnappings. Ravenscroft alleged that these victims, mostly Jews or communists, were "sacrificial victims" in rites of "Astrological Magic" carried out by Dietrich Eckart and the inner circle of the Thule Society. He claimed it was a "well-known fact" that the Thulists were a "Society of Assassins," which would link them to the Assassins of Hasan bin Sabah and hence to the Knights Templar and the Illuminati. Assassins or not, it is true that on April 7, 1919, when communist revolutionaries held Munich for a short period proclaiming a Bavarian Soviet Republic, the only people they rounded up and executed as dangerous subversives were Thule Society members, including its young secretary and Prince von Thurn und Taxis. There have even been accusations that Hitler was an Illuminati operative. In 2005, author Greg Hallett published a book entitled *Hitler Was a British Agent* in which he quoted several retired intelligence officers who claimed Hitler was recruited into British Intelligence when he visited his English sister-in-law, Bridget Hitler, in 1912–1913. This issue was confirmed by Hitler's English nephew, William Patrick Hitler, who added an astounding comment. In the late 1930s, William hinted to newsmen that the German Fuehrer had a Jewish background linked to the Rothschilds. Hans Frank, Hitler's personal attorney, confirmed this scandalous information but the name Frankenberger was substituted for Rothschild. When no record of a Frankenberger could be found in Vienna, the matter was quietly dropped by all but Hitler. Historians have long noted that the question of possible Jewish ancestry haunted Hitler throughout his life. It is astounding that Hitler's Jewish blood might be traced to a Rothschild.

Could it be that the man who caused the Holocaust, Adolf Hitler, actually had a family background that included a grandmother with Rothschild blood?

Dr. Walter C. Langer, a psychologist who produced a wartime psychoanalysis of Hitler for American intelligence, reported that secret pre-war Austrian police reports proved Hitler's father was the illegitimate son of a peasant cook named Maria Anna Schicklgruber, who at the time she conceived her child was "employed as a servant in the home of Baron Rothschild" in Vienna. Upon learning of her pregnancy in 1837, she left Vienna and gave birth to Hitler's father of record, Alois. Five years later, she reportedly married an itinerant miller named Johann Georg Hiedler. Yet Alois carried his mother's name of Schicklgruber until nearly forty years of age when Hiedler's brother, Johann Nepomuk Hiedler, offered him legitimacy. Due to the illegible writing of a parish priest in changing the birth register, the name Hiedler became Hitler, either by mistake or to confuse authorities. Alois Hitler led a sad and morose life, chiefly as a government bureaucrat, and married his own second cousin, Klara Poelzl, in 1885, after obtaining special episcopal dispensation. Adolf was born in Braunau, Austria, in 1889, when Alois was fifty-two years old.

The incredible story of Hitler's heritage might be written off as fanciful wartime propaganda except for the fact that U.S. intelligence never made this story public, indicating the tale may have linked Hitler to top globalist financiers and thus been considered too sensitive to make public.

In case someone might question if a Rothschild would consider dallying with the servants, it is instructive that Rothschild biographer Ferguson stated that the son of one of Salomon's senior clerks "recalled that by the 1840s, [the Viennese Rothschild] had developed a somewhat reckless enthusiasm for young girls."

The late Philippe Rothschild in 1984 published memoirs revealing his "scandalous love life." He wrote, "I was a tremendous success ... leaping from bed to bed like a mountain goat.... I was always convinced (my father) had won his spurs riding my grandmother's chambermaids."

Author Epperson pondered, "It is possible that Hitler discovered his Jewish background and his relation to the Rothschilds, and aware of their enormous power to make or break European governments, re-established contact with the family. This would partially explain the enormous support he received from the international banking fraternity, closely entwined with the Rothschild family [and Illuminated societies such as Thule], as he rose to power."

Author Hallett's claim that "Hitler was a British Agent" has been amplified by New World Order writer Henry Makow, who wrote, "When Hallett says 'British,' he means Illuminati, the Masonic cult of super rich bankers who control an interlocking network of cartels. This cult is based in the City of London but uses England and most nations as sock puppets in a Punch and Judy show called history."

Hallett's claim might clarify the many improbable events in World War II, such as the 335,000 Allied soldiers Hitler allowed to escape at Dunkirk. This action has been explained away as a peace overture, but most historians believe England would have been more agreeable to a negotiated peace if its army were prisoners of the Nazis. Makow explained, "Hallett's hypothesis explains (1) Why Hitler was able to expand into the Rhineland etc. without fear of retaliation. (2) Why the Nazi war machine was financed and built by the Bank of England and a Who's Who of Anglo American corporations controlled by the Illuminati. (3) Why Hitler never sealed the Mediterranean at Gibraltar; and why the Spanish dictator Franco remained neutral, despite the huge debt he owed the Nazis from the Civil War. (4) Why I. G. Farben headquarters in Frankfurt was never bombed. This became CIA headquarters. (5) Why the Bank of England rewarded Hitler for taking Prague by giving him the Czech gold reserves held in London."

Makow sees the extremely wealthy elite as having organized themselves into a "Satanic cult" to make prey of mankind and establish their permanent hegemony over the entire globe. "Put yourself in the central bankers' shoes," he postulated. "The nations of the world owe you trillions based on money you printed for the cost of paper and ink. The only way to protect this 'investment' is to establish a thinly disguised dictatorship, using sophisticated methods of social and mind control. This is the true meaning of the 'War on Terror.' It's not directed at 'Muslim terrorists.' It's directed at you and me."

According to several conspiracy writers, World War II achieved the goals of the Illuminati—the nations of Germany, Italy, and Japan, along with their economies, were devastated; the world population reduced as some sixty million people, mostly civilians, perished; the Jewish Holocaust prompted the establishment of the Rothschild's world government headquarters in Israel; Libertarians and peace candidates from both ends of the political systems were killed; and all the nations involved, smothered under debt, were easily brought into the newly formed United Nations.

On a bizarre note, even today's music scene may be the product of a pre-World War II Nazi/Illuminati plan to change music to replace tranquility and harmony with discontent and aggressiveness. And we are not talking about head-banging or rap music exclusively. It is all music and the story goes like this: About 1939 the German Nazis fundamentally changed music to negatively impact our lives, how we feel, and how we interact with our environment.

Up until 1939, the most preferred pitch in music was 432 Hertz (Hz). This frequency has been found in the world's oldest flutes, some dating back to the time of the Neanderthals. According to Gary Vey, writing for *Viewzone*, "An interesting story claims that the lyres of the temples of Greece were an integral part of the ceremonies worshiping Isis and other so-called mystery schools. Cult members were aroused to states of ecstasy by the sounds of this 432 Hz tuned music which, in the case of the Eleusinian Mysteries, made them filled with compassion and altruism. For this reason, according to the story, the war-like state of Sparta had all the lyres re-tuned to a higher frequency, thus nulling the anti-war sentiments."

It has been understood for some time that a change in musical frequencies can cause a change in human responses, both physical and psychological.

In 1962, Dr. T. C. Singh, head of the Botany Department at India's Annamalai University, studied the effect of musical sounds on the growth rate of plants. He found that balsam plants exposed to music grew at a rate of 20 percent higher than normal and developed 72 percent more in biomass. Singh first experimented with classical music but later moved to *raga* music, composed of rhythms and notes played on flute, violin, harmonium, and the *reena*, an Indian instrument, where he found the music created similar effects.

Music creates sound waves that travel through the air at different frequencies. When these frequencies reach our eardrums, the brain interprets them as sound and music. When a plant is exposed to music, it also receives the same sound waves, which create a vibration that can be picked up by plants. The plant does not hear the music. It feels the vibration of the sound wave.

On a bizarre note, even today's music scene may be the product of a pre-World War II Nazi/Illuminati plan to change music to replace tranquility and harmony with discontent and aggressiveness.

Interestingly enough, it has been found that different music produces different results in plants. In 1973, while a student, Dorothy Retallack, experimented with three groups of plants exposed to various types of music, she played the note F for an eight-hour period for one group. A second group was played the same note for three hours, while the third controlled group received no note. The first group died within two weeks, while the second group was much healthier than the controlled group.

Singh also discovered that when seeds were exposed to music, after germination they would produce more leaves, grow to greater size, and exhibit other improved characteristics. Music appeared to change the plant's genetic makeup.

Others experimented with different types of music. Plants exposed to classical music (still in the 432 Hz range) by such composers as Hayden, Beethoven, Brahms, and Schubert actually grew to entwine themselves around the speakers. But when modern rock music was played, another plant group grew away from the speakers, as if trying to escape the music. Rock music was tried on different varieties of plants and found to produce abnormal growth and smaller leaves. It was discovered that no matter which way they were turned, the plants leaned away from the rock music source. Similar experiments produced the same effects as described in the 1973 book *The Secret Life of Plants* by Peter Tompkins and Christopher Bird.

> The effects of different forms of music on plants may be explained by the diverse sound wave frequencies....

Interestingly, country music did not seem to affect plants. They exhibited no unusual growth reaction. Jazz, on the other hand, seemed to provide beneficial effects with improved growth. The effects of different forms of music on plants may be explained by the diverse sound wave frequencies that then provide varying degrees of pressure and vibration. Louder music, like rock, features greater pressure, promoting detrimental effects on plants. The hosts of the science television show *MythBusters*, after some experimentation, concluded that plants reacted pretty much the same to any type of music but their methodology has been questioned and their results contested. With the understanding that musical frequencies can alter behavior in both plants and humans, we turn to John Calhoun Deagan, a musician who almost singlehandedly changed the world of music by increasing the historical 332 Hz pitch to 440. Deagan, who died in 1934, developed many of the percussion instruments still in use today—including the xylophone, organ chimes, aluminum chimes, aluminum harp, Swiss hand bells, orchestra bells, and the marimba.

Deagan's work began in earnest after he heard a series of lectures in London by German physicist Hermann von Helmholtz that prompted an interest in the science of music. Helmholtz in the mid-1800s had published a tract entitled *On the Sensations of Tone as a Physiological Basis for the Theory of Music*. Studying this work, Deagan developed the first scientifically tuned glockenspiel.

In 1910 Deagan persuaded the American Federation of Musicians, at its annual convention, to adopt the musical letter A at 440 Hz as the standard universal pitch for orchestras and bands. It was also accepted by the U.S. government and generally throughout the world.

In the years following, popular support grew enormously for Thomas Edison's inventions of the radio and moving pictures. Audiences were polled to determine what effects were generated by movie soundtracks, especially after "talkies" (movies in which viewers could hear the actors speaking and singing) came on the scene in the late 1920s. It was found that propaganda films were most effective when using the 440 Hz frequency.

According to Vey: "At the beginning of the 1930s, the potential of 440 Hz to combat altruism and stimulate nationalism, narcissism and aggression was fueled by the new science of Psychology. Freud's psychoanalysis in Europe was mainly for the elite but his theories of mass hysteria found their way to America through his nephew, Edward Bernays, who successfully used Freud's theories and mind control techniques in advertising and politics. He was the first to note that only about 8–10 percent of a population was needed to be convinced of a new idea for it to eventually become unanimously accepted. This has been called the '10 percent Solution.'" Vey explained that the Rockefeller Foundation and the Rothschild's banking syndicate were most interested in such mind-control techniques. Their representatives approached the Nazi minister of propaganda, Dr. Joseph Goebbels, who was quite attentive as he already was using many of Bernays's propaganda methods to promote the Nazi Party.

"With their support, and with the reminder that the British were heavily in debt to their banks, the Illuminati sponsored Goebbels to promote the adoption of the 440 Hz standard by the British Standards Institute which would apply to all musicians playing in Europe. This measure reluctantly passed in 1939 despite being three months after Hitler invaded Poland," reported Vey, adding, "Technically, Germany had started WWII and was an axis [enemy] of Britain, but this had little impact on their ultimate decision."

Joseph Goebbels, Hitler's Minister of Propoganda, was interested in Edward Bernays's methods of controlling the minds of the masses.

Vey sought to determine why 432 Hz, the intuitive tuning frequency used since the inception of human music, was so undesirable to the Rockefellers, Rothschilds (Illuminati), and Nazis.

The answer may be found in the argument of proponents of 432 Hz, who claim this frequency stimulates the best attributes of the right brain, resonates with the Heart Chakra (one of seven centers of spiritual power in the human body described in literature in India), repairs DNA, and restores both spiritual and mental health.

Critics of the 440 Hz system say it is unnatural and therefore creates subtle disharmony in listeners leading to irritation, discomfort, anger, and aggressiveness. This argument is supported by Cymatics experiments, in which sand or water is placed on a plate and exposed to various frequencies. Under 432 Hz tones, distinct patterns emerge indicating that the frequency resonates with the natural world. The 440 Hz frequency creates indistinct patterns revealing a lack of coherence. Since the human body is about 78 percent water, it is apparent that sound waves can impact both the health of the physical body as well as cognizance.

Few scientific papers have been produced on the effects of 432 Hz vs. 440 Hz but in January 2014, a paper entitled "Amelioration of psychiatric symptoms through exposure to music individually adapted to brain rhythm disorders—a randomized clinical trial on the basis of fundamental research" was published in *Cognitive Neuropsychiatry*. After subjecting fifty psychiatric patients to classical music on CDs for over eighteen months, the investigators found that "patients in the experimental group showed significantly decreased BSI [Brief Symptom Inventory] scores compared to control patients. Intriguingly, this effect was not only seen for symptoms of psychoticism and paranoia but also for anxiety, phobic anxiety and somatization."

The key part of this experimentation was that the experiment was carried out using "adapted music," the 432 Hz frequency. "This 'Mozart effect' can be intensified by playing the music composition slightly decelerated (as practiced in the days of Mozart). Furthermore, the instruments are tuned to the old French pitch of 432 Hz which corresponds to the harmonic ratio of natural body rhythms...." noted the paper.

Further studies found non-musicians appreciate a melody and harmony because they are processed in the right hemisphere of the brain, but trained musicians perceive it in the left hemisphere, most probably because this is to what they have been conditioned. "Musicians have different [auditory] networks than non-musicians," explained Vey, "and those who listen to a particular type of music can develop networks specific to that genre." Vey concluded that research conducted with grants from the Rockefeller Foundation determined that 440 Hz music was "good at making people work harder and fostered personality traits more in tune with *Star Trek*'s Vulcan character, Spock. These are pure left brain traits which stifle creative thought and null the emotions. It is clear why these traits were desirable in the Third Reich. It also might explain why modern music, which changed to the 440 Hz standard in 1939, has had such a negative effect on today's culture."

The early symptoms of psychosis, such as depression, anxiety, and paranoia, are widespread in today's society. Such discomfort can only benefit the giant pharmaceutical

> **F**urther studies found non-musicians appreciate a melody and harmony because they are processed in the right hemisphere of the brain, but trained musicians perceive it in the left hemisphere....

corporations who charge billions for medications claiming to relieve these symptoms.

Once the population understands this long and pervasive effort to alter our music and behavior, they may never listen to music in public places, at a concert, or on their cell phone in the same way again.

It should be noted that music designed to alter the consciousness is not the only mind-control technique in use today. Aside from CIA-developed behavior modification programs using hypnosis and drugs such as MKUltra and Project Monarch, one need only look at our society today with its constant TV and radio programming promoting consumerism, hyper-sexuality (the porn industry), alcohol and drug consumption, and daily virtual killing via video games—all to desensitize the soul. Department of Defense private contractors today are involved in a variety of deniable programs using sophisticated psychotronics such as cell phone towers, pulsed beam microwaves, ELF, scalar waves, gang-stalking, and sophisticated chemicals and drugs secretly administered to "targeted individuals" as well as sleeper agents. Such tactics are designed to entrain thought, emotions, attitudes, and actions in the mind, which in turn shape the consciousness and actions of the masses to conform to the Illuminati-minded operational goals.

The Nazi rocket scientists who were brought to the United States just after the war under Project Paperclip, facilitated by then-CIA director Allen Dulles and his mentor, High Commissioner of Germany John J. McCloy, were accompanied by the Nazi mind-control specialists.

The war ended with the atomic destruction at Hiroshima and Nagasaki, Japan. The Illuminati-minded globalists returned to their pre-World War I plan of gaining power, control, and profits by pitting a socialist East against a capitalist West. It was called the Cold War.

Following the fruitless wars in Korea and Vietnam by America, and Russia's invasion in Afghanistan in the 1980s, the extreme socialist philosophy of communism collapsed under its financial burdens. In 2008, the United States moved into an inflationary depression after several corporate failings.

James H. Billington, a Rhodes Scholar and the Librarian of Congress Emeritus, authored a 1980 book entitled *Fire in the Minds of Men: Origins of the Revolutionary Faith*. In this work, he stated that "the modern revolutionary tradition" stems from "Bavarian Illuminism." Author William H. McIlhany added, "Among the subversive and revolutionary 19th- and early 20th-century movements created by the Illuminati (primarily through European Grand Orient Freemasonry, not British and American Freemasonry) were the Marxian and 'utopian' socialist movements; anarchism; syndicalism; Pan Slavism; Irish, Italian and German 'nationalism'; German Imperialism; the Paris Commune; British 'New Imperialism'; Fabian Socialism; and Leninist Bolshevism."

Today in America, socialist programs with the same objectives espoused by Marxists, communists, and national socialists are marketed under new names like "liberals," "leftists," "Progressives," and even "neocons," or "neo-conservatives," which is merely an innovative label for National Socialists. Where Americans once joined together and celebrated their Americanism, they now are being divided into left-wing and right-wing ideologies. Politics cannot be diagramed on a straight line, but on a circle where the extreme left and extreme right eventually join together.

While all these movements appear to be separate philosophies, upon close inspection it seams they all stem from the doctrines of Illuminism.

Whistleblowers

Although the official Bavarian Order of the Illuminati no longer exists, even today many people claim to have been in contact with or members of a group that emulates the ideals of Illuminism.

More than ten years ago, Gaylon Ross, a Texas researcher who has done considerable investigation of modern secret societies, was allowed to make a copy of what purports to be an Illuminati membership card for one R. J. Higgins dated December 17, 1903. Ross said he has no further knowledge as to the authenticity of the card or its origins. Is this evidence that some form of an Illuminati society still exists?

A most unbelievable website appeared in December 2005, posted by Mimi L. Eustis, the daughter of Samuel Todd Churchill, said to be a high-level member of a New Orleans secret Mardi Gras society connected to the Illuminati. Her information was gained by making recordings and notes of her father as he lay painfully dying from lung cancer. She only agreed to have her father's information published after she was diagnosed with terminal breast cancer.

According to Eustis, Illuminati agents fatally poisoned Presidents William Henry Harrison and Zachary Taylor. They also poisoned President James Buchanan in 1857 but he survived. She said these three men were obstructing the U.S. Civil War plans of the Illuminati and the House of Rothschild.

"Behind the pretense of the Cowbellion de' Rakin Society [named after the cow bells used in the Mardi Gras festival and founder of the festival] which originated in 1835 as parading revelers through the streets of New Orleans, these men were in actuality Yankee bankers from New England. They used the idea of this Cowbelli[o]n society to create a front for an international banking cartel, the House of Rothschild, headquartered in Europe, as well as for Skull

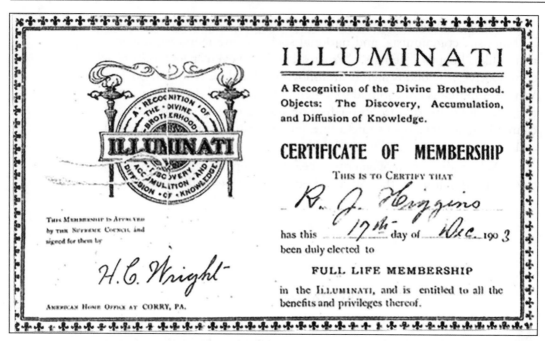

A membership certificate from the Illuminati.

and Bones, a branch of the German Illuminati established by William Russell in 1832 at Yale University. The name of this newly formed secret group was the Mystick Krewe of Comus," wrote Eustis. This New Orleans society, which reorganized during Mardi Gras festivities in 1857, was a chapter of the Skull and Bones, she wrote. It is believed that it began as a front for the activities of Masons Albert Pike, Judah Benjamin, and John Slidell, who became leaders of the Confederacy. "In 1857, Judah Benjamin was an agent of the House of Rothschild living in New Orleans. His job was to fund the Confederacy and help foster a devastating Civil War," wrote Eustis. "Judah Benjamin started in the Confederate government as Attorney General and later became Secretary of State. Judah Benjamin also became head of the Confederate intelligence and was a key player in the assassination of Abraham Lincoln." "The House of Rothschild was fearful that the new United States Republic would begin printing its own money and have a central bank not tied into the House of Rothschild. This would weaken the House of Rothschild's control over the monetary currencies of the world. They had already established a secret bloodline elitist society, incorporating thirteen of the world's most wealthy families, to eventually establish a New World Order with control over the world's economy," explained Eustis. Recall these words echoed a similar statement from German chancellor Otto von Bismarck.

Various individuals have publicly claimed to be a part of the Illuminati, the inner elite, or whatever name one would like. Most are dubious characters with little or no real credentials or evidence. However, their stories tend to support the accounts of various conspiracy researchers and their stories are surprisingly consistent. Such whistleblowers offer fascinating insights into the workings of such an elite.

Bill Ryan, initially with a social sciences project called Project Camelot, interviewed one of these self-proclaimed elite members. "In the summer of 2010, I was approached by a very unusual man," Ryan explained. "I've called him 'Charles.' He's spent many years working for the elite group that considers it their responsibility to run the planet. He's not an academic, a historian, or a scientist. But he wanted to communicate some important information: about the worldview and philosophy of this group."

Ryan quoted his source as explaining, "They are a controlling group of 33 individuals who meet frequently to make strategic decisions about humanity and the planet. They are *not* the 'Illuminati,' which is a lower-level secret society—of which are there many, like the Knights of Malta, the Rosicrucians, Skull and Bones, the Priory of Sion, numerous Masonic groups, and more. The 33 can be compared to a Board of Directors of a very large global corporation. Like a real Board, there is a 'Number One Man' who makes final policy decisions, having consulted his colleagues, all of whom have expertise and who have earned a right to participate. There are differences of opinion sometimes—and different personalities, as in any group of people—but basically they are very much aligned with the overall purpose, which is (using this analogy) to ensure that Corporation Plant Earth continues to expand and prosper. All in line with the Corporation's 'mission statement'—which is about optimizing the human genome."

Charles explained that each of these representatives of the thirty-three bloodlines is so powerful, and control so much wealth and so many assets, that they could be regarded almost as nation-states in their own right. They regard it as their responsibility to "manage" planet Earth. He said they are party to a great deal of hidden history through their private possession of ancient documents and artifacts, many located in the Vatican Library.

> Charles explained that each of these representatives of the thirty-three bloodlines is so powerful ... that they could be regarded almost as nation-states in their own right.

"The history and lineage of the human race is not—*at all*—what the public has been told. It has been decided a long time ago that the human race could not handle these truths. This information is regarded as a kind of 'sacred knowledge.' Safeguarding this knowledge is taken extremely seriously, and, as Charles explained, there is a great deal of tradition and historical culture—going back thousands of years—which is almost inextricably interwoven with the way the group functions," reported Ryan. "As Charles also tried to explain, they do not see time as you and I do. Delaying something by a year, or a decade, or a hundred years, means very little. They do not operate to a calendar. Only to unfolding events."

Fritz Springmeier, the controversial author of *Bloodlines of the Illuminati*, reports that the modern Illuminati is led by thirteen prominent families. He gives the names Astor, Bundy, Collins, DuPont, Freeman, Kennedy, Li, Onassis, Rockefeller, Rothschild, Russell, Van Duyn, and Merovingian with others, such as Reynolds, Disney, Krupp, and McDonald as intermarried extended families. He wrote, "From the ancient Middle East, some of the families ended up in Venice. From Venice these families then moved to Switzerland, Russia, London, and Amsterdam.... Families from these groups have tended toward Gnoticism (also known as Luciferianism) and cults that are abnormal 'Christian' deviations."

Springmeier opined, "I do not fear the Illuminati taking over this country and doing away with the Constitution, because they took over this country long ago, and the Constitution has not technically been in effect due to Presidential emergency decrees since W.W. II (and before that too). Don't think for a moment you are going to vote the Illuminati out of office. They control the major and minor political parties. They control the process of government, they control the process of information flow, they control the process of creating money and finally they control Christendom. (However, God controls the hearts of His people.)"

Springmeier went on to explain that during the past few centuries there has been an organized program to hide the bloodline lineages of the Illuminati families. "This program includes: secret conceptions, children being switched at birth, twins being raised separately and secretly, bloodline children being adopted out into both Illuminati and non-Illuminati families, surnames being changed, genealogy and public records being altered, bloodlines being carried via the mothers, and finally special brooder families that are used to breed elite bloodlines secretly. These devices mean that even if useful genealogical material is assembled, it may not reflect the hidden reality which is kept recorded in the Illuminati's own hidden genealogical books."

Going by the name Cisco Wheeler, one professed Illuminati defector is Linda Anderson, who, with Springmeier, co-authored *The Illuminati Formula Used to Create an Undetectable Mind Controlled Slave*. This book related how trauma-based conditioning and mind-control techniques, such as those used by the CIA in Project Monarch, were used to create Illuminati slaves. Both said this activity is carried on through Illuminati families.

"My father came from a trans-generational satanic family. My life was planned according to a particular structure, from the beginning, as my father was a programmer for the Illuminati and the U.S. government," said Wheeler in a radio interview. "[M]y Great Uncle was General Earl Grant Wheeler, he was a direct descendant of Ulysses Grant. General Earl Wheeler was the head of the American military in the Vietnam War. He was the Joint Chief of Staff so we had a very strong political background. My father was also a Grand Master within the Illuminati. He worked on the west coast during the Vietnam War with his uncle who headed the military, to run drugs into this country to create a drug culture. The purpose of that was to destroy the structure within the family unit. The drug culture was the real purpose behind the Vietnam War."

Wheeler said she has spent years in therapy and helping other survivors of Illuminati mind control but has never broken completely free. "We are continually harassed by external threats. We get a lot of phone calls, we get bullets in our windows, we get run off the road, we get letters, we get people that walk up to us in the grocery store and they threaten us. They let us know in their little way that they know where I am, what I am doing, and what I am up to, and that it's not over until they say it's over. They are calling the shots," she said.

Wheeler said her conditioning began even before she left the womb and was facilitated by a "Dr. Green," who she later learned was the famous escaped Nazi war criminal Dr. Josef Mengele. "They knew from A to Z what they wanted to do with my life and how they wanted to structure, what they wanted me to be, and what they wanted me to become. That is slavery. I had to deal with the body, soul and spirit because all parts of myself have been raped. I continually have to deal with memories; with spirit issues; issues within me—in my programming; how they dehumanized me; how they shamed me; how they traumatized me to the point that I didn't even know who I was, what I was, where I was going. I didn't even know I was a little girl at some points in my traumatization," she explained.

Looking to the future, Wheeler said, "I believe that the people in the world are going to wake up some day very soon and realize that the stock market has crashed, that financially the world has been crushed. They are going to realize that their food and grain has been contaminated, that their medical field has been dominated by the Illuminati medical force because the Illuminati has infiltrated every aspect of our lives. They are going to realize that we don't have the freedom to even speak for our children, that the government has more to say in regards to our children than we do, they can take them and control them at any given point. We are going to realize that the

The infamous Nazi Dr. Josef Mengele, who orchestrated the deadly medical experiments at Germany's concentration camps, also conditioned people to be Illuminati slaves, according to Cisco Wheeler, who claimed to be one such victim.

churches are not what they seem to have been—that the churches have been infiltrated. There is nothing left. There is nothing that has not been touched by the Illuminati and its family.... They have already accomplished it ... by taking our constitutional rights away from us ... by having a government within a government, like a box within a box. By creating famines, by having wars and rumors of wars, by the American people and the Canadian people no longer having the freedoms that once were theirs."

Other individuals have gone public anonymously with similar claims. One middle-aged registered nurse who goes by the pseudonym of "Svali" claimed to have escaped the Illuminati after working for years as a high-level programmer and trainer. She has given some of the most detailed and riveting disclosures concerning a modern Illuminati.

Svali said that her mother and stepfather were Illuminati members. According to her, the Illuminati have six chairs on their "ascended masters council"—Sciences, Government, Leadership, Scholarship, Spiritual, and Military. She claimed that her mother sat on a Washington, D.C., area regional council and served as spiritual chair.

Beginning in 2000, Svali began writing a monthly Internet site dedicated to survivors of Illuminati ritual abuse. This public effort prompted the editor of CentrExNews.com, H. L. Springer, to contact Svali and arrange an eighteen-part interview in which Svali detailed the organization of an Illuminati group, which she said can be found in every major city in the United States. "I am convinced she is the real McCoy," Springer wrote later. "I have personally relayed numerous email messages to her from other members—ritually abused, brainwashed, raped, sexually abused people; you name it—some of them confirming to me her story. So I have absolutely no doubt that Svali has been part of the Illuminati since childhood."

Svali explained that the Illuminati are involved in a Luciferian faith known as "enlightenment." It teaches its followers that their roots go back to the ancient mystery religions of Babylon, Egypt, and Celtic druidism. "They have taken what they consider the 'best' of each, the foundational practices, and joined them together into a strongly occult discipline. Many groups at the local level worship ancient deities such as El, Baal, and Ashtarte, as well as Isis and Osiris and Set.... I do know that these people teach and practice evil," she stated.

In an interesting sidelight, it was announced that in the spring of 2016 a reproduction of a Temple of Baal was to be built in New York's Times Square and another in London's Trafalgar Square. Reproductions of the fifty-foot arch that formed the temple's entrance are said to be a tribute to the 2,000-year-old structure in the Syrian town of Palmyra destroyed by the Islamic State [ISIS] in 2015, enraging scholars worldwide. But after plans for this temple broke in the media, it was pointed out that according to the Bible (See Jeremiah 19:46), Baal's Temple was the site where children were sacrificed by fire. Public opposition grew causing a change of plans. The reproductions now will be of Palmyra's Arch of Triumph, also destroyed by Muslim fanatics. Christian author and publisher Michael T. Snyder credited the surprising change of plans on public backlash. "Of course let us not underestimate the prayers of God's people. Once this story went viral, Christians all over America started praying against this arch. From personal experience, I know that the prayers of righteous men and women are extremely powerful, and we may never know how much of an impact they had on this situation. So let us celebrate this victory, but let us also understand that what this country is facing is not going to fundamentally change unless there is true repentance. Because even though a monument to Baal is not going up in New York City next month, we continue to embrace the ways of Baal as a nation."

The whistleblower Svali describes the modern Illuminati as a sadistic satanic cult led by the richest and most powerful people in the world. She claimed the Order is filled with homosexuals and pedophiles and that the Illuminati works hand-in-glove with the CIA and Freemasonry to control the world traffic in drugs, guns, pornography, and prostitution. It has even been accused of being the power behind political assassination, and "terrorism," including the events of September 11, 2001. "Svali's courageous testimony explains why our children are no longer taught civic values, why they are being habituated to homosexuality and violence, and why our 'culture' is descending into nihilism and sexual depravity," commented one researcher.

Svali said it is not true that Adam Weishaupt founded the Illuminati in Germany in 1776. "[T]hey chose him as a figurehead and told him what to write about. The financiers, dating back to the bankers during the times of the Templar Knights who financed the early kings in Europe, created the Illuminati. Weishaupt was their 'gofer,' who did their bidding," she stated.

Addressing the Illuminati belief in "enlightenment," Svali explained. "There are 12 steps to this, also known as 'the 12 steps of discipline' and they also teach traveling astral planes, time travel, and other metaphysical phenomena. Do people really do this, or is it a drug induced hallucination? I cannot judge. I saw things that I believe cannot be rationally explained when in this group, things that frightened me, but I can only say that it could be a combination of cult mind control, drug inductions, hypno-

The Illuminati have been blamed for acts of terrorism, including the 9/11 attacks.

> She said the Illuminati are international and funded by wealthy people. Like the Bavarian Illuminati, the watchword is secrecy.

sis, and some true demonic activity. How much of each, I cannot begin to guess. I do know that these people teach and practice evil.

"At the higher levels, the group is no longer people in robes chanting in front of bonfires. Leadership councils have administrators who handle finances (and trust me, this group makes money. That alone would keep it going even if the rest were just religious hog wash). The leadership levels include businessmen, bankers, and local community leaders. They are intelligent, well educated, and active in their churches. Above local leadership councils are the regional councils, who give dictates to the groups below them, help form the policies and agendas for each region, and who interact with the local leadership councils."

She said the Illuminati are international and funded by wealthy people. Like the Bavarian Illuminati, the watchword is secrecy. "The first thing a child learns from 'family,' or the 'Order' as they are called, is 'The first rule of the Order is secrecy.' This is why you don't hear from more survivors who get out," she explained. "The lengths that this group goes to, to terrify its members into not disclosing, is unbelievable.... Try being buried in a wooden box for a period of time (it may have been minutes, but to a four year old it is an eternity), and then when the lid is lifted, being told, 'if you ever tell, we'll put you back in forever.' The child will scream hysterically that they will NEVER EVER [emphasis in the original] tell. I was that child, and now I am breaking that vow made under psychological duress. Because I don't want any other children to go through what I did, or have seen done to others." Svali presented this picture of present-day Illuminati undertakings:

The Illuminati are present in every major metropolitan center in the United States. They have divided the United States up into seven major regions, and each has a regional council over it, with the heads of the local councils reporting to them. They meet once every two months, and on special occasions.... They also have excellent lawyers who are well paid to help cover their tracks. There are also people in the media paid to help keep stories from coming out. I know of three people in San Diego who worked for the *Union Tribune* who were faithful Illuminists, and who also wrote frequent articles attacking local therapists who worked with RA (Ritual Abuse) survivors. I remember leadership boasting they had "run so-and-so out of town" because of a media blitz, and being quite happy about it.

The Illuminati believe in controlling an area through its banks and financial institutions (guess how many sit on banking boards? You'd be surprised). Local government: guess how many get elected to local city councils? Law: children are encouraged to go to law school and medical school. Media: others are encouraged to go to journalism school, and members help fund local papers.

According to Svali, the leaders of the national Illuminati councils report to a Supreme World Council, which acts as a prototype of one that will rule when the New World Order comes into being. "It meets on a regular basis to discuss finances, direction, policy, etc. and to problem-solve difficulties that come up," she said. "Once again, these leaders are heads in the financial world, old banking money. The Rothschild family in England, and in France, has ruling seats. A descendant of the Hapsburg dynasty has a generational seat. A descendant of the ruling families of England and France has a generational seat. The Rockefeller family in the US holds a seat." She added the Illuminati leadership believe they are descended from royal bloodlines, as well as unbroken occult heritage. She explained the structure of control within the Illuminati:

> [M]y understanding was: The Hanoverian / Hapsburg descendants rule in Germany over the *Bruderheist*. They are considered one of the strongest lines for occult as well. The British line is just under them, with the royal family. Definitely, they rule the UK branch under the Rothschilds in the occult realm, even though parliament rules the country openly. In France, again, descendants of the royal families are also in power in the occult realm, but the French Rothschilds hold the reigns over all of them. The U.S. is considered lower, and younger, than the European branches. This is why the children of leaders are ALWAYS sent to Europe for part of their training; the education is considered better and the U.S. families want to renew their affiliation with the European forebears [recall Bill Clinton of Arkansas was given a Rhodes scholarship to the University of Oxford].

Svali's most shocking revelations concern a coming economic collapse followed by martial law in some parts of the United States. She said each region of the country contains military compounds and bases that are hidden in remote, isolated areas or on large private estates. "These bases are used intermittently to teach and train generational Illuminati in military techniques, hand-to-hand combat, crowd control, use of arms, and all aspects of military warfare. Why? Because the Illuminists believe that our government, as we know it, as well as the governments of most nations around the world, are destined to collapse," she wrote, adding these will be planned collapses, and they will occur in the following ways:

> The Illuminati has planned first for a financial collapse that will make the Great Depression look like a picnic. This will occur

through the maneuvering of the great banks and financial institutions of the world, through stock manipulation, and interest rate changes. Most people will be indebted to the federal government through bank and credit card debt, etc. The governments will recall all debts immediately, but most people will be unable to pay and will be bankrupted. This will cause generalized financial panic, which will occur simultaneously worldwide, as the Illuminists firmly believe in controlling people through finances.

Doesn't sound pleasant, does it? I don't know the exact time frame for all of this, and wouldn't want to even guess. The good news is that if a person is debt-free, owes nothing to the government or credit debt, and can live self-sufficiently, they may do better than others. I would invest in gold, not stocks, if I had the income. Gold will once again be the world standard, and dollars will be pretty useless (Remember after the Civil War? Our money will be worth about what Confederate money was after the collapse).

Next there will be a military takeover, region by region, as the government declares a state of emergency and martial law. People will have panicked, there will be an anarchical state in most localities, and the government will justify its move as being necessary to control panicked citizens. The cult trained military leaders and people under their direction will use arms as well as crowd control techniques to implement this new state of affairs…. Military bases will be set up, in each locality (actually, they are already here, but are covert). In the next few years, they will go above ground and be revealed. Each locality will have regional bases and leaders to which they are accountable. The hierarchy will closely reflect the current covert hierarchy.

Svali said the United Nations was created to help overcome one of the biggest barriers to a one-world government—nationalism, or pride in one's country. However, following the global collapse, it will be the leadership of the Illuminati, not the UN, who will rule the New World Order.

She also was very clear that the Illuminati agenda is not a Jewish conspiracy. "Yes, there are some very powerful Jewish people in this group. For instance, the Rothschild family literally runs the financial empire in Europe (and indirectly the States), and are a well-known Jewish family. I have also known people whose parents were Jewish diamond merchants in the group, and at every level. But to rise to power in the Illuminati, a Jewish person at night would be forced to renounce their faith, and to give their first allegiance to Lucifer and the beliefs of the Illuminati," she explained. She added, "I have always wondered this, though, why some of the highest ranking financial fami-

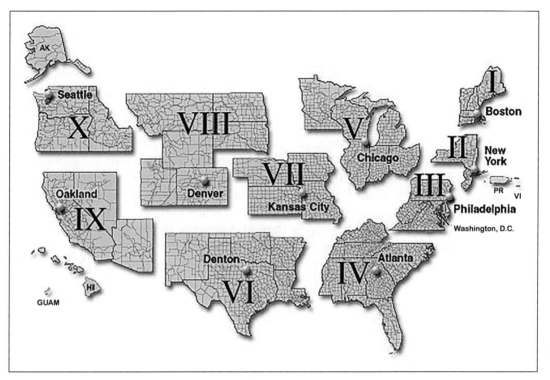

The Federal Emergency Management Agency (FEMA) is under the Department of Homeland Security and was created in 1978 initially to coordinate response to any disaster within the USA. Although the governor of any stricken area must seek FEMA's aid after a state of emergency has been declared, the feds may take the initiative if such disaster occurs on government property or to government assets.

lies in the group … are Jewish, yet the group espouses hatred of their own race." This could be because dedicated Zionists, largely Ashkenazi Jews, despise Orthodox Jews, who largely oppose Zionism.

According to Svali, the Freemasons and the Illuminati work hand in glove. "I don't care if this steps on any toes, it's a fact. The Masonic temple at Alexandria, Virginia (the city itself was named after Alexandria, Egypt, and is a hotbed of Illuminati activity) is a center in the Washington, D.C., area for Illuminati scholarship and teaching. I was taken there at intervals for testing, to step up a level, for scholarship, and high ceremonies. The leaders in this Masonic group were also Illuminists. This has been true of every large city I have lived in. The top Freemasons were also top Illuminists." But she explained that all Masons are not Illuminati. "[E]specially at the lower levels, I believe they know nothing of the practices that occur in the middle of the night in the larger temples. Many are probably fine businessmen and Christians. But I have never known a 32 degree or above who wasn't Illuminati, and the group helped create Freemasonry as a 'front' for their activities."

Svali described the Illuminati as a "very political and back stabbing group, a 'dog-eat-dog' mentality; everyone wants to move up. These are NOT nice people and they use and manipulate others viciously. They cut their eyeteeth on status, power, and money. They never openly disclose their agenda, or their cult activities, as often they are amnesic to them. These are well-respected, 'Christian' appearing business leaders in the community. The image in the community is all-important to an Illuminist; they will do anything to maintain a normal, respected facade, and DESPISE exposure" [emphasis in the original]. Pop culture, especially TV and rock music, is used as a tool to influence the masses, said Svali. "It cannot create a total personality change in the average citizen, but it can desensitize us increasingly to violence, pornography and the occult, and influence the perceptions of young children." She said the Illuminati have kept their secrecy intact because the public simply won't believe that this could be happening. "I am [now] a strong Christian, and in Revelations, it says that right before the return of Jesus, people will be acting as if nothing has happened, that all is normal, in spite of evidence to the contrary," she said. "You could show people a video taken of a ritual, and they would declare: 'it has to be a fake; people just don't do those things.' You can show them a site with pentagrams, buried bones, and other evidence, and they would say, 'Oh, that is just teenagers playing around." ... They can be shown the scars on a survivor's body, from cigarette burns in childhood, and old lash marks that have healed on their back, and the question would be 'Are you sure it wasn't self-inflicted?'

"The evidence is there, but in my opinion, the average person does not want to know, and even when confronted with it, will look the other way. The Franklin case [a 1988 scandal involving child abuse, Satanism, and murder in Nebraska] is a point. How much evidence has come out? Or the MK-Ultra [the CIA mind-control program] documents that have been declassified, shown as real, and people ignore it.... We as human beings want to believe the best of our race, not the worst...."

Hidden Hand also contradicted British author David Icke's belief that this family was filled with reptilian creatures.

Another anonymous whistleblower from within the elite entered the AboveTopSecret Forum in the fall of 2008 using the avatar "Hidden Hand." Hidden Hand said he was a member of "The Family," a group of elitists aligned with extraterrestrials. They are alternately called the Illuminati, Nephilim, Custodians, Watchers, and Advanced Beings and all are the product of distinct bloodlines that have passed along wealth and power from one generation to another.

"I am a generational member of a Ruling Bloodline Family," Hidden Hand proclaimed. "Our lineage can be traced back beyond antiquity. From the earliest times of your recorded 'history,' and beyond, our Family has been 'directing' the 'play' from behind the scenes, in one way or another. Before the rise and fall of Atlantis (Yes, that was indeed perfectly real). We are 'born to lead.' It is part of the design for the current paradigm.... There are 13 'base' or 'core' original bloodlines. Yet there are many, many other lines that spring from these, as do rivers from the oceans. If you imagine the 13 original lines as primary colors, that can be mixed to create a vast array of other colors, then you will have some comprehension. Again, no competition, just family."

Hidden Hand also contradicted British author David Icke's belief that this family was filled with reptilian creatures. "We are most certainly not Reptilian," Hidden Hand stated. "And there is nothing remotely reptilian about the True Power Bloodlines." He also said the British royalty are not the most powerful bloodline. "There are others above these lineages in the hierarchy," he explained. "You will not know the names of these lines." Icke explained that the Illuminati creator is not the "devil" or "Satan" but rather "Lucifer, the Light Bearer." This is actually a group soul or "Social Memory Complex." "We (our Bloodline Families), as a Group Soul or Social

In order for humans to be able to ascend to higher levels of existence they had to understand polarity and have the ability to choose. Thus, the Garden of Eden included forbidden fruit.

Memory Complex (Lucifer), were on the verge of Seventh Density Ascension, though at this level, before Harvest comes, we have the choice to progress higher, or, to return to help others of lower densities with their own evolution, by passing down our knowledge and Wisdom (Light) to those that call upon us for assistance, with their own Free Will," he said. He noted that without polarity, opposites derived from Free Will, there is only the Unity of Love and Light, and no choice to experience anything other than that. "So, we [the Luciferian group soul] were to be the Catalyst for change, in order to provide that choice, thus bringing polarity. Yahweh [the deity of the ancient Israelites] agreed that we would introduce the concept of Free Will to Earth's inhabitants, by offering them an initial choice, as to whether they 'wanted' it or not. Hence, the Tree of the Knowledge of 'Good and Evil' (or more accurately, the Knowledge of Polarity, of Positive or Negative). Yahweh takes his inhabitants to a new 'garden' and tells them you can do anything you like, except this one thing, thus creating the desire to do the one thing there are told they cannot. Hence, a 'Choice.'

We provide the Catalyst by telling them the benefits of attaining Knowledge, they eat from the tree, and the rest is history." Hidden Hand also explained the current state of humanity and warned:

> Thought is creative energy, focused. You get exactly what you put out. Why do you think the Media is so important to us? You have (as a society), in your hypnotized comatose state, given your Free Will consent to the state your planet is in today. You saturate your minds with the unhealthy dishes served up for you on your televisions that you are addicted to, violence, pornography, greed, hatred, selfishness, incessant "bad news," fear and "terror." When was the last time you stopped, to think of something beautiful and pure? The planet is the way it is, because of your collective thoughts about it. You are complicit in your inaction, every time you "look the other way" when you see an injustice. Your "thought" at the sub-conscious level of creation to the Creator, is your allowance of these things to occur. In so doing, you are serving our purpose. It is very important to us, that the Polarization of this planet is Negative at the time of the Great Harvest. That means Service to Self orientated, as opposed to Positive, Service to Others. We require a Negative Harvest, and you are doing a fine job of helping us to attain our goal. We are very grateful.

Asked what role "God" plays in the scheme of the Illuminati, Hidden Hand responded:

> Religion is either actually created, or at very least, heavily influenced by us. There is no such thing as "god." "God" is a human concept, which is a misunderstanding of the original concept of "Creator." This is further confused, as there are many macrocosmic level Creators, or Logos…. "God" implies some separate entity which is "outside" of you, which you must supplicate to and worship. Our One Infinite Creator, and almost all of our Logos and sub-Logos, do not want your worship. They want you to understand Creation, and your place within it, as a Co-Creator. Ultimately, there is a "Supreme Being," in the form of the One Infinite Creator, but we are all a part of It, rather than its subjects. None of the names given for this "Supreme Being" by your religions are the true name, but they are indeed correct, in that there is One Supreme Being, namely the Infinite Creator. They just have different concepts about It, which spring from the texts their religion is based upon. Do not "worship" your Infinite Creator, but rather live in a state of Thanksgiving and Service to It, for bringing you into Being, and for this amazing Game It has

Created, in which we may forget who we really are, in order to remember, and know ourself one again, as the Creator.

Hidden Hand's posts were compiled and published by Michael E. Salla, who is the founder of the Exopolitics Institute, which studies the politics of the impact of extraterrestrial life on humanity. In 2004, Salla was dismissed from his position with the Center for Global Peace in Washington's American University for his research on UFOs. Salla interpreted the Hidden Hand as suggesting that there is a "Luciferian group soul that is working in our Galaxy that has established power not only on our planet, but on other worlds. Reptilian worlds under the influence of the Family, or Luciferian entity, would be as highly manipulated as our own by off-world bloodlines."

"This appears uncannily similar to the Star Wars saga where a group of dark spiritual entities called the Sith secretly infiltrate and take over political and spiritual organizations in the Galaxy," remarked Salla. "If the Hidden Hand and his Luciferian peers belong to something similar to the Sith, is there a positive counterpart similar to the Jedi Knights? This is how the Hidden Hand describes the modern equivalent of the Jedi Knights—a positive polarity 'Family.'"

According to Hidden Hand, all youngsters born into Illuminati families are carefully schooled in the areas of the military, government, spiritual, scholarship, leadership, and sciences. "[W]e hold key positions in all these main areas of importance," he said. "With the addition of a complicit Media machine and ownership of your financial establishments, all bases are covered." After Hidden Hand's posts, the *AboveTopSecret* website was soon filled with cries of "Hoax!" and "disinformation." But after studying the lengthy dialogs with Hidden Hand, Salla concluded, "In my opinion, it is a genuine revelation by an insider belonging to an organization called 'The Family' that has both Earthly human and extraterrestrial membership. The Family has been secretly involved in ruling both the Earth and other planets through highly placed elites in key social and political institutions."

Another reported ranking Illuminati defector is Leo Lyon Zagami, a former Grand Master of the Ordo Illuminatorum Universalis ("Universal Order of the Illuminati"), headquartered in Florence, Italy, and considered by some as the good side of the Illuminati in the Vatican. Zagami is a former member of the Comitato Esecutivo Massonico (the "Masonic Executive Committee") of Monte Carlo, and a thirty-third-degree Freemason. He was a senior member of the infamous P2 Lodge, which in the 1980s was revealed as a seditious organization, involving figures connected to Freemasons, the Vatican, and the CIA, attempting to bring about a fascist state in Italy. Zagami claimed to be born of a

In 2004, Salla was dismissed from his position with the Center for Global Peace in Washington's American University for his research on UFOs.

According to Zagami, illuminated thinkers have been around since the days of the legendary civilization of Atlantis.

Scottish-Sicilian Illuminati aristocratic bloodline and has been involved in the Illuminati Order since childhood.

In 2016, Zagami published a book entitled *Confessions of an Illuminati,* in which he described Illuminati rituals, rites, and his perspective of the Illuminati's "web of deceit and total world control." He said his confession was "an attempt to bring to light a reality considered by most, unfortunately, non-existent, and even the object of derision by so-called academics, often controlled and manipulated by secret societies themselves, as they succeed in silencing the truth at the source, on behalf of the elite." He described "the occult and millenarian groups of power made of societies more or less secret, which have governed the world since the dawn of civilization.

"In fact, while it is true that the Order of the Illuminati of Bavaria, created by Adam Weishaupt, was apparently short-lived amongst the Western systems of initiation, it is equally true that they were just another enactment of the same mystery school from ancient times, a school of 'illuminated' thinkers, which have been around since the days of legendary Atlantis, and were present in the Egyptian Mystery School, called the 'School of the Right Eye of Horus' in Alexandria, Egypt," he wrote. "It has been confirmed by many historians and scholars of Freemasonry, that in the decades following the official demise of the Bavarian Illuminati, many other cells of this organization were reactivated from time to time within Freemasonry, but rarely called themselves according to Weishaupt's tradition. In the USA there is the Skull and Bones, created out of prestigious Yale University in 1832, and the Bohemian Club in California, founded in 1872, so as not to risk persecution by the growing anti-Masonic movement in the USA."

Zagami reported that in 1972 a significant Congress of the World Synod of Bishops of Gnostic Succession and Communion was conducted in Liege, Belgium. Here met representatives of some of the many Illuminati offshoot organizations. Zagami listed these little-known groups:

- The Monastery of the Seven Rays
- The Ecclesia Gnostica Spiritualis
- The Memphis Misraim Rite
- The Ecclesia Gnostica Ophitica

- The Universal Martinist Federation of Initiates
- The Albigensian Gnostic Rite of Haiti
- Gnostic and Magic Christians
- Gnostic and Theurgic Ontology
- The Esoteric Rite of the Rose-Croix
- The Church of Mandala of Giordano Bruno
- The Fraternitas Hermetica
- The American Synod of Gnostic Bishops
- The QBLH [Cabalistic] Alchemist Church
- The Martinist Order of the Rose-Croix and Adelph-Initiates
- The Interior Synuary of the Elus Cohens
- The Naasenian Gnostic Brotherhood of Initiates and Adepts.

Zagami noted that it is unclear what connection such organizations have to the Bavarian Illuminati as most were unheard of prior to 1973. He also illustrated how some occult organizations can be infiltrated and turned to different directions. "He said only a few months after the 1973 congress, "several members of the 'Monastery of the Seven Rays' adopted [Aleister] Crowley's Law of Thelma … [which] is the key moment for the secret conversion of a Catholic Monastery based in Spain, into a homosexual magickal sect." Zagami credited this change to Michael P. Bertiaux, a former Seattle Episcopalian minister who established a Voodoo church and was a longtime member of the Ordo Templi Orientis Antiqua, a pseudo-initiatic gnostic-magical order reportedly founded in Haiti in 1921. Zagami said Bertiaux's teachings were derived from "Gnostic sources, Bon'pa [a Tibetan sect], Tantric, Voodoo, Cabbalistic and even extraterrestrial."

This explanation of modern Illuminism was offered by Zagami:

The Illuminati sects operating in the occult and sexual magick circles united people ranging from the ex-terrorist to the fundamentalist Catholic; ready to manipulate sects, new religions, state secrets, and anything else they can get their hands on for profit and power. *The two big players, The Vatican on one side; and the Jewish lobby on the other, play a daily game of chess with the destiny of all of humanity* [emphasis in the original].… Many of the sects of the Illuminati network … use the occult to get rich off the backs of the poor and the ignorant that fall into their trap. There are also those immersed in demonic practices who, in some cases, influence adepts to promote human sacrifice. Although organizations of this type (those that practice human sacrifice) are a minority, they usually consist of very influential members of high society, people who will never be prosecuted for such horrible actions.

In his obtuse and exhaustive book, Zagami designated Aleister Crowley and his O.T.O. as a primary funnel of Illuminati mysticism and explained that in Crowley's publications "we find the initials, A.A., which used the Masonic custom to abbreviate certain words with their initial, followed by three dots arranged in an equilateral triangle." He explained that these initials represent an "ultra-secretive sect of powerful telepaths known as the *Argentium Astrum* or the Silver Star of Sirius … because it is linked to the very origins of our species: the Annunaki."

Yet another Illuminati whistleblower, who some disregard as simply a disgruntled ex-wife, is Katharine "Kay" Griggs, a devout Christian formerly married for eleven years to U.S. Marine Colonel George Raymond Griggs. Mrs. Griggs claims to have heard from her husband, usually while drunk, accounts of military assassination squads, drug running, illegal weapons sales, and sexual perversions within both the military and federal government connected to secret societies.

Aleister Crowley wearing the formal clothing of the Ordo Templi Orientis.

"I became a whistle blower and received death threats," explained Griggs in an interview. "I finally wound up living for safety reasons with Sarah [McClendon], the dean of the White House Press Corps, who had been with every president since FDR and was in Army intelligence and also an attorney's daughter from Texas." She added, after 9/11, the war in Iraq, the London bombings, and the fear of terrorism, the "American people are at a point where they are ready and willing to hear the truth."

"My former husband, George, who is a trained assassin, calls the people he is involved with the members of The Firm or The Brotherhood. If you are in the clique, you are above the law and literally can get away with murder. For years, mostly when he was drinking, he told me how he and others in this elite military group would kill people," said Griggs, who has mentioned several prominent names as those behind sexual perversion, murder, brainwashing, and mind control. She said all these activities are sanctioned, participated in, and condoned by a group of military and political elite operating on the same principles as the Illuminati.

She said her ex-husband stated that The Brotherhood contains many members of secret societies such as "Cap and Gown" at Princeton and "Skull and Bones" at Yale. In interviews, Griggs revealed that members of The Brotherhood operate in a world of treachery, deceit, lies, murder, drug running, sex slavery, and illegal weapon sales, all in the name of forming a New World Order. "In general, they are first generation German sons, mostly who run things in the military through tight friendships made in Europe and at war colleges. Psyops [psychological operations] is a controlling group and [former Deputy Secretary of Defense and president of the World Bank] Paul Wolfowitz is a major player, as are the many Zionists on this side of the Atlantic.

"As far as the sheer numbers of people involved in this cap and gown, skull and bones secret society, it's hard to say. But it is based on old friendships, college and prep school relationships, covering up secrets and sexual perversion. My husband told me about all the sexually perverted rituals, like anal and oral sex in coffins at drunken parties and running naked in the woods at Bohemian Grove," she reported, describing this clique as "a very, very small group and a rather homogenized group of global top-down existentialist Zionists and socialists. In short, Nazis who came to the U.S. when Hitler, their boy, turned on them in 1933.

"After what I heard all those years and now putting it into perspective after 9/11, I think they are trying to destroy America. Their whole game is all about war, selling weapons and creating a militaristic society. I know firsthand from listening to my husband, they will do anything—I mean anything including murder—to get what they want."

From overheard conversations between her husband and others, Griggs said, "I am sure 9-11 was a joint and combined military operation, using boys who were recruited via A[bdul] Q[adeer] Khan's Israeli network in Pakistan and South Africa through Zionists in Hamburg. I believe that certain MI6 British Zionists … were also involved in funding and recruiting these guys. It was a large and ongoing operation to set up and involved lots of CIA Zionists and lots of funny money."

Following several interviews, Kay Griggs dropped from sight and in mid-2016, controversy continued on the Internet as to whether she was still alive or not.

There have been several other persons, always anonymous, who claimed to have been in the Illuminati and their revelations range from the ridiculous to the sublime.

One person, who was never identified but whose story has been repeated on several websites, recounted how he was recruited while still a student at Harvard in the early 1960s. "I was a member of the Illuminati for 47 years. I was recruited when I was 19 years old," he stated. "The information that I am about to unfold is very revealing and very dangerous. I am one of seven people in the history of the Illuminati that have performed the 'Departure Ritual.' I knew that I needed to get out when I had something revealed to me at a meeting in June of 2010. For years I was in line with the beliefs, motives, and actions of the Illuminati, but it recently became too much for me to bear, and I had to extinguish my sacred contract."

This self-styled whistleblower spoke on conspiracies that resonate with many Internet surfers—secret space flights, nuclear missiles at moon bases, deep underground bunkers reserved for the very wealthy, how Abraham Lincoln lived and spent his last years in a Mexican bunker, how the Illuminati created Hurricane Katrina and the Gulf Oil Spill, how Israel is "the grand puppet state of the Illuminati," how some epidemics (including the Spanish Flu of 1918) were actually engineered by the Illuminati, and how "scientists working for the Illuminati have found a way that they can 'shut' off the sun." destroying all life on Earth within nine years. He even accused Alex Jones, the popular anti-Establishment conspiracy broadcaster, of secretly being an Illuminati member.

Despite all the negative press concerning the Illuminati, there have been some recent attempts at resurrecting the beneficial aspects of the old Order. One such is called Congressional Illuminism, which is expounded upon in a trilogy entitled *Spirit Builders* by Tau Palamas, reportedly taking the name from fourteenth-century monk Gregory Palamas, a saint in the Eastern Orthodox Church. The books present a synthesis of many esoteric practices derived from a variety of occult practices.

According to Palamas, Congressional Illuminism is "a non-hierarchical and non-authoritarian approach to spirituality. Essentially this is a spiritual organization without the priest. No grand poohbahs, no secret chiefs, no blessed leader, and no boss. The group is composed of individuals seeking to facilitate the spiritual development of others. Folks united in a common goal of spiritual growth and communion."

At least one conspiracy writer, one with a credible work record, has offered hopeful solace to gloomy conspiracy researchers. Benjamin Fulford sees the modern Illuminati on the run. Fulford worked in Japan as a correspondent for Knight Ridder, the *International Financing Review*, the *Nihon Keizai Shimbun* English edition, and

A NASA photo shows the extent of the oil spill in the Caribbean off the Mississipi Delta. The environmental disaster was the result of yet another Illuminati plot, according to some.

the *South China Morning Post* before moving to *Forbes* magazine, where he was the Asian Bureau chief from 1998 to 2005. He then began reporting on the pending collapse of the Illuminati's scheme of world control, predicting a complete revision of the global financial system. He argued the Illuminati plans for a New World Order are imploding, thanks to the revelations now available on the Internet and countermoves by wealthy Chinese in the White Dragon Society.

Fulford said escalating world events have "prompted the Rothschild family, the Chinese communist party, the gnostic illuminati, the Pentagon and others to send representatives to negotiate with the White Dragon Society," and that Fulford, due to his knowledge and experience in Asia, was selected to be the society's public spokesman. Since that time, he has published a series of predictions and analyses of events he described as an unfolding plan to break the centralized power of what he termed the "Khazarian crime syndicate" or "Nazionists," a cabal of Nazis, Zionists, and the wealthy elite of Europe and America. He said the countermove is to develop a new global financial system.

> **Fulford said the creation of an Asian Infrastructure Investment Bank along with the recent formation of a BRICS-nation [Brazil, Russia, India, China, and South Africa] development bank will provide an alternative**

"There are rapidly accelerating indications the Khazarian crime syndicate that illegally seized power in the United States and many European countries is being systematically dismantled," he wrote in 2015. He cited several factors, indicating a take-down of the Illuminati conspiracy, including a New York court ruling that members of the George W. Bush administration may be sued and face criminal charges (especially in regard to the 9/11 attacks), a senior member of the Rothschild family being questioned about fraud by French police, the premature death of more than a dozen JP Morgan bankers, and the sudden resignations of several hundred corporate CEOs over the past few years.

"Despite all the fudged numbers and smoke and mirrors coming out of Western governments, the Western financial system (the Federal Reserve Board) is already bankrupt," he stated. "The Fed's corporate subsidiary, the United States of America Corporation headed by 'acting president' Barack Obama has been issuing fake financial data for years now to create the appearance all is well."

Fulford said the creation of an Asian Infrastructure Investment Bank along with the recent formation of a BRICS-nation [Brazil, Russia, India, China, and South Africa] development bank will provide an alternative to the current Rothschild-led Illuminati financial system. However, he warned, this move is being accompanied by major cyber warfare. "A lot of it is being reported in the corporate media in the form of stories about data being stolen on all U.S. Federal employees etc.... plentiful anecdotal evidence suggests the real cyber-warfare is taking place between world financial networks.... This is all anecdotal but the fact that most of the over 50 bankers who have recently died suddenly and mysteriously were IT experts shows that financial cyber-warfare is moving out of cyberspace."

Corroborating Fulford's account of bankers suddenly dying is an article from SecretsOfTheFed.com in 2015 listing leading bankers, along with scientists and investigative reporters, who died, many under unusual circumstances, in that year. "The deaths of 48 high level bankers just within the last year is even more strikingly bizarre due to the sheer number and manner of deaths. What are the odds these high-level, multi-millionaire bankers who are often described as happy people would kill themselves in the most odd of ways? Are these bankers being killed in order to stave off prosecution by the banks? Our entire monetary system is a Ponzi scheme, are big banks scared of a whistle-blower coming forward to expose all the corruption, leading to a loss of confidence and crash of the system?" noted this site.

"The fact is the BRICS know that time is on their side because the Western countries no longer have the industrial or resource base needed to support their world domination. In other words, there is not enough reality to support their money illusion any more. That is why the Khazarian mafia controlled Western economic and financial systems are slowly imploding. This can be seen with the fall in stock markets, commodity prices etc. and the desperate move to negative interest rates," Fulford explained.

"The British, the Swiss, the Germans, the French and the Vatican have already abandoned the Khazarians and allied with the WDS [White Dragon Society] and BRICS alliance," said Fulford. "The collapse of their global debt slavery regime is accelerating and their immunity from prosecution for mass murder is evaporating along with their funny money."

Fulford's optimistic view is echoed by David Wilcock, a "New Age" author and lecturer whom some claim to be the reincarnation of the famous "sleeping prophet" of the early twentieth century, Edgar Cayce. Wilcock outlined a plan that "has been meticulously followed for at least 300 years.

"The economic, political and social concerns we struggle with today are the result of a plan that was systematically put into practice as of 1776, with the founding of the Order of the Illuminati in Bavaria. This group networked, infiltrated, consolidated and enacted plans that had been in place for much longer periods of time. They created the hidden infrastructure, secrecy, membership, documentation and blueprints necessary to effectuate what they had hoped would be a global takeover—in the hopes of declaring a New World Order."

Wilcock said for many years he has had hundreds of dreams in which he sees "a massive, unprecedented exposure and arrest of this cabal on a worldwide level … this will indeed be of tremendous, unprecedented, positive benefit to humanity."

But, he said the will of good people must be gained to bring an end to Illuminati rule. He said such a plan for the mass arrest of criminally guilty parties within government and the corporate world have been in development since the Coup of 1963—the assassination of President John F. Kennedy. "This plan requires the will of the people to succeed," he explained. "Otherwise, our supporters within the military and the justice system do not have the legal precedent to perform such actions. After many years, the public outrage is now sufficiently high that the will of the people has become more than sufficient to take these steps. Elements within our civilian and military sectors alike have had enough—and are taking a stand. US marshals from the Department of Justice

Katy Perry's half time performance at Superbowl XLIV in 2015 supposedly included Illuminati symbolism. Her riding a lion in this scene was compared to Egyptian art depicting the goddess Isis.

and peace officers will carry out the arrests, with the assistance of military personnel—in the event of any unforeseen disturbances. By assisting a legal civilian operation in this manner, the military personnel are following their Oath of Enlistment—to protect and defend the US Constitution against all enemies, foreign and domestic. This will be a point of no return for the cabal … the mass arrests will generate a situation from which there is no turning back for the Cabal. Once the truth is exposed, there will be no further walls of secrecy for them to hide behind. That is why they are so terrified right now."

But it was not just the financial and corporate systems that reveal the machinations of Illuminati operatives in whichever secret society they belong. Both Wilcock and Fulford saw Illuminati influence seeping into all forms of public entertainment. "Both the Super Bowl [XLIV] half-time show and the [2016] Grammy Awards ceremony … featured blatant Luciferian rituals," Wilcock wrote.

Other whistleblowers who claim to have been Illuminati insiders include John Todd, Arizona Wilder, Bill Schnoebelen, Joseph "Doc" Marquis, Mark Cleminson, and Carolyn Hamlett. Though usually lacking in documentation or hard evidence, their stories are generally and remarkably consistent. Yet there is one publicly known secret society, often mentioned by self-professed Illuminati insiders, that has been definitely linked to the Bavarian Illuminati—Yale University's Skull and Bones.

Skull and Bones

Skull and Bones is more than a fraternity. It is a secret society that evolved from a group of senior students from Yale University. Its trappings and rites are so close to those of the Illuminati that some believe it is a modern reincarnation of the Order. Like the Illuminati, this society is sometimes thought to play a critical role in global conspiracies that aim to dominate the world. Each year, only fifteen Yale juniors are selected to participate in Skull and Bones during their senior year. In addition to extraordinary secrecy—Skull and Bones members are required to leave the room if anyone should mention the group—the Order has its own membership designations. Neophyte members are called Knights, after the fashion of earlier secret societies such as the Knights Templar, Knights of Malta, or Knights of St. John. Once a full member, he is known as a Patriarch, one honored as a founding father. Outsiders are derogatorily referred to as "gentiles" or "vandals."

Antony Sutton, author of *America's Secret Establishment: An Introduction to the Order of Skull & Bones*, noted that active membership in Skull and Bones comes from a "core group of perhaps 20–30 families.... First we find old line American families who arrived on the East coast in the 1600s, e. g. Whitney, Lord, Phelps, Wadsworth, Allen, Bundy, Adams and so on," he wrote. "Second, we find families who acquired wealth in the last 100 years, sent their sons to Yale and in time became almost old line families, e. g. Harriman, Rockefeller, Payne, Davison."

The flow of financial power was not always channeled through direct membership in Skull and Bones. "The Order controls the substantial wealth of Andrew Carnegie, but no Carnegie has ever been a member of The Order," wrote author Sutton. "The Order used the Ford wealth so flagrantly against the wishes of the Ford family that two Fords resigned from the board of the Ford Foundation. No Ford has been a member of The Order. The name Morgan never appeared on the membership lists, although some of Morgan partners are with the inner core, for example, [Henry P.] Davison and [John] Perkins."

This Order, a highly-secret fraternal order apparently only found at Yale, has been the source of an unprecedented number of government officials who have furthered the globalist aims of their brethren in other covert groups, such as Wolf's Head and Scroll and Key. According to conspiracy researchers, anyone in the Eastern Establishment who does not belong to Skull and Bones almost assuredly belongs to one of these other groups. But none has the demonstrable blood and wealth connections of Skull and Bones. The senior class of Yale founded the organization in 1832 to show its resistance to the debating societies of the university—Linonia, Brothers in Unity, and the Calliopean Society. Known variously as Chapter 322, the "Brotherhood of Death," "The Order," or more popularly as "Skull & Bones," or simply "Bones," the Order was brought from Germany to Yale in 1832 by General William Huntington Russell and Alphonso Taft.

Russell's cousin, Samuel Russell, was an integral part of the British-inspired Opium Wars in China. Taft, secretary of war and attorney general during under President Ulysses S. Grant and U.S. minister to Austria-Hungary and Russia under President Chester A. Arthur, was the father of William Howard Taft, the only person to serve as both president and chief justice of the United States. Another prominent Bones member was W. Averell Harriman, U.S. ambassador to Russia during World War II and who played a prominent role in the establishment of the American empire.

A pamphlet detailing an 1876 investigation of Skull and Bones by a rival secret society stated, "… its founder [Russell] was in Germany before Senior Year and formed a warm friendship with a leading member of a German society. He brought back with him to college authority to found a chapter here…. Thus was Bones founded."

The secret German society may have been none other than the infamous Illuminati. Ron Rosenbaum—a former Yale student and one of the few journalists to take a serious look at Skull and Bones—took note that the official skull and crossbones emblem of The Order, the naval ensign of the Knights Templar, was also an icon of the Illuminati. In an investigative piece for *Esquire* magazine, Rosenbaum wrote, "I do seem to have come across definite, if skeletal, links between the origins of Bones rituals and those of the notorious Bavarian Illuminists … [who] did have a real historical existence … from 1776 to 1785 they were an esoteric secret society with the more mystical free-thinking lodges of German Freemasonry."

Rosenbaum wrote how another fraternity gave him a dossier on Bones rituals that revealed that a Bones initiate is placed in a coffin, which is carried to a central part of their building, called "the Tomb." This new man is chanted over and said to be "reborn" into society after being removed

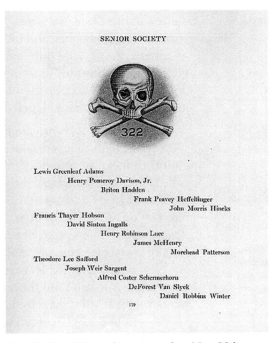

SENIOR SOCIETY

Lewis Greenleaf Adams
Henry Pomeroy Davison, Jr.
Briton Hadden
Frank Peavey Heffelfinger
John Morris Hincks
Francis Thayer Hobson
David Sinton Ingalls
Henry Robinson Luce
James McHenry
Morehead Patterson
Theodore Lee Safford
Joseph Weir Sargent
Alfred Coster Schermerhorn
DeForest Van Slyck
Daniel Robbins Winter

119

The Skull and Bones has appeared on Nazi SS banners and pirate ships. Here it is on a 1920 Skull and Bones Society program. Two of the people here—Briton Hayden and Henry Robinson Luce—were founders of *Time* magazine.

from the coffin and given robes covered with symbols. "A bone with his name on it is tossed into bone heap at start of every meeting [and] initiates plunged into mud pile," stated the notes reported by Rosenbaum. He added that part of the initiation ceremony "is devoted exclusively to sexual histories. They don't leave out anything these days.... [T]he sexual stuff is totally explicit and there's less need for fabricating exploits to fill up the allotted time. Most ... sessions start with talk of prep school masturbation and don't stop until the intimate details of Saturday night's delights have come to light...."

Other similarities between Skull and Bones and Weishaupt's Illuminati include a reading list of books venerated by both orders. One of these, *The Life and Opinions of Tristram Shandy*, involves a character named "Uncle Toby," the same name given to the Bonesman who directs the Order's initiation ceremonies. Like the Illuminati, Bones members are given code names based on historical or mythical figures. "George H. W. Bush (class of 1948) was supposedly assigned *Magog*," noted author Melanson. "Averell Harriman (1913), *Thor*; Charles Seymour (1908) *Machiavelli*. Some of the recurring aliases throughout the years, such as *Dr. Slop, Yorick*, and *Sancho Panza* also can be traced to characters and references in Laurence Sterne's 1760 novel *Tristram Shandy.*"

As in the old Illuminati, Bones members are required to keep personal diaries, called "Life Histories," in which to record their day-to-day experiences, deepest thoughts, and feelings. In addition to such diaries, which can be accessed by Bones superiors, each Bonesman must stand in front of the membership and confess his innermost secrets, including his sexual history. This is done in front of a painting of a woman entitled "Connubial Bliss" and is recorded by the current "Uncle Toby."

Obviously, such private matters on file with the Order could be used at some future date to leverage, if not outright blackmail, members. Yet another connection can be found in a report made years ago by a rival secret society called File and Claw, whose members once broke into the Bones' Tomb to learn its secrets. In its documentation, "They go on to describe a German slogan painted 'on arched walls above the vault' of the sacred room 322," reported Rosenbaum. "The slogan appears above a painting of skulls surrounded by Masonic symbols, a picture said to be 'a gift of the German chapter.' '*Wer war der Thor, wer Weiser, Bettler oder Kaiser? Ob Arm, ob Reich, im Tode gleich*,' the slogan reads, or, 'Who was the fool, who the wise man, beggar or king? Whether poor or rich, all's the same in death.' Imagine my surprise when I ran into that very slogan in a 1798 Scottish anti-Illuminatist tract reprinted in 1967 by the John Birch Society. The tract *Proofs of a Conspiracy* by John Robison) prints alleged excerpts from Illuminist ritual manuals supposedly confiscated by the Bavarian police when the secret order was banned in 1785." According to *U.S. News & World Report*, one of the Bonesmen's traditional songs is sung to the tune of the German National Anthem, *Deutschland Uber Alles*.

Other researchers agree that The Order is merely the Illuminati in disguise, since Masonic emblems, symbols, the German slogan, even the layout of their initiation room—all are identical to those found in Masonic lodges in Germany associated with the Illuminati. "Skull & Bones is an entry point into the Illuminati," declared Fritz Springmeier, author of the voluminous *Bloodlines of the Illuminati*, which traces the bloodline families through the years. "Researchers have noticed the Skull & Bones, but there are a lot of other organizations which are entry points. Rhodes Scholars, a group in Oxford, there are number of different fraternal organizations. Skull & Bones is not the only one—but that's the one George Bush joined. There is also Scroll & Key, Berzelius, and some other fraternal organizations [such as Wolf's Head, Book and Snake, and many others]."

Researchers have noticed there are membership crossovers between Skull and Bones and the CIA. In addition to the aforementioned former president George H. W. Bush, who was named CIA director in 1976 by President Gerald Ford, and his son, George W. Bush, who became president in 2001, we find McGeorge Bundy (The Order, 1940), a national security adviser, and William Bundy (1939), a longtime CIA analyst. Other Bonesmen who became CIA officials included director of personnel F. Trubee Davison (1918); Beirut CIA station chief James Buckley (1944); Rhodes scholar and deputy director for plans Hugh Cunningham (1934), and poet Archibald MacLeish (1915), who helped Office of Strategic Services (OSS) director William Donovan form the CIA in the late 1940s. "Yale has influenced the Central Intelligence Agency more than any other university, giving the CIA the atmosphere of a class reunion," stated Yale history professor Gaddis Smith. Rosenbaum made a point of mentioning that Yale slang for a secret society member is "spook," the same term used in the CIA for an undercover operative.

It should also be noted that this one society has produced national leaders and opinion shapers far outside the statistical norm. Members have included extremely powerful men, such as Henry Stimson, secretary of war under President Franklin D. Roosevelt, and described as "a man at the heart of the heart of the American ruling class"; publisher Henry Luce; author and

Father and son presidents, George W. Bush (left) and his father, George H. W. Bush, have connections to the Illuminati. There is also the CIA–Illuminati connection, so it is no coincidence that the elder Bush was a CIA director.

commentator William F. Buckley Jr. ; and J. Richardson Dilworth, longtime manager of the Rockefeller fortune.

The previously mentioned Jacob Schiff financed the purchase of the Union Pacific for railroad magnate Edward H. Harriman, whose control over railroad transport costs aided John D. Rockefeller in monopolizing the petroleum industry in the late 1800s. He is the father of Bonesman and world statesman W. Averell Harriman, who played a prominent role in the rise of communism in Russia, both before and after World War II. The elder Harriman's two sons attended Yale and were inducted into the Order of the Skull and Bones—William Averell (1913) and Edward Roland Noel (1917). During the 1930s, W. Averell's banking firm of W. A. Harriman & Company merged with the private international banking firm of Brown Brothers creating Brown Brothers, Harriman & Company, a longtime partner of which was Prescott Bush (1917), father of George H. W. Bush and grandfather of George W. Bush. The Harrimans were mentors to the Bush family.

Yet another modern secret society with ties to the Illuminati that has been accused of having more reach and power than its small size should dictate is the Knights of Malta.

Knights of Malta

Another modern secret society, linked to the Knights Templar and hence the Illuminati, is the Knights of Malta, reportedly one of the most powerful of the modern societies, with members reaching into the highest levels of Catholicism, governments, and intelligence agencies.

These Knights survived medieval persecution by allying themselves with the Vatican and even participating in the persecution of its enemies. Likewise, many of Europe's royal families, themselves usurpers of the thrones of the Merovingians and others, worked in partnership with the Vatican to maintain the status quo. These royals are referred to as the "Black Nobility." With the papal condemnation of the Knights Templar beginning in 1307, many Templars simply doffed their distinctive red-cross mantles and secreted themselves within other orders, such as the Knights of Christ, the Teutonic Knights, or the Hospitallers, an order that mutated into the Knights of Malta.

The Hospitallers began about 1070 when a group of Italian merchants established a hospital in Jerusalem dedicated to Saint John long before the First Crusade. After Crusaders took the city in 1099, the Hospitallers reorganized as an order and a Grand Master was selected. While not initially a military order, the Knights of St. John became more militant as the Templars rose to prominence. After the destruction of the Templars, the Hospitallers acquired much of their property, which only increased their already prosperous and powerful order. With the loss of the Holy Land, the Hospitallers fell back to Cyprus along with the Templars. Later they were forced to retreat to Rhodes. When a third siege by the Turks finally took the island in 1522, the order relocated to the island of Malta, where they would become the Sovereign and Military Order of Malta, or simply the Knights of Malta.

The coat of arms of the Knights of Malta, who evolved from the Hospitallers in the early sixteenth century, when they moved to Malta.

Today, the Knights of Malta are headquartered in Rome under the direct supervision of the pope and are recognized by more than forty countries as a sovereign nation. A British offshoot, known as the Knights of St. John of Jerusalem, is a Protestant order headquartered in London and headed by the queen. Prominent Americans connected to the Knights of Malta include the late CIA directors William Casey and John McCone, former Chrysler chairman Lee Iacocca, columnist William F. Buckley, Joseph P. Kennedy, U.S. ambassador to the Vatican William Wilson, Clare Boothe Luce, and former U.S. Secretary of State Alexander Haig. Dr. Luigi Gedda, the head of Catholic Action, was decorated by the Knights of Malta for his liaison work between the Vatican, the CIA, and the European Movement of Joseph Retinger, the "Father of the Bilderbergers." The Knights of Malta are believed to be one of the primary channels of communication between the Vatican and the CIA. The Knights of Malta, Hospitallers, Knights of St. John, Freemasonry, and the Rosicrucians, and perhaps others, all trace their lineage to the Knights Templar with their esoteric knowledge recovered from under Solomon's Temple.

Scandals involving the Knights of Malta go back to the time of John J. Raskob, one of the thirteen founders of the American Order of the Knights of Malta. He was involved in the abortive coup against President Roosevelt in the early 1930s, foiled only after Marine Major General Smedley Butler blew the whistle on the scheme.

During the Reagan administration, the Knights of Malta were involved in the infamous P2 Lodge scandal, in which this Masonic organization attempted to subvert the government of Italy. *Propaganda Masonica Due (2),* better known as the P2 Lodge, was founded in Italy in 1877 to serve Italian Freemasons visiting Rome.

According to Robert Anton Wilson's website, the Knights of Malta currently act as couriers between the Vatican and the CIA. "According to Covert Action Information Bulletin, recent members of the Knights of Malta have included: Franz von Papen, who persuaded von Hindenburg to resign and make Hitler the Chancellor of Germany; General Reinhard Gehlen, Hitler's chief of Intelligence, and later head of the CIA's Russian penetration bureau; General Alexander Haig, major architect of foreign policy in both the Nixon and Reagan regimes; Alexandre de Marenches, former chief of French Intelligence; William Casey, head of the CIA during the Iran-Contra conspiracy; Otto von Habsburg, also a member of the Bilderbergers and part of the Merovingian bloodline ... and Licio Gelli, Roberto Calvi and Michele Sindona, leaders of the P2 Conspiracy in Italy."

According to whistleblower Zagami, the Knights of Malta are "the most powerful group known to man." He stated, "If you think Illuminati and Freemasons are the ones ruling our world, then you better check your real history books again. Who are Knights of Malta? They are your CIA, your politicians, your lobbyists, your previous, present and future presidents. Medici family, which produced four popes for the Vatican church are not just powerful, they are the family related to the Black Pope. Black pope is the most powerful pope in the world. If you think your regular [pope] is the main pope, then you are missing it big. If the white pope, your regular media pope is the CEO, then the Black Pope is the President of the company, who has the authority to fire the CEO."

Considering what this one German professor achieved in the 1700s, it is clear why recent conspiracy writers have expressed a concern over what a modern Illuminati might accomplish, armed with technology and influence over the mass media. It is also abundantly clear that world government and corporate leaders produced from the Knights of Malta, Skull & Bones, and other secret societies improbably outweigh their small size and numbers.

"Even though the Illuminati faded from public view, the monolithic apparatus

Banker and Chase Manhattan Corporation CEO David Rockefeller is seen here in 1953 with First Lady Eleanor Roosevelt. Members of the wealthy, powerful Rockefeller family have long been influential in American politics.

set in motion by Weishaupt may still exist today," commented journalist William T. Still. "Certainly, the goals and methods of operation still exist. Whether the name Illuminati still exists is really irrelevant."

Oddly enough, one of those persons often named as a luminary of the Illuminati, former Chase CEO and banker David Rockefeller, in his 2003 *Memoirs* appeared to support the conspiracy view of some when he wrote, "For more than a century ideological extremists at either end of the political spectrum have seized upon well-publicized incidents such as my encounter with Castro to attack the Rockefeller family for the inordinate influence they claim we wield over American political and economic institutions. Some even believe we are part of a secret cabal working against the best interests of the United States, characterizing my family and me as 'internationalists' and of conspiring with others around the world to build a more integrated global political and economic structure—one world, if you will. If that's the charge, I stand guilty, and I am proud of it."

Of less provenance is a statement attributed to Rockefeller at the 1991 Bilderberg meeting, in which he was quoted as saying, "We are grateful to the *Washington Post*, the *New York Times*, *Time Magazine* and other great publications whose directors have attended our meetings and respected their promises of discretion for almost 40 years.... It would have been impossible for us to develop our plan for the world if we had been subjected to the lights of publicity during those years. But, the world is more sophisticated and prepared to march towards a world government. The super-national sovereignty of an intellectual elite and world bankers is surely preferable to the national auto-determination practiced in past centuries."

So it should be clear that the age-old dream of world domination— whether by military conquest or corporate takeover—is still very much alive, especially within the hearts of individuals who practice the doctrine of Illuminism.

Dr. John Coleman, the controversial author of *Conspirators' Hierarchy: The Story of the Committee of 300* and *The Tavistock Institute of Human Relations: Shaping the Moral, Spiritual, Cultural, Political and Economic Decline of the United States of America*, has claimed to have been a member of British intelligence with insider knowledge but some conspiracy authors have accused Coleman of plagiarizing their work. As an author and lecturer, he has detailed some of the goals of modern Illuminists. Sounding eerily similar to the much-reviled *Protocols*, Coleman has listed some of the goals of present-day Illuminati, which essentially are to create a One World Government or New World Order, to administer a unified church and monetary system.

He said this could be brought about through the political chaos caused by the total collapse of the world's economies. This is based on the old Masonic motto "Order out of chaos." Such chaos would necessitate the elimination of all national sovereignty, identity, and national pride.

The Illuminati will support "religious liberation" across the world to undermine all existing religions, but specifically Christianity, which they seek to replace with humanistic Luciferianism, according to Coleman. He added that Illuminism fully supports supranational institutions such as the United Nations, the International Monetary Fund, the Bank of International Settlements, and the World Court and it hopes such organizations will supplant local institutions by gradually phasing them out or bringing them under the mantle of the UN. The education system will be controlled and eventually destroyed by "Outcome Based Education" programs such as No Child Left Behind and Common Core.

Coleman stated that the Illuminati seek to bring about the end to all industrialization with the exception of the computer and service industries. All U.S. industries will be exported to third-world counties. "Unemployables in the US, in the wake of industrial destruction, will either become opium-heroin and/or cocaine addicts, or become statistics in the elimination of the 'excess population' process we know of today as Global 2000 [a 1980 presidential report warning of increasing climate changes and hunger in the years to come and advocating a U.S population reduction of 100 million by 2050.] All scientific development will be suppressed that might interfere with the Illuminati's "limited natural resources" agenda, including nuclear and other alternative energy sources.

The moral fiber of nations will be weakened and mass unemployment will demoralize workers in the labor class. Coleman explained that as jobs dwindle due to the post-industrial zero-growth policies introduced by the Club of Rome, demoralized and discouraged workers will resort to alcohol and drugs, increasing crime and the need for police forces. "The youth will be encouraged by means of rock music and drugs to rebel against the status quo, thus undermining and eventually destroying the family unit," noted Coleman.

He added that to keep people from determining their own destinies, crisis after crisis will be created with attendant government management "to confuse and demoralize the population to the extent where, faced with too many choices, apathy on a massive scale will result."

Anyone paying attention to news headlines undoubtedly will see these goals manifested in today's world.

Summary

It has been shown how the principles of the Illuminati continued to thrive long after the demise of the Bavarian Order.

The assassination of Austrian Archduke Franz Ferdinand, which precipitated World War I, has been attributed to European Illuminized Freemasonry, the followers of whom began planning for war before 1912. Masonic author Albert Pike, a former Confederate general, reportedly predicted three world wars, although this claim has been contested. As previously mentioned, Freemasonry was dabbling in practices such as the veneration of Lucifer, called the Light Bringer, the Illumined One, as admitted by Pike. What is not contested is the fact that warring secret societies brought on World War II, seen by many as merely an extension of the First World War. Many books and articles have been written about the Nazi involvement with the occult and the search for mystical artifacts. As with any cult, the Nazi cult viewed competing cults as their enemies. And the cult of National Socialism (Nazi) grew out of older groups, including the Bavarian Illuminati, the *Germanenorden*, Freemasonry, the Teutonic Knights, and others.

One instigator of Nazism was Dietrich Eckart, a publisher who circulated *The Protocols of the Wise Men of Zion* and founded the German Worker's Party, which evolved into the National Socialist German Workers Party, the acronym of which is NAZI. Eckart also was among the prominent members of

Anti-Serbian riots occurred in Sarajevo in 1914, shortly after the assassination of Archduke Franz Ferdinand that would spark World War I. It was one of many incendiary incidents that have been blamed on the Illuminati.

the Thule Society, a group of wealthy German aristocrats linked to the Assassin cult, who placed fellow member Adolf Hitler in power. Hitler may have provided yet another connection to the Illuminati and Zionism. An American wartime intelligence report by Dr. Walter C. Langer, and confirmed by Hitler's English nephew, William Patrick Hitler, stated that Hitler's father was the illegitimate son of Maria Anna Schicklgruber, who at the time she conceived her child was working as a cook in the home of Salomon Baron Rothschild in Vienna. If true, this means the Fuehrer of the Third Reich had Jewish ancestry and was connected to the Rothschilds. At least one researcher believed it was this Rothschild connection that may explain the considerable support Hitler received early on from banks in Paris, London, and New York. It would appear from the results of World War II that the Illuminati achieved its goals—the nations of Germany, Italy, and Japan, along with their economies, were devastated and the world population reduced by some sixty million people. The Jewish Holocaust prompted the establishment of the Rothschild enterprise called Israel. All the nations involved, smothered under debt, were easily brought into the newly formed United Nations. The Illuminati may have used the Nazis to substantially change our music. Prior to 1939 the preferred pitch in music was 432 Hertz (Hz). This frequency has been found in the world's oldest flutes, some dating back into pre-history. It is well known how the pitch and frequency of music can affect both the minds and emotions of humans. Even plants have been shown to either excel or languish under various types of music.

The work of John Calhoun Deagan, who developed many of the percussion instruments still in use today, along with Freudian psychology demonstrated that an altered pitch—440 Hz—would change feelings of altruism and compassion to those of nationalism, narcissism, and aggression. In 1939, the British Standards Institute adopted the 440 Hz standard to all musicians playing in Europe. This measure reluctantly was passed in late 1939 despite the fact that the Nazis had been using this basic pitch in their martial music and it was only shortly after Hitler invaded Poland. Sound frequencies, now and in the past, have been used as weapons. The biblical Joshua toppled the walls of Jericho with horns and drums. Today the U.S. Defense Department is actively developing sonic cannons and other auditory weapons. Sound also affects the civilian population. The daily deluge of 440 hz music, along with constant TV and radio programming promoting consumerism, hyper-sexuality (the porn industry), alcohol and drug consumption, and daily virtual killing via video games, desensitizes the population and causes widespread physical and mental illnesses. With the United States becoming more like socialist Russia and the failing economy there causing the collapse of communism, the Illuminati globalists began to put together their next step toward one world socialism— the creation of the European Union. Attempts also began for the creation of a North American Union, composed of Canada, the United States, and Mexico. Such plans are being implemented through so-called free trade agreements sanctioned by non-government entities, such as the North American Free Trade Agreement (NAFTA), the Central America Free Trade Agreement (CAFTA),the Security and Prosperity Partnership of North America (SPP), and the proposed Trans-Pacific Partnership (TPP).

The biblical Joshua toppled the walls of Jericho with horns and drums. Today the U.S. Defense Department is actively developing sonic cannons and other auditory weapons.

Much of the information concerning the activities of Illuminati-related operations today comes from whistle-blowers, who contend that some version of the Illuminati still exists. An unverified Illuminati membership card from 1903 suggests that some sort of organization using the Illuminati name was active that year.

Other claims of Illuminati activity do not boast such hard evidence. On a website appearing in 2005, one Mimi L. Eustis claimed her father, Samuel Todd Churchill, was a member of the Cowbellion de Rakin Society, a New Orleans secret Mardi Gras order connected to the Illuminati. Based on notes and recordings left by her dying father, Eustis learned that Illuminati agents fatally poisoned Presidents William Henry Harrison and Zachary Taylor. They also poisoned President James Buchanan in 1857 but he survived. She said these three presidents were obstructing Illuminati and House of Rothschild plans for the U.S. Civil War. She added the Cowbellion was connected to Yale University's Skull and Bones society, which is merely a branch of the Illuminati. She said it all began as a front for the activities of Masons Albert Pike, Judah Benjamin, and John Slidell, who became leaders of the Confederacy. Eustis echoed the words of German chancellor Otto von Bismarck by saying the House of Rothschild banking dynasty, fearful the United States would begin printing its own money and create a central bank not connected to the Rothschilds, employed a secret society, the Knights of the Golden Circle, to create conflict in America, which led to the War Between the States. She also stated that thirteen bloodline families established a secret elitist society with the goal of ruling the entire Earth through a New World Order. Like so many other tales of the Illuminati, Eustis provided no third-party verification for her claims. Likewise, Bill Ryan, a founder of Project Camelot, could not verify the claims of one anonymous self-proclaimed member of a globalist elite, known only as "Charles." According to Charles, a group of thirty-three individuals meet regularly to make decisions for controlling the world. They can be compared to the board of directors of any large corporation, he said, adding that the Illuminati is a lower-level society than this group. Charles related how this small group regards it as their responsibility to "manage" planet Earth. Some of their control comes because they know the hidden history behind world events due to their possession of ancient documents and artifacts, many located in the Vatican Library. He also noted that this group works for long-term projects. They do not see time as we do. "Delaying something by a year, or a decade, or a hundred years, means very little," he explained. "They do not operate to a calendar. Only to unfolding events."

The controversial author of *Bloodlines of the Illuminati*, Fritz Springmeier, while not a whistleblower, nevertheless has offered up an abundance of information on the Illuminati. Some of his information aligns with that of Charles. Like Mimi Eustis, Springmeier states that the modern Illuminati is led by thirteen prominent families. He said these included names like Astor, Bundy, Collins, DuPont, Freeman, Kennedy, Li, Onassis, Rockefeller, Rothschild, Russell, and Van Duyn. Springmeier said he does not fear the Illuminati taking over the United States because it already took control long ago and the Constitution has not been in effect since the presidential decrees of World War II. He also explained how the lineage of the bloodline families has been obscured by children being switched at birth, the impregnation of servants, twins raised separately, altered genealogical and public records, and even special families used to breed bloodline children. Linda Anderson, under the name Cisco Wheeler, is another self-proclaimed whistleblower who with Springmeier co-authored a book entitled *The Illuminati Formula Used to Create an Undetectable Mind Controlled Slave*. In it she described being raised in a "trans-generational Satanic family," with her father, a Grand Master of the Illuminati, serving as a programmer of the minds of individuals. Wheeler said her programming began as a child and was conducted by a "Dr. Green," who she later learned was the famous escaped Nazi war criminal Dr. Josef Mengele. She said the trauma of her life resulted in years of therapy. "I had to deal with the body, soul and spirit because all parts of myself have been raped."

She said one day very soon the people of the world will awaken to learn that nothing—the schools, churches, governments, medicine, food, and water—has escaped the touch of the Illuminati.

Another anonymous whistleblower using the pseudonym of "Svali" is a registered nurse who claims to have escaped the Illuminati after years serving as "a high-level programmer and trainer." She said the Illuminati have six chairs on their "ascended masters council"—Sciences, Government, Leadership, Scholarship, Spiritual, and Military. Her mother sat on a Washington, D.C., area regional council and served as spiritual chair, she said. Svali explained that the Illuminati is involved in a Luciferian faith known as "enlightenment," which teaches that its roots go back to the ancient mystery religions of Babylon, Egypt, and Celtic druidism. Some groups worship ancient deities such as El, Baal, Ashtarte, as well as Isis and Osiris and Set. It is indeed interesting to note that a small scandal ensued in the spring of 2016 when it was announced that a replica archway of the Temple of Baal was to be erected in New York's Times Square. After the story went viral on the Internet pointing out that children were sacrificed to Baal, the plans were changed to a reproduction of Palmyra's Arch of Triumph.

Svali's account of the Illuminati as a Satanic cult led by the wealthiest and most powerful people in the world has been supported by other researchers who saw in her testimony a possible explanation for why civic values are no longer taught to children. She claimed Adam Weishaupt did not originate the Illuminati but was merely a figurehead chosen for the task by European financiers who traced their lineage back to the Knights Templar and beyond. She gave detailed information on the regions, councils, Supreme World Council, and general structure of the Illuminati, which she claimed is represented in every major city. She also revealed the basis of the secrecy imposed by the Illuminati. She said the first thing an Illuminati child is taught is secrecy, often through terrifying means. "This is why you don't hear from more survivors who get out," she explained. Like other former members, Svali said the Illuminati leadership is composed of old banking money, including the Rothschilds in England and France, along with the royal families, a member of the Hapsburg dynasty, and the Rockefellers in the United States. And she predicted a coming widespread economic collapse precipitating martial law in some regions of America. Following this global collapse, she said the Illuminati, not the United Nations, will rule the New World Order. The Illuminati will be working closely with Freemasonry, she added.

> Svali explained that the Illuminati is involved in a Luciferian faith known as "enlightenment" ...

Amplifying Svali's bizarre story was the account of another anonymous whistleblower who in 2008 began posting his Illuminati experiences on the AboveTopSecret Forum. Using the code name "Hidden Hand," this person claimed to have come from a group called simply "The Family," thirteen inner-core bloodline families who can be traced back beyond antiquity and who are aligned with extraterrestrials alternately called Illuminati, Nephilim, Custodians, Watchers, and Advanced Beings.

Hidden Hand claimed many other bloodline-related individuals as well as families have branched off from the original thirteen families. Unlike some critics of the New World Order, Hidden Hand asserted that none of the members of his "Family" are "Reptilian" aliens. He said they are in reality a Luciferian "Group Soul" that decided to come to this lower-density Earth plane to help with the evolution of the human species by passing along their knowledge and wisdom. He explained the problems in the world come from the polarity (opposites derived from Free Will) experienced by humans. He added, without polarity (positive vs. negative) there would only be the Unity of Love and Light with no opportunity to experience anything else. This source also predicted fearsome troubles for humanity in the near future but said the race has the option to choose between service to self or service to others, to live in fear and terror, or to live in love and freedom. He did say that his "Family" knows that there exists a Universal Creator of which we are all a part, but that the idea of a God-like entity outside ourselves has been made up by humans in the past and used as a control mechanism. Michael E. Salla is founder of the Exopolitics Institute, a nonprofit organization dedicated to the study of extraterrestrial life. After a study of Hidden Hand's testimony, Salla concluded Hidden Hand's story was "a genuine revelation by an insider." He added his account sounded uncannily like the plot of *Star Wars*, in which a group of dark spiritual entities called the Sith secretly infiltrate and take over political and spiritual organizations in the Galaxy. "If the Hidden Hand and his Luciferian peers belong to something similar to the Sith, is there a positive counterpart similar to the Jedi Knights?" asked Salla.

> He added his account sounded uncannily like the plot of *Star Wars,* in which a group of dark spiritual entities called the Sith secretly infiltrate and take over political and spiritual organizations in the Galaxy.

Then there is Leo Lyon Zagami, a former grand master of the *Ordo Illuminatorum Universalis* [Universal Order of the Illuminati], headquartered in Florence, Italy. In his 2016 book entitled *Confessions of an Illuminati*, Zagami detailed Illuminati rituals, rites, and his perception of the Illuminati's "web of deceit and total world control." He too claimed secret societies have governed the world since before the dawn of human civilization. He described the Bavarian Illuminati as merely a short-lived organization of "illuminated" free thinkers carrying on the knowledge and traditions covertly handed down since before the time of the Atlantis. After naming a number of organizations said to be offshoots of the Illuminati, Zagami said the connections between these groups and the old Illuminati are unclear but that they appear to be intertwined with Illuminism doctrines, including occult practices. He added that while such groups are very much in the minority, their memberships often include wealthy and influential members of high society. He also links the origin of humankind to the space-faring Anunnaki described by the ancient Sumerians. Another person claiming insider knowledge of modern Illuminati activities is Katharine "Kay" Griggs, a devout Christian married eleven years to a U.S. Marine colonel, whom she said would describe illegal activities with a military group connected to both government and secret societies. He said this clique was called "The Firm" or "The Brotherhood" and was above the law and employs assassinations. She said her husband, in a drunken state, would tell of assassination squads, drug running, illegal weapons sales, and sexual perversions within both the military and federal government, conducted and condoned by a group of military and political elite operating on the same principles as the Illuminati.

Griggs characterized this group as "a very, very small group and a rather homogenized group of global top-down existentialist Zionists and socialists. In short Nazis who came to the U.S. when Hitler, their boy, turned on them in 1933."

In 2016, controversy continued on the Internet as to the truthfulness of Griggs's accounts and even whether she was still alive or not.

Yet another anonymous whistleblower, never identified but published on several websites, was a man who claimed to have been recruited by the Illuminati while still a student at Harvard in the early 1960s. This person said he faithfully served the Illuminati for years until it "became too much for me to bear" and he participated in a "Departure Ritual." His claims ran from the ridiculous to the sublime—secret space flights, nuclear missiles on the moon, how Abraham Lincoln lived on in Mexico after his assassination, how the Illuminati created Hurricane Katrina and the Gulf Oil Spill, how the Illuminati plans to shut off the sun, and how alternative media star Alex Jones is a secret Illuminati member. Other whistleblowers who claim to have been Illuminati insiders include John Todd, Arizona Wilder, Bill Schnoebelen, Joseph "Doc" Marquis, Mark Cleminson, and Carolyn Hamlett. Though usually lacking in documentation or hard evidence, their stories are generally and remarkably consistent. One recent incarnation of the Illuminati said to be beneficial is an ideology called Congressional Illuminism, detailed in a trilogy entitled *Spirit Builders* by Tau Palamas, a nom de plume taken from the Eastern Orthodox fourteenth-century monk Gregory Palamas. Sounding eerily similar to the description of Hidden Hand, Palamas wrote that Congressional Illuminism is composed of individuals with the common goal of facilitating the spiritual development of others.

Benjamin Fulford, a former Asian Bureau chief for *Forbes* magazine, is not a whistleblower but a journalist who claims to be in contact with a Chinese secret society called the White Dragon Society. He said he is bringing a message of hope by reporting indications that what he described as "the Khazariaan crime syndicate," or "Nazionists," who have seized power in the United States and many European nations, is today being systematically dismantled. As proof of this claim, Fulford pointed to indications of a take-down of the Illuminati conspiracy, which included a recent New York court ruling that members of the George W. Bush administration may be sued and face criminal charges in regard to the 9/11 attacks, that a senior member of the Rothschild family was questioned about fraud by French police, and the premature death of more than a dozen JP Morgan bankers, along with the sudden resignations of several hundred corporate CEOs over the past few years.

He said the creation of an Asian Infrastructure Investment Bank along with the recent formation of a BRICS-nation [Brazil, Russia, India, China, and South Africa] development bank will provide an alternative to the current

If there is one mod-ern group that can be linked directly to the old Bavarian Illumi-nati it is Yale Universi-ty's fraternity, Skull and Bones....

Rothschild-led Illuminati financial system, although it has prompted major cyber warfare between nations. Recent declines in stock markets and commodity prices along with the move to negative interest rates are seen by Fulford as signs the Western economic and financial systems are slow-ly imploding.

"The British, the Swiss, the Germans, the French and the Vatican have already abandoned the Khazarians and allied with the WDS [White Dragon Society] and BRICS alliance. The collapse of their global debt slavery regime is accelerating and their immunity from prosecution for mass murder is evaporating along with their funny money," Fulford said.

Such optimism was echoed by "New Age" author and lecturer David Wilcock, who stated the economic, political, and social concerns of today are the result of a plan that was systematically put into practice as of 1776, with the founding of the Order of the Illuminati in Bavaria. Wilcock said in hun-dreds of dreams he has envisioned "a massive, unprecedented exposure and arrest of this cabal on a worldwide level [which] will indeed be of tremendous, unprecedented, positive benefit to humanity." He added that public outrage over this plan is now sufficiently high enough to permit overt action against those trying to control the world.

If there is one modern group that may be linked directly to the old Bavarian Illuminati it is Yale University's fraternity, Skull and Bones, whose active membership of Yale students originate from a core of twenty to thirty wealthy families, mostly from the East Coast, America's "Old Money." Known variously as Chapter 322, the "Brotherhood of Death," "The Order," or more popularly as "Skull & Bones" or simply "Bones," the Order was brought from Germany to Yale in 1832 by General William Huntington Russell and Alphonso Taft. It has been reported that Russell was granted the authority of a German secret society to form a chapter at Yale.

Ron Rosenbaum, in an investigative article for *Esquire* magazine, wrote he discovered "definite, if skeletal, links between the origins of Bones rituals and those of the notorious Bavarian Illuminists." Even books on their reading list, German slogans on the walls, and music played in their headquarters, known as the "Tomb," are identical to those found in the old Illuminati.

Rosenbaum's article outlined bizarre initiation rites of Skull and Bones, such as members given mud baths and being placed in coffins where they are ordered to reveal every intimate detail of their sex lives, a device thought to provide future blackmail material.

Author Fritz Springmeier wrote that along with some other groups, such as Rhodes Scholars, Wolf's Head, and Scroll & Key, "Skull & Bones is an entry point into the Illuminati." It is true that both Presidents George H. W. Bush and his son, George W. Bush, were Bonesmen and that an inordinate number of order members have achieved ranking positions within government agencies, particularly the CIA.

The Knights of Malta is another modern society composed of prominent and wealthy members who hold some of the highest positions within governments and intelligence agencies. The Knights, once linked to the Knights Templar, survived persecution by becoming allies with the Vatican, and many former Templars simply disappeared into the ranks of the Knights of Saint John, established in 1099 as an order in the recently-captured city of Jerusalem. Although not founded as a military order, the Knights of St. John, popularly known as Hospitallers, grew as militant as the Templars. Expelled from the Middle East by the Muslims, the Knights of Malta finally set up their headquarters in Rome under the direct supervision of the pope. Prominent Americans connected to the Knights of Malta include the late CIA directors William Casey and John McCone, former Chrysler chairman Lee Iacocca, columnist William F. Buckley, Joseph P. Kennedy, U.S. ambassador to the Vatican William Wilson, Clare Boothe Luce, and former U.S. Secretary of State Alexander Haig. Dr. Luigi Gedda, the head of Catholic Action, was decorated by the Knights of Malta for his liaison work between the Vatican, the CIA, and the European Movement of Joseph Retinger, the "Father of the Bilderbergers." Scandals have plagued the Knights of Malta, including exposure of the P-2 Freemason Lodge of Italy found to be plotting treason against the Italian government during the Reagan years. Illuminati whistleblower Zagami claims the Knights of Malta are "the most powerful group known to man," comprised of "your CIA, your politicians, your lobbyists, your previous, present and future presidents."

According to many theorists today, while the Bavarian Illuminati may have faded away, its goals and doctrines continue on through various individuals and groups seeking to control the world.

Prominent banker David Rockefeller apparently admitted this when he wrote in his 2003 *Memoirs*, "Some even believe we are part of a secret cabal working against the best interests of the United States, characterizing my family and me as 'internationalists' and of conspiring with others around the world to build a more integrated global political and economic structure—one world, if you will. If that's the charge, I stand guilty, and I am proud of it."

With comments such as this from knowledgeable people coupled with the research now available, it is little wonder the name of the Illuminati crops up quite frequently in popular culture.

Pop Culture

Considering the ongoing controversies and extensive literature surrounding the Illuminati, it's no surprise this infamous Order continuously pops up in popular fiction, whether in books, comics, or even as a plot devise in TV shows and films.

As in the real world, the Illuminati in the media is incongruously portrayed as a serious and sinister organization bent on world conquest on the one hand, but as a spoof playing on paranoid conspiracy notions on the other.

One of the earliest, and still best, examples of the Order in fiction is *The Illuminatus!*, a tongue-in-cheek, yet largely truthful and highly entertaining trilogy written by Robert Shea and Robert Anton Wilson in 1975. It has rightly been termed required reading for any conspiracy buff.

The series is humorously surreal and takes the reader on a wild ride into the world of the Illuminati. The story begins in *The Eye in Pyramid*, continues in *The Golden Apple*, and finally concludes in *Leviathan*. The literate reader knows he or she has stepped off the deep end from the first sentence of the first book: "It was the year when they finally immanentized the Eschaton." *Eschaton* merely means attempting to bring about the end of the world as we know it and was popularized by conservative William F. Buckley and used by rebellious anti-war demonstrators in the 1960s.

From this perplexing beginning, the storyline continues to be steeped in mystery and conspiracy—very apropos for a book on the Illuminati. The reader is introduced to a pair of New York City-based police detectives, Barney Muldoon and Saul Goodman. They are assigned to get to the bottom of a terrorist-like attack on the offices of a left-wing magazine called *Confrontation*. Finding the editor of the magazine—a man named Joe Malik, who has mysteriously vanished—is a central part of the mystery. As Muldoon and Goodman dig further into the murky case, they quickly learn that *Confrontation*'s staff had been seriously researching some of the most hotly-debated assassinations of the twentieth century, including the killings of President John F. Kennedy and civil rights leader Martin Luther King Jr. The trail led not to lone and unhinged gunmen, but to the Illuminati.

This conclusion has reached into the real world. Kris Milligan, the son of a CIA official and publisher of TrineDay books, has written, "A four-tiered network of power interests was responsible for the Killing of the King of Camelot, with the all-seeing eye of the Illuminati at the top of the pyramid. Hanging from the Illuminati puppet strings are the Masons, Mafia and other secret societies, followed by the national security state apparatus/subculture. A rogue's gallery of various commercial, ideological, political and bureaucratic partners fills out the foundation of this conspiracy."

The reader is soon introduced to the world of the Discordians, a group that worships Eris, or Discordia, the Greek goddess of strife and chaos. In the real world, Discordianism came into being in 1963, thanks to two young 1960s radicals, Kerry Thornley and his childhood friend Greg Hill.

The pair created Discordianism as a counterculture religion. Using the pen names of Malaclypse the Younger and Omar Khayyam Ravenhurst, Thornley and Hill in 1963 published their "holy" book entitled *Principia Discordia,* which proposed three primary principles—the Aneristic Principle, interpreted as apparent order; the Eristic Principle, apparent disorder; and the

The Lovecraftian monster Yog-Sothoth makes an appearance in *The Illuminatus!*, a tongue-in-cheek fictional tale of the Illuminati

idea that both are manmade concepts to mask sheer chaos. As if such arcane notions were not mind-boggling enough, all copies of the original edition were made on a Xerox machine in the office of Jim Garrison, the New Orleans district attorney who, in 1968, sought to bring the assassins of President John F. Kennedy to justice. In a further twist, Thornley, in 1962, had written a manuscript called *The Idle Warriors* based on the life of one of his fellow Marines—Lee Harvey Oswald.

In the Shea-Wilson storyline, the Discordians are led by Freeman Hagbard Celine, a man who travels the planet in a submarine made of gold. His goal? To bring to an end the world-manipulating activities of the Illuminati. Add in an anthrax scare in Las Vegas (shades of the post-9/11 anthrax attacks), the appearance of H. P. Lovecraft's legendary fictional monster Yog-Sothoth, human sacrifice, and a surprising twist ending, and you have one of the most mind-bending examples of the intermixing of Illuminati fact and fiction in popular culture. The *Illuminatus!* trilogy has greatly influenced many modern authors, musicians, and even game makers. In 1982, Steve Jackson Games introduced *Illuminati*, a card game that paid homage to the trilogy. This was followed by other games based on the Order, a series of trading cards called *Illuminati: New World Order*, and a stand-alone game entitled *Illuminati: Crime Lords*.

As if Steve Jackson had some sort of prior knowledge of Illuminati plans, his 1995 game *Illuminati: New World Order* contained cards clearly depicting explosions at New York's World Trade Center and the Pentagon on fire. Indicating this was not simply a wild guess made six years in advance, in the background of the twin-towers card is a building displaying the Illuminati's all-seeing eye in a pyramid symbol. The card's title refers to a "Terrorist Nuke," and while officially, no nuclear devices were involved in the Trade Center attacks, a growing number of researchers now believe that a small nuclear device in the basements may have disintegrated the forty-seven steel core beams of the towers. In 1983, Robert Shea wrote an introduction to one game, stating, "Maybe the Illuminati are behind this game. They must be—they are, by definition, behind everything."

One particularly entertaining and thought-provoking Illuminati novel is Italian philosopher Umberto Eco's *Foucault's Pendulum*, published in 1988. The noteworthy storyline revolves around the activities of three friends, Diotallevi, Casaubon, and Belbo. Not only friends, they all work in the fields of writing and publishing. After digesting far too many conspiracy-themed manuscripts penned by would-be authors, they decide to lighten things up by creating their very own fictional conspiracy known simply as The Plan. Like *Illuminatus!*, they combine historical events with concocted tales in a distinctly satirical fashion.

But The Plan attracts more than a few conspiracy theorists and soon, even the inventors begin to believe their creation is all too real. The Plan also attracts powerful and ruthless secret society members who see Diotallevi, Casaubon, and Belbo as a threat. Suddenly, the three are faced with death, occult rites, sinister rituals, and dangerous characters, including the legendary Comte de Saint-Germain. A gripping tale, *Foucault's Pendulum* demonstrates what may happen if one gets too close to certain dark truths of history.

More recently, author Dan Brown's 2003 novel *The Da Vinci Code*, which was made into a major film starring Tom Hanks in 2006, has probably done more to bring the Illuminati to public attention than any other endeavor. Brown's story of Professor Robert Langdon, who uncovers insidious plots connecting the Vatican, the Templars, and the Order, reached millions around the world, eclipsing the work of Eco, Shea, and Wilson. It also focused public attention on

Author Dan Brown made it big in 2003 with his bestselling novel *The Da Vinci Code*, a tale about a devastating secret involving a blood line tracing back to Jesus Christ.

Brown's novel of 2000, *Angels and Demons*, which was made into a movie in 2009, again with Hanks in the starring role.

The intriguing plot of *Angels and Demons*, as in the earlier works on the Illuminati, combined historical fact with a fanciful story of conspiracy, murder, and even a mystery of science. In Dan Brown's story, the Illuminati is in possession of a stolen canister of anti-matter, a canister that will detonate—with a force close to that of an atomic weapon—within twenty-four hours. Worse still, the canister is somewhere in Vatican City. It's up to Langdon and Vittoria Vetra, an expert on anti-matter and an employee of CERN, the European Organization for Nuclear Research, to save the day. Rich with symbolism, Vatican secrets, and cold-blooded murder, *Angels and Demons*, both as a book and a movie, exposed millions of readers and viewers to the shadowy world of the Illuminati.

Horror-writer Michael Romkey is the author of numerous vampire-themed novels, including *I, Vampire*; *The Vampire Virus*; *The London Vampire Panic*; and *American Gothic*. Romkey placed a new spin on the Illuminati when he presented them as key figures in the secret existence of the vampire. In Romkey's world, there are both malevolent and benevolent vampires, such as those within the Illuminati, whose membership includes both Beethoven and Mozart. It is truly an alternative take on the Illuminati.

Even comic books have turned to the Illuminati, at least by name, as a plot device and even connected it to the realm of the superheroes. The Order first surfaced in Marvel Comics' *New Avengers* in July 2005, and to a far greater degree in *New Avengers: Illuminati* in May 2006. This updated Illuminati membership includes Thunderball, the Mad Thinker, and the Enchantress, while previous members of Marvel's Order included Captain America, Iron Man, and Professor X, of X-Men fame. The Marvel Illuminati, like its real-life counterpart, operates strictly in secret, in stealth, and behind the scenes.

A comic version of Adam Weishaupt as George Washington appeared in Dave Sim's allegorical graphic novel *Cerebus the Aardvark*. In 2014, Tom A. Hidell published both in print and online *Adam Weishaupt and the Secrets of the Bavarian Illuminati* and an ambitious illustrated history of the Order simply titled *Illuminati*. More details on conspiracy and the Illuminati are found on Hidell's website, www. illuminatirex.com/.

Blue Exorcist is a Japanese graphic novel that debuted in 2009 in the pages of Japan's *Jump SQ* magazine. The story tells of the True Cross Order, a group overseen by the Vatican, whose role it is to wipe out deadly demons terrorizing the Earth. Members of the True Cross Order must not only battle supernatural but also the Illuminati, which is attempting to bring demons to the Earth to create a single nightmarish world ruled by the Devil himself. The Illuminati has also appeared in major films. Celebrity actress Angelina Jolie crossed paths with the Order in her role as Lara Croft in the 2001 movie *Lara Croft: Tomb Raider*. In this story, Croft thwarts an Illuminati plot to harness awesome and mysterious powers at the height of a planetary alignment, which occurs only every 5,000 years during a solar eclipse. Naturally, she saves the day from the overtly named Illuminati.

Other films, while not specifically naming the Order, nevertheless have definite Illuminati overtones. Some of these include *V for Vendetta, The X-Files: Fight for the Future, Dark City*, George Orwell's classic *Nineteen Eighty-Four, The Matrix, The Devil's Advocate, They Live*, and even the *Star Wars* saga, in which an unscrupulous politician lays secret plans to overthrow the Old Republic and install an imperial dictatorship.

The Illuminati has even become the subject of comedy, such as in the February 2007, episode of FOX's hit cartoon comedy show *American Dad!* Entitled "Black Mystery Month," the animated program focuses not on the Illuminati, but on the "Illuminutty." In this screwy scenario Steve Smith and his dad Stan (the American dad) are studying the life of botanist George Washington Carver, when Steve stumbles upon the "most dangerous secret in American history"—that peanut butter actually was the brainchild of Abraham Lincoln, not Carver.

Whether in comedy, drama, or fiction, the name of the Illuminati continues to surface in the popular media, in some instances with serious implications. Many people, especially conservative Christians, see Illuminati influence in just about everything, especially in the entertainment world. Movies that some claim to have incorporated Illuminati symbols include the Harry Potter series (which involves magic and witchcraft anyway), *The Wizard of Oz*,

The Oscar statuette presented for Academy Awards is said to get its name from the Egyptian god Osiris.

the aforementioned Stanley Kubrick film *Eyes Wide Shut,* and such early Walt Disney classics as *Fantasia, The Sorcerer's Apprentice,* and *Alice in Wonderland.*

Author and lecturer Jordan Maxwell viewed nearly the entire film industry as a means of offering a platform for Illuminati symbolism. "Magic wands were always made out of the wood of a Holly tree. It's made out of Holly wood. Hollywood is a Druidic establishment and the symbols, the words, the terms, the stories, are designed," he charged. Others claim the Oscar statue of the Academy Awards derived its name from Ausar or Osiris, the Egyptian god, always pictured as a golden standing figure with arms folded across the chest and holding a scepter.

Andrew Dilks, a contributor to the whatculture.com website, listed several popular recent movies believed to contain Illuminati symbolism. These include *Captain America: The Winter Soldier, The Cabin in the Woods, The Imaginarium of Doctor Parnassus, Hide and Seek, Now You See Me,* and the Kubrick classic *A Clockwork Orange.* Dilks wrote:

> The Illuminati. It's a name that strikes fear and dread in the hearts of some and laughter and mirth in others, but whatever your opinion of the reality of this decidedly sinister organization, there's no denying that it has become a part of the cultural landscape.
>
> While there's no denying the historical existence of the Order of the Illuminati as established by Adam Weishaupt in Bavaria in 1776, the evidence for their continued existence to this day is rather more difficult to come by. It's perhaps immaterial whether or not they exist under that title—it's become a convenient term for many relating to the perceived shadowy group of powerful individuals at the heart of banking, politics and corporate interests which exert their control over much of the world.
>
> The existence or otherwise of the Illuminati hasn't stopped plenty of people from seeing their presence in Hollywood movies. When judging the "Illuminati stamp" in films often all it takes is for something vaguely occult or esoteric to be featured—a pyramid here, an all-seeing eye there—and conspiracy theorists will declare it the work of this shadowy organization. Of course, it's just as likely to be production designers including this imagery because it fits the film, or even to wind up those who see signs of the Illuminati in every movie.

Yet viewers continually see Illuminati signs and symbols in entertainment. Geoffrey Grider, writing on the religious website *Nowtheendbegins,* pointed to the statement on the inevitability of world government by James Paul Warburg, the German-born "father" of the Federal Reserve System. Warburg said: "We shall have World Government, whether or not we like it. The only question is whether World Government will be achieved by conquest or consent. Grider wrote, "Whatever you call them—New World Order, the Illuminati, Bilderbergs, CFR—they are all the same and all seek to achieve the same purpose. The above quote by James Warburg illustrates this perfectly. A One World Government led by a single individual is exactly what the Bible said would take place in the end of time. Our time. What all these groups are doing is setting the stage for the coming Antichrist who will deceive the whole world and force them to take his mark. Their favorite medium of communication for broadcasting clues about their plans is the Hollywood media industrial complex which has been producing Predictive Programming 'entertainment' for the past 50 years, laced with more clues than you could shake a stick at."

Predictive programming has been defined as a subtle form of psychological conditioning provided by the media to condition the public to events and societal changes planned by the globalists and often ascribed to the Illuminati. In this manner, when such events or changes take place, the public will have been familiarized with the prospect and will offer less public resistance. Such programming should be considered as a veiled form of preemptive mass manipulation or mind control.

Numerous corporate logos said to contain Illuminati symbols.

"An excellent example of Hollywood predictive programming [is] making the truth seekers look like insane conspiracy nuts, and painting the New World Order masters as the good guys," said Grider. He added, "In Hitler's Nazi Germany, they loved to taunt their victims in a Satanic game of cat and mouse, it gave them great pleasure to let them know what was in store for them before it actually happened. In much the same way, the NWO—Illuminati—CFR people are doing the same thing...."

Some especially suspicious researchers see Illuminati symbolism even in corporate logos. Such ideas are prevalent among those who see the Order behind global corporatism, what they term the New World Order.

In the music world, *The Vigilant Citizen* website staff on February 23, 2016, noted how the Jackson singing family reflects Illuminati influence within the music industry. They wrote, "The Jacksons' 1984 video 'Torture' is a nightmarish ordeal laced with a whole lot of Illuminati mind-control symbolism. Does the video symbolically reveal the secret life of the Jacksons, particularly the family's most famous member, Michael?"

Another site describes Justin Bieber in a Comedy Central skit falling to the ground with angel wings as a "Satanic Illuminati" reference to Satan's fall from Heaven. Bieber is even accused of causing young girls to harm themselves for his attention. This and other such allegations prompted Bieber in a YouTube video to give the Illuminati two-handed triangle sign but declare, "I'm not in the Illuminati."

Other celebrities, such as Rihanna, Madonna, Lady Gaga, Katy Perry, and Beyoncé, have added to the clamor over Illuminati infiltration of the entertainment industry by being pictured with Illuminati symbols and words. Whenever a celebrity dies unexpectedly, such as Heath Ledger and Michael Jackson, the elusive Illuminati is blamed. Others drop hints of their lives being controlled by the Order.

Beyoncé has admitted in interviews to being guided by a separate personality named Sasha Fierce. In one interview she explained that her hands in the shape of a pyramid was the "Roc-A-Fella sign." This was explained by Shawn "Jay Z" Carter, a hip-hop artist and Rihanna's producer, as the sign of his Roc-A-Fella Records. Many believed Jay Z was connected to the Illuminati when he was pictured wearing a black sweatshirt with the words "Do what thou wilt," the Assassin maxim that passed through the Illuminati to Crowley's OTO.

Some have actually claimed (perhaps facetiously) to being a member or having intimate knowledge of the Illuminati. Madonna, for example, has frequently been accused of being a member of the Order. In an interview with *Rolling Stone* magazine, Madonna, who released a record entitled "Illuminati," said, "People often accuse me of being a member of the Illuminati, but the thing is, I know who the real Illuminati are."

Singer Katy Perry told *Rolling Stone* she was flattered to be named among the Order's membership. "I guess you've kind of made it when they think you're in the Illuminati!" she said, adding she was tolerant of people who wanted to believe her Illuminati connection because "I believe in aliens."

Various hand signs used by the old Illuminati are mimicked frequently not only by entertainment celebrities but by sports figures and politicians. Such signs include the thumb and forefingers of both hands placed in the shape of a triangle or pyramid and a close fist with the index and little fingers extended (a Satanic symbol for horns or in Texas the sign for "Hook'em, Horns," reflecting support for the University of

Ancient Levite priests using the pyramidal handsign as prayer to God. This same gesture has been seen being made by various celebrities and world leaders.

Texas Longhorns). By crooking the thumb and holding up two fingers, one has made the familiar sign for "Victory," as popularized by the Master Mason Winston Churchill during World War II. Or, as claimed by some, did Churchill learn this sign, which is said to make the shadow of the devil or a horned god, during his initiation into the Ancient Order of Druids of Ox in 1908? Another sign is produced by touching your thumb with your index finger, making a circle. The other fingers follow the index's shape thus forming the tail of two 6s, or the biblical number of the anti-Christ Beast—666. Or again, this sign might just symbolize "A-Okay."

It is difficult for the average person to know when a hand gesture is innocent, a coincidence, or the use of an Illuminati hand sign. Song lyrics and occult symbols occasionally just crop up unintentionally, such as the University of Texas's "Hook'em, Horns" hand sign misread as a similar Satanic salute.

Sometimes a pyramid is just a pyramid. Like seeing animals in the clouds. What some might consider Illuminati symbols may be simply in the eye of the beholder. And, sometimes, symbols seen in the mass media are simply intentional jokes. Such was the case of one graphic artist who until recently worked developing standardized graphics for use by affiliates of NBC, ABC, CBS, FOX, and local news segments. Speaking anonymously to writer Gabriella Garcia, the artist explained how he intentionally injected occult symbols in some graphics.

> When I was working for a major broadcasting conglomerate, I passed the time sneaking cult symbols into its affiliates' news graphics. I don't really know why I did it. Maybe because I'm just easily amused…. I'd find a way to incorporate something in the

graphics, usually small and out of the way—maybe a reference to the Illuminati or Freemasonry—just to fuck with anyone who noticed it. I also liked using symbols created by John Dee, who was a 16th century alchemist and occultist, like the esoteric Monas Hieroglyphica, or just simple, but well-known things like the pentagram or the eye in the pyramid. I wasn't doing it because the news was so obviously right-wing, but doing it made me feel a little bit better about myself at the end of the day, because I was working for a company that was diametrically opposed to the generally lefty, generally pro-human rights views that I cared about.

I had to do a graphic for this "Our news travels the world" promo that had three red comets flying across the globe, and, well, I just had to make them draw a giant Anarchy "A." When I had to make a Halloween promo, I just couldn't help myself from throwing a Masonic pyramid eye on one of the tombstones, you know just to keep people who were looking for that kind of thing on their toes. There were a couple of Discordian references like the Sacred Chao's apple and pentagon that I'd throw in, which would really only be obvious to anyone who knew about Robert Anton Wilson's *Illuminatus!* trilogy.

Comedian John Oliver once took the phenomenon of seeing Illuminati symbols everywhere to an absurd level by showing how Cadburgy Creme Eggs were a tool of the Illuminati.

Although the artist never was called out for his graphic insertions, someone (within the Illuminati?) must have noticed because he was eventually fired. "Apparently someone complained about picking my nose at a meeting. That's really all the information I was given at my termination; by the time I got back to my desk my computer had already been removed, and then I had to awkwardly ask the person who fired me for bus fare because I had carpooled to work that morning," he recalled.

Over and above misinterpretations and practical jokes, one sure-fire method of deflecting public attention from a serious subject is to make it the object of ridicule. For example, during Easter 2016, British Emmy Award-winning comedian John Oliver delivered an amusing, but condescending and belittling, soliloquy regarding YouTube conspiracy videos. He presented, of all things, Cadbury Creme Eggs as a dark Illuminati conspiracy. With great gusto, Oliver explained:

> The average Cadbury Creme Egg weighs 34 grams, the same number of streets as *Miracle on 34th Street*. That's one of the most beloved Christmas movies of all time; coincidentally, the Christmas carol "12 Days of Christmas" talks about "five golden rings" as one of the ideal holiday gifts. Germany has Europe's largest supply of gold, and Cadbury Creme Eggs are made in the United Kingdom—in other words, only a quick, affordable flight apart. That connection is actually more of a distraction, however; the "truth" lies in the fact that Cadbury Creme Eggs were originally called Fry Creme Eggs. Why change the name? Perhaps because "Fry" is a word with three letters—the same number as the sides of a triangle. And if you cut a Creme Egg in half and put it at the top of a triangle, it greatly resembles the Illuminati pyramid. There: Cadbury Creme Eggs are a tool of the Illuminati.

But, as has been demonstrated in the preceding pages, the Illuminati—and especially Illuminati theology—is nothing to laugh about.

As the controversies and allegations continue to fly in the public over celebrity involvement with the Illuminati and the claims of both accusers and defenders clash in the social media, the philosophies of the Order quietly continue to spread.

Conclusions

First, it must be acknowledged that the Perfectibilists, or the Order of the Bavarian Illuminati, as a cohesive German organization no longer exists.

But, secondly, it should be understood that the doctrines and philosophies expounded by the Order predate the Bavarian Illuminati by millennia. These traditions and beliefs can be traced back through the Freemasons, Rosicrucians, Knights Templar, Mystery Schools of Greece and Egypt, to ancient Sumer and their accounts of the possibly extraterrestrial Anunnaki.

These theologies carry on today as the doctrine of Illuminism, which is simply another "ism," similar to capitalism, socialism, communism, Zionism, liberalism, feminism, and Nazism. It is a philosophy, a mindset.

A thorough search of the pockets of Hillary Clinton and Dick Cheney will not produce a membership card in the Illuminati. They might not even recognize the name. But both practice Illuminism. They both have exhibited acceptance of the Illuminati maxim "the end justifies the means." And we saw how that doctrine turned out when the Nazis carried it to its logical extreme. Also know that Clinton has attended meetings of the secretive Bilderberg group as far back as 1997.

Like many historical organizations, the German National Socialists (Nazis) started out with plans to make their nation a better place. Under Hitler, a national highway system was built (the *Autobahn*), the first pollution control laws were put into effect, and there was national healthcare and gun registration. Hitler, himself, was the epitome of many liberals today—he was a vegetarian, an animal lover, an environmentalist, a teetotaler, and nonsmoker.

But with the concentrated centralized power Hitler gained as *fuehrer* (leader) of his country came corruption, cronyism, and the overthrow of basic

A growing number of the public today are waking up to the fact that a virtual handful of international bankers and financiers ... control the global economy and, hence, most governments.

human rights. In their zeal to force their ideology unto whole populations, the Nazis brought on World War II with its unimaginable death and destruction. It was a classic example of altruism being corrupted by the inhuman Illuminati creed of the "end justifies the means" and the quest for total power and control.

We have seen the same process displace other promising movements—from the crumbling of the Roman and British Empires to Russian socialism right on to the ongoing loss of individual freedom in American democracy.

Through the ages, there have always been those who consider themselves "enlightened." They have sought to extricate themselves from the restrictions of other people. Since such activity does not sit well with the established religious and political elite, such free thinking by necessity has been forced to become secretive, to go underground.

Today, the term "Illuminati" has become ambiguous. It means different things to different people. "There is a multitude of different versions of what exactly the Illuminati is, but most researchers agree that the group consist mainly of the upper crust of the world's financial and political elite. Generally, it's used as a catch-all term to describe the One Percenters, the oligarchs, the plutocrats, or the ruling class whose combined wealth and power influence every aspect of our daily lives," wrote Tom Hidell of Illuminatirex.com.

A growing number of the public today are waking up to the fact that a virtual handful of international bankers and financiers, the ones who set the rules for the world's financial institutions and interest rates, control the global economy and, hence, most governments. But it was as the Bavarian Illuminati that, for the first time in modern history, "enlightened" men, who believed themselves superior to the masses, created a unified movement against church and state to overthrow the old order and establish control over entire nations.

Though the Bavarian Illuminati was crushed, Illuminism subsequently expanded its influence worldwide. This was accomplished without much difficulty because long before the Illuminati arrived, a few wealthy and powerful bloodline families, whose greed, ingenuity, and ruthlessness gave them indescribable economic control, had managed to manipulate world events since the time of the Mesopotamian sky gods, the Anunnaki. For further details on the Anunnaki, see this author's 2013 book *Our Occulted History*. Then there is a matter of interpretation. Beginning with the anti-Illuminati screeds of the eighteenth-century Christian writers Augustin Barruel and John Robison right up to Nesta Webster and Texe Marrs, a number of authors clearly viewed Illuminism as a Satanic attack on Christianity and the state.

Others held a more sympathetic view. Founding Father Thomas Jefferson perhaps echoed the earliest and truest intentions of the Freemasons and even the Illuminati when he wrote in the Declaration of Independence, "We hold these truths to be self-evident, that all men are created equal; that they are endowed by their Creator with inherent and inalienable Rights; that among these, are Life, Liberty, and the pursuit of Happiness; that to secure these rights, Governments are instituted among Men, deriving their just powers from the consent of the governed; that whenever any Form of Government becomes destructive of these ends, it is the Right of the people to alter or abolish it, and to institute new Government, laying its foundation on such principles, and organizing its powers in such form, as to them shall seem most likely to effect their Safety and Happiness."

But as in so many instances in the past, basic truths such as these are manipulated and twisted by power-hungry individuals, members of secret societies, and hypocrites who speak the language but practice something entirely different.

Just as the United States today seems to have lost its earlier belief in individual freedom as well as the egalitarian spirit of its Founding Fathers, so did the Illuminati lose sight of its original purposes to its more narrow-minded and manipulative members. The Order towards the end was ruled by an inner elite, which some believe originated it in the first place, that twisted its activities to their benefit, just as the United States today is ruled by a shadowy and unelected elite of extremely wealthy persons, many from bloodline families.

And it is not just odd-ball conspiracy theorists who hold such views. In a 1932 letter to Sigmund Freud, Albert Einstein indicated he too understood the world was ruled by a small but powerful clique. He wrote, "… the ruling class at present, has the schools and press, usually the Church as well, under its thumb. This enables it to organize and sway the emotions of the masses, and make its tool of them."

But Einstein failed to acknowledge the evil in such rulers by blaming the victims. He wrote, "Yet even this answer does not provide a complete solution. Another question arises from it: How is it these

The famous mathematician and physicist Albert Einstein came to conclude, too, that the world was ruled by a small group of people.

devices succeed so well in rousing people to such wild enthusiasm, even to sacrifice their lives [in wars]? Only one answer is possible; because people have within them a lust for hatred and destruction. In normal times this passion exists in a latent state, it emerges only in unusual circumstances; but it is a comparatively easy task to call it into play and raise it to the power of a collective psychosis."

Einstein in 1932 could not have imagined that by the second decade of the twenty-first century virtually all news and information delivered to the American public, including publishing, movies, music, TV, and networks, would be controlled by a few owners of only six multinational corporations. These six conglomerates are General Electric (NBC), Time Warner, Disney, News Corporation, Bertelsmann of Germany, and Viacom (former owner of CBS). This media monopoly may not tell the public how to think, but it certainly sets the agenda for what to think about. The monopoly creates an electronic "matrix" all around us.

Topics such as climate change, gender identity ambiguity, anti-gun legislation, harmful prescription drugs and vaccines, and genetically modified organisms (GMOs) continually fill the media owned by these corporate giants only because such issues keep society divided and in conflict, which serves to divert public attention from the true rulers of the world.

In the words of Internet commentator Rich Scheck, "Whether you label it the New World Order, the Deep State, the Military-Industrial Complex, or The Huxwellian World of 2016 as I do, a careful review of the current landscape demonstrates clearly that we are governed by a 'power elite' of corporate oligarchs and global bankers who dominate the decision making process through their lobbyists, control of elected officials irrespective of party affiliation and ownership of the means of communication."

Researchers have encountered too many connections and coincidences, along with statements from world leaders, to simply write off the notion of an attempt at global control by a small but dedicated group. "When one takes an honest look at the machinations currently taking place on this sphere we refer to as planet Earth, it becomes obvious that such trickery is the result of a carefully planned and coordinated effort being practiced by top-level leaders in many key governments worldwide," noted Dr. John Reizer, founder of the *NoFakeNews* website, adding that the majority of citizens cannot comprehend the idea of powerful central control over the Earth, "not because they are stupid individuals [but] mostly due to the fact that most people, and their understanding of life and societal structure, are far removed from what is actually taking place in the world.... Once you control and directly influence the perspective of reality that a civilization has embraced through strategically delivered media content, you control everything for all intents and purposes."

Commentator Henry Makow mused, "We are reminded of a soldier marching out-of-step in a parade who has the chutzpah, money and media to convince the other marchers that it is they who are out-of-step. Extrapolate this image to a cosmic level and you will understand the New World Order."

Anyone from a small town understands the concept of a "pecking order," that one man or a few can set the agenda for the whole community. This may be the newspaper editor, leading banker, or most prosperous business owner. And such leaders need not give orders. Just by letting their will be known, subordinates tend to fall into line. This same structure can be applied to whole nations. But while most people can relate to or understand this structure on a small scale, they balk at the idea of it occurring on a large scale. While secrecy is a vital part of Illuminati theology, it is not the ultimate goal, which is keeping the whole plan "unbelievable" to the public. Control over the mass media plays a huge role in this. To evaluate the success of this objective, just ask friends and neighbors their thoughts on the Illuminati. Chances are they won't know what you are talking about, much less have any particular views on the subject. It must also be acknowledged that the scheming of secret societies, whether "illuminized" or not, is not the product of some Jewish conspiracy. While Zionism, as has been demonstrated, has played a large role in secret society manipulation, devout Jews more often have been the victims of such machinations.

> While secrecy is a vital part of Illuminati theology, it is not the ultimate goal, which is keeping the whole plan "unbelievable" to the public.

There appears to be something darker behind the effort to subjugate humanity and wreck the environment than simple corporate greediness or political power grabs. Even animals know not to dirty their own nests. Why would corporate leaders want to kill the Golden Goose that provides golden eggs by poisoning the Earth and killing its inhabitants?

Authors Gardiner and Osborn noted it all seems to go back to knowledge of the ancient Sky gods. From the Illuminati, Knights of Malta, Opus Dei, and today's Bilderberg group back through the Freemasons, Rosicrucians, Knights Templar, and the ancient Mysteries of Greece, Egypt, and Sumer, "they have all essentially arisen from the same hub or stem: The Catholic Church, which in turn, in our view, can be traced back to ancient Sumer and the Shining Ones," they noted.

"We have found the Shining Ones in every culture of the world over a period that reaches back into the days of ancient Sumer and Egypt.... We had discovered that down [through] the ages many organizations, however seemingly diverse and contradictory, had all been various fronts or derivatives of the Shining Ones," they added.

After years of study, Dr. Reizer said he has come to the same "uncomfortable conclusion" as Gardiner and Osborn, namely that control over the Earth is being carried out by persons not of the planet. He said the answer to the Big Question of who or what really controls this Planet is "quite honestly *out of this world!*" [Emphasis in the original].

By the 1920s, Charles Fort had spent twenty-seven years at the British Museum and the New York Public Library researching old scientific journals, periodicals, and newspaper clippings. In 1919, Fort published *The Book of the Damned* (meaning those who were excluded from true knowledge). Here he presented this startling conclusion:

I think we are property.

I should say we belong to something:

That once upon a time, this earth was No-man's Land, that other worlds explored and colonized here, and fought among themselves for possession, but now it's owned by something. That something owns this earth—all others warned off … that all this has been known, perhaps for ages, to certain ones upon this earth, a cult or order, members of which function like bellwethers to the rest of us, or as superior slaves or overseers, directing us in accordance with instructions received—from Somewhere else—in our mysterious usefulness.

This astounding conclusion is supported by the recent work of Chris Hardy, who holds a doctorate degree in psychological anthropology and is a former researcher at Princeton's Psychological Research Laboratories. After closely studying Sumerian lore through many sources, Hardy was persuaded that the ancient Anunnaki, or Sky gods, or Shining Ones, are the very "forces that wanted to keep us as working donkeys—producing riches and metals that they would dispose of, without even paying for those or for the work—these shadow powers took all possible actions to impede us from reaching this understanding, and when a few insightful individuals did, they were quick to silence them in the name of reason and good sense, of statistics and laws of 19th-century physics, or of religious incompatibility with their dogmas and worldviews."

Interest in aliens visiting the Earth is not limited to *Star Trek* fans and fantasists. Many knowledgeable and credible persons are on the public record. Paul T. Hellyer, an aeronautical engineer who served as Canada's defense minister from 1963 to 1967, has stated, "They've been visiting our planet for thousands of years." He said they have given us advanced technology such as the microchip, night vision, and Kevlar body armor, although "much of the media won't touch [this subject]."

The late Edgar Mitchell, the sixth man to walk on the moon, was convinced that extraterrestrials have visited the Earth. Mitchell, who founded the Institute of Noetic Sciences in 1973, also said we have gained technology from the crashed ships of aliens but that governments, particularly the U.S. government, have been covering up this fact for many years.

If the accounts of the Anunnaki sky gods are in any way truthful, then early humans were ruled over by extraterrestrial astronauts. If this is so, what happened to them, since they do not appear in evidence today? Did they all depart the Earth at some point or are at least some still here?

The answer may be found by simply reviewing human history. We are taught that humans slowly evolved from hunter-gatherers to farmers who gathered in city-states, which became nations and empires. Yet, a close scrutiny of history also tells of legends of marvelous lost civilizations, amazing artifacts, and reports from around the world of gods flying in ancient times—the flying dragons of the Chinese, the *vimanas* of the Hindus, the soaring boats of the Egyptians, the flying shields of the Romans, the airships of the 1800s, and the UFOs of today. Someone has been with us all through recorded history. It has been demonstrated that a mere handful of bloodline-fixated individuals hiding behind corporate fronts, foundations, and government bureaucrats are seeking to control the wealth and knowledge of the planet. Here there seem to be but three possibilities: the ruling elite are using modern technology in an effort to contact the ancient gods; they already have contacted the ancient gods and are being guided, or controlled, by them; or they *are* the ancient gods, the Anunnaki, the Advanced Beings, the Shining Ones of antiquity.

The current condition of our world may well have been outlined in a website claiming channeled information from an entity named "Matthew," whose words rang true when he declared:

> Freedom burns in the heart of humankind, yet rarely have Earth's peoples lived freely. For long ages strongmen [from "off-planet sources"] increased their landholdings and power by brutal conquest— troops were forced into battle; untold numbers were killed, captured, or sold into slavery; and all except the privileged few lived at bare subsistence level. After governing systems were labeled, the Illuminati made a mockery of democracy by putting ones within their ranks as candidates; rigging elections; and bribing, blackmailing, threatening or assassinating members of governments. They declared what country must be fought to keep *us* safe from *that* kind of government or *that* ideology [emphasis in the original], and they started civil and international wars.
>
> Like their forbearers, they thrived on war. By producing and selling weapons, ammunitions and other war machinery to both sides, they profited hand-

It has been demonstrated that a mere handful of bloodline-fixated individuals hiding behind corporate fronts, foundations, and government bureaucrats are seeking to control the wealth and knowledge of the planet.

somely. By setting new national borders or simply taking over a country and subjugating its populace, they kept expanding their empire. By infiltrating governments, military forces, intelligence agencies, judicial and economic systems, religions, education, media, commerce, multinational corporations, the medical field, film industry and entertainment venues, eventually they controlled everything that impacts life in your world. By relentlessly creating fear, grief, unjustness and poverty, conditions that produce the energy that fuels them, they have kept your world in their clutches.

Today, the attempt at global control comes more from financial manipulation rather than religion, at least in the Western nations. In the Third World, despotism and religious fanaticism still reign. Such financial control is centered in less than two dozen multinational banks owned by a mere handful of individuals. These persons must be identified and addressed. Fortunately for humankind, consciousness is rising around the world. More and more people are becoming more knowledgeable as to the realities of life on Earth today. Much of the credit for this goes to the ever-expanding Internet. With communication between the populations, traditional thinking is breaking down in a wide range of fields—from party politics and centralized government to dogmatic religiosity and our views of human origins. Considering the previously described connections between certain wealthy families—particularly the Rockefellers and the Rothschilds, who have shown such interest in Sumerian lore and artifacts—the idea that at least some among the ruling elite may not be entirely human should not be summarily dismissed. After all, it can be clearly demonstrated that the policies and practices of such families and their corporations do not appear to be in the best interests of this world's citizens or environment. The evidence of ancient nonhuman visitation is compelling, almost overwhelming. Cave drawings, cuneiform tablets of stone, biblical descriptions, ancient writings, and anomalous artifacts around the world attest to the reality of such a presence down through history. Since it has been shown that a mere handful of bloodline-fixated individuals hiding behind corporate fronts are seeking to control the wealth and power of the planet, it may be time we ask in all seriousness: Are they even us?

Whatever the answer may be, it is Illuminism, the theology of deceit and the power-seeking, that is the thread connecting the ancient astronauts and their knowledge to the Bavarian Illuminati and the illuminized organizations of today. And it is this Illuminism philosophy, not just the attendant societies and orders, that must be resisted for the sake of peace, harmony, and true individual freedom.

The old Illuminati is no more, but Illuminism still casts its shadow across the world.

FURTHER READING

Adachi, Ken. "The New World Order (NWO): An Overview." *Educate Yourself.* http://educate-yourself.org/nwo/. (Accessed December 12, 2016.)

"Adam Weishaupt." *Biblioteca Pleyades.* http://www.bibliotecapleyades.net/sociopolitica/ esp_sociopol_illuminati_0a.htm. (Accessed March 2, 2017.)

"All Roads Lead to Babylon." *Above Top Secret*, January 2, 2012. http://www.abovetop secret.com/forum/thread792178/pg1.

Allen, Gary. *None Dare Call It Conspiracy.* Seal Beach, CA: Concord Press, 1971.

"The All-Seeing Eye." *Grand Lodge of British Columbia and Yukon.* http://freemasonry .bcy.ca/symbolism/eye.html. (Accessed March 8, 2017.)

Antelman, Marvin S. *To Eliminate the Opiate*, Volume II. Jerusalem, Israel: Zionist Book Club: 2002, p. 121.

Baigent, Michael, Richard Leigh, and Henry Lincoln. *Holy Blood, Holy Grail.* New York: Dell Publishing, 1983, p. 368.

———. *The Messianic Legacy.* New York: Dell Publishing, 1986.

Barrett, David V. *A Brief History of Secret Societies.* London: Constable & Robinson, 2007, pp. xiii- xiv.

Barruel, Augustine. *Mémoires pour servir à l'histoire du Jacobinisme* ("Memoirs Illustrating the History of Jacobinism"). Fraser, MI: American Council on Economics and Society, 1995, p. 441.

"The Bavarian Illuminati." *Masonic Dictionary.* http://www.masonicdictionary.com/ illuminati.html. (Accessed March 4, 2017.)

Bierce, Ambrose. "Freemasons." *The Devil's Dictionary.* www.thedevilsdictionary.com/ ?f=#!. (Accessed March 7, 2017.)

"Bilderberg's Silent Takeover of Britain's $60bn Defense Budget." *RT*, May 16, 2014.

Bollyn, Christopher. "Iraqis Robbed." *American Free Press*, April 21, 2003.

Brecher, Edward M., and the editors of *Consumer Reports, Licit and Illicit Drugs.* Mount Vernon, NY: Consumers Union, 1972.

Brzezinski, Zbigniew. "America and Europe." *Foreign Affairs*, October, 1970, p. 29.

————. *Between Two Ages: America's Role in the Technetronic Era.* New York: Viking, 1970, p. 9.

Bullamore, George W. "The Beehive of Freemasonry." *Grand Lodge of British Columbia and Yukon.* https://www.freemasonry.bcy.ca/aqc/beehive.html. (Accessed November 15, 2016.)

Butler, Trent C., ed., *Holman Bible Dictionary.* Nashville, TN: Holman Bible Publishers, 1991, p. 992.

Carr, William Guy. *Pawns in the Game.* Willowdale, Ontario: Federation of Christian Laymen, 1958, p. 2.

————. *Satan, Prince of this World.* (unfinished manuscript published by his son, W.J. Carr, Jr. in 1966), pp. 15-16.

Carroll, Robert Todd. "Illuminati, The New World Order & Paranoid Conspiracy Theorists (PCTs)." *The Skeptic's Dictionary.* http://skepdic.com/illuminati.html. (Accessed February 2, 2017.)

Chamish, Barry. "Chamish—Rabbi Antelman Is Back." *Rense.com*, March 10, 2002. http://www.rense.com/general20/rabb.htm.

Childress, David Hatcher. *Technology of the Gods: The Incredible Sciences of the Ancients.* Kempton, IL: Adventures Unlimited Press, 2009, pp. 231–232.

Churchill, Winston. *The World Crisis.* New York: Scribner's Sons, 1949, p. 300.

————. "Propaganda in the Next War." *What Really Happened.* http://whatreallyhappened.com/WRHARTICLES/PROPAGANDA_IN_THE_NEXT_WAR_FOREWORD.html. (Accessed January 22, 2017.)

————. "Zionism versus Bolshevism." *Illustrated Sunday Herald*, February 8, 1920, p. 5. http://www.fpp.co.uk/bookchapters/WSC/WSCwrote1920.html.

Cirucci, Johnny. "Illuminati Unmasked: Everything You Need to Know about the 'New World Order' and How We Will Beat It." *JohnnyCirucci.com.* (Accessed November 20, 2016.)

Coghlan, Andy, and Debora MacKenzie. "Revealed—The Capitalist Network That Runs the World." *New Scientist*, October 19, 2011. https://www.newscientist.com/article/mg21228354.500-revealed—the-capitalist-network-that-runs-the-world.

Cook, Nick. *The Hunt for Zero Point.* London: Century, 2001, p. 164.

Coppens, Philip. "Best Evidence?" *Philip Coppens.* http://philipcoppens.com/bestevidence.html. (Accessed March 1, 2017.)

Cuddy, Dennis L. "The Illuminati." *Kjos Ministries*, January 17, 2012.

————. "The Illuminati: Part 6." *News with Views*, January 10, 2011. http://www.newswithviews.com/Cuddy/dennis198.htm.

Daraul, Arkon. *Secret Societies.* New York: MJF Books, 1961, p. 226.

"Dead: 125 Scientists, 75 High-Level Bankers, & 3 Investigative Journalists within 24 Hours." *Secrets of the Fed.com.* http://www.secretsofthefed.com/dead-125-scientists-75-high-level-bankers-and-within-24-hours-3-investigative-journalists/. (Accessed March 4, 2017.)

"Decoding Illuminati Symbolism." *IlluminatiWatcher.com*, August 19, 2014. http://illuminatiwatcher.com/decoding-illuminati-symbolism-the-all-seeing-eye/.

Dubay, Eric. *The Atlantean Conspiracy: Exposing the Global Conspiracy from Atlantis to Zion.* AtlanteanConspiracy.com, 2015.

Durden, Tyler. "Deep State: Inside Washington's Shadowy Power Elite." *ZeroHedge*, January 30, 2016. http://www.zerohedge.com/news/2016-01-30/deep-state-inside-washingtons-shadowy-power-elite.

Dwilson, Stephanie Dube. "Edgar Mitchell & Aliens: 5 Fast Facts You Need to Know." *Heavy.com*, February 5, 2016. http://heavy.com/news/2016/02/edgar-mitchell-ufo-aliens-exist-are-real-ed-et-roswell-conspiracy-coverup-cover-up-died-noetics-esp/.

Easen, Nick. "New Technology from 'Black World.'" *CNN.com*, September 8, 2003. http://www.cnn.com/2003/TECH/09/05/wow.tech.black.world/.

Eddy, Patricia G. *Who Tampered with the Bible?* Nashville, TN: Winston-Derek Publishers, 1993, pp. 222–223.

Elinoff, Jonathan. "'33 Conspiracy Theories That Turned Out to Be True, What Every Person Should Know....'" *Infowars*, January 6, 2010. http://www.infowars.com/33-conspiracy-theories-that-turned-out-to-be-true-what-every-person-should-know/.

Epperson, A. Ralph. *Masonry: Conspiracy against Christianity*. Tucson, AZ: Publius Press, 1997, pp. 18-19.

———. *The New World Order*. Tucson, AZ: Publius Press, 1990, pp. 33, p. 56.

———. *The Unseen Hand: An Introduction to the Conspiratorial View of History*. Tucson, AZ: Publius Press, 1985, p. 7.

Eringer, Robert. *The Global Manipulators*. Bristol, England: Pentacle Books, 1980, p. 61.

Evans, Medford. *The Assassination of Joe McCarthy*. Los Angeles: Western Islands, 1970, p. 113.

Farmer, John. *The Ground Truth: The Untold Story of America Under Attack on 9/11*. New York: Riverhead Books, 2009, pp. 2, 4.

Ferguson, Niall. *The House of Rothschild*. New York: Viking, 1998, p. 9.

Fest, Joachim C. *Hitler*. New York: Harcourt Brace Jovanovich, 1974.

"The First Encounters." *Biblioteca Pleyades*. http://www.bibliotecapleyades.net/sitchin/divine_encoun/divine_encounters01.htm. (Accessed December 10, 2016.)

Fisk, Robert. "Robert Fisk: A Civilisation Torn to Pieces." *Information Clearing House*, April 13, 2003. http://www.informationclearinghouse.info/article2908.htm.

Ford, Brian. *German Secret Weapons: Blueprint for Mars*. New York: Ballantine Books, 1969, p. 22.

"Former Illuminist Witch Reveals Strong Witchcraft Tie to Freemasonry: Doc Marquis, Former Illuminist Witch, Answers the Top 25 Questions He Receives during His Seminars on Illuminati, Witchcraft, and Freemasonry." *Cutting Edge Ministries*. http://www.cuttingedge.org/free14.html. (Accessed October 23, 2016.

Freedman, Benjamin H. "Benhamin H. Freedman 1961 Speech." *YouTube*. https://www.youtube.com/watch?v=x8OmxI2AYV8. (Accessed November 3, 2016.)

"The French Revolution." *The Judeo-Masoni Conspiracy*. http://judeo-masonic.blogspot.com/2010/02/5-french-revolution.html. (Accessed February 23, 2017.)

Fulford, Benjamin. "Benjamin Fulford: Bush, Rothschild Prosecutions, New Disclosures, Greece, All Signs of Accelerating Cabal Take Down." *The Event Chronicle*. http://www.theeventchronicle.com/intel/benjamin-fulford-bush-rothschild-prosecutions-new-disclosures-greece-all-signs-of-accelerating-cabal-take-down/#. (Accessed March 3, 2017.)

———. "Benjamin Fulford Update—March 1, 2016." *Ascension with Mother Earth and Current State of Affairs*, February 29. 2016/ http://www.ascensionwithearth.com/2016/02/benjamin-fulford-update-march-1-2016.html.

Garcia, Gabriella. "I Hid Illuminati Symbols in Broadcast News Graphics Because I Was Bored." *Hopes and Fears*. http://www.hopesandfears.com/hopes/now/media/214739-illuminati-conspiracy-news-hidden. (Accessed February 10, 2017.)

Gardiner, Philip, and Gary Osborn. *The Shining Ones: The World's Most Powerful Secret Society Revealed*. London: Watkins Publishing, 2006, pp. 86, 250, 265.

Gardner, Laurence. *Bloodline of the Holy Grail*. Rockport, MA: Element Books, 1996.

———. *Genesis of the Grail Kings*. London: Bantam Press, 1999, pp. 219–220.

———. *The Shadow of Solomon: The Lost Secret of the Freemasons Revealed*. London: HarperElement, 2005, pp. 43, 116.

Gilliland, James. *Anunnaki Return, Star Nations and the Days to Come*. Trout Lake, OR: ECETI, 2016, p. 16.

Glancy, Josh. "Chaim Weizmann and How the Balfour Declaration Was Made in Manchester." *The JC*, November 1, 2012. http://www.thejc.com/lifestyle/lifestyle-features/89026/chaim-weizmann-and-how-balfour-declaration-was-made-manchester.

Glass, Sandra. "The Conspiracy." *Teenset*, March, 1969, pp. 34-40.

"The Global Propaganda Arm of the New World Order." *Zona de Libre*. http://myspace gabyven.fullblog.com.ar/the-global-propaganda-arm-of-the-new-world-order-791213437632.html. (Accessed February 10, 2017.)

Goldwater, Barry. *With No Apologies*. New York: William Morrow and Company, 1979, p. 278.

Good, Timothy. *Alien Contact*. New York: William Morrow, 1993, p. 143.

Greer, John Michael. *The Element Encyclopedia of Secret Societies*. London: HarperElement, 2006, pp. 360-361.

Griffin, G. Edward. *The Creature from Jekyll Island*. Westlake Village, CA: American Media, 1994.

Hale, William Harlan. "When Karl Marx Worked for Horace Greeley." *American Heritage*, 8:1 (April 1957). http://www.americanheritage.com/content/when-karl-marx-worked-horace-greeley.

Hall, Manly P. *America's Assignment with Destiny*. Los Angeles: The Philosophical Research Society, 1951, pp. 49–50.

———. *What the Ancient Wisdom Expects of Its Disciples*. Los Angeles: The Philosophical Research Society, 1982, p. 23.

———. *The Secret Teachings of All Ages*. Los Angeles: The Philosophical Research Society, 1988 , p. 76.

Harbinson, W. A. *Inception*. New York: Dell Publishing, 1991, p. xi.

Hardy, Chris H. *Wars of the Anunnaki: Nuclear Self-Destruction in Ancient Sumer*. Rochester, NY: Bear & Company, 2016, p. 5.

Harrison, Elizabeth. "9 Things You Didn't Know about the Declaration of Independence." *History.com*, July 4, 2012. http://www.history.com/news/9-things-you-may-not-know-about-the-declaration-of-independence.

Healey, Denis, quoted in http://www.goodreads.com/quotes/40800-world-events-do-not-occur-by-accident-they-are-made. (Accessed February 4, 2017).

Healthzombie, "Reality Check—America's Destiny, Part 6." *Calling Yisrael*, October 27, 2012. https://israelinprophecy.wordpress.com/2012/10/27/reality-check-americ-as-destiny-part-6/.

Heiden, Konrad, *Der Fuehrer*. Boston: Houghton Mifflin Company, 1944.

Heller, Steven. "The Secret History of Secret Societies." *The Atlantic*, April 26, 2012. https://www.theatlantic.com/entertainment/archive/2012/04/the-secret-history-of-secret-societies/256392/.

Hill, Miriam Joan. "Everything Is Under Control: The Encyclopedia of Conspiracy Theories." *The Robert Anton Wilson Website*. http://www.rawilson.com/undercontrol.html. (Accessed March 3, 2017.)

Hitler, Adolf. *Mein Kampf*. New York: Houghton Mifflin Company, 1940, p. 424.

"Hoodoo Dreams 10: Work Begins with Spirit Builders." *The Art of Stealing fire: Trickster as Magician*. https://theartofstealingfire.wordpress.com/2015/08/20/spirit-builders-the-work-begins/. (Accessed March 9, 2017.)

Horn, Arthur David. *Humanity's Extraterrestrial Origins*. Mount Shasta, CA: A & L Horn, 1994. p. 104.

Horowitz, Mitch. "The Illuminati Rules?: Sorry, Conspiracy Theorists, but 'Secret Societies' Do Not Run the World." *Salon*, January 31, 2016. http://www.salon.com/2016/01/31/the_illuminati_rules_sorry_conspiracy_theorists_but_secret_societies_do_not_run_the_world/.

"How the Pyramid Side of the Great Seal Got on the One-Dollar Bill in 1935." *GreatSeal.com*. http://greatseal.com/dollar/hawfdr.html. (Accessed October 13, 2016.)

"How to Join the Illuminati." *IlluminatiRex*. http://www.illuminatirex.com/join-illuminati/. (Accessed March 9, 2017.)

Hudson, David. "Superconductivity and Modern Alchemy: Has the Philosopher's Stone Been Found?" *SubtleEnergies*. http://www.subtleenergies.com/ormus/presentations/Dallas1.htm. (Accessed October 15, 2016.)

"Hylan Takes Stand on National Issues." *The New York Times*, March 27, 1922, p. 3.

"The Illuminati." *Promise of His Coming*. http://www.promiseofhiscoming.com/r134illuminati.htm. (Accessed March 4, 2017.)

"Illuminati Conspiracy Part One: A Precise Exegesis on the Available Evidence." *Conspiracy Archive*. http://www.conspiracyarchive.com/2014/01/29/illuminati-conspiracy-part-one/. (Accessed November 1, 2016.)

"The Illuminati–Freemason Connection." *Biblioteca Pleyades*. http://www.bibliotecapleyades.net/sociopolitica/illuminati/svali2_04.htm. (Accessed February 12, 2017.)

"The Illuminati: Subverting the Body Politic." *Meta Religion*. http://www.crossroad.to/articles2/2012/cuddy/illuminati-1.htm. (Accessed March 8, 2017.)

"The Illuminati Symbol, the Great Seal and the One Dollar Bill." *IlluminatiRex.com*, April 22, 2014. http://www.illuminatirex.com/illuminati-symbol-great-seal-one-dollar-bill/.

"The Illuminati—Triumph of Treachery." *Biblioteca Pleyades*. http://www.bibliotecapleyades.net/sociopolitica/signscorpion/signscorpion02.htm. (Accessed January 5, 2017.)

Inquire Within, *Light-Bearers of Darkness*. TGS Publishing, 2006.

"The Ismaili Community." *The Ismaili*. http://www.theismaili.org/community. (Accessed March 1, 2017).

"I Was in the Illuminati … Now I Am Telling All (Obama, Space Flights, Denver, Aliens)." *AnonyMags*, February 24, 2015. http://www.anonymousmags.com/illuminatinow-telling-obama-space-flights-denver-aliens/.

Jason. "With Loving Greetings from All Souls at This Station, This Is Matthew." *Ashtar Command Tribe*, April 22, 2016. http://www.ashtarcommandcrew.net/forum/topics/with-loving-greetings-from-all-souls-at-this-station-this-is.

"Jedediah Morse and the Illuminati." *Grand Lodge of British Columbia and Yukon*. http://freemasonry.bcy.ca/anti-masonry/morse.html. (Accessed November 20, 2016.)

"Jefferson on Weishaupt." *Grand Lodge of British Columbia and Yukon*. http://freemasonry.bcy.ca/anti-masonry/jefferson.html. (Accessed March 2, 2017.)

"Jewish Attitudes toward Non-Jews." *Judaism 101*. http://www.jewfaq.org/gentiles.htm. (Accessed March 8, 2017).

Jiang, Peter, and Jenny Li, "Scientists Confirm Extraterrestrial Genes in Human DNA." *The Canadian*, January 26, 2007. http://www.agoracosmopolitan.com/home/Frontpage/2007/01/26/01340.html.

Johannsen, R. W., ed. *The Lincoln–Douglas Debates of 1858*. New York: Oxford University Press, 1965.

"John F. Kennedy Speeches: The President and the Press: Address before the American Newspaper Publishers Association, April 27, 1961." *John F. Kennedy Presidential Library and Museum*. https://www.jfklibrary.org/Research/Research-Aids/JFK-Speeches/ American-Newspaper-Publishers-Association_19610427.aspx. (Accessed January 3, 2017.)

Jones, E. Michael. *The Jewish Revolutionary Spirit and Its Impact on World History*. South Bend, IN: Fidelity Press, 2008, p. 255.

———. *Libido Dominandi: Sexual Liberation & Political Control*. South Bend, IN: St. Augustine's Press, 1999, pp. 11-12.

"Justifications for War against Iraq." *Mt. Holyoke*. https://www.mtholyoke.edu/acad/intrel/bush/iraqjust.htm. (Accessed February 22, 2017.)

Kakutani, Michiko, "It's a Plot! No It's Not: A Debunking." *New York Times*. February 15, 2010.

Kant, Immanuel. "What Is Enlightenment?" *Columbia University Sources of Medieval History*. http://www.columbia.edu/acis/ets/CCREAD/etscc/kant.html. (Accessed December 15, 2016.)

Kaplan, Karen. "DNA Ties Ashkenazi Jews to Group of Just 330 People from Middle Ages." *Los Angeles Times*, September 9, 2014. http://www.latimes.com/science/sciencenow/la-sci-sn-ashkenazi-jews-dna-diseases-20140909-story.html.

"Karl Marx—Evil's Idol." *Biblioteca Pleyades*. http://www.bibliotecapleyades.net/sociopolitica/signscorpion/signscorpion03.htm. (Accessed March 8, 2017.)

Katz, Jacob. *Jews and Freemasonry in Europe*. Boston: Harvard Press, 1970, p. 246. https://historyofconspiracy.wordpress.com/2011/10/19/1782-congress-of-wilhelmsbad/.

Kirchubel, Michael A. *Vile Acts of Evil*, Volume 1: *Banking in America*. CreateSpace, 2009, pp. 101-102.

Kiyosaki, Robert. "Illuminati History in 6 Minutes." *The Financial Armageddon*. (Accessed January 13, 2017.)

Knight, Christopher. *The Hiram Key*. New York: Barnes & Noble, 1998, p. 240.

Koestler, Arthur. *The Thirteenth Tribe: The Khazar Empire and Its Heritage*. New York: Random House, 1976, p.136.

Langer, Walter C. *The Mind of Adolf Hitler: The Secret Wartime Report*. New York, London: Basic Books, 1972.

Lett, Donald G. Jr. *Phoenix Rising: The Rise and Fall of the American Republic*. Bloomington, IN: Authorhouse, 2008.

Levenda, Peter, *Unholy Alliance*. New York: Avon Books, 1995.

Levy, Joel. *The Little Book of Secret Societies: 50 of the World's Most Notorious Organizations and Wow to Join Them*. New York: Metro Books, 2012, p. 15.

Livingston, David. "The Shabbatean Frankists." *Conspiracy School*. http://www.conspiracyschool.com/illuminati. (Accessed October 22, 2016.)

Luchet, Jean-Pierre-Louise de. *Essai sur la secte des illuminés*. [France], 1789.

Luckert, Steven. *Jesuits, Freemasons, Illuminati, and Jacobins: Conspiracy Theories, Secret Societies, and Politics in Late Eighteenth-Century Germany*. Binghamton, NY: State University of New York, 1993.

Lukas, J. Anthony. "The Council on Foreign Relations—Is It a Club? Seminar? Presidium? 'Invisible Government'?" *New York Times Magazine*, November 21, 1971, p. 125.

Mackey, Albert G., "Comte de Virieu: 1782 Congress of Wilhelmsbad, The Illuminati-Masonic Alliance." *History of Conspiracy*, October 19, 2011.

———. *Encyclopedia of Freemasonry*. Richmond, VA: Macoy Publishing, 1966, p. 1099.

———. *The History of Freemasonry*. New York: Gramercy Books, 1996, p. 236.

Mackey, Albert Gallatin, Edward L. Hawkins, and William James Hughan, *An Encyclopedia of Freemasonry and Its Kindred Sciences*, Volume 2. New York: The Masonic History Company, 1919.

Makow, Henry. "Illuminati Defector Details Pervasive Conspiracy." *HenryMakow.com*. October 14, 2002. http://www.henrymakow.com/141002.html.

———. "The Illuminati: The Cult That Hijacked the World." *AntiMatrix*. http://antimatrix.org/Convert/Books/Henry_Makow/Henry_Makow_Illuminati_The_Cult_that_Hijacked_the_World.html#THE_ILLUMINATI. (Accessed November 14, 2016.)

———. "Independent Historian Unveils Cabalist Conspiracy." *HenryMakow.com*, September 1, 2007. http://www.henrymakow.com/002159.html.

———. "Jacob Schiff Ordered Czar and Family Murdered." *HenryMakow.com*, July 9, 2011. http://www.henrymakow.com/jacob_schiff_ordered_murder_of.html.

———. "Meditation on 'The Jewish Revolutionary Spirit' by E. Michael Jones." *HenryMakow.com*, June 27, 2008. http://www.henrymakow.com/meditations_on_the_jewish_revo.html.

———. "USSR—Illuminati Experiment Was 'Social Catastrophe.'" *HenryMakow.com*, May 20, 2009. http://www.henrymakow.com/ussr_-_a_social_catastrophe_bu.html#sthash.55ig3lCF.dpuf.

———. "Was Hitler an Illuminati Agent?" *HenryMakow.com*, January 12, 2016. http://henrymakow.com/001399.html.

———. "Were Illuminati Jews behind the Nazis?" *HenryMakow.com*, March 4, 2015. http://henrymakow.com/were_illuminati_jews_responsib.html.

Marchetti, Victor, and John D. Marks. *The CIA and the Cult of Intelligence.* New York: Dell Publishing, 1974, p. 267.

Marrs, Jim. "All Roads Lead to Sumer." http://astroeth.atspace.org/digitalsea/web/all-roads-lead-to-sumer.html. (Accessed March 1, 2017.)

———. *Circle of Intrigue.* Austin, TX: Living Truth Publishers, 1995.

———. *Dark Majesty.* Austin, TX: Living Truth Publishers, 1992, p. 101.

———. "Illuminati Mystery Babylon." *Power of Prophecy.* http://www.texemarrs.com/082003/illuminati_mystery_babylon.htm. (Accessed January 22, 2017.)

———. "The Murder of America." *Power of Prophecy*, August 1, 2006. http://www.texemarrs.com/082006/murder_of_america.htm. (Accessed November 17, 2016).

Maxwell, Jordan. *Matrix of Power: How the World Has Been Controlled by Powerful People without Your Knowledge.* Escondido, CA: The Book Tree, 2000.

"Maxwell Taylor: 'Write Off a Billion.'" *Executive Intelligence Review*, September 22, 1981, p. 56.

Mazza, Ed. "John Oliver Exposes the Dark Illuminati Conspiracy behind Cadbury Cream Eggs." *The Huffington Post*, March 29, 2016. http://www.huffingtonpost.com/entry/john-oliver-cadbury-creme-eggs-illuminati_us_56f8caaee4b0a372181a4474.

McIlhany, William, "A Primer on the Illuminati." *The New American.* June 12, 2009. http://www.thenewamerican.com/culture/history/item/4660-a-primer-on-the-illuminati.

McKeown, Trevor. "A Bavarian Illuminati Primer." *Grand Lodge of British Columbia and Yukon.* http://Freemasonry.bcy.ca/texts/illuminati.html. (Accessed March 1, 2017.)

"Meaning of Numbers in the Bible: The Number 13." *Bible Study.org.* http://www.biblestudy.org/bibleref/meaning-of-numbers-in-bible/13.html. (Accessed January 7, 2017.)

Melanson, Terry. "Albert Pike to Mazzini, August 15, 1871: Three World Wars?" *Conspiracy Archive*, January 10, 2015. http://www.conspiracyarchive.com/2015/01/10/albert-pike-to-mazzini-august-15-1871-three-world-wars/.

———. "Masonic Congress of Wilhelmsbad." *Conspiracy Archive*, August 11, 2008. http://www.conspiracyarchive.com/2015/07/06/masonic-congress-of-wilhelmsbad/.

———. "Owl of Wisdom: Illuminati, Bohemian Club, Schlaraffia, James Gordon Bennet Jr." *Conspiracy Archive*, April 18, 2015. http://www.conspiracyarchive.com/2015/04/18/owl-of-wisdom-illuminati-bohemian-club-schlaraffia-james-gordon-bennett-jr/.

———. *Perfectibilists: The 18th Century Bavarian Order of the Illuminati.* Walterville, OR: Trine Day, 2009.

Meyer, Edgar, and Thomas Mehner. *Das Geheimnis der deutschen Atombombe.* Rottenburg, Germany: Kopp Verlag, 2001, p. 122.

Michel, Jean. *Dora: The Nazi Concentration Camp Where Space Technology Was Born and 30,000 Prisoners Died.* New York: Holt, Rinehart and Winston, 1980, pp. 290, 296–297.

Miller, Edith Starr (under pen name Lady Edith Queenborough). *Occult Theocracy* [published posthumously], 1933.

Moe, "The Illuminati Hand Sign of the Pyramid." *Gnostic Warrior,* June 9, 2015. http://gnosticwarrior.com/illuminati-hand-sign.html.

Molinet, Jason. "Worldwide 'Cabal' of Leaders Is Covering Up Aliens: Pol." *New York Daily News,* April 23, 2015. http://www.nydailynews.com/news/world/world-wide-cabal-leaders-covering-aliens-pol-article-1.2195513.

Morris, Wayne, "Cisco Wheeler Interview." *The Forbidden Knowledge.* http://www.the-forbiddenknowledge.com/hardtruth/cisco_wheeler_interview.htm. (Accessed February 24, 2017.)

Moscow, Alvin. *The Rockefeller Inheritance.* Garden City, NY: Doubleday & Company, 1977, p. 225.

Müller, W., G. Haffelder, A. Schlotmann, A. T. Schaefers, and G. Teuchert-Noodt. "Amelioration of Psychiatric Symptoms through Exposure to Music Individually Adapted to Brain Rhythm Disorders—A Randomised Clinical Trial on the Basis of Fundamental Research." *Cognitive Neuropsychiatry,* 2014, 19(5): 399-413. http://www.ncbi.nlm.nih.gov/pubmed/24460405.

Myers, Gustavus Myers. *History of the Great American Fortunes.* New York: Random House, 1936.

Nataf, Andre. *The Wordsworth Dictionary of the Occult.* Hertfordshire, UK: Wordsworth Reference, 1994, p. 37.

Oglesby, Carl. *The Yankee and Cowboy War.* http://educationforum.ipbhost.com/index.php?showtopic=22107. (Accessed October 23, 2016.)

Penre, Wes. "Dialogue with 'Hidden Hand,' Self-proclaimed Illuminati Insider." *Illuminati News.* December 27, 2008. http://illuminati-news.com/00363.html.

"The Philosopher's Stone." *Library of Alexandria.* http://www.halexandria.org/dward483.htm. (Accessed December 3, 2016.)

Picknett, Lynn, and Clive Prince. *The Templar Revelation.* New York: Touchstone, 1997, p. 142.

Pike, Albert. "Instructions to the 23 Supreme Councils of the World," as recorded by Abel Clarin de La Rive. *La Femme et l'Enfant dans la Franc-maçonnerie Universelle.* 1894, p. 588.

———. *Morals and Dogma of the Ancient and Accepted Scottish Rite of Freemasonry* Washington, DC: The Roberts Publishing Company, 1871, pp. 839-840.

Poisuo, Pauli, and M. Asher Cantrell. "5 Ridiculous Origins of Famous Urban Legends." *Cracked,* May 2, 2012. http://www.cracked.com/article_19800_5-ridiculous-origins-famous-urban-legends_p2.html.

"Prologue: Genesis." *Mars-Earth Connection.* http://www.mars-earth.com/12planet.htm. (Accessed February 15, 2017.)

The Protocols as Historic Truth: Konrad Heiden, Der Fuehrer. Boston: Houghton Mifflin Company, 1944.

Protocols of the Learned Elders of Zion, originally published in 1903, CreateSpace Independent Publishing Platform, 2014.

Prouty, L. Fletcher. *The Secret Team: The CIA and Its Allies in Control of the United States and the World.* Englewood Cliffs, NJ: Prentice-Hall, 1973, pp. 2-3.

"Putin: First Soviet Government Was Mostly Jewish." *Times of Israel*, June 19, 2013. http://www.timesofisrael.com/putin-first-soviet-government-was-mostly-jewish/.

Quigley, Carroll. *Tragedy and Hope: A History of the World in Our Time*. New York: MacMillan, 1966, p. 290.

Ravenscroft, Trevor. *The Spear of Destiny*. York Beach, MA: Samuel Weiser, Inc., 1973.

Reed, Douglas. *The Controversy of Zion*. Torrence, CA: The Noontide Press, 1985, p. 163.

Reizer, John. "The Big Picture: Who or What Really Controls This Planet?" *NoFake-News.net*, July 17, 2013. https://nofakenews.net/2013/07/17/the-big-picture-who-or-what-really-controls-this-planet/.

Reynolds, John Lawrence. *Secret Societies: Their Mysteries Revealed*. Chichester, West Sussex: Summersdale Publishers, 2006, p. 61.

Rivera, David Allen. *Final Warning: A History of the New World Order*. Oakland, CA: InteliBooks Publishing, 2004, pp. 36-37.

Robison, John. *Proofs of a Conspiracy Against All the Religions and Governments of Europe*. New York: George Forman, 1798.

Rose, Mark. "Interviews: A Conversation with Matthew F. Bogdanos." *Archaeology Archive*, Octber 16, 2003. http://archive.archaeology.org/online/interviews/bogdanos/.

Rosenbaum, Ron. "The Last Secrets of Skull and Bones." *Esquire* (September, 1977) pp. 87-88.

Ryan, Bill, "Welcome to Project Avalon." *Project Avalon*, January 29, 2017. http://www.projectavalon.net/. (Accessed February 4, 2017.)

Sachar, Howard. *A History of the Jews in America*. New York: Alfred A. Knopf, 1992, p. 92.

Salla, Michael E. "Antarctica's Secret History—Extraterrestrial Colony Created Elite Bloodline Rulers." *Exopolitics.org*, March 1, 2017. http://exopolitics.org/author/dr-michael-salla/.

Schoenman, Ralph. "The Hidden History of Zionism." *Reds—Die Roten*. http://www.marxists.de/middleast/schoenman/ch06.htm. (Accessed March 4, 2017.)

Sepher, Robert. *Redemption through Sin*. Encino, CA: Atlantean Gardens, 2015, p. 15.

Shearer, S. R., "The Origins of the Illuminist Myth: The Fabrication of the Protocols of the Learned Elders of Zion." *Antipas Ministries*. http://www.antipasministries.com/html/file0000130.htm. (Accessed February 13, 2017.)

Silver Bear, Johnny. "The Illuminati and the House of Rothschild." *Red Ice Creations*, August 23, 2005. http://www.redicecreations.com/specialreports/2005/08aug/redshield.html.

Sitchin, Zecharia Sitchin. *The 12th Planet*. New York: Avon Books, 1976, p. 381.

Sklar, Dusty. *The Nazi's and the Occult*. New York: Thomas Y. Crowell Company, 1977.

Smith, Sally Bedell. "Empire of the Sons," *Vanity Fair*, January 1997, p. 102.

Speer, Albert. *Infiltration: How Heinrich Himmler Schemed to Build an SS Industrial Empire*. New York: Macmillan, 1981, pp. 207–208.

Spencer, John, ed. *The UFO Encyclopedia*. New York: Avon Books, 1991, p. 103.

Springmeier, Fritz. *Bloodlines of the Illuminati*. Austin, TX: Ambassador House, 2002.

Stamp, Jimmy, "American Myths: Benjamin Franklin's Turkey and the Presidential Seal." *Smithsonian.com*, January 25, 2013. http://www.smithsonianmag.com/arts-culture/american-myths-benjamin-franklins-turkey-and-the-presidential-seal-6623414/?no-ist.

Stauffer, Vernon L. "The European Illuminati." *Grand Lodge of British Columbia and Yukon.* http://freemasonry.bcy.ca/anti-masonry/stauffer.html. (Accessed November 15, 2016.)

———— "The European Order of the Illuminati." *Conspiracy Archive.* http://www.con spiracyarchive.com/NWO/Stauffer_Illuminati.htm. (Accessed November 16, 2016.)

————. *New England and the Bavarian Illuminati.* New York: Columbia University: 1918.

Still, William T. *New World Order: The Ancient Plan of Secret Societies.* Lafayette, LA: Huntingnton House Publishers, 1990, p. 108.

Sullivan, Martin E. Sullivan. "Martin Sullivan's Letter of Resignation as Chairman of the President's Advisory Committee on Cultural Property." *Washington Report on Middle East Affairs,* April 14, 2002. http://www.wrmea.org/2003-june/letter-of-res ignation.html.

Sutton, Anthony C. *America's Secret Establishment: An Introduction to the Order of Skull & Bones.* Billings, MT: Liberty House Press, 1986.

Sutton, William Josiah. *The Illuminati 666.* Brushton, NY: TEACH Services, 1983.

Swift, Art. "Majority in U.S. Still Believe JFK Killed in a Conspiracy." *Gallup,* November 15, 2013. http://www.gallup.com/poll/165893/majority-believe-jfk-killed-conspiracy.aspx.

Szymanski, Greg. ""Kay Griggs, Former Marine Colonel's Wife, Talks Again about Military Assassin Squads, Drug Running, Illegal Weapon Deals and Sexual Perversion Deep within the Highest Levels of U.S. Military and Government." *Arctic Beacon,* July 25, 2005. http://www.arcticbeacon.com/articles/25-Jul-2005.html. (Accessed January 15, 2017.)

"'Torture': A Creepy Video about the Jacksons Being Subjected to Mind Control." *The Vigilant Citizen,* February 23, 2016. http://vigilantcitizen.com/musicbusiness/tor ture-creepy-video-jacksons-subjected-trauma-based-mind-control/.

Tsarion, Michael. *The Irish Origins of Civilization.* http://www.irishoriginsofciviliza-tion.com/. (Accessed March 6, 2017.)

Vesco, Renato, and David Hatcher Childress. *Man-Made UFOs: 1944–1994 50 Years of Suppression.* Kempton, IL: Adventures Unlimited Press, 1994, p. 225.

Vey, Gary, "It Hertz So Bad: Are We All Listening to Nazi-engineered Music?" *View-zone,* 2014. http://www.viewzone.com/432hertz.html. (Accessed March 4, 2017.)

Von Ward, Paul. *We Have Never Been Alone.* Charlottesville, VA: Hampton Roads Publishing Company, 2011, p. 285.

Waite, Arthur Edward. *A New Encyclopedia of Freemasonry.* New York: Wings Books, 1996, p. 386.

Warburg, James Paul. [Appearance before the U.S. Senate Committee on Foreign Relations.] February 17, 1950.

Washington, George. *The Writings of George Washington,* Volume 14: *1798-1799.* New York: G. P. Putman's Sons, 1893.

Weber, Mark. "The Jewish Role in the Bolshevik Revolution and Russia's Early Soviet Regime." *Institute for Historical Review*. http://www.ihr.org/jhr/v14/v14n1p-4_Weber.html. (Accessed February 3, 2017.)

Webster, Nesta H. *Secret Societies and Subversive Movements*. Palmdale, CA: Omni Publications, 1924, p. iv.

———. *World Revolution: The Plot against Civilization*. Boston: Small, Maynard & Company, 1921, p. 37.

"Who Are the Illuminati and What Do They Control?" *The Week,* July 7, 2016. http://www.theweek.co.uk/62399/who-are-the-illuminati-and-do-they-control-the-music-industry.

"Who Was Albert Pike?" *Three World Wars*. http://www.threeworldwars.com/albert-pike2.htm. (Accessed December 3, 2016.)

Wilcock, David. "Financial Tyranny: Defeating the Greatest Cover-Up of All Time." *Divine Cosmos*, January 13, 2012. http://www.divinecosmos.com/start-here/davids-blog/1023-financial-tyranny?start=1.

———. "Major Event: Liens Filed against All 12 Federal Reserve Banks." *Divine Cosmos*, April 13, 2012. http://www.divinecosmos.com/start-here/davids-blog/1047-liens.

Wildie, Duane L. *Government: A Christian's Civic Responsibility*. Bloomington, IN: Westbow Press, 2014.

Wilmshurst, Walter Leslie. *The Meaning of Masonry*. New York: Bell Publishing Company, 1980, p. 173.

Wilson, Derek Wilson. *Rothschild: The Wealth and Power of a Dynasty*. New York: Charles Schribner's Sons, 1988, p. 11.

Wilson, Robert Anton. *Cosmic Trigger: Final Secret of the Illuminati*. New York: Pocket Books, 1977, pp. xvi–xvii.

Winrod, Gerald B. *Adam Weishaupt—A Human Devil*. Wichita, KS: Defender Publishers, 1935, p. 9.

"Winston Churchill on Rosa Luxemburg, Jews and 'The Worldwide Conspiracy for the Overthrow of Civilization.'" *Rosaluxemburgblog*, July 23, 2012. https://rosaluxemburgblog.wordpress.com/2012/07/23/churchill-on-rosa-luxemburg-2/.

Wisse, Ruth. "Was Lenin Jewish?" *My Jewish Learning*. http://www.myjewishlearning.com/article/was-lenin-jewish/ (Accessed March 4, 2017.)

Witkowski, Igor. *Truth about the Wunderwaffe*. Warsaw: European History Press, 2003, p. 184.

Wurmbrand, Richard. *Marx & Satan*. Crossway Books, 1986.

Zagami, Leo Lyon. *Confessions of an Illuminati*. San Francisco, CA: Consortium of Collective Consciousness Publishing, 2016.

———. "Confessions of an Illuminati." *Just Energy Radio*, December 24, 2015. http://justenergyradio.com/confessions-illuminati-leo-lyon-zagami/.

Index

Note: (ill.) indicates photos and illustrations.

THE ILLUMINATI: THE SECRET SOCIETY THAT HIJACKED THE WORLD